BLITZKRIEG IN THE GULF

ARMOR OF THE 100-HOUR WAR

by YVES DEBAY

CONCORD COLOR SERIES

CONTENTS

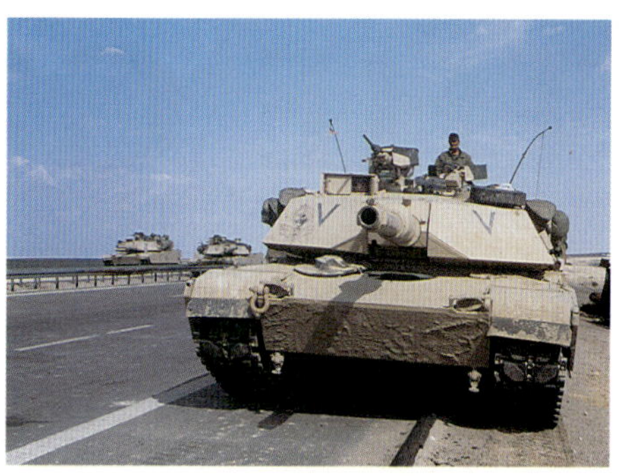

Of the 1,956 M1 tanks deployed for Operation Desert Sabre, only four were lost, two to friendly fire from other M1A1 tanks. Four others received repairable damage, mostly by antitank mines.

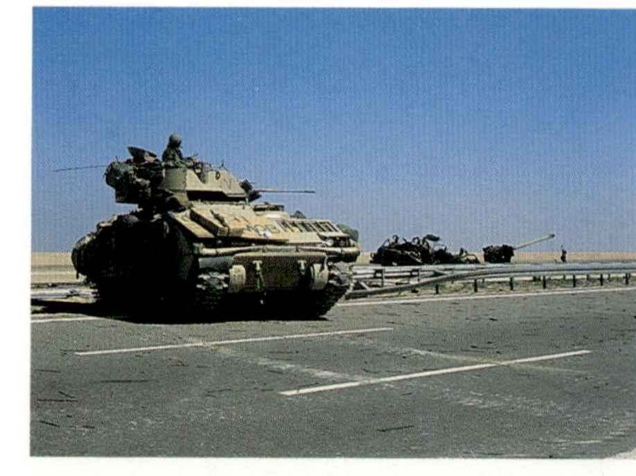

M2 Bradleys of the 24th Mechanized Infantry Division, nicknamed the "Victory Division", reached the Baghdad-Basra highway on February 28, 1991, isolated the KTO from reinforcement and cut-off the Iraqi Republican Guard units.

All photos by Yves Debay unless noted.
The author would like to thank Michael Green and the photographers of the U.S. Army, Marine Corps, Air Force and Navy for their cooperation.

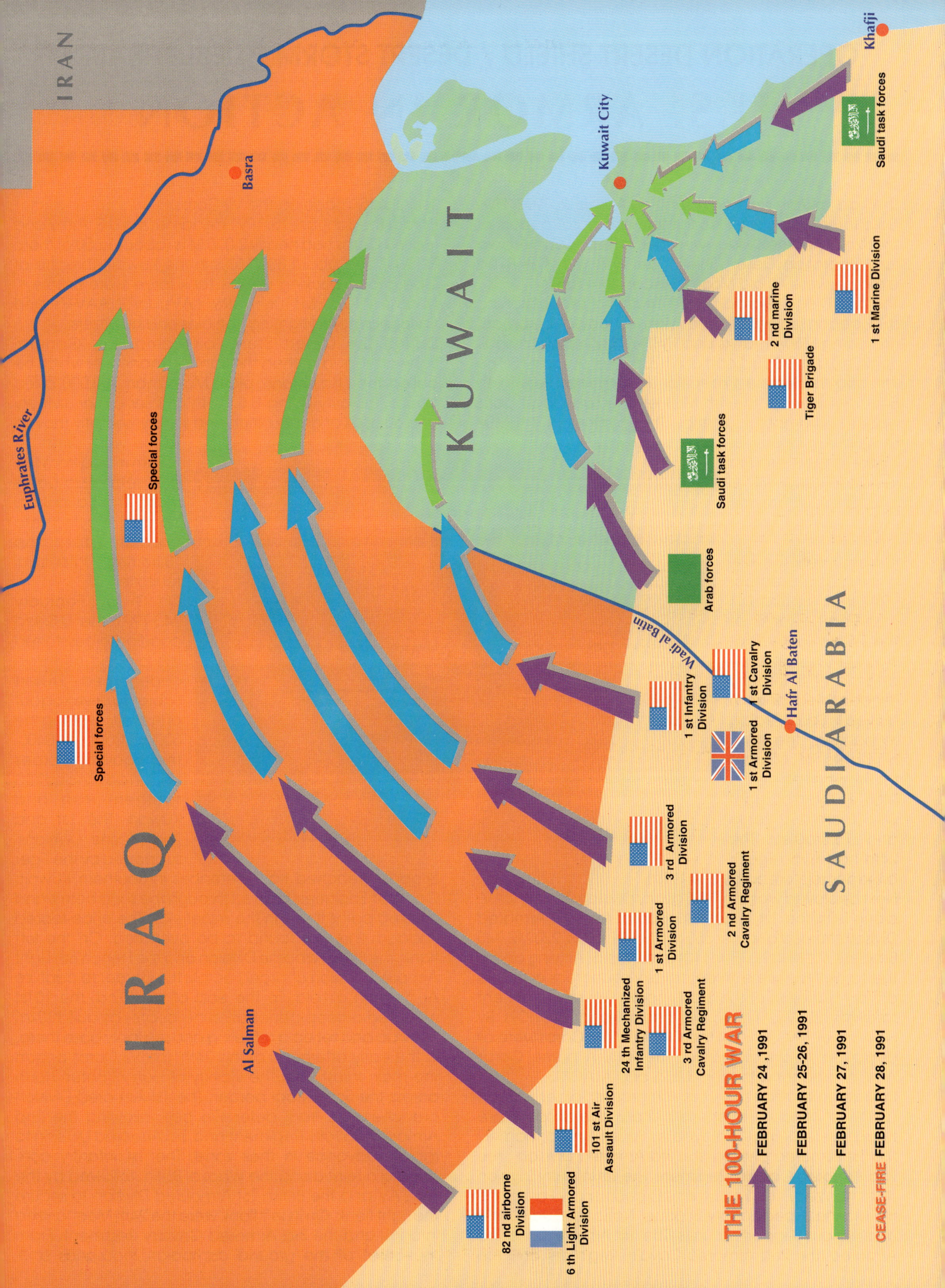

IRAN
Basra
Euphrates River
Special forces
Special forces
Special forces
KUWAIT
Kuwait City
Khafji
Saudi task forces
2 nd marine Division
1 st Marine Division
Tiger Brigade
Saudi task forces
Arab forces
Wadi al Batin
1 st Cavalry Division
1 st Infantry Division
1 st Armored Division
Hafr Al Baten
SAUDI ARABIA
3 rd Armored Division
2 nd Armored Cavalry Regiment
1 st Armored Division
24 th Mechanized Infantry Division
3 rd Armored Cavalry Regiment
Al Salman
I R A Q
101 st Air Assault Division
82 nd airborne Division
6 th Light Armored Division
THE 100-HOUR WAR
FEBRUARY 24, 1991
FEBRUARY 25-26, 1991
FEBRUARY 27, 1991
CEASE-FIRE FEBRUARY 28, 1991

U.S. ARMOR IN ACTION

The Iraqi military overran Kuwait on August 2, 1990. Five days later, American F-15 fighters and paratroopers of the 82nd Airborne Division were deployed to Saudi Arabia for "Operation Desert Shield". Arriving with the 82nd airborne were 40 old M551 Sheridan light tanks.

The first Diego Garcia-based maritime prepositioning ship began unloading the Marine heavy equipment (including M60A1 tanks and LVTP-7 amphibious assault vehicles) at the Saudi port of A1-Jubayl on August 15. The 7th and 1st Marine Expeditionary Brigades flew in to Saudi Arbia while the 4th MEB left the East Coast ports aboard 13 amphibious ships. The Marines of 7th MEB were the first combat forces on the ground in Saudi Arabia with a credible armored/mechanized offensive capability.

It wasn't until the beginning of September 1990 that the first M1 main battle tanks of the 24th Infantry Division (Mechanized) and the 197th Infantry Brigade (Mechanized) arrived in Saudi Arabia to back up the small numbers of Marine M60s and Airborne M551s. They brought with them 290 tanks and 275 Bradleys. The 24th had two regular brigades reinforced by the 197th.

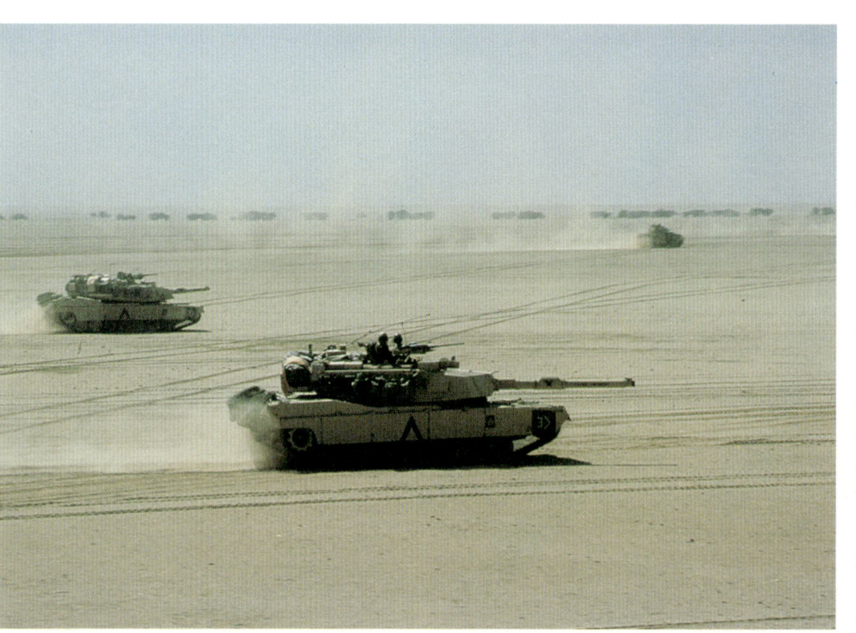

Next deployed was the 1st Cavalry Division. The 1st CAV, along with the 1st "Tiger" Brigade of the 2nd Armored Division, fielded another 350 M1/M1A1 tanks, 220 M2/M3 Bradleys, 72 M109s, 12 M110s and 9 MLRS. Arriving about the same time were three cavalry squadrons and one artillery battalion of the 3rd Armored Cavalry Regiment totalling 120 M1A1s, 115 M3 Bradleys and 24 M109s. By November 1990, units of the XVIII Airborne Corps were all deployed to Saudi Arabia. The XVIII Airborne Corps Artillery brought with them MLRS and ATACMS.

In order to provide the coalition ground forces with an ability to conduct offensive military operations, more troops were being deployed to Saudi Arabia, namely the 1st Armored Division, the 3rd Armored Division , the 2nd Armored Cavalry Regiment, the 1st Infantry Division (Mechanized), the 2nd Marine Expeditionary Force, the 5th Marine Expeditionary Brigade, National Guard units and various supporting units. The 1st Armored, the 3rd Armored, the 2nd Armored Cavalry Regiment and the

1st Infantry made up the VII Corps.

Before the January 15, 1991 deadline, the U.S. Army and Marine Corps had nearly 2,000 M1s (about 1,650 of them M1A1s) and about 300 M60s in the Kuwaiti Threatre of Operations. Backing up this tank force were Bradleys, M113s, M109s, M110s, MLRS, LAVs, LVTP/AAV-7s and various armored fighting vehicles and howitzers.

During the Desert Storm air campaign, General Schwarzkopf launched the flanking maneuver which he called the "Hail Mary" play. More than 150,000 allied troops, majority being U.S., with all thier armor, artillery and 60 days of ammunition and supply, secretly moved to the west, as far as 500km inland from the gulf, setting up bases along the Saudi-Iraqi border, moving into position for the "Blitzkrieg" into Iraqi territories.

On G-day, February 24, 1991 the U.S.-led coalition forces started the air-land offensive codenamed "Desert Sabre" to drive Iraq out of Kuwait. All along the 500km front, at 0400, the coalition forces began advancing into southern Iraq and Kuwait. The 1st and 2nd Marine Divisions, supported by the Tiger Brigade, breached Iraqi defences in Southern Kuwait. Combat Engineers blasted through the sand berms and cleared paths through the minefields. The once feared Saddam line was found to be overrated. On the left flank, the 82nd Airborne Division and the French 6th Light Armored Division charged across the border to capture Al Salman airfield. To the east of the 82nd, the 101st mounted a deep-penetration helicopter assault 110km into Iraq and set up a refueling and resupply base there. In the early afternoon of the 24th, the VII Corps began the main thrust from the vicinity of Hafr Al Baten north across the Saudi-Iraqi border. The 1st Armored Division breached the Iraqi defensive belt, allowing the 2nd Armored Cavalry Regiment and 3rd Armored Division to rapidly advance in their zone. The 1st Infantry conducted a feint along the Wadi al Batin, followed by the 1st CAV and the British 1st Armoured Division to secure the right flank. On its left flank were the 24th Mechanized Infantry and the 3rd Armored Cavalry Regiment. From the onset of the ground campaign, thousands and thousands of Iraqi troops surrendered, allowing rapid advance in all sectors.

The next two days, the 25th and 26th , all units continued to advance in rapid pace. The 82nd Airborne took position to guard the left flank. The 101st Air Assault and 24th Mechanized Infantry dashed to the Euphrates to link up and to cut off any Iraqi retreats. The VII Corps swung east and raced towards Kuwait. In a night battle on 25th, M1A1s of the 1st Cavalry, 1st Armored Division and 3rd Armored Division enveloped the Republican Guard's Tawakalna Armored Division and destroyed it without a loss. While the Marines pushed north to Kuwait City, tanks from the 1st Marine Division engaged 50 to 60 Iraqi tanks near the Burgan oil field and destroyed all enemy tanks without loss.

The following day, February 27, 1991 two major tank battles occured. The 1st Marine Division ran into a major Iraqi armored force near the Kuwait International Airport but managed to destroy all 100 Iraqi tanks that they engaged. The other major tank battle took place in Iraqi 80km west of Basra where 700 U.S. tanks and armored vehicles of VII Corps and the 24th Mechanized Infantry took on a Republican Guard division's 300 tanks. All Iraqi tanks were destroyed with few casualties to the American. By the 28th, it was over, President Bush ordered a suspension of all offensive action. In 100 hours of ground combat, U.S. forces, using a combination of armored, light, and special operation forces in joint and combined missions, defeated the fourth most powerful army in the world.

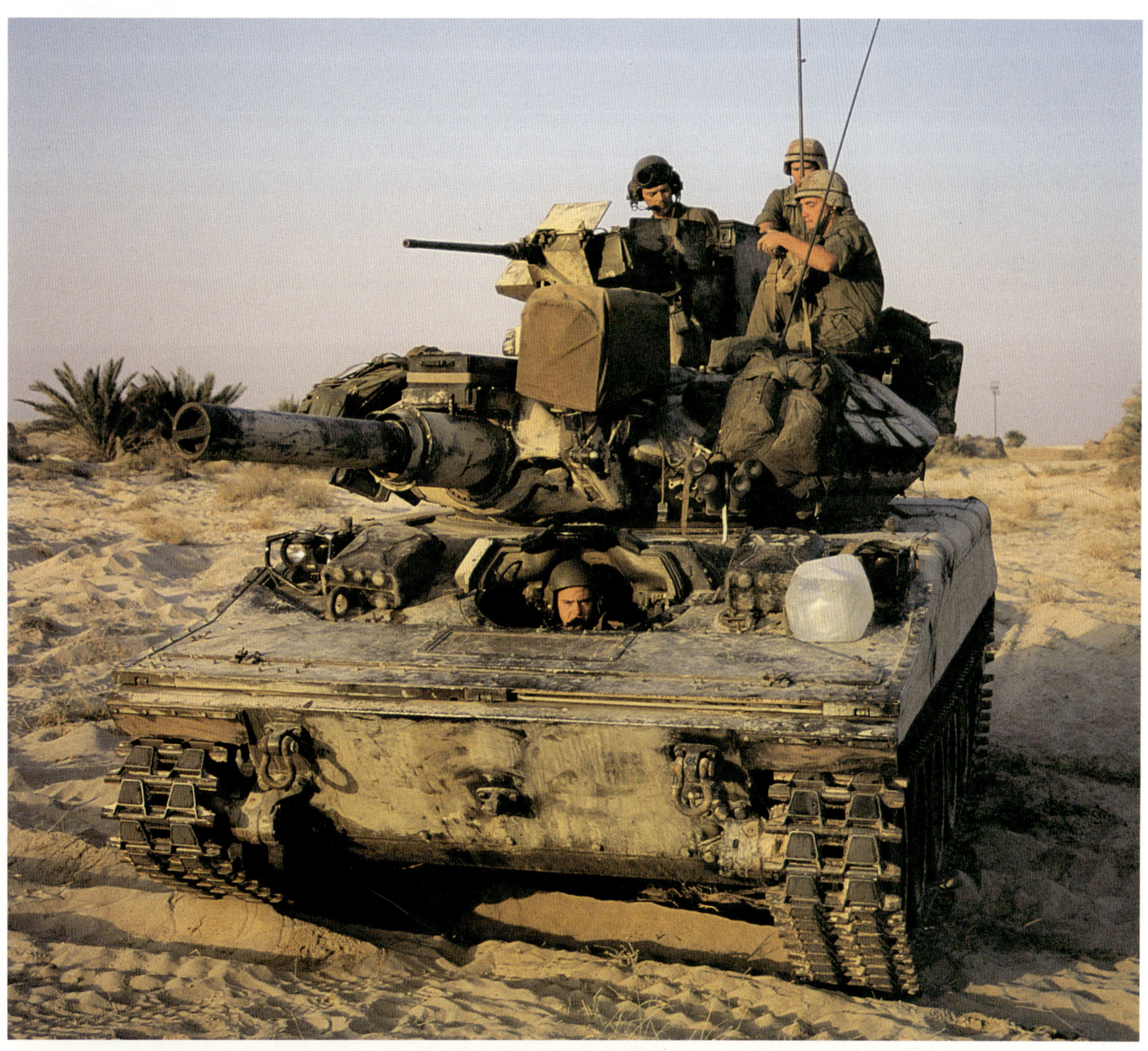

The main armament of the M551 Sheridan is the M81 152mm gun/launcher which can fire the Shillelagh missile or a number of conventional rounds. However, in practical, the recoil generated by firing a convential round usually damages the missle guidance system, making the launcher inoperative. This and other problems contributed to the phase-out of the M551 from general service, leaving the 82nd Airborne the only user of the Sheridans.

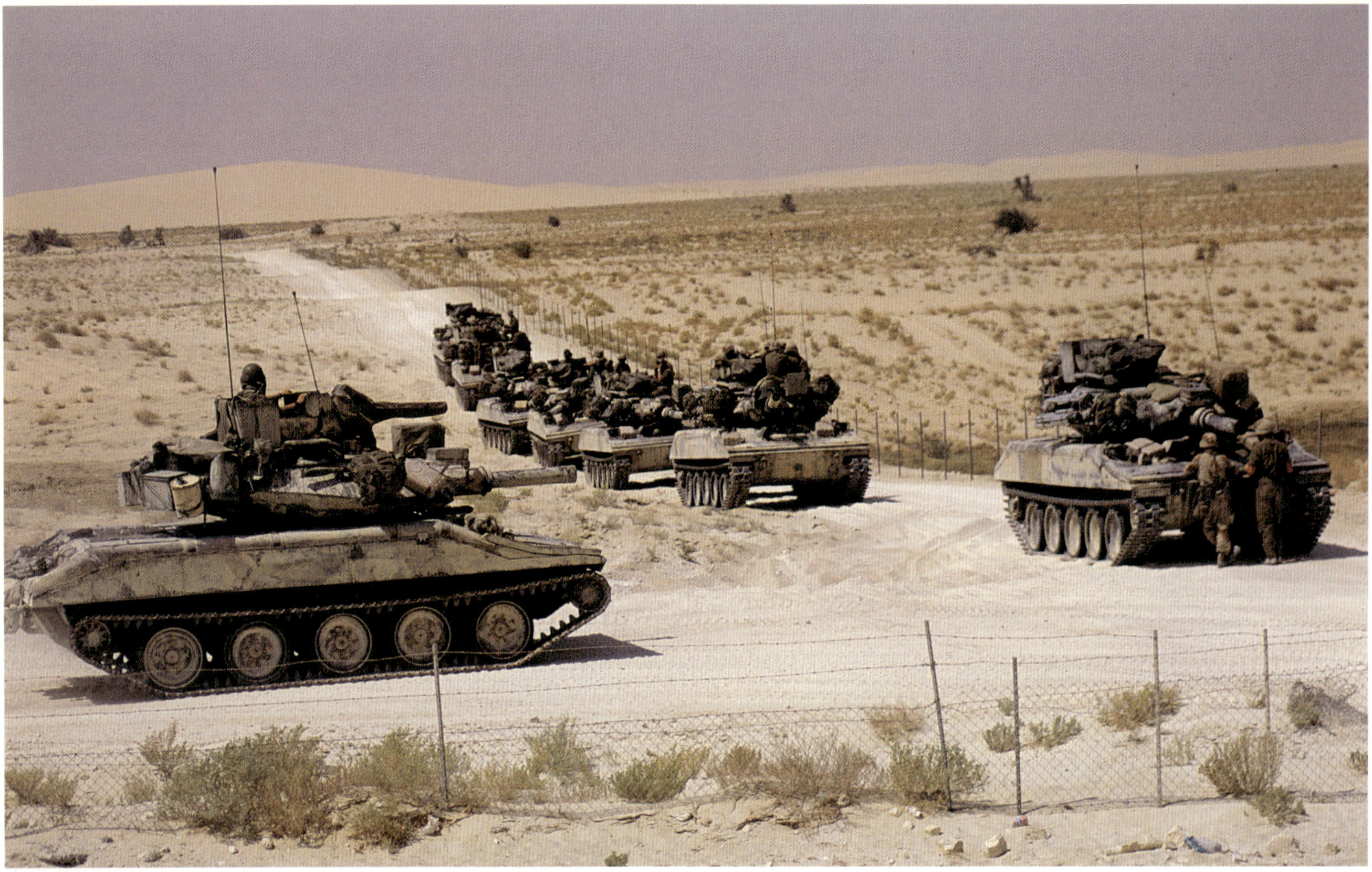

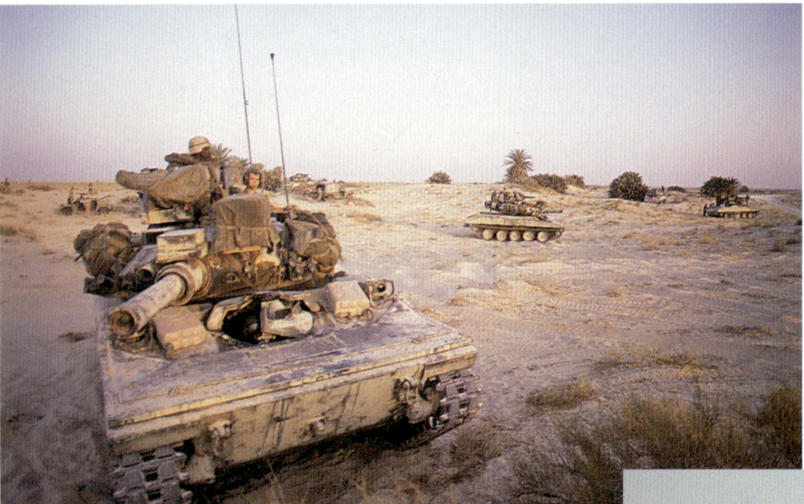

A column of M551s in the Saudi desert. 40 Sheridans were deployed to Saudi Arabia. Before the arrival of the M1s of the 24th Mechanized Infantry, these M551s had to face the huge fleet of 4,280 Iraqi tanks.

The M551 Sheridan Armored Reconnaissance/Airborne Assault vehicles (AR/AAV) were the first armored vehicles deployed to Saudi Arabia for Operation Desert Shield. The 82nd Airborne Division has a battalion of M551A1 Sheridans, the 3rd Battalion, 73rd Armor Regiment which is the only unit that uses this light tank.

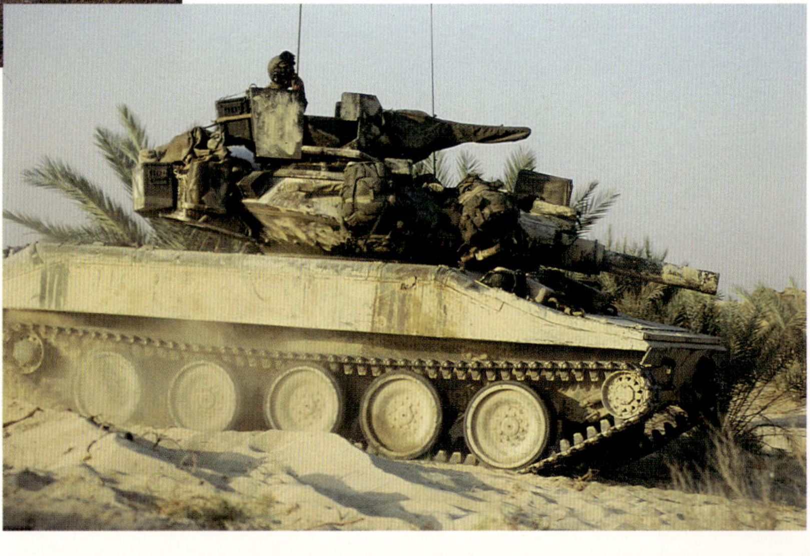

The improved external storage racks on the turret rear are a reminder of the M551's cramped interior. The Sheridan has an all-welded aluminium hull and a crew of four.

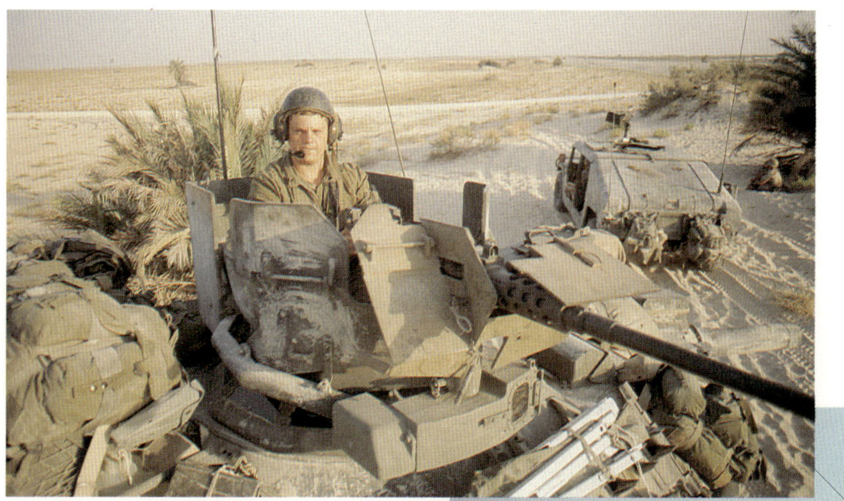

The turret of the M551 is of all welded steel armor, with the commander and gunner seated on the right and the loader on the left. A .50 caliber M2 machine gun is mounted on the commander's cupola enclosed by armor shields to give the commander some protection.

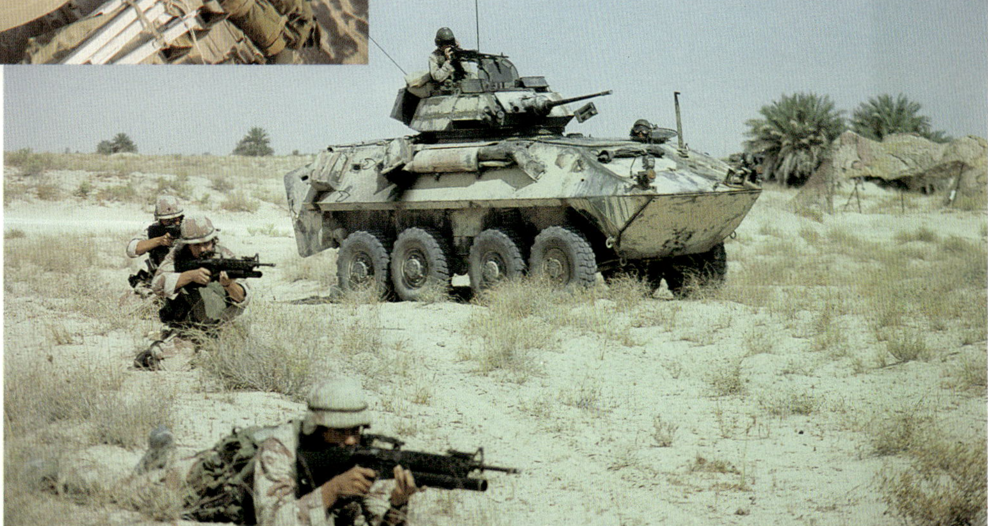

The 82nd Airborne has a scout platoon of LAV-25 Light Armored Vehicles for reconnaissance role. Shown is an LAV-25 on exercise with the "All Americans" paratroopers in Saudi Arabia.

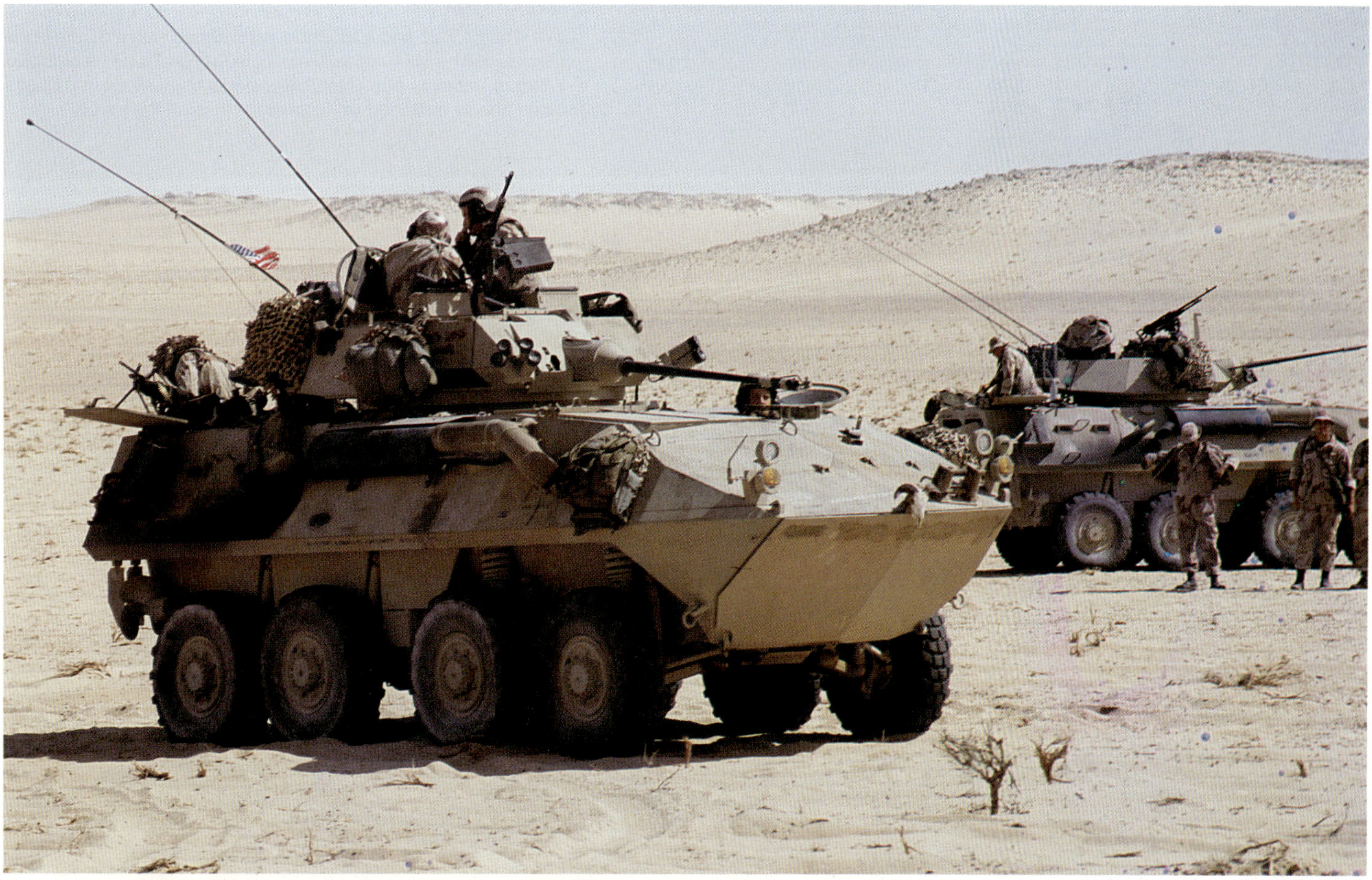

LAV-25s of the Marine 3rd LAI (Light Armored Infantry) Battalion soon after their deployment to Saudi Arabia. Originally a Swiss Mowag design, the 8-wheeled "Piranha" is built under licence in Canada with the new name of LAV (Light Armored Vehicle).

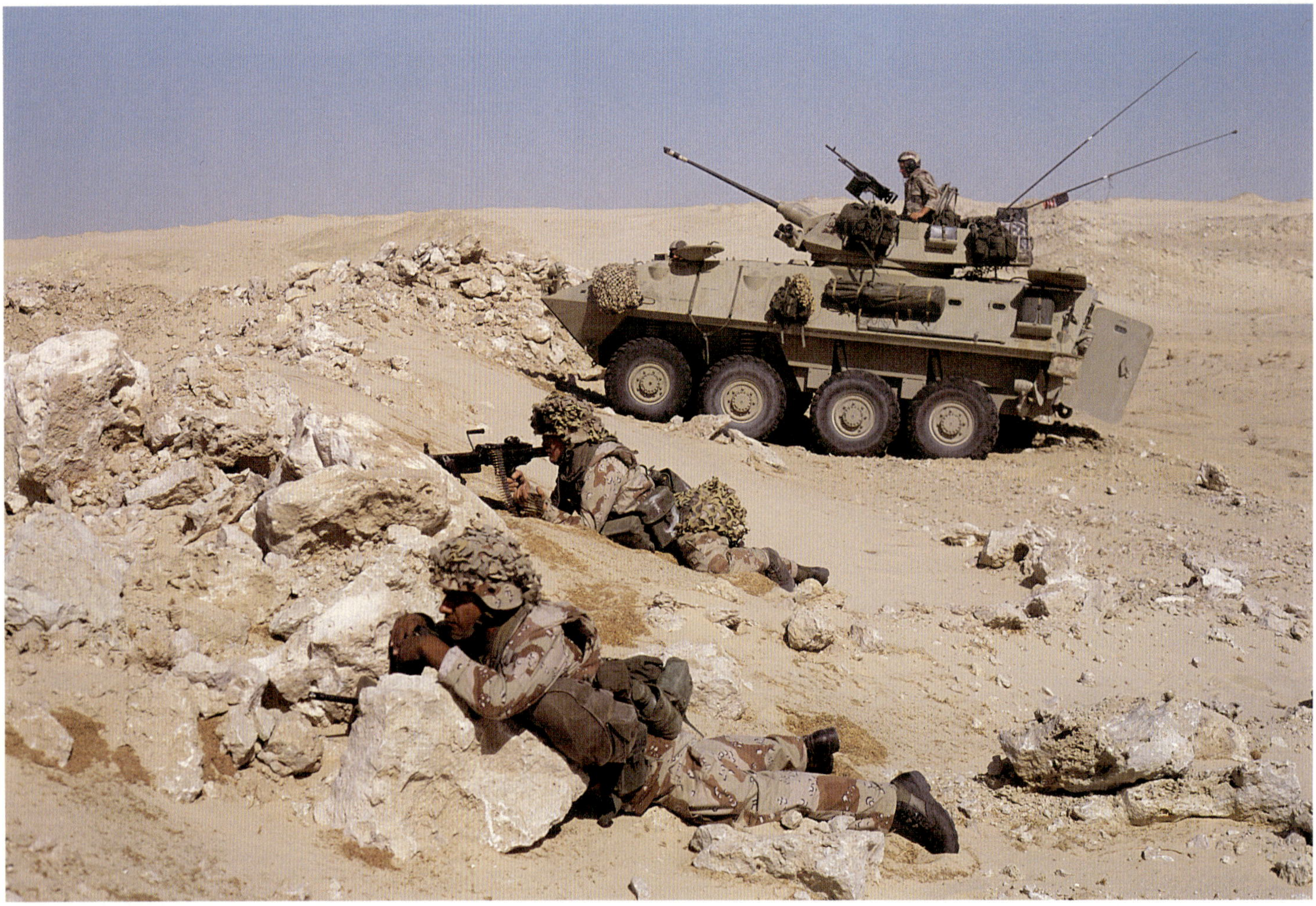

The LAV is amphibious and air-deployable. The Marine Corps CH53E transport helicopter can transport one LAV in the sling position.

The LAV-25 has a two-man turret armed with a 25mm chain gun, a 7.62mmM240 coaxial machine gun and a pintle mounted 7.62mm machine gun. A stabilization system allows the 25mm chain gun to be aimed while the vehicle is on the move.

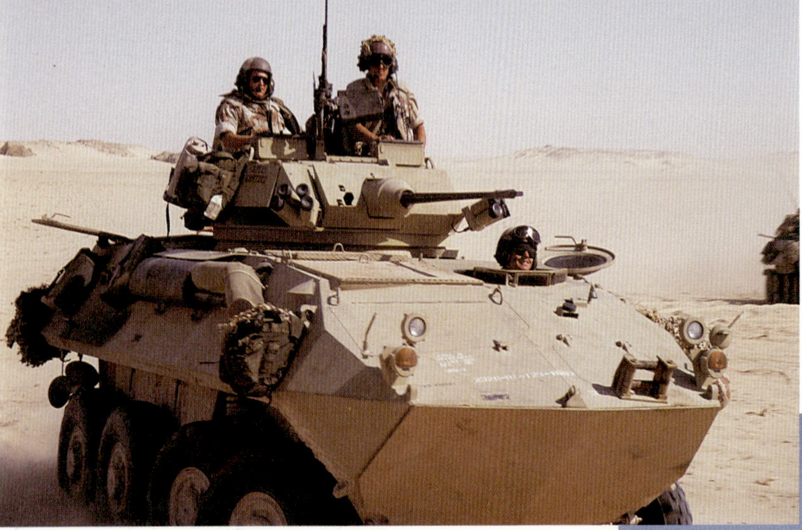

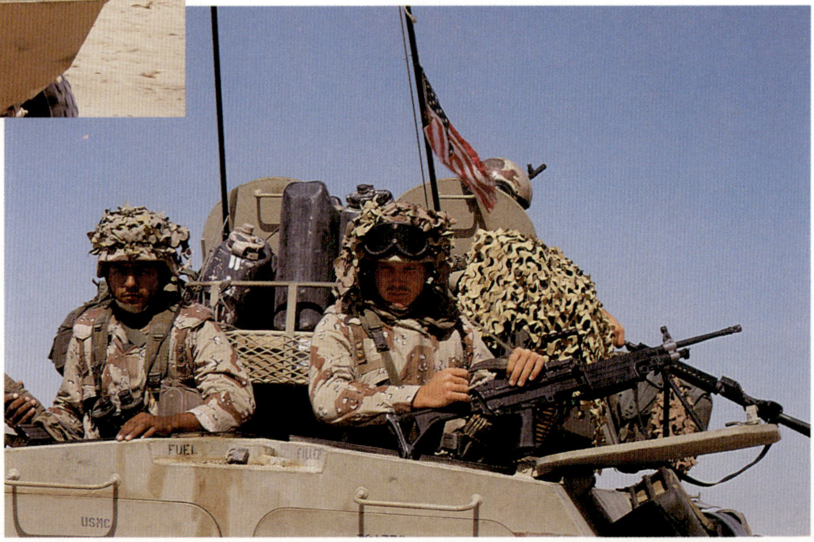

The LAV-25 has a crew of three and can carry six fully equipped Marines inside its armored hull. The two large rear doors allow the troops to disembark quickly. Pictured are two Marines in desert BDUs on guard with the roof hatches opened.

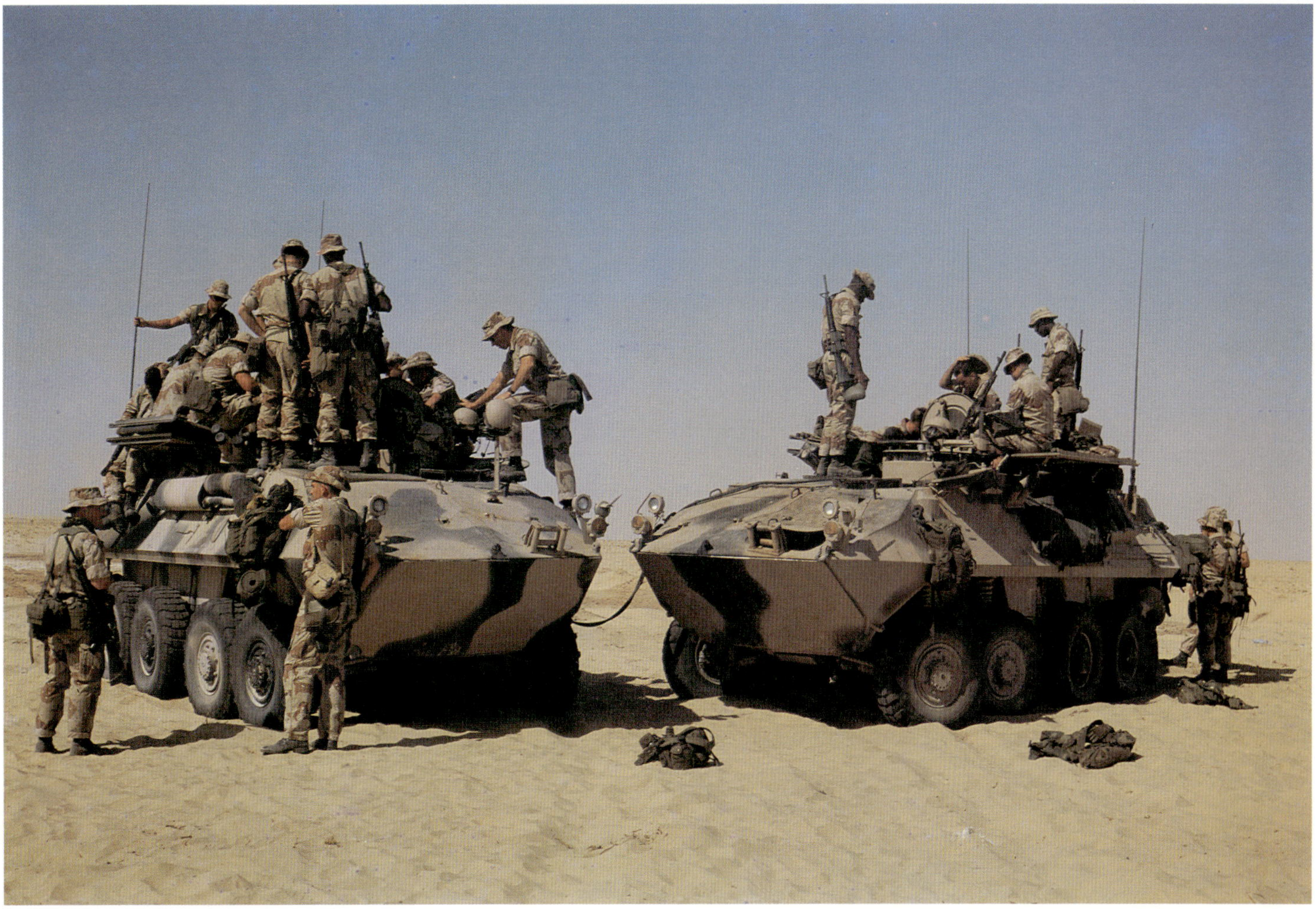

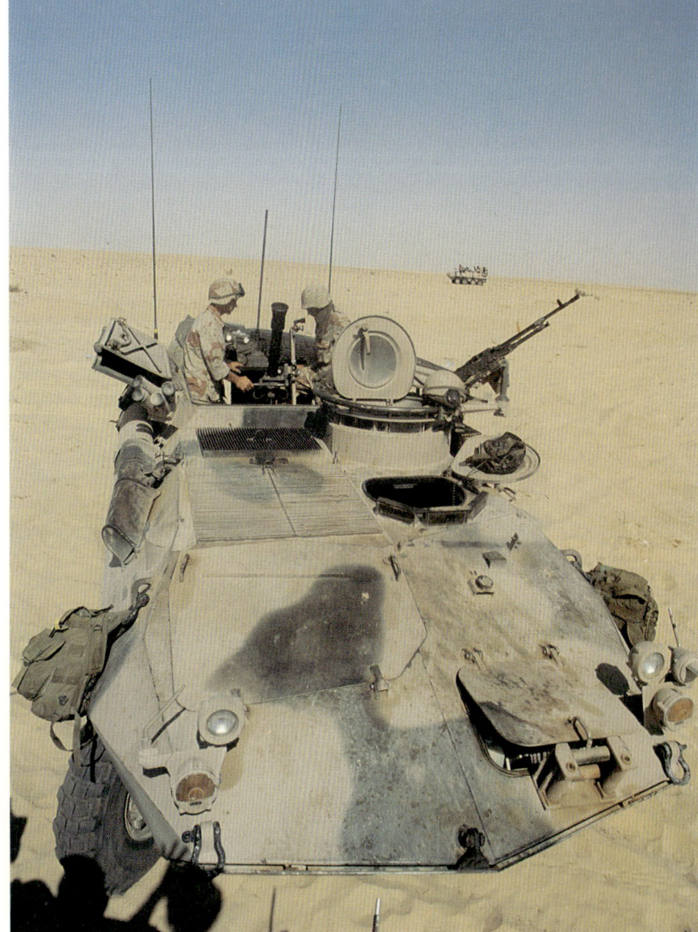

▲ Marines of 3rd LAI crowded around two LAV Mortar Carriers. Each LAV(M) has a crew of four consisting of a commander, a driver and two mortar troops. Each LAI Battalion is equipped with a weapons company with eight LAV(M)s.

▶ The LAV Mortar Carrier variant is fitted with an 81mm mortar mounted in the center of the vehicle and fires through the roof hatch. It can carry 94 rounds of 81mm mortars.

▼ The LAV(AT) Anti-tank version has an Emerson twin TOW launcher mounted on the hull top. It has two ready-to-launch TOW missiles in the launcher and another 14 missiles stored in the hull. The vehicle also carries a gound mount for the TOW.

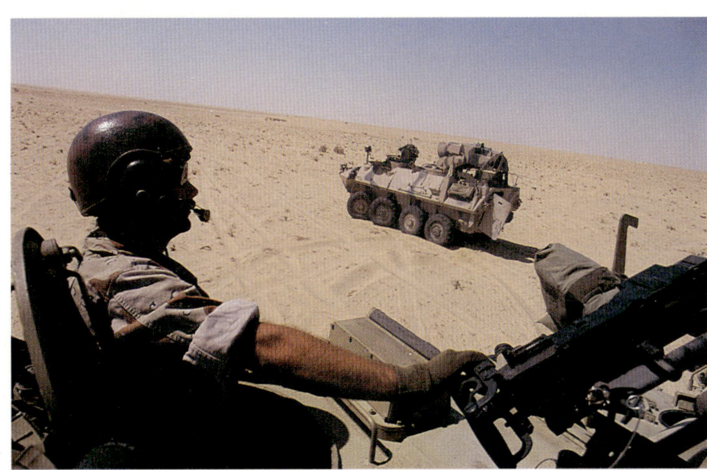

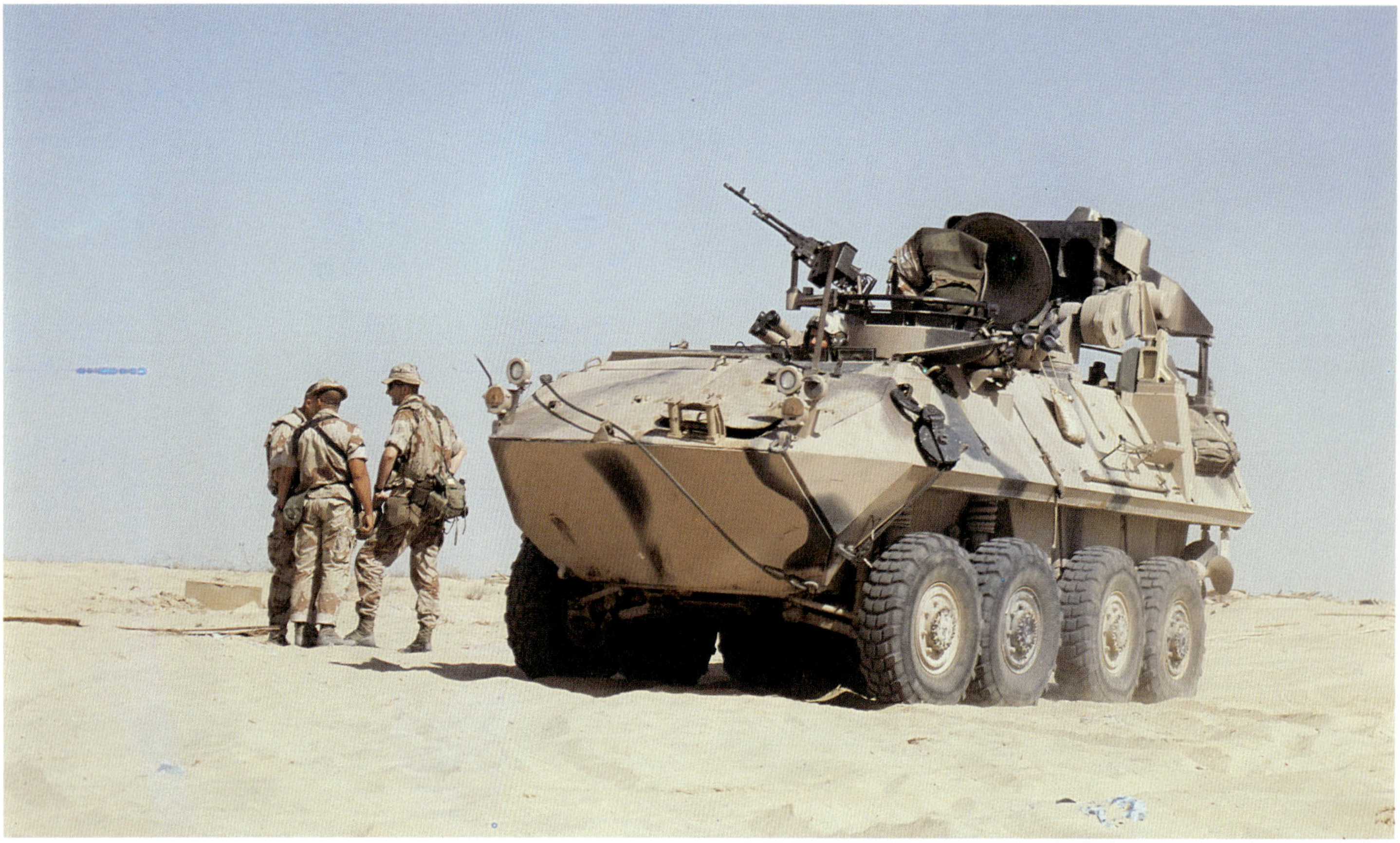

The LAV(AT) has a crew of four, namely the commander, the driver, the gunner and the loader. The vehicle has a pintle mounted 7.62mm machine gun for self defense.

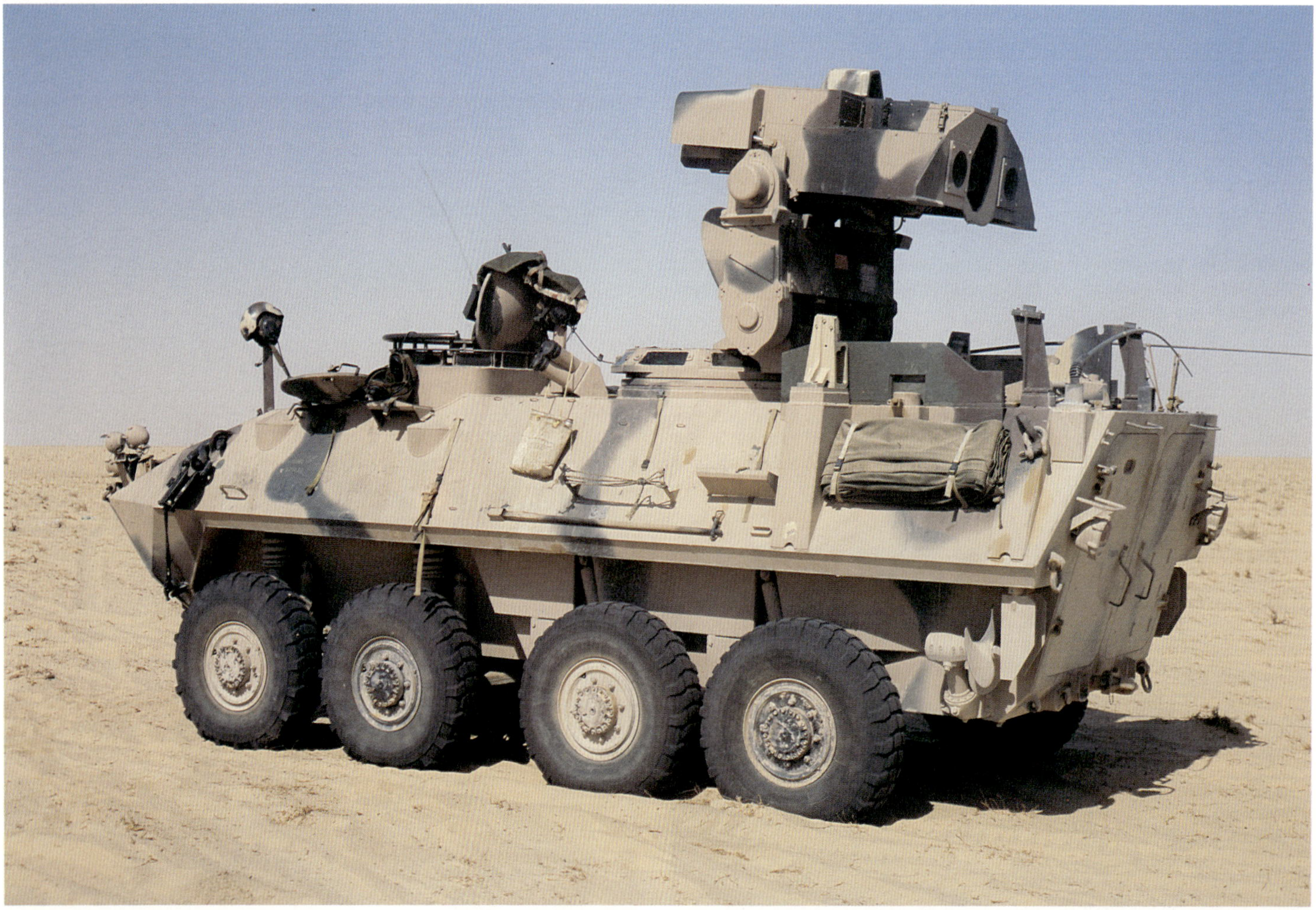

An LAV(AT) of the Marine Corps 3rd LAI Battalion with the TOW launcher erected in training somewhere in Saudi Arabia. The weapons company of 3rd LAI Battalion has 16 of the LAV(AT) vehicles.

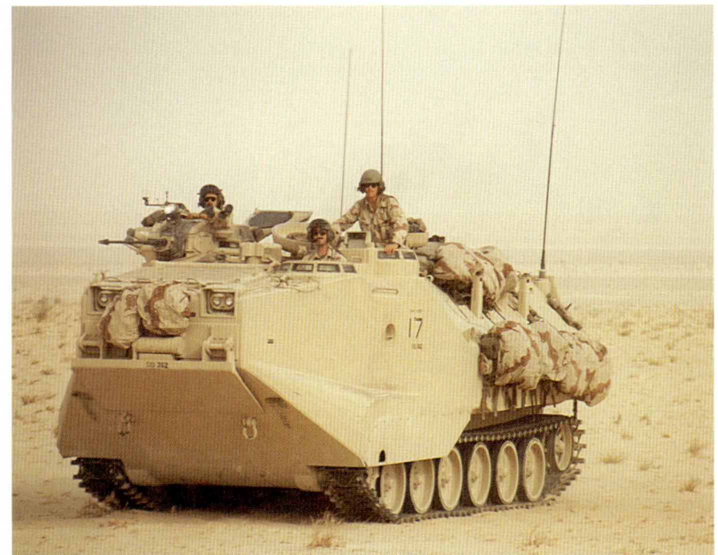

The AAV-7A1 (Assault Amphibious Vehicle 7) is the key transport of the Marines in an amphibious landing. It has the capacity to transport 25 fully equipped Marines plus a crew of three. Its all-welded aluminium hull provides ample protection to its passengers.

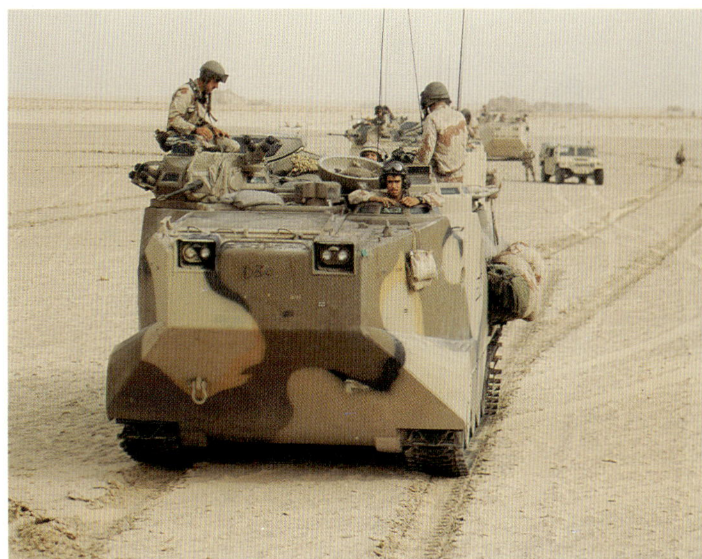

The AAV-7 is fully amphibious without preparation, being propelled in the water by two water jets. The tracks can also be used to propel the vehicle when afloat.

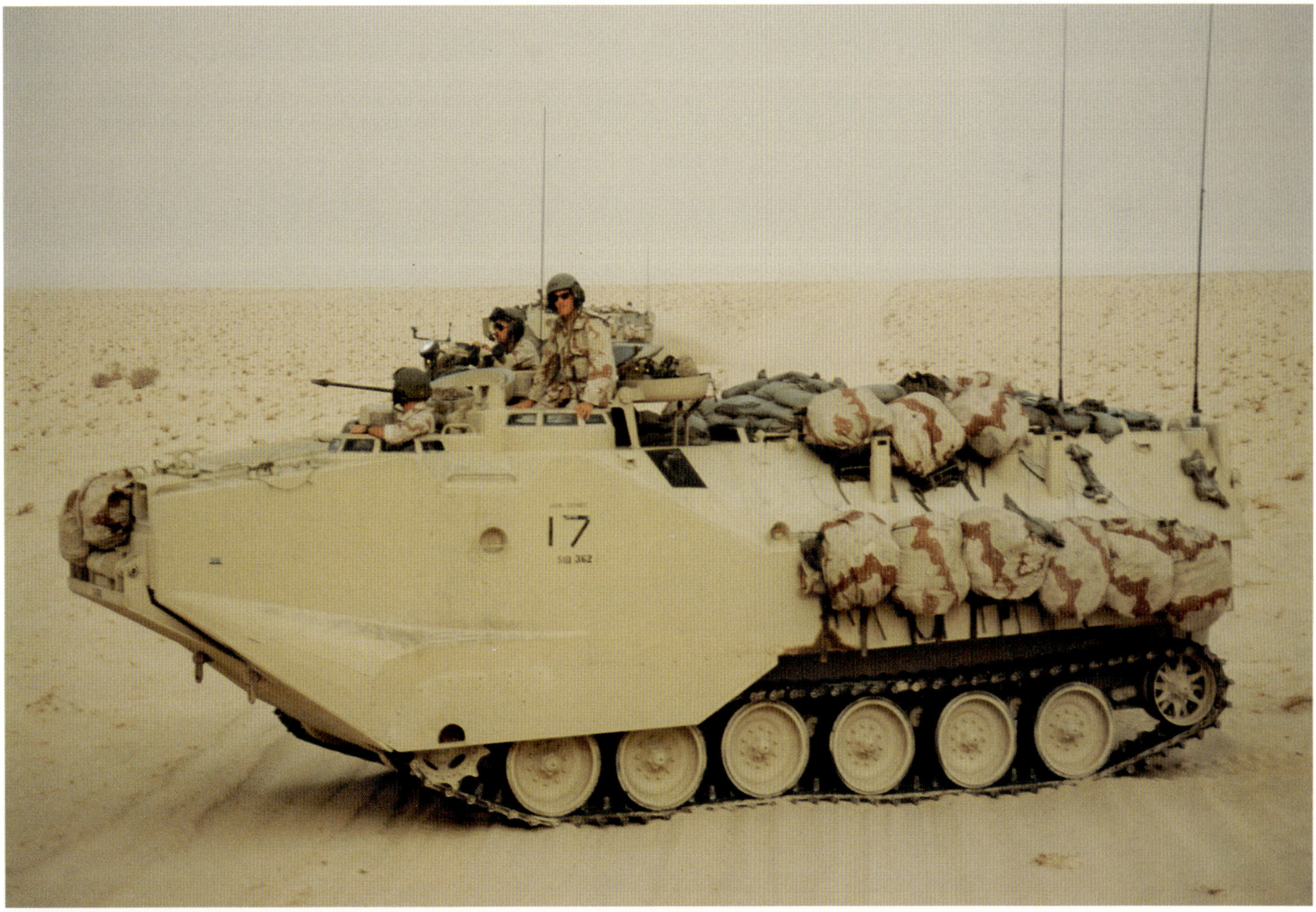

AN AAV-7 in Saudi-Arabia. Note the troops' gear hanging on the side of the vehicle. The turret is armed with a 12.7mm machine gun. Some AAV-7s deployed to Saudi-Arabia were fitted with P-900 applique armor and a new turret armed with 12.7mm machine gun and 40mm grenade launcher.

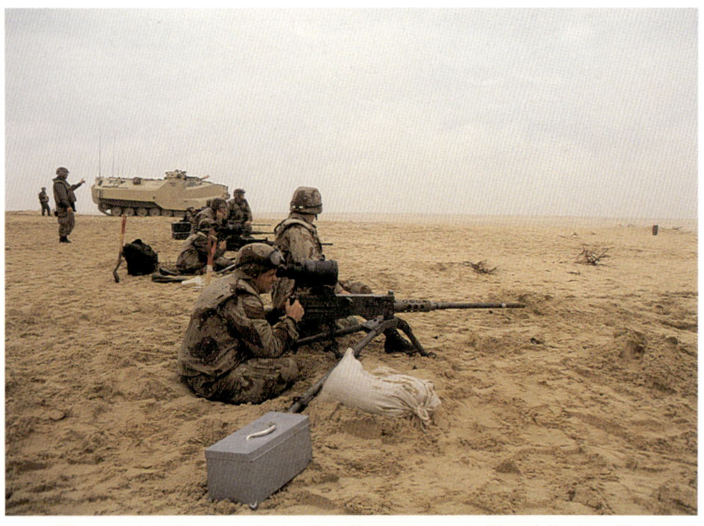

Dismounted Marines during live fire exercise in Saudi Arabia. Their .50 caliber machine guns are fitted with night sights. Their AAV-7 transport is at the back.

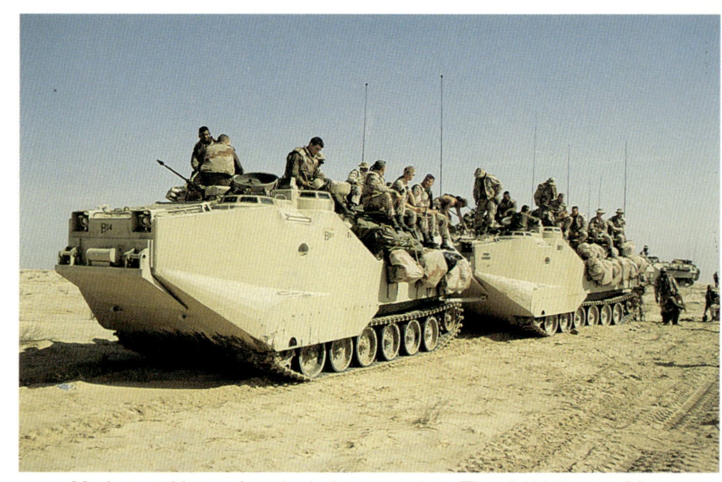

Marines taking a break during exercise. The AAV-7s provide armor protection, command and control, and repair capabilities while transporting troops and cargo from ship to shore, while negotiating ten-foot plunging surf, difficult beaches, and rough terrain. The AAV-7 is often called the "Marine taxi", each Marine division has a battalion of these vehicles attached.

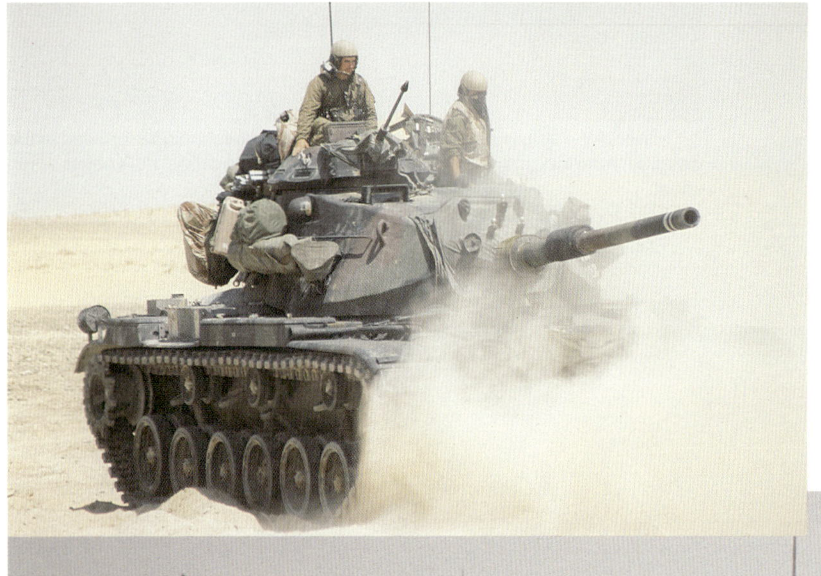

◄ With a crew of four, the M60A1 has a weight of 45 tons and can reach a speed of 52km/hr on flat ground. It has a 105mm gun with a coaxial 7.62mm machine gun, and another 12.7mm(.50 caliber) machine gun mounted on the commander's cupola.

▼ The first American main battle tanks to arrive in Saudi-Arabia for Operation Desert Shield were the Marine Corps M60A1 tanks. These tanks belonged to the 1st Marine Tank Battalion and were prepositioned on board ships based at Diego Gracia.

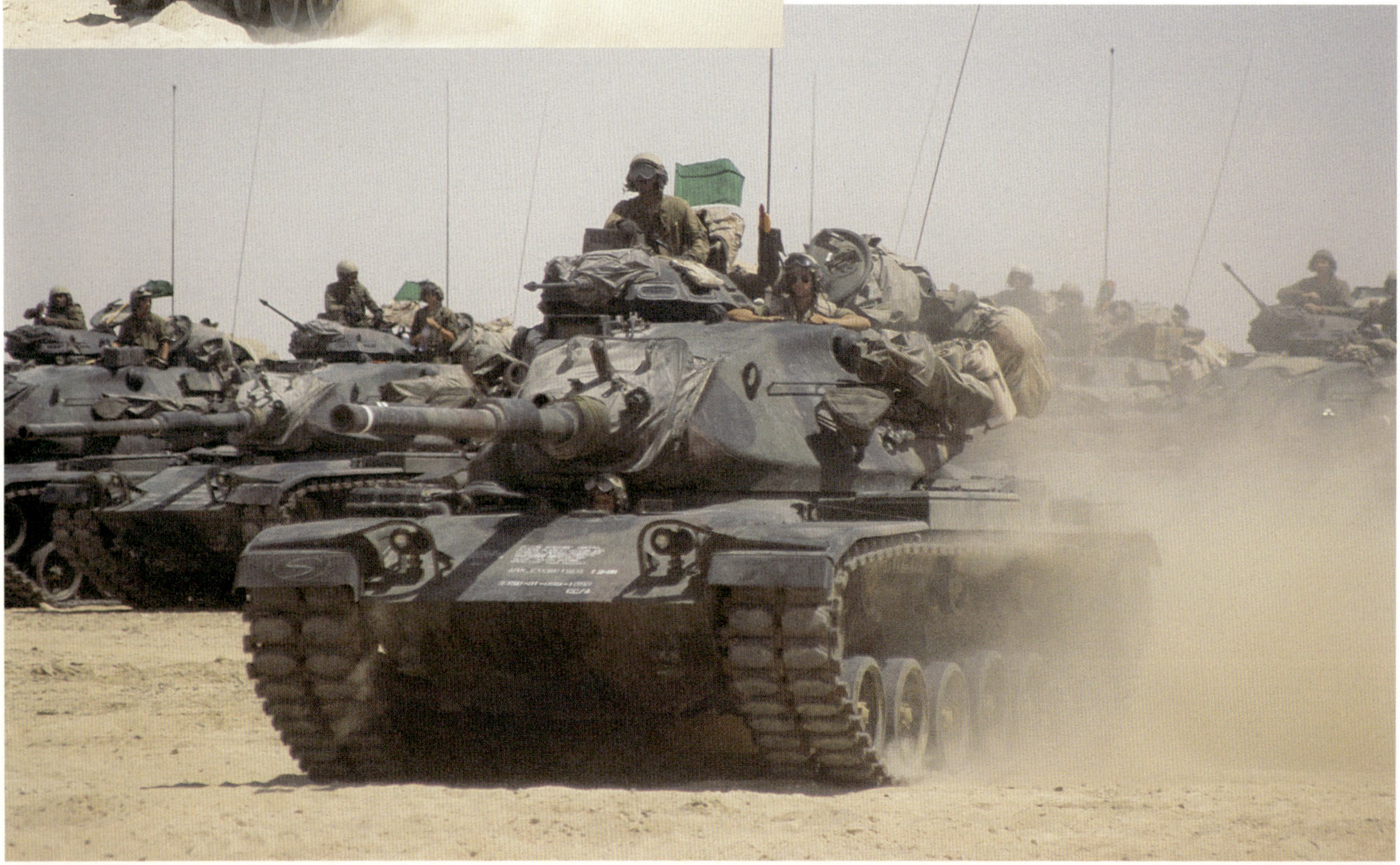

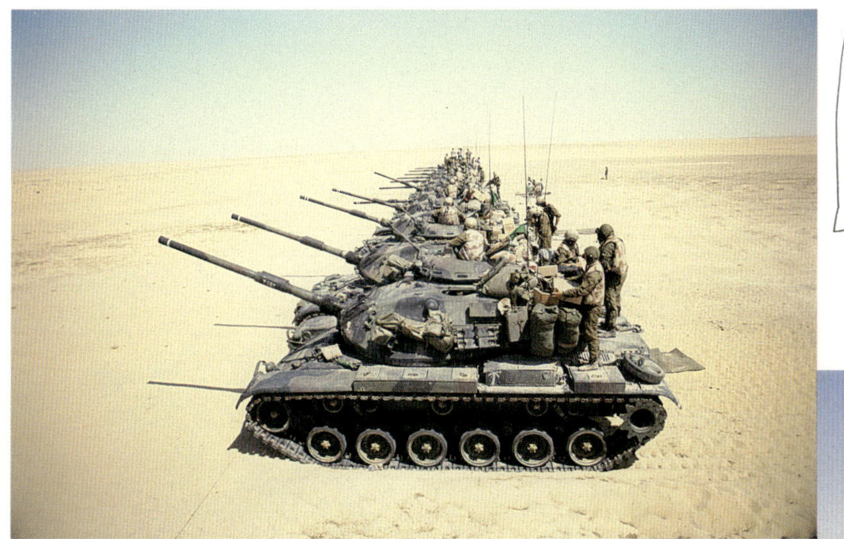

A row of Marine M60A1 tanks test firing their 105mm guns after their deployment to the Saudi desert. Since its introduction in the 1970s, the M60A1 had gone through a three-part improvement program to upgrade its performance. The final product after the improvement program was the M60A1(RISE/PASSIVE).

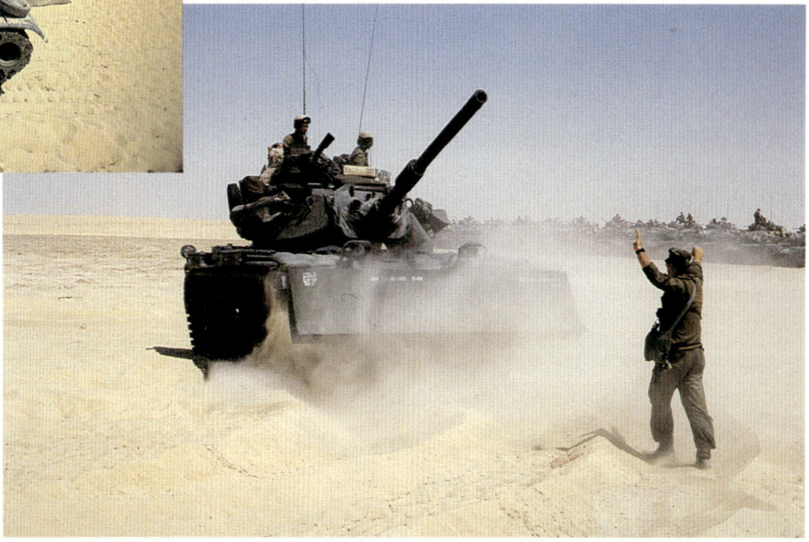

An M60A1 of the 1st Marine Tank Battalion fitted with a dozer blade backing up to fall into position to form a row with the other tanks.

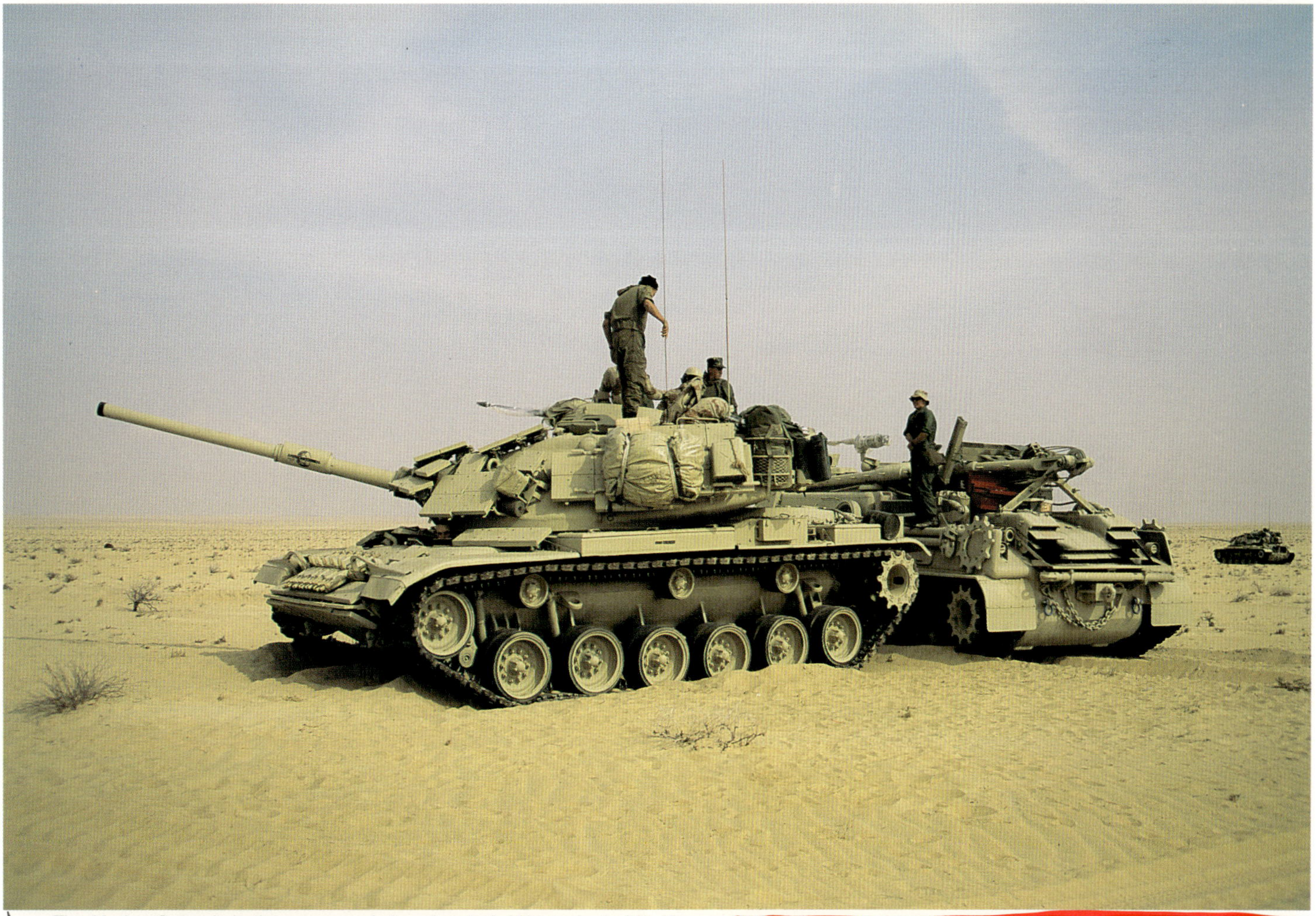

The Marine Corps is in the process of changing their M60 tanks to M1 Abrams. Before the switch-over is complete, reactive armor tiles is a stop-gap measure to improve survivability to the M60A1 (RISE/PASSIVE)tanks used by the Corps.

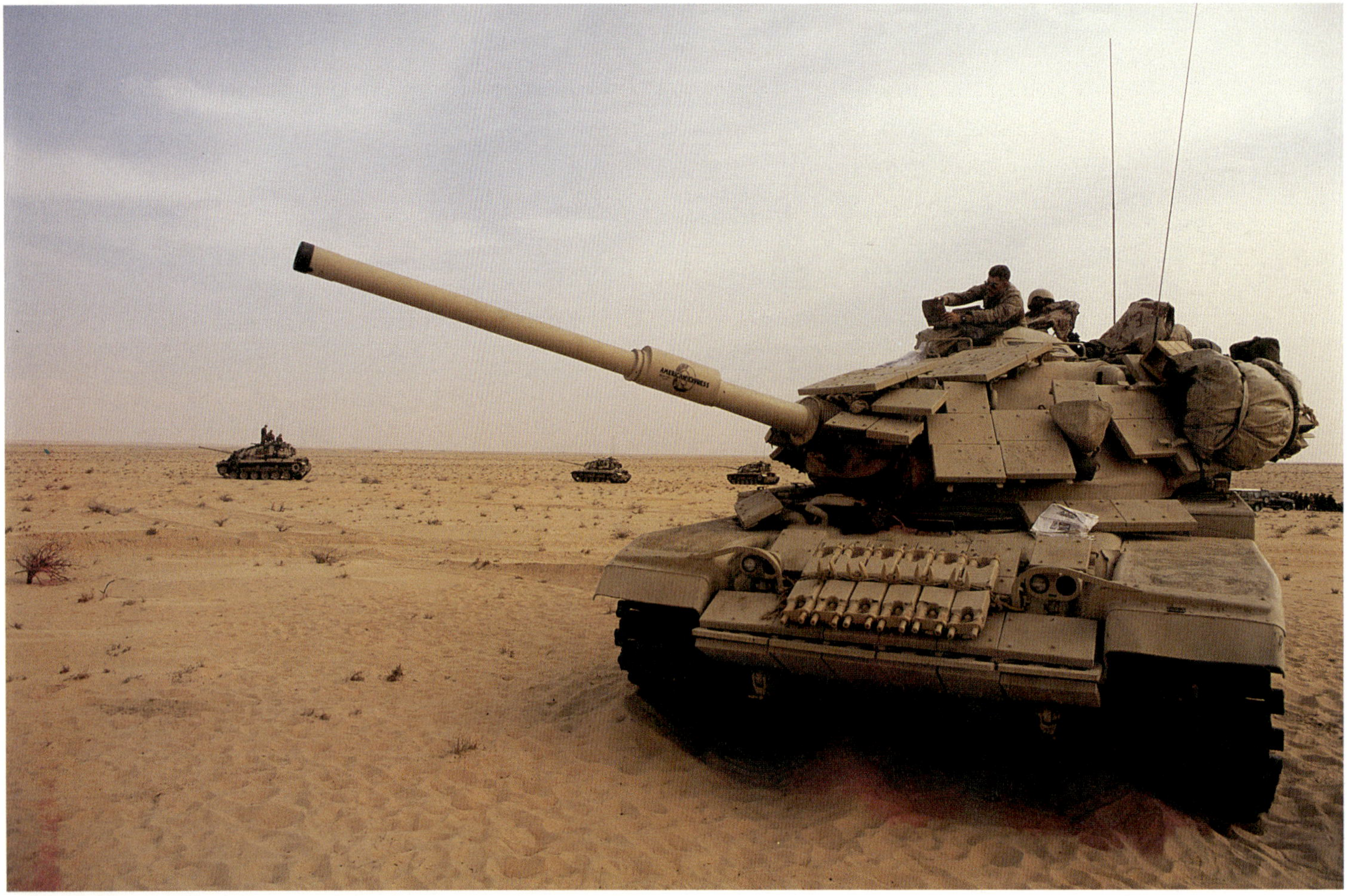

▲ Bombing up of "American Express" prior to a live firing exercise in Saudi Arabia. "American Express" is fitted with reactive armor tiles.

◄ The reactive armor tiles are mounted to the exterior of the tank's hull and turret, and consists of 91 armor tiles (49 M1 tiles and 42 M2 tiles) which attach to mounting hardware using retaining clips and machine bolts. Some of the outside tow cables and brackets have had to be modified and/or relocated due to the installation of reactive armor tiles.

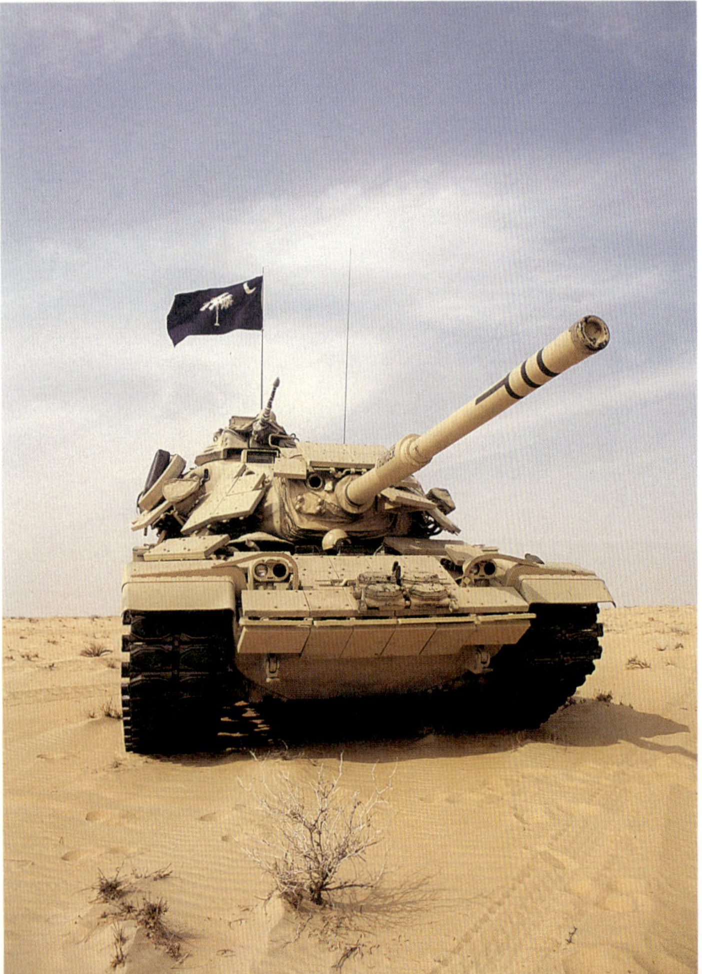

▼ M60A1 tanks of the 8th Marine Tank Battalion lining up for a gunnery match.

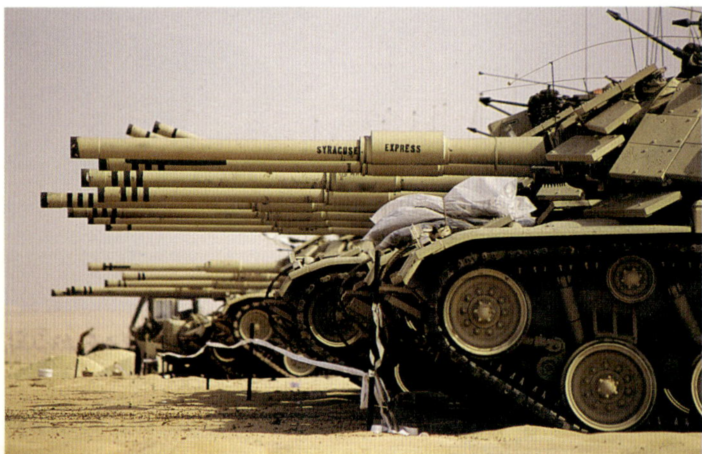

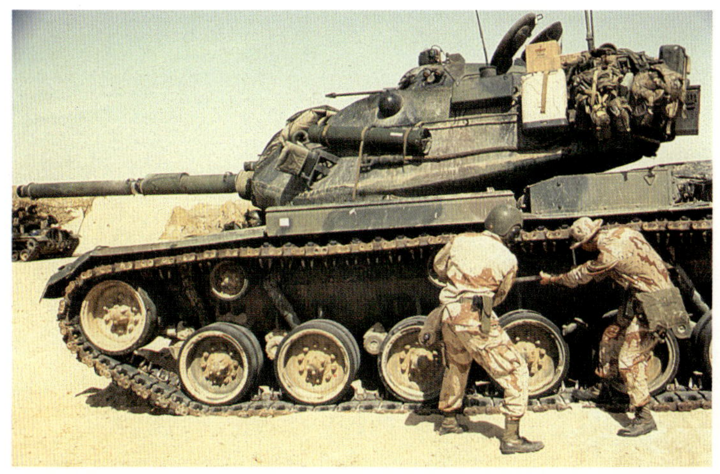

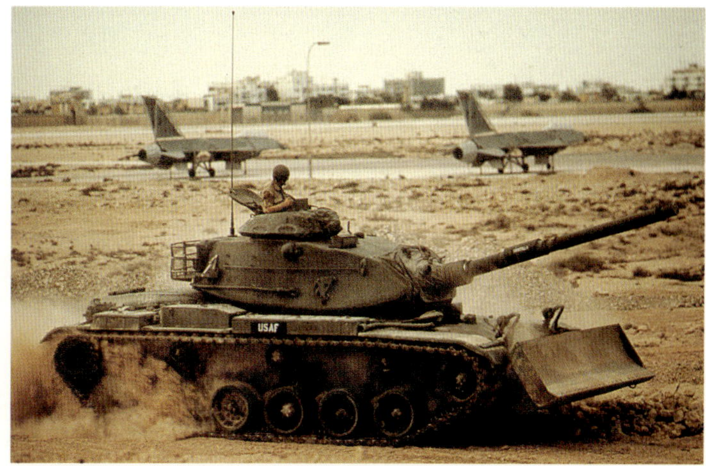

▲ While most U.S. Army main battle tanks in Saudi Arabia were either M1 or M1A1 tanks, five M60A3 tanks belonging to the 197th Infantry Brigade were deployed in the country.(DoD)

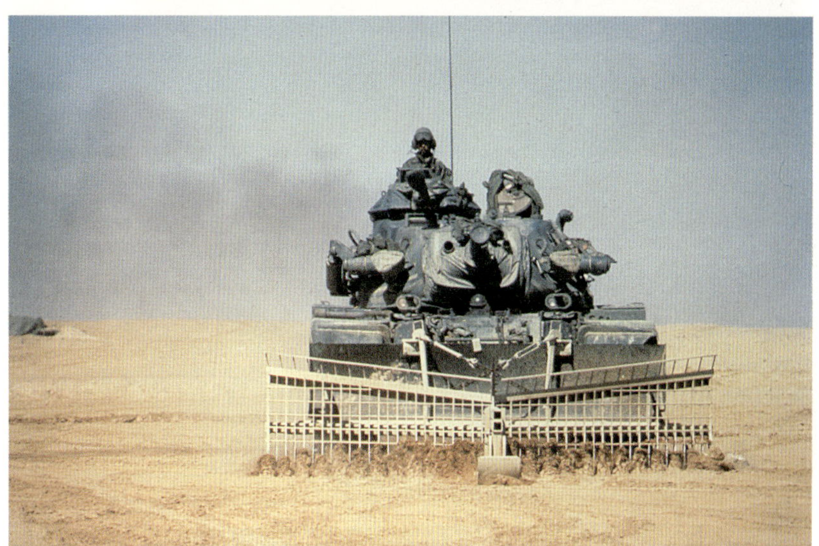

▲▶ The strangest M60 tank deployed to Saudi Arabia during Operation Desert Shield, was this first-of-its-kind United Stated Air Force M60A3 tank. Notice the USAF marking on the side of the tank. Also notice the decoy F-16 fighter planes in the background.(DoD)

▼▶ The 24th Mechanized Infantry Division deployed a number of M728 Combat Engineer Vehicles to Saudi Arabia. The vehicles were mounted a brand-new mine clearing rake. Created for sand or loose soil, the 12-inch rake was used by both Army and Marine combat engineers in Saudi Arabia to breach a 180-inch path through Iraqi minefields. This is wide enough to allow an M1A1 to pass. (DoD)

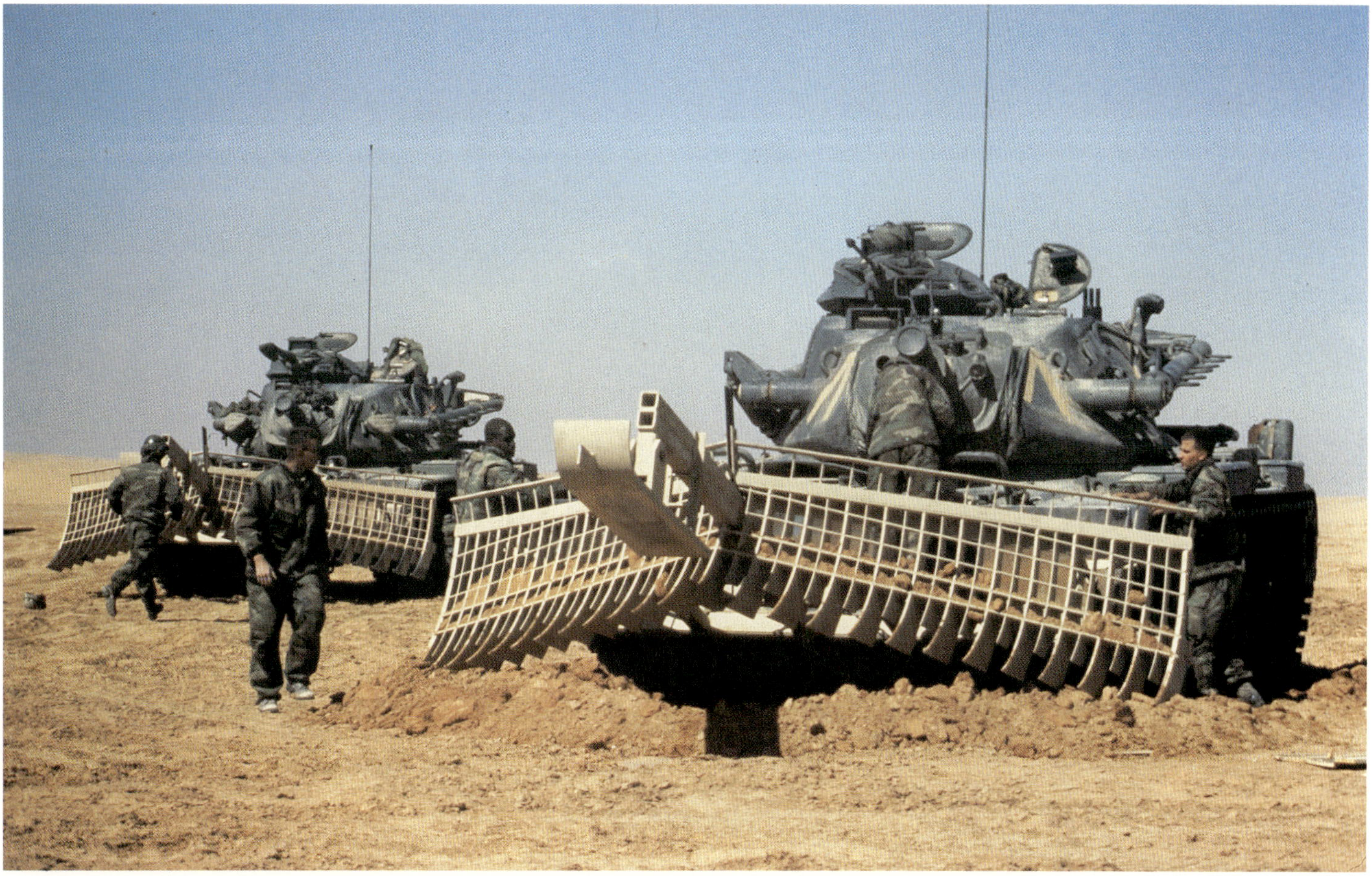

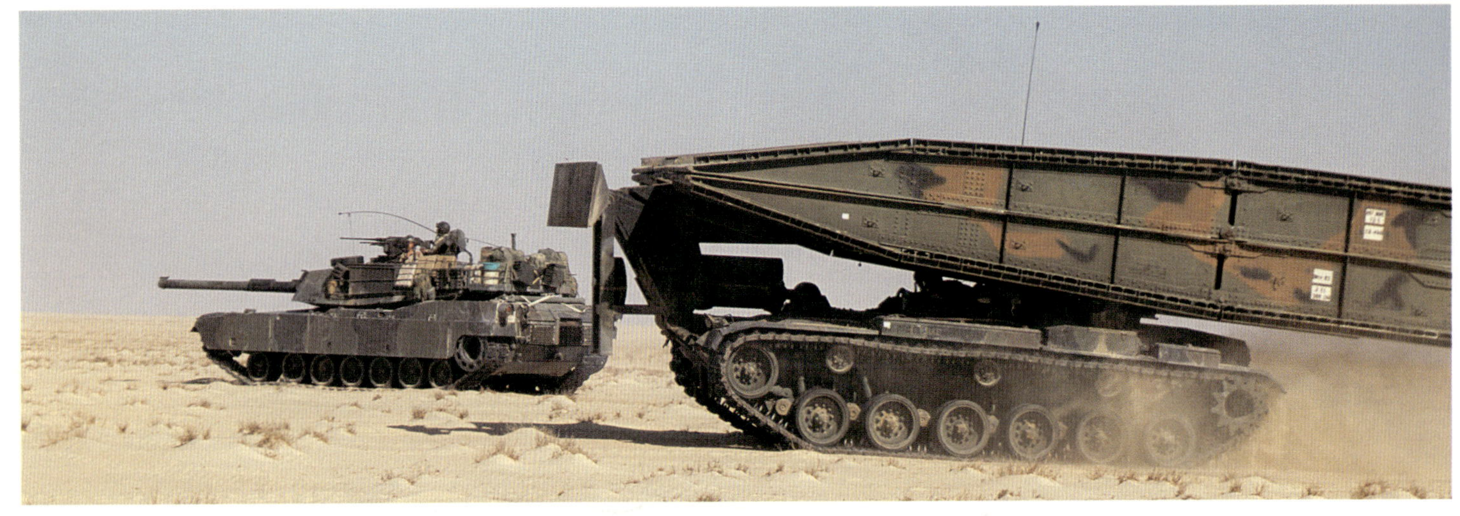

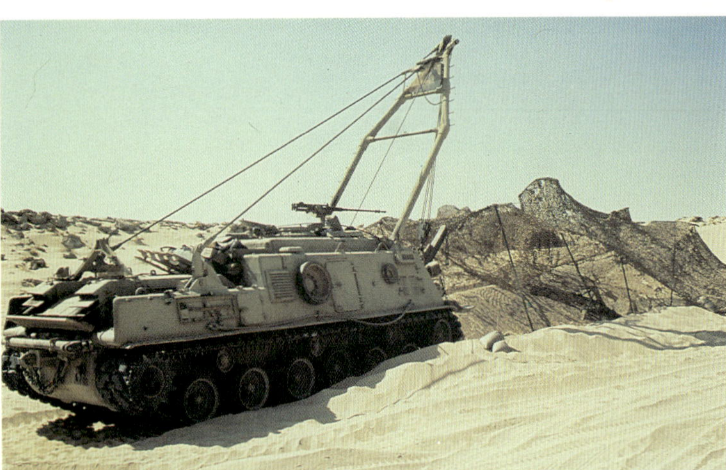

▲ Pictured is an M1 of the 197th Mechanized Infantry Brigade covering an M60 AVLB (Armored Vehicle Launched Bridge) while it approaches a ditch it will span. The M60AVLB is fitted with a hydraulic launching mechanism and the aluminium scissors bridge takes only two minutes to lay and can span a ditch of up to 18.288m.

◄ Used in Saudi Arabia by both the Army and Marine Corps was the M88A1 armored recovery vehicle. (DoD)

▼ An M578 Light Armored Recovery Vehicle towing an M548 tracked cargo carrier. The M578 has a turret at the rear of the hull fitted with a crane which can be traversed through 360 degrees.

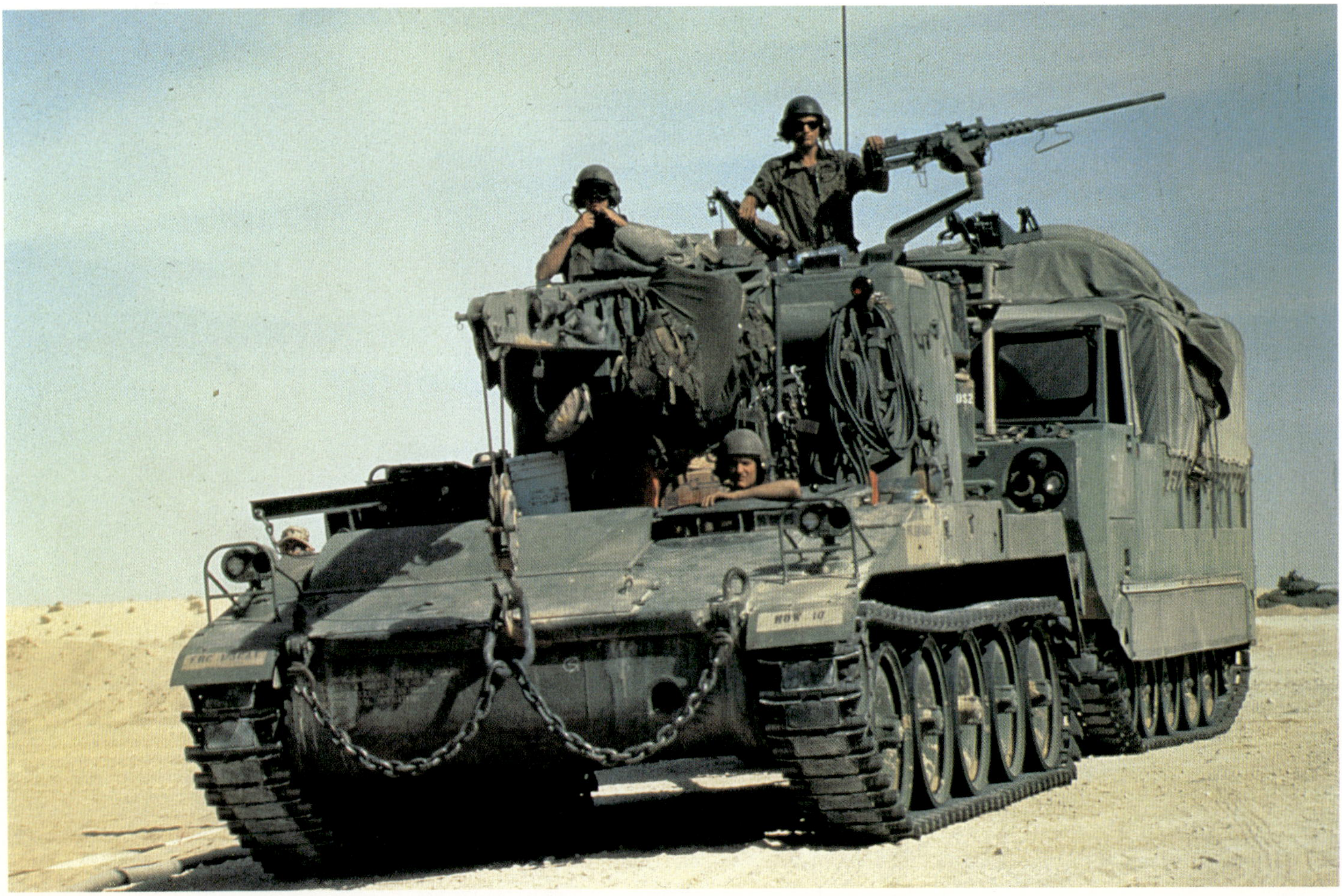

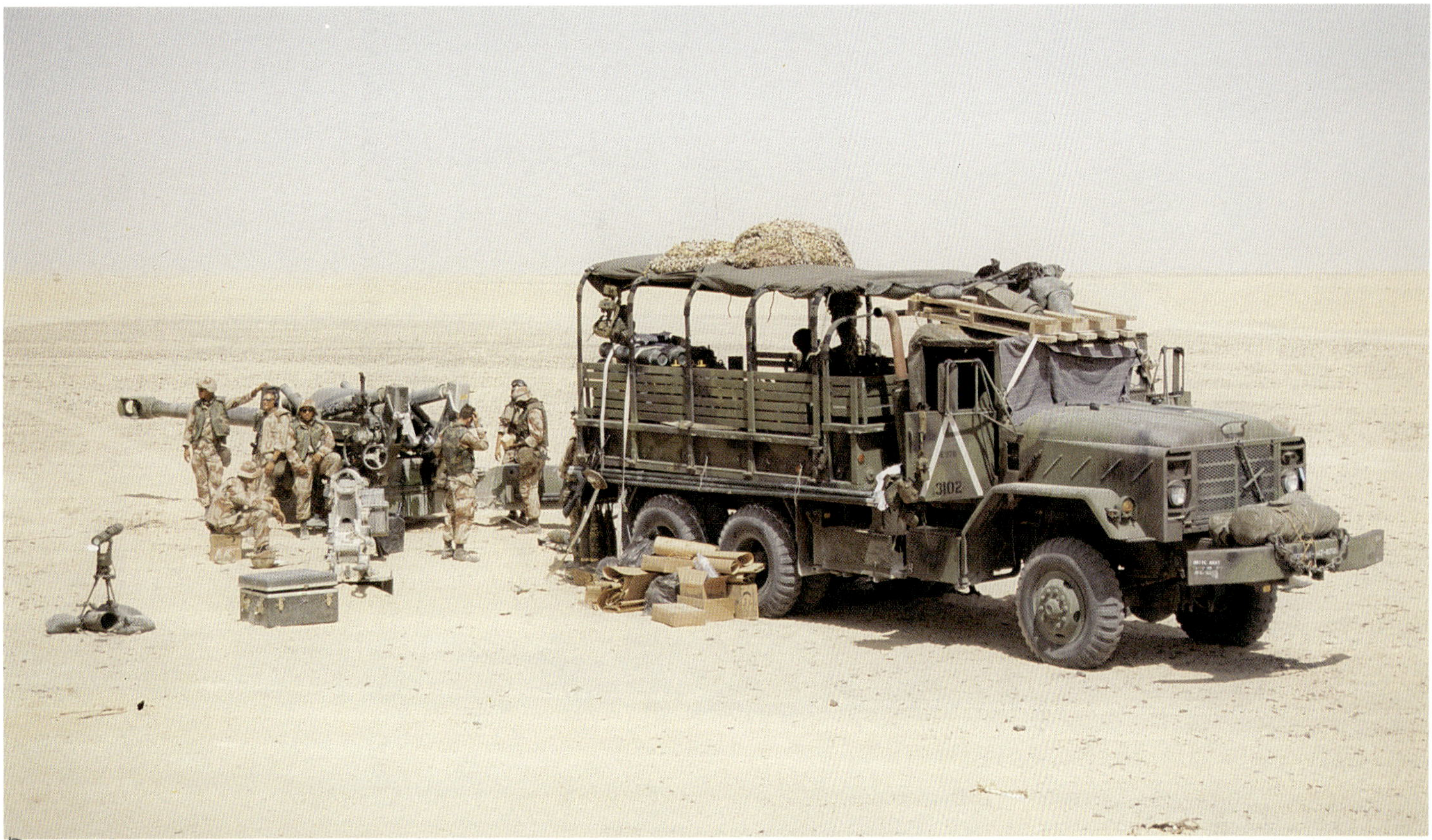

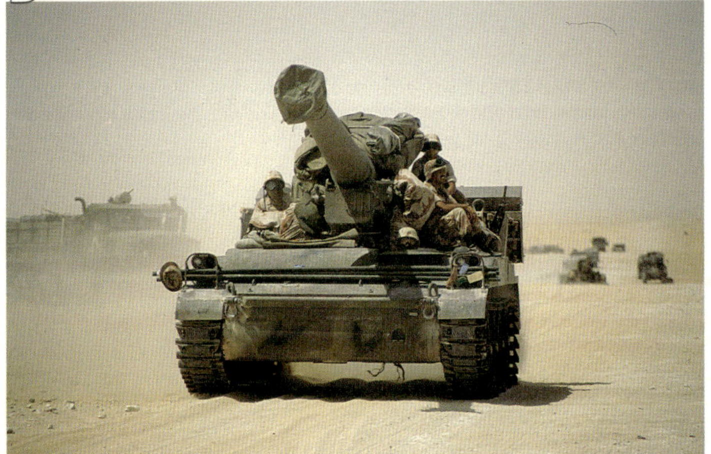

The 155mm M198 howitzer is the standard gun of the Marine Corps. It is towed by the M939 truck and can be put into battery position in 10 minutes time.

The M110A2 self-propelled gun is the biggest artillery piece used by the Marines. Shown is an M110A2 of the 13th Marine Artillery Regiment.

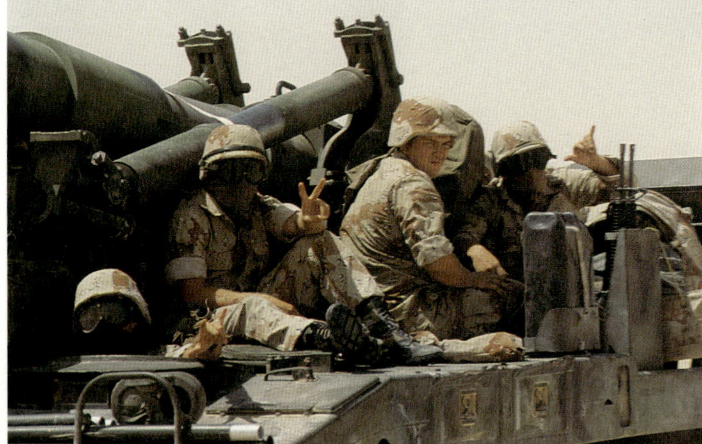

The M110A2 is operated by a 13 crew, of which the commander, the driver and three gunners are carried on the gun. It is armed with a 203mm (8-inch) howitzer. Each Marine Artillery Regiment has twelve M110A2 self-propelled howitzers.

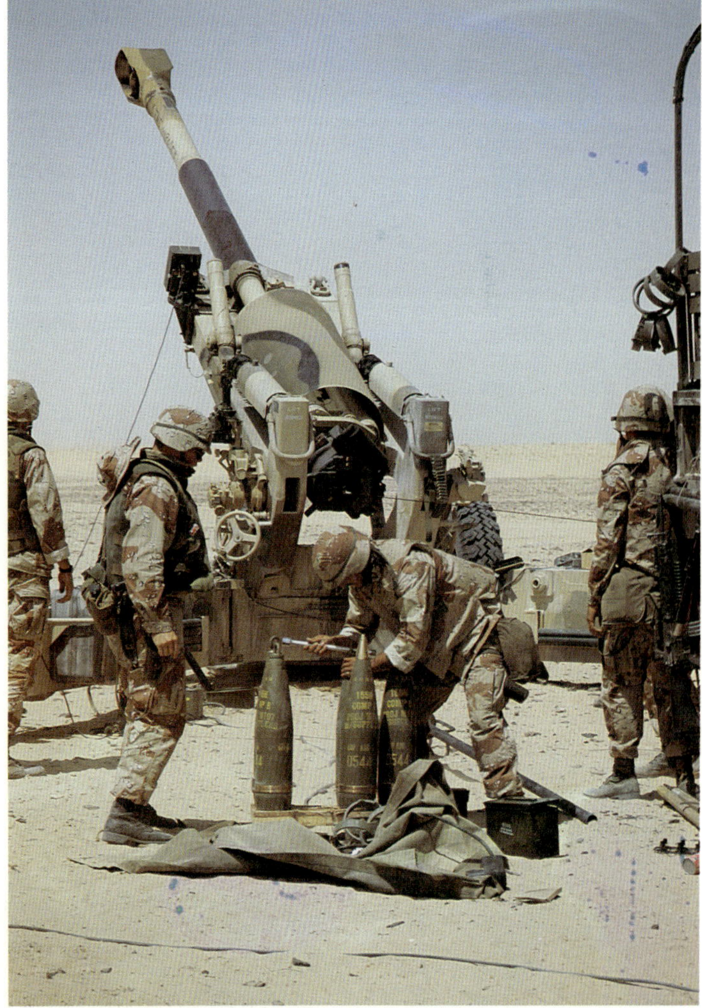

M198 155mm howitzer of the 13th Marine Artillery Regiment in action in Saudi Arabia. The range is 24km but with certain projectiles the M198 can reach an improved range of 30km. The rate is 4 rounds per minute.

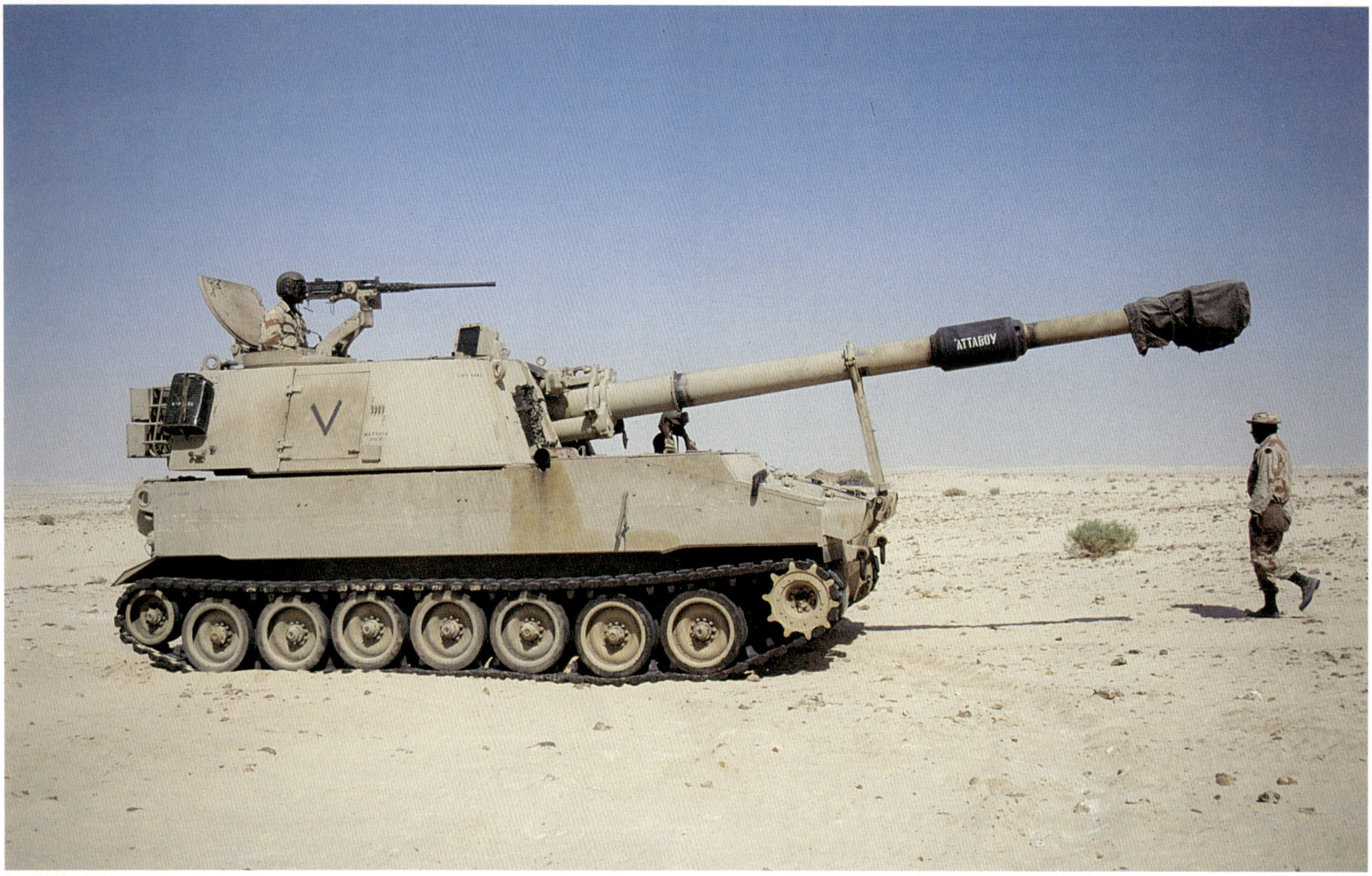

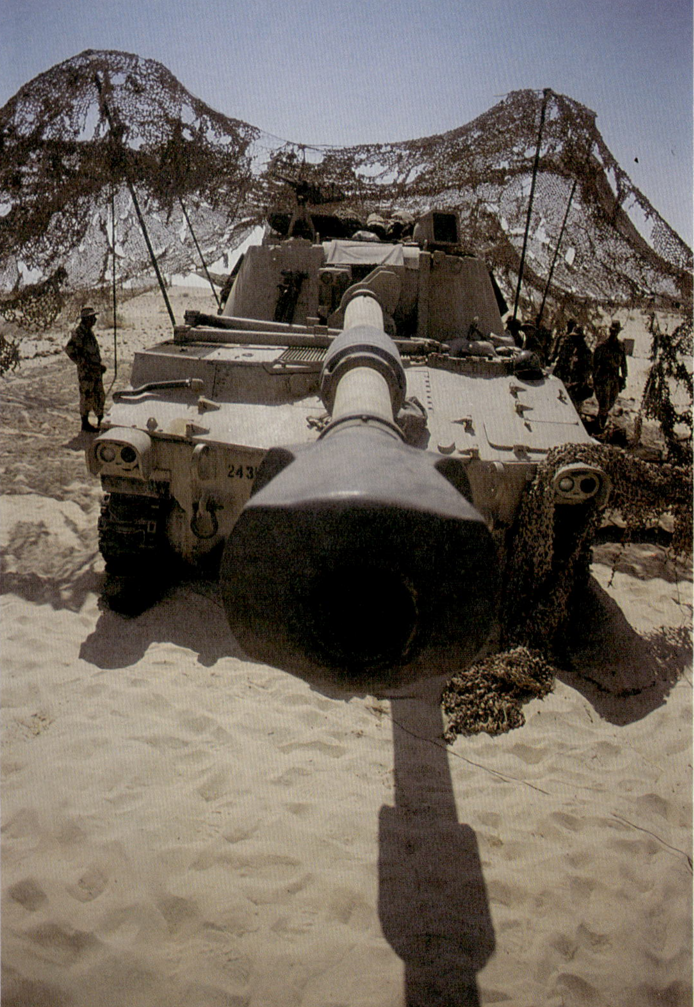

▲ The M109A2 155mm self-propelled howitzer is an aluminium-armored, air-transportable field artillery weapon system. The vehicle has a top speed of 35 mph and a cruising range of 220 miles.

◄ All of the M109s of the 24th Mechanized Infantry Division are of the M109A2 variant. Each brigade of the 24th ID has an M109A2 battalion, and there are 24 M109A2s in a battalion. Shown is an M109A2 of the 3/41st Artillery under a camouflaged net in Saudi Arabia.

▼ The M548 Tracked Cargo Carrier is used as an ammunition resupply vehicle for the M109 and M110 self-propelled artillery units. It is fitted with a .50 caliber machine gun for self defense. (DoD)

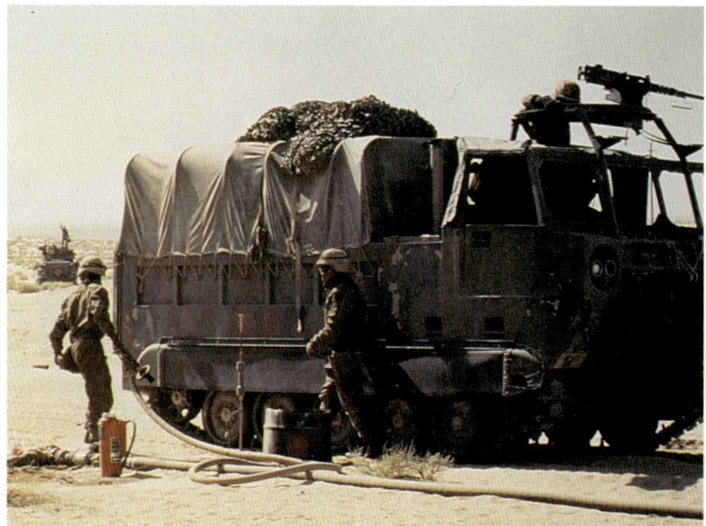

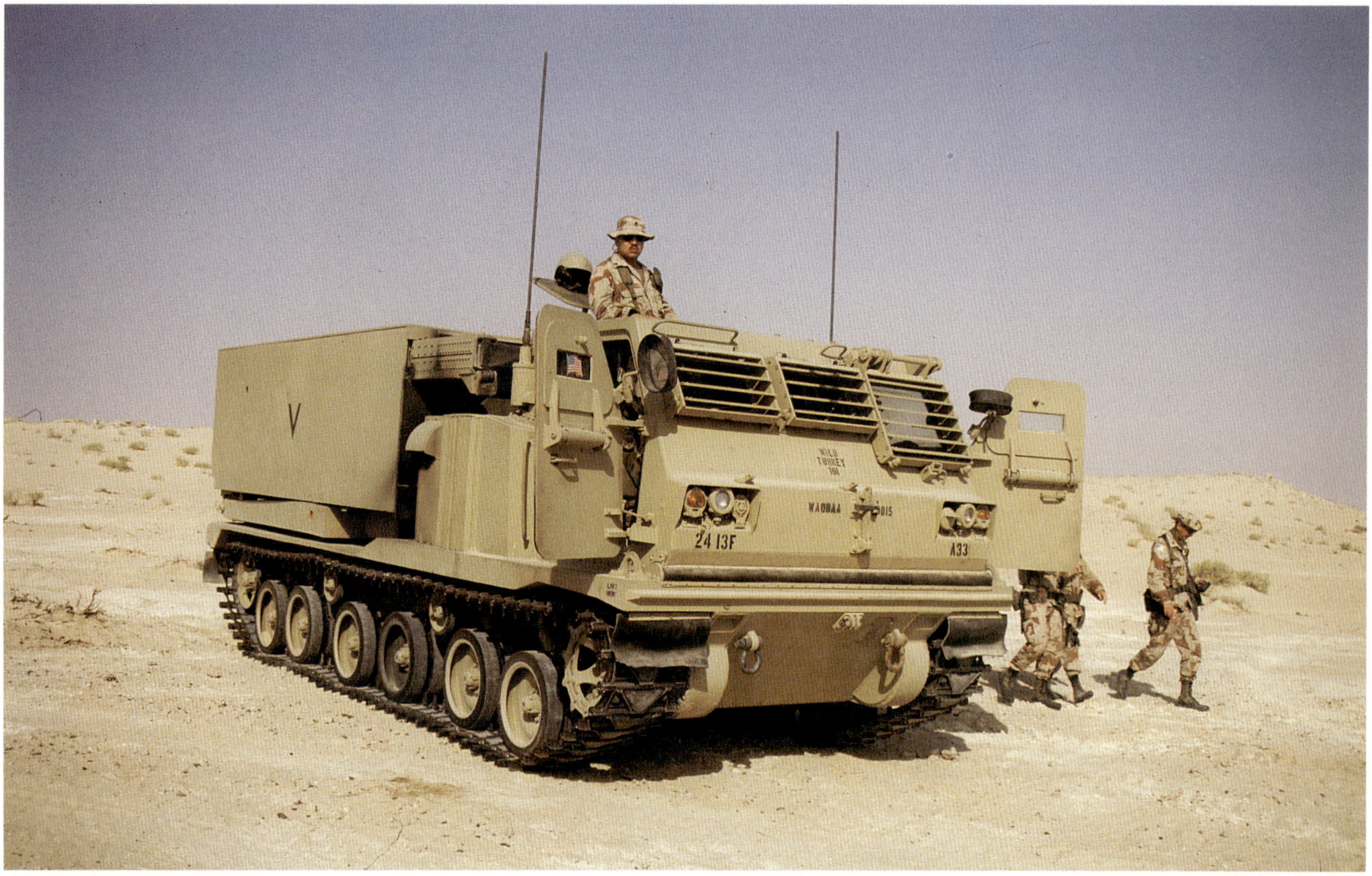

▲ The 24th Mechanized Infantry Division had a Multiple Launch Rocket System (MLRS) battery attached to it in Saudi Arabia. The MLRS battery is attached to the 17th Field Artillery. Each MLRS battery is divided into three groups of three MLRS vehicles each.

▼ M548 Tracked Cargo Carrier of the 3/41st Artillery, 24th ID under a camouflage net in Saudi Arabia. The M548 can carry a maximum load of 5,443kg and is amphibious.

▶ The MLRS is a free-flight artillery rocket system that greatly improves the conventional indirect fire capability of the field army. Its primary mission is to counter fire and suppression of enemy artillery and air defense systems. Shown is an MLRS of the 24th ID.

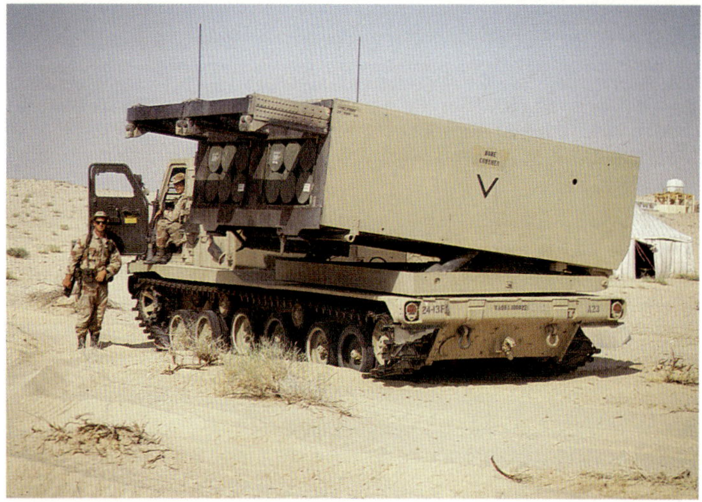

▶▼ An MLRS of the 24th ID ready to be reloaded with 2 six-round pack of rockets.

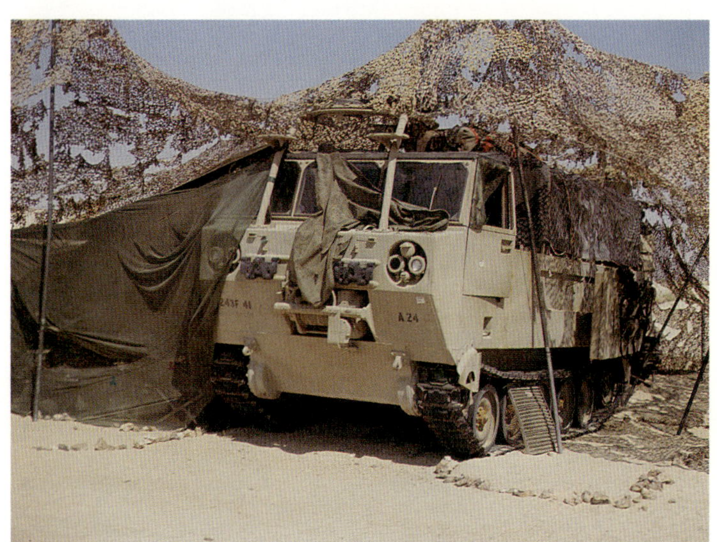

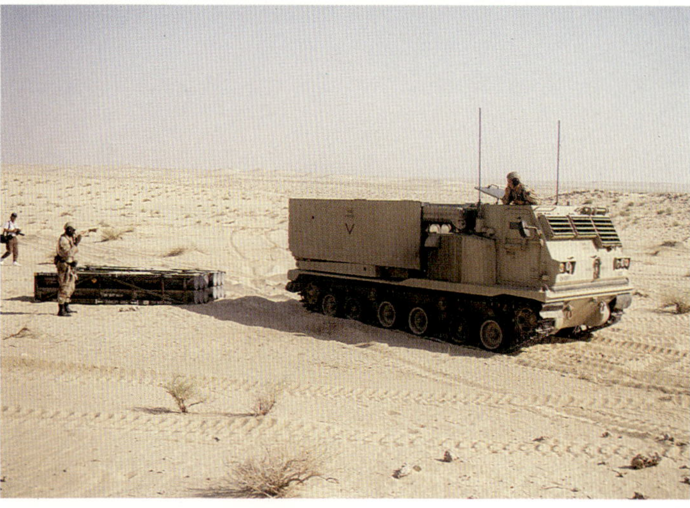

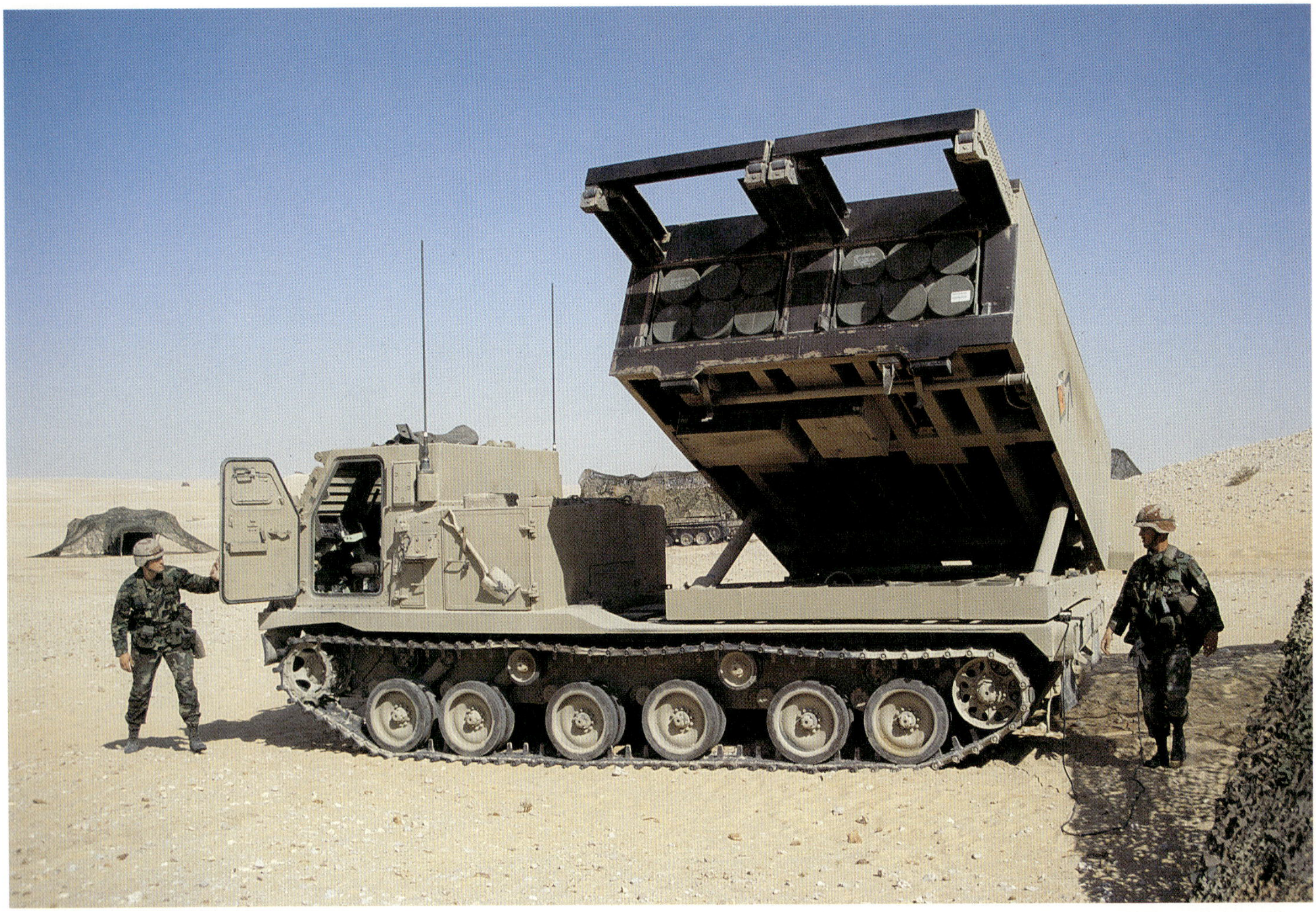

▲ Shown is an MLRS of the 1st Cavalry in firing position. The MLRS consists of a 12-round launcher mounted on a highly mobile, tracked vehicle and is capable of firing rockets one at a time or in rapid ripples to ranges of more than 30km.

▼ The MLRS rocket launcher system is mounted on a Bradley-type chassis known as the M987 Fighting Vehicle System (FVS) carrier. The FVS carrier armored cab seats three people. Armor protection is provided by the aluminium cab and ballistic front windows. Pictured is an MLRS of the 1st Cavalry on the move.

▶ An Avenger air defense system arriving a Saudi Arabia seaport. A pedestal-mounted Stinger missile system is being fitted to a HMMWV chassis.

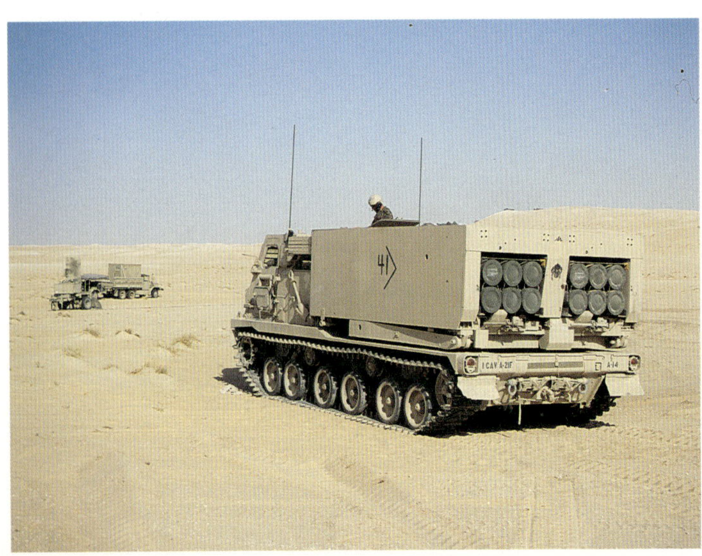

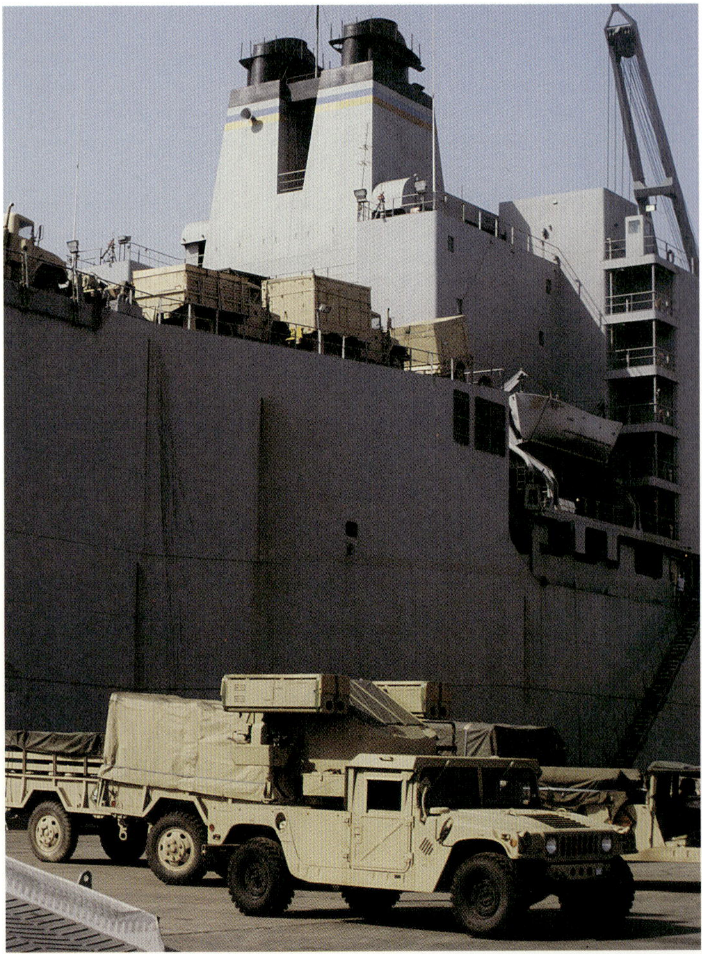

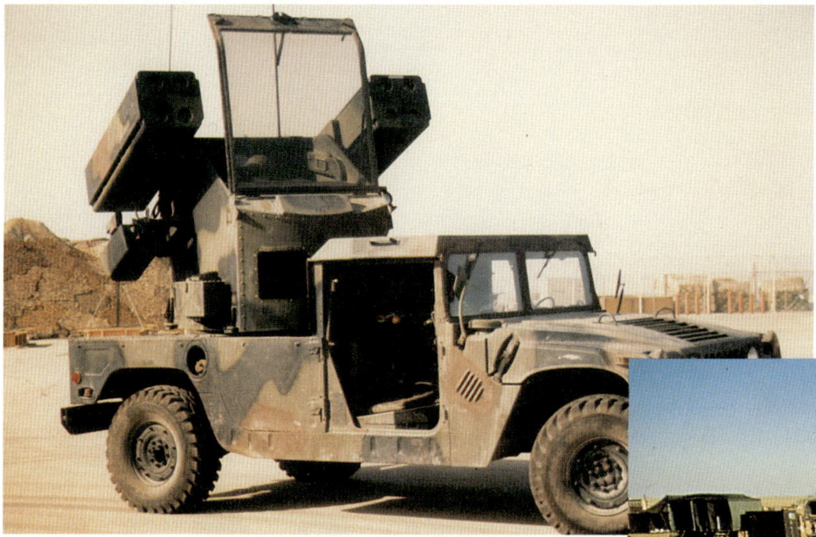

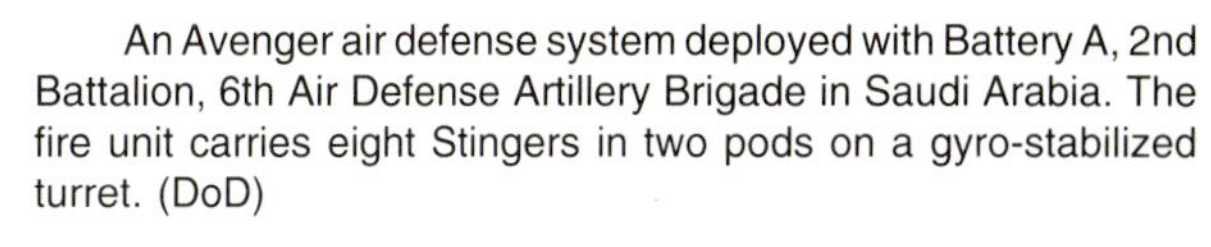

An Avenger air defense system deployed with Battery A, 2nd Battalion, 6th Air Defense Artillery Brigade in Saudi Arabia. The fire unit carries eight Stingers in two pods on a gyro-stabilized turret. (DoD)

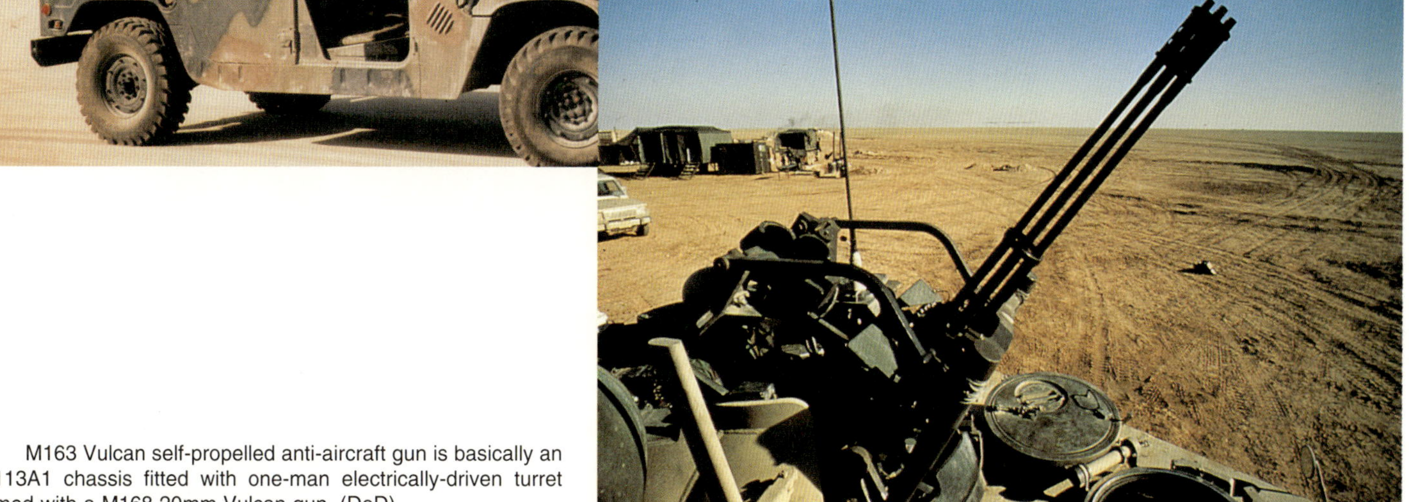

M163 Vulcan self-propelled anti-aircraft gun is basically an M113A1 chassis fitted with one-man electrically-driven turret armed with a M168 20mm Vulcan gun. (DoD)

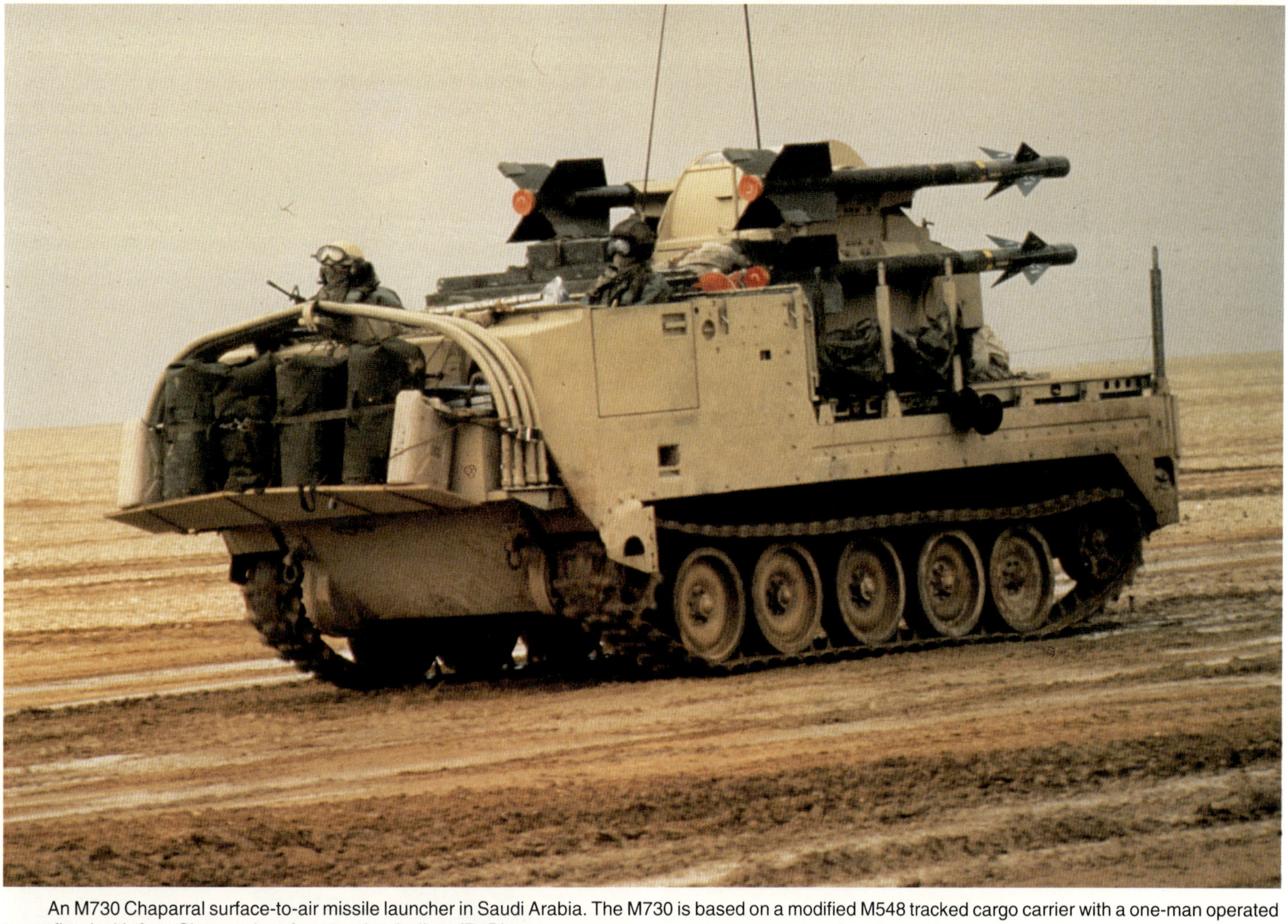

An M730 Chaparral surface-to-air missile launcher in Saudi Arabia. The M730 is based on a modified M548 tracked cargo carrier with a one-man operated turret fitted with four Chaparral surface-to-air missiles. (DoD)

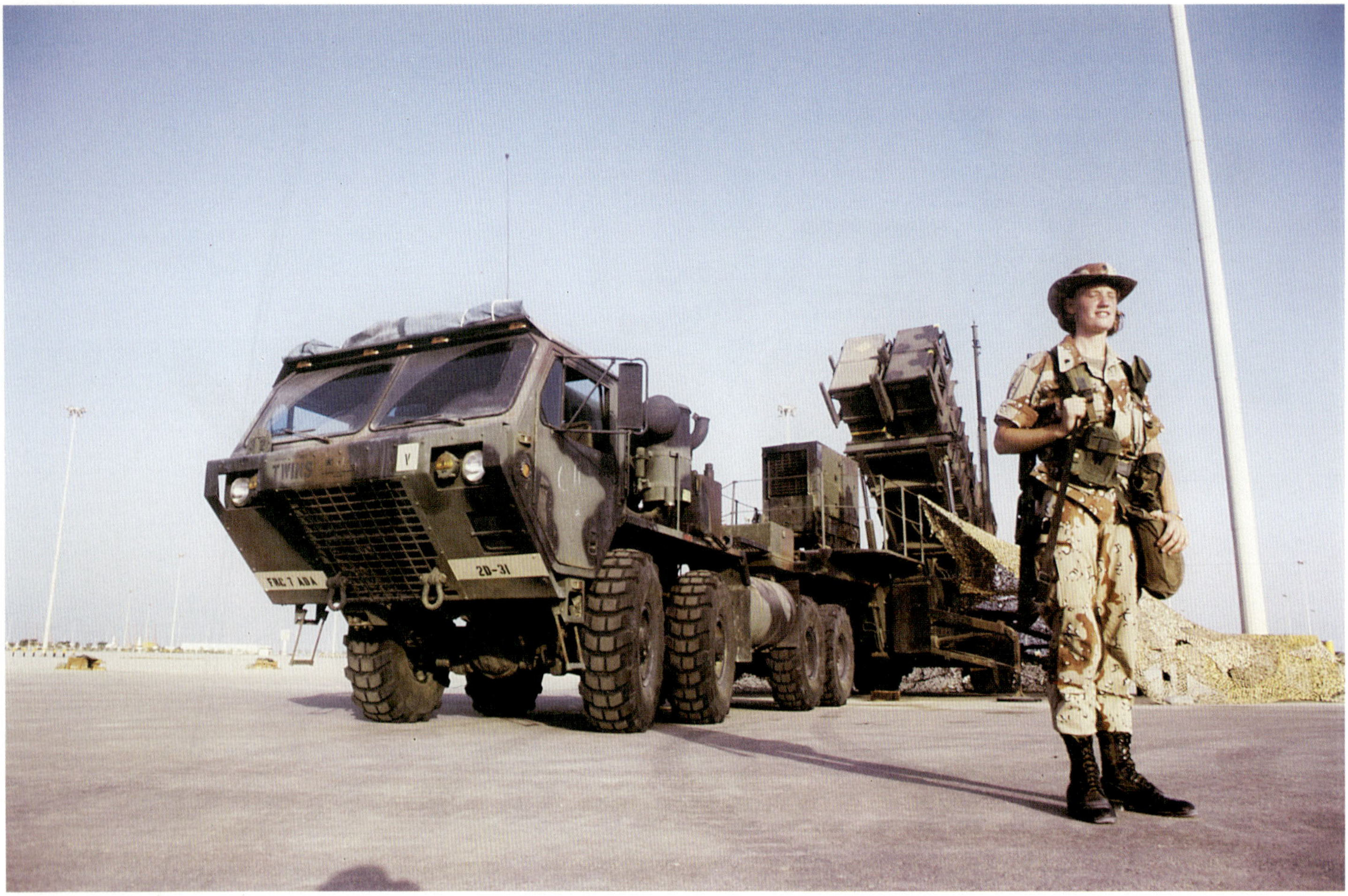

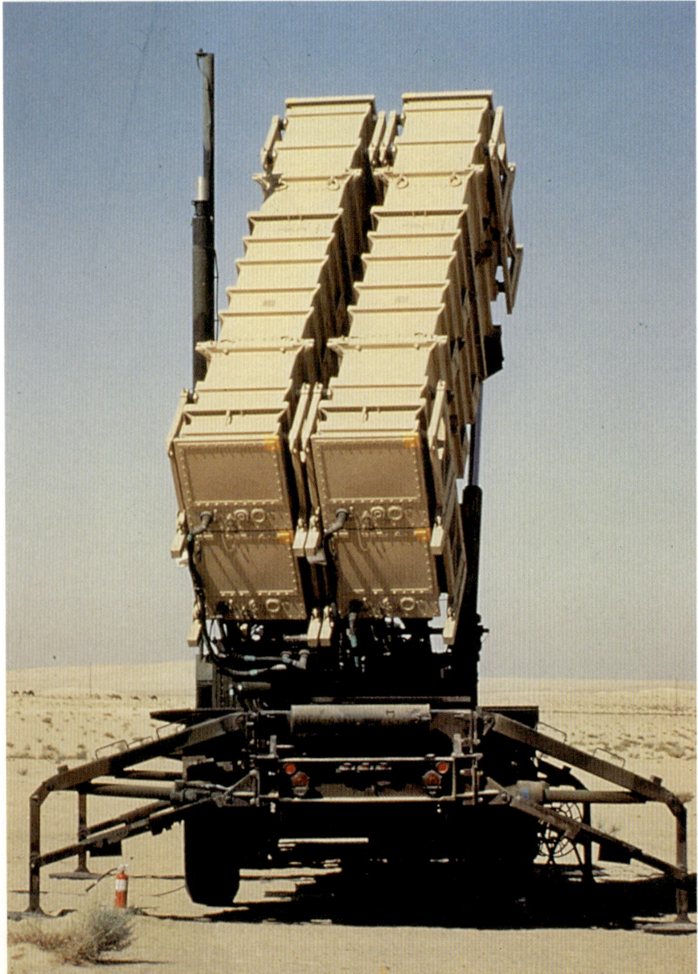

▲ The Scud killer! The all-weather Patriot featured a high kill ratio of Iraqi Scud missiles during the Gulf War. Here, a four-round Patriot surface-to-air M901 missile launcher with its Oshkosh tractor in Saudi Arabia being guarded by a female soldier.

◄ Patriot is the Army's medium and high-altitude ground-to-air missile that provides primary air defense to military bases and vital landmarks.(DoD)

▼ An M730 Chaparral SAM launcher with four Chaparral surface-to-air missiles in ready-to-launch position.(DoD)

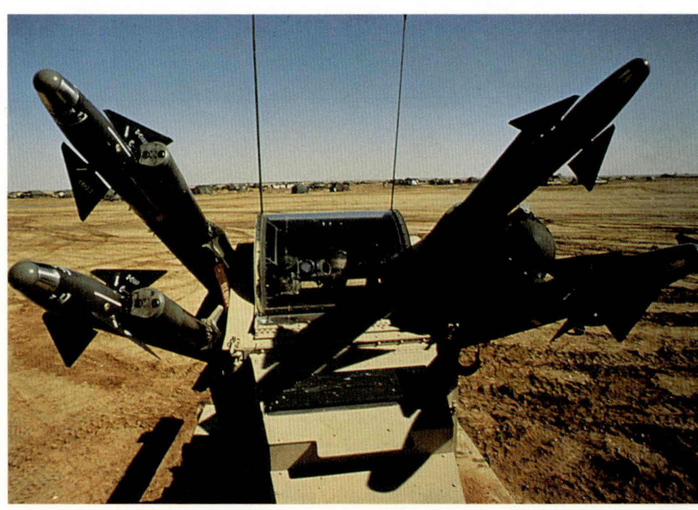

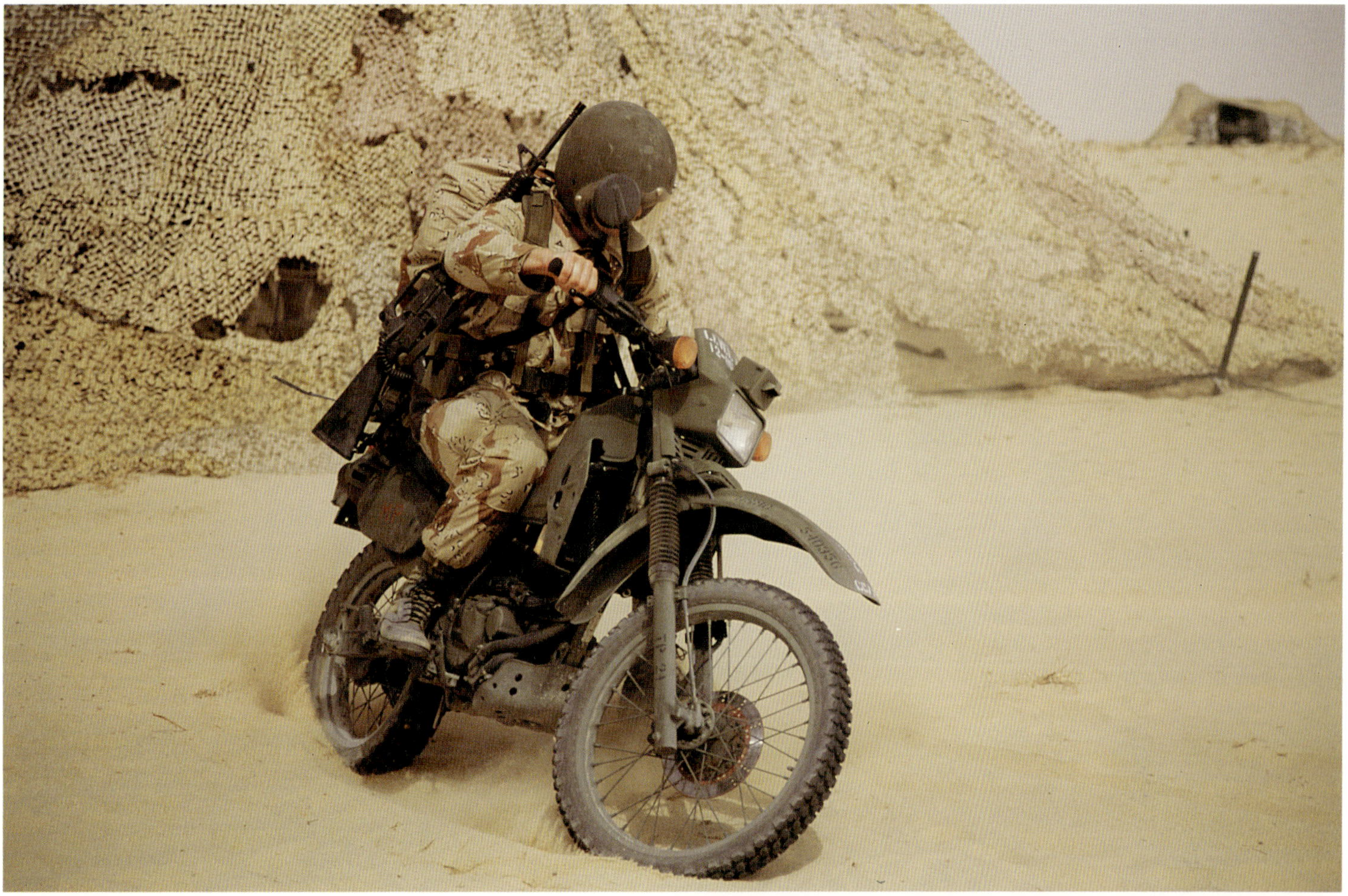

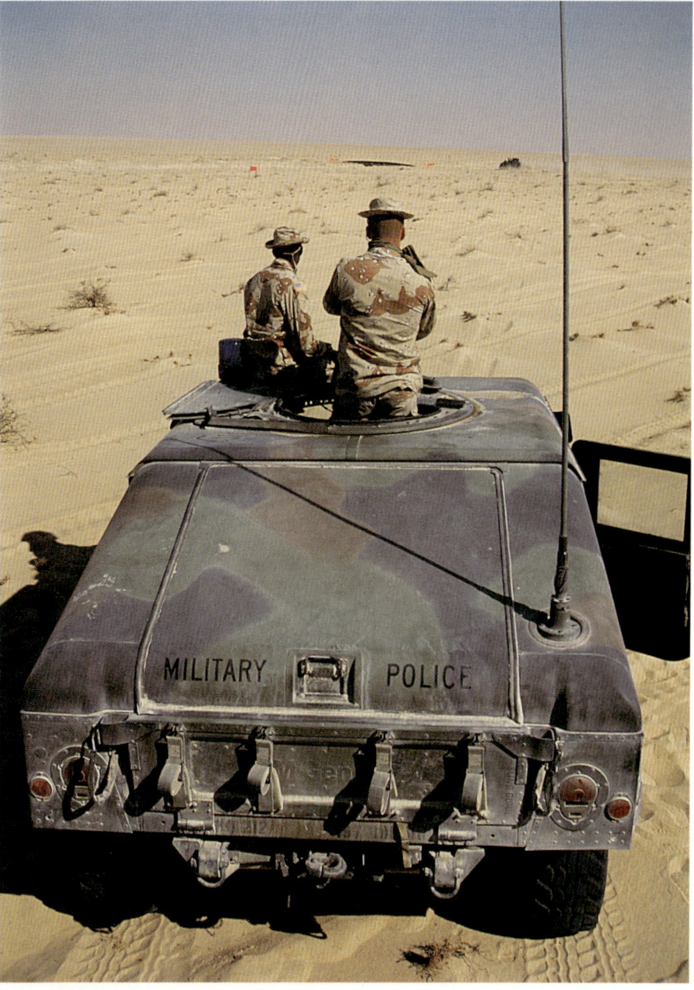

▲ A Military Police riding a Kawasaki KXT 250c.c. motorcycle which has excellent off-road mobility.

▼ Three-round I-HAWK (Improved-Homing All the Way Killer) M192 missile launcher of the Marines deployed in the Saudi desert. The Marine Corps light anti-aircraft missile I-HAWK battalions are attached to the Marine Air Wings.

▶ A Military Police HMMWV (High Mobility Multi-purpose Wheeled Vehicle) on the look-out while an M901 practices going over a scissor bridge in the middle of a dummy minefield.

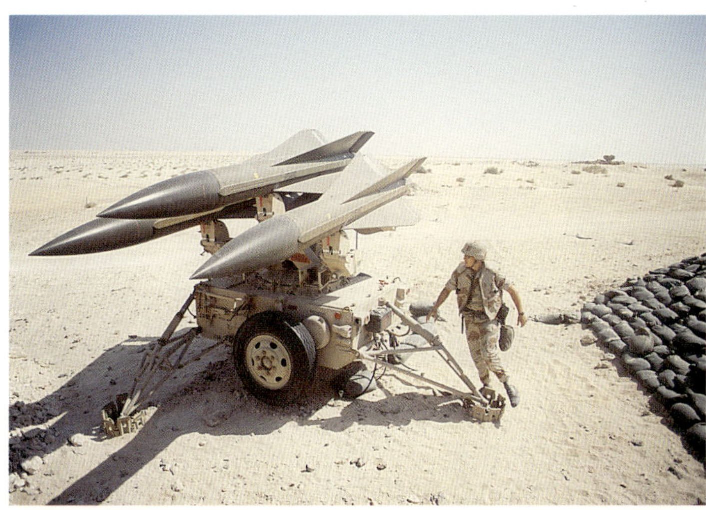

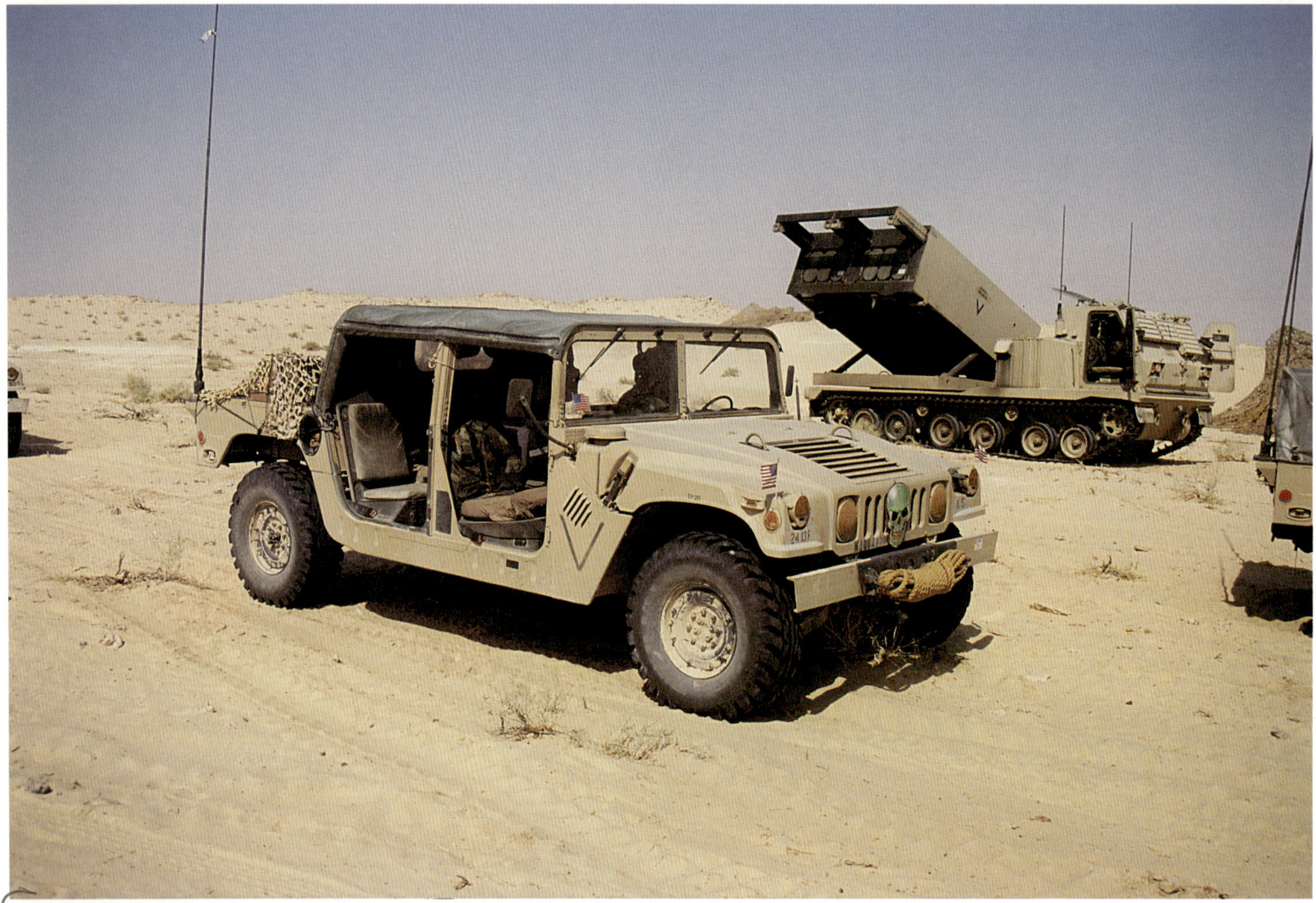

A HMMWV of the 13th Field Artillery, 24th Mechanized Infantry Division decorated with a skull above its bumper celebrating the Halloween.

A Marine Corps HMMWV with a .50 caliber machine gun mounted on its roof.

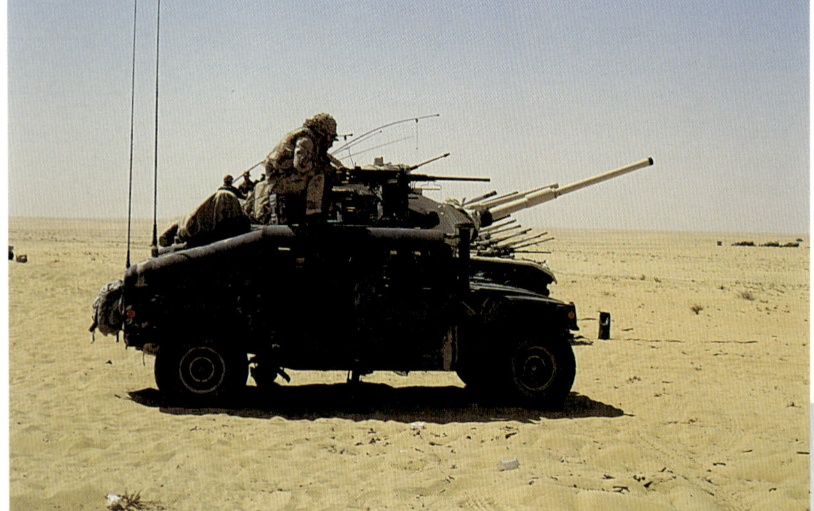

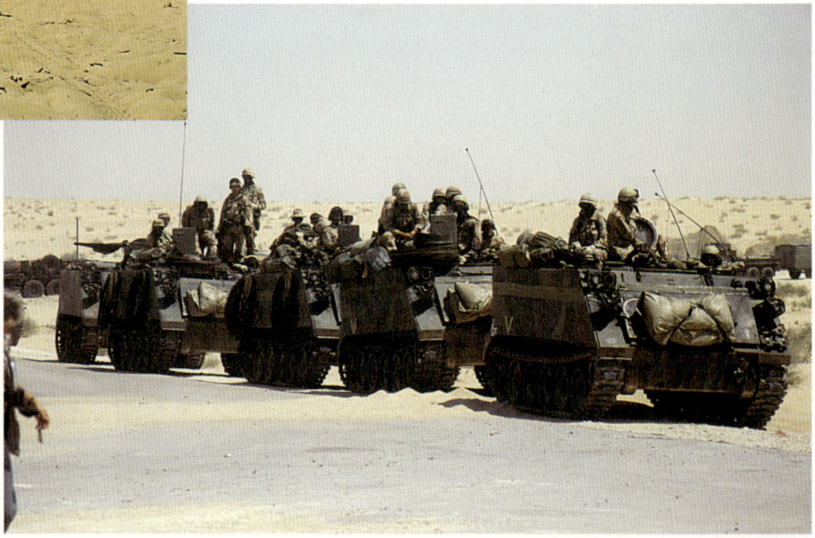

M113A2 armored personnel carriers of the 2/18 Infantry, 197th Mechanized Infantry Brigade just after their arrival in Saudi Arabia in October 1990.

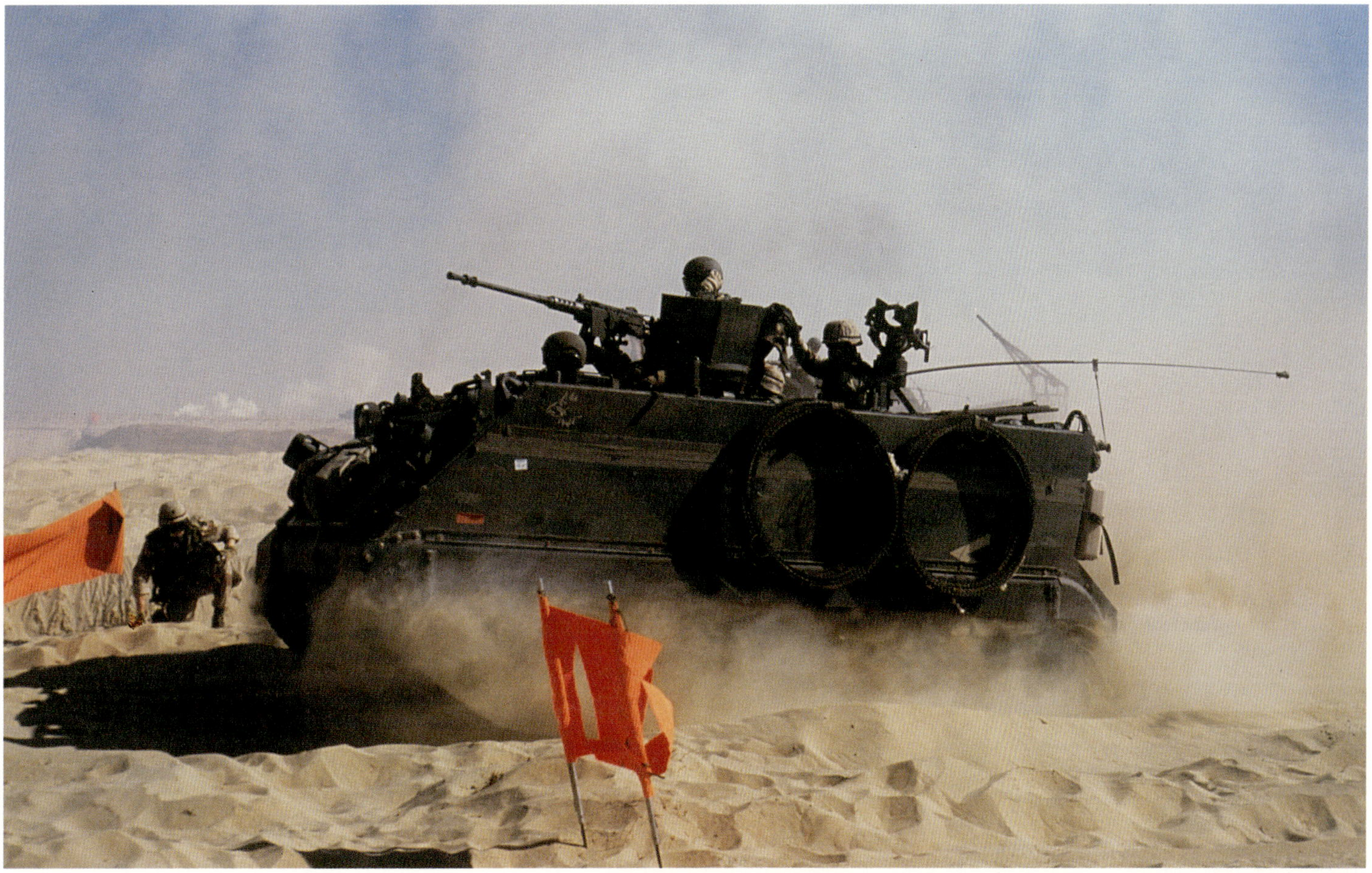

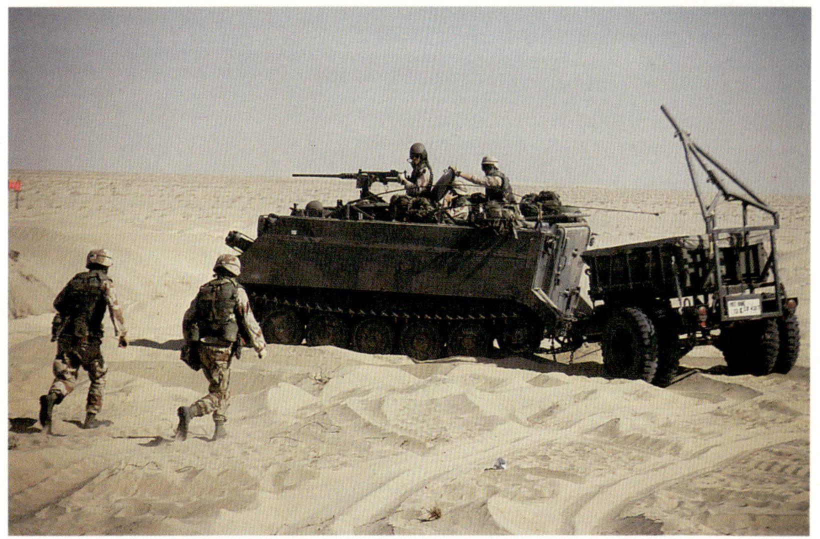

▲ Shown is an M113A2 vehicle being used by engineers of the 197th Mechanized Infantry Brigade while practicing assault through a dummy minefield. The rolls of barbed wire is for nightime security use.

▶ An Engineer's M113A2 towing a Mine-Clearing Line Charge M58A4 (MICLIC) trailer. The M58A4 is used to clear a path through a minefield for the passage of tanks, APCs and vehicles.

▼ An M113A2 being used in the ambulance role.

▼▶ M577A1 Command Posts of the 2nd Armored Cavalry Regiment. The M577A1 is essentially an M113A1 with a higher roof. A tent can be erected at the rear of the hull for additional space. (DoD)

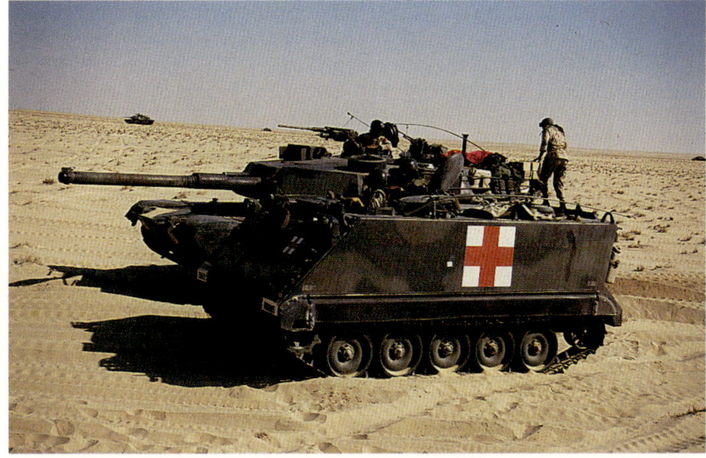

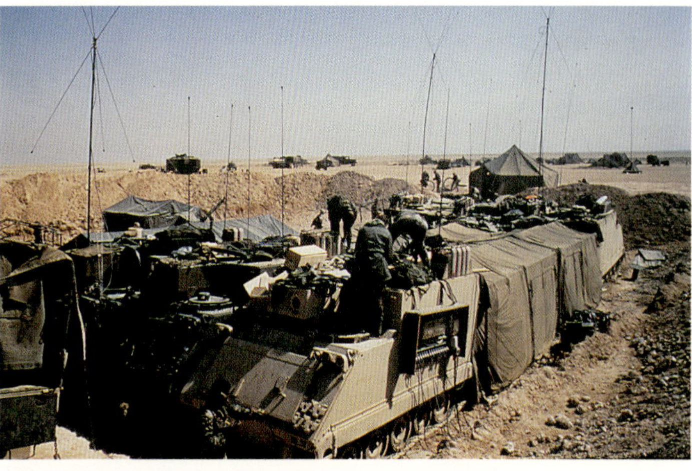

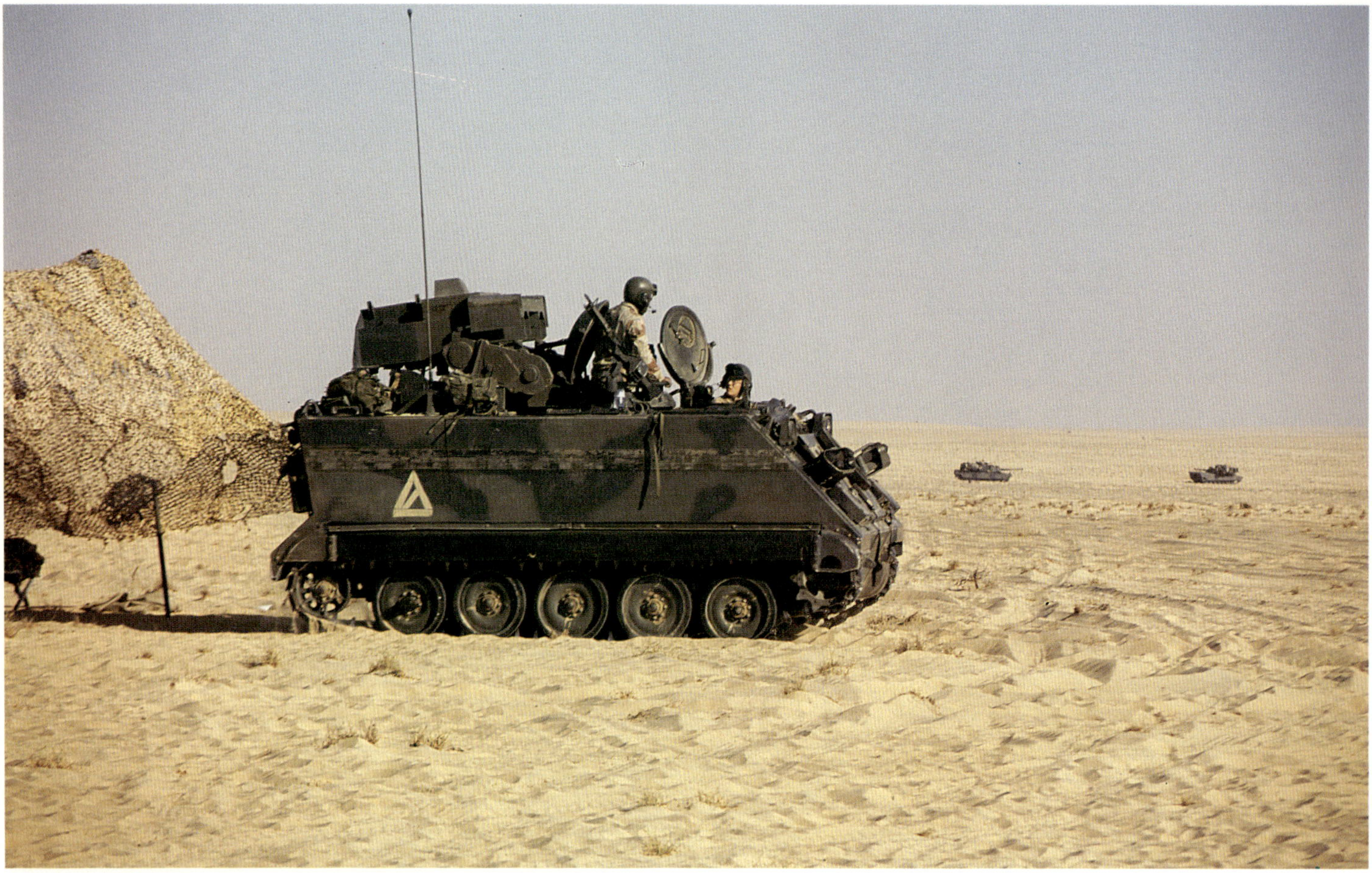

An M901 Improved TOW Vehicle (ITV) of the 197th Mechanized Infantry Brigade with the TOW launcher unit in the stowed position.

The M901 is basically an M113A2 armored personnel carrier fitted with an elevating two-launcher TOW turret which allows the anti-tank missile to be fired from hull defilade with the gunner and his assistant under armor protection. Here, an M901 of the 1st Cavalry towing an M105 cargo trailer after its deployment to Saudi Arabia.

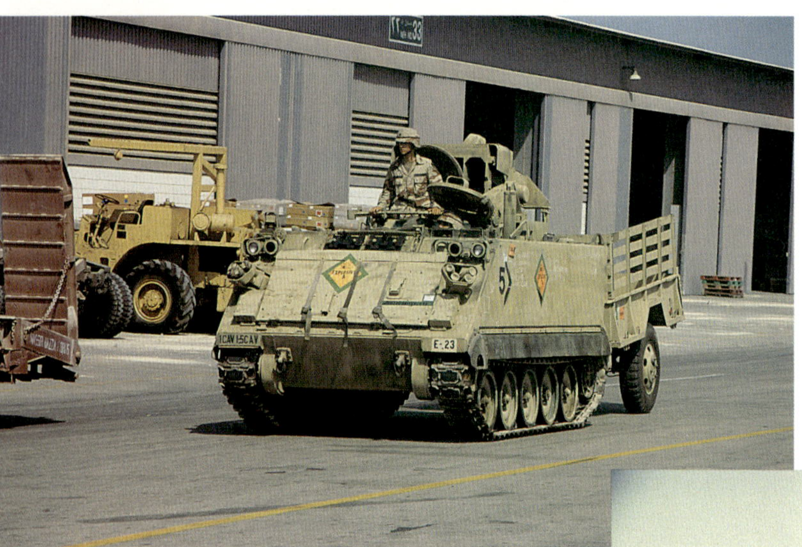

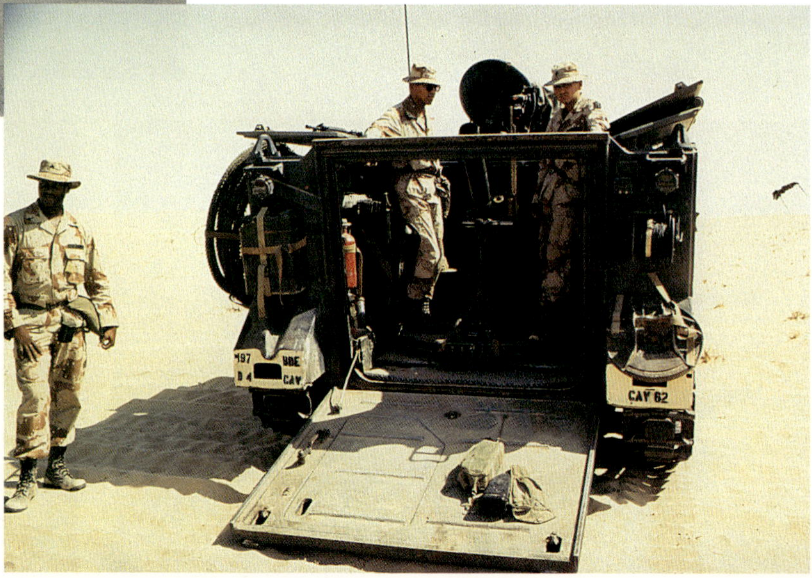

An M106 Mortar Carrier fitted with a 107mm mortar with the roof hatch opened and the ramp lowered at the rear. This vehicle belongs to the 197th Mechanized Infantry Brigade. (DoD)

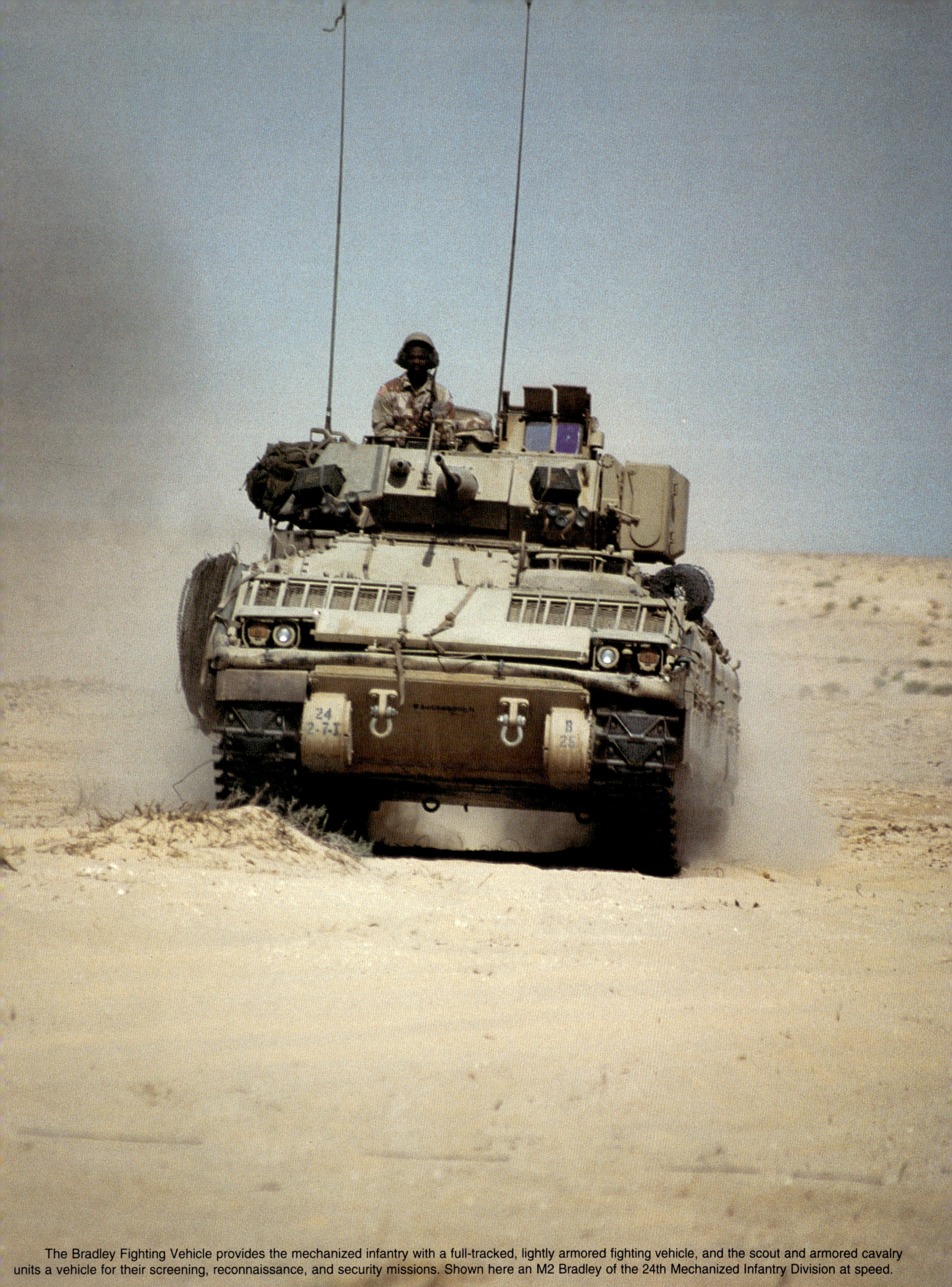

The Bradley Fighting Vehicle provides the mechanized infantry with a full-tracked, lightly armored fighting vehicle, and the scout and armored cavalry units a vehicle for their screening, reconnaissance, and security missions. Shown here an M2 Bradley of the 24th Mechanized Infantry Division at speed.

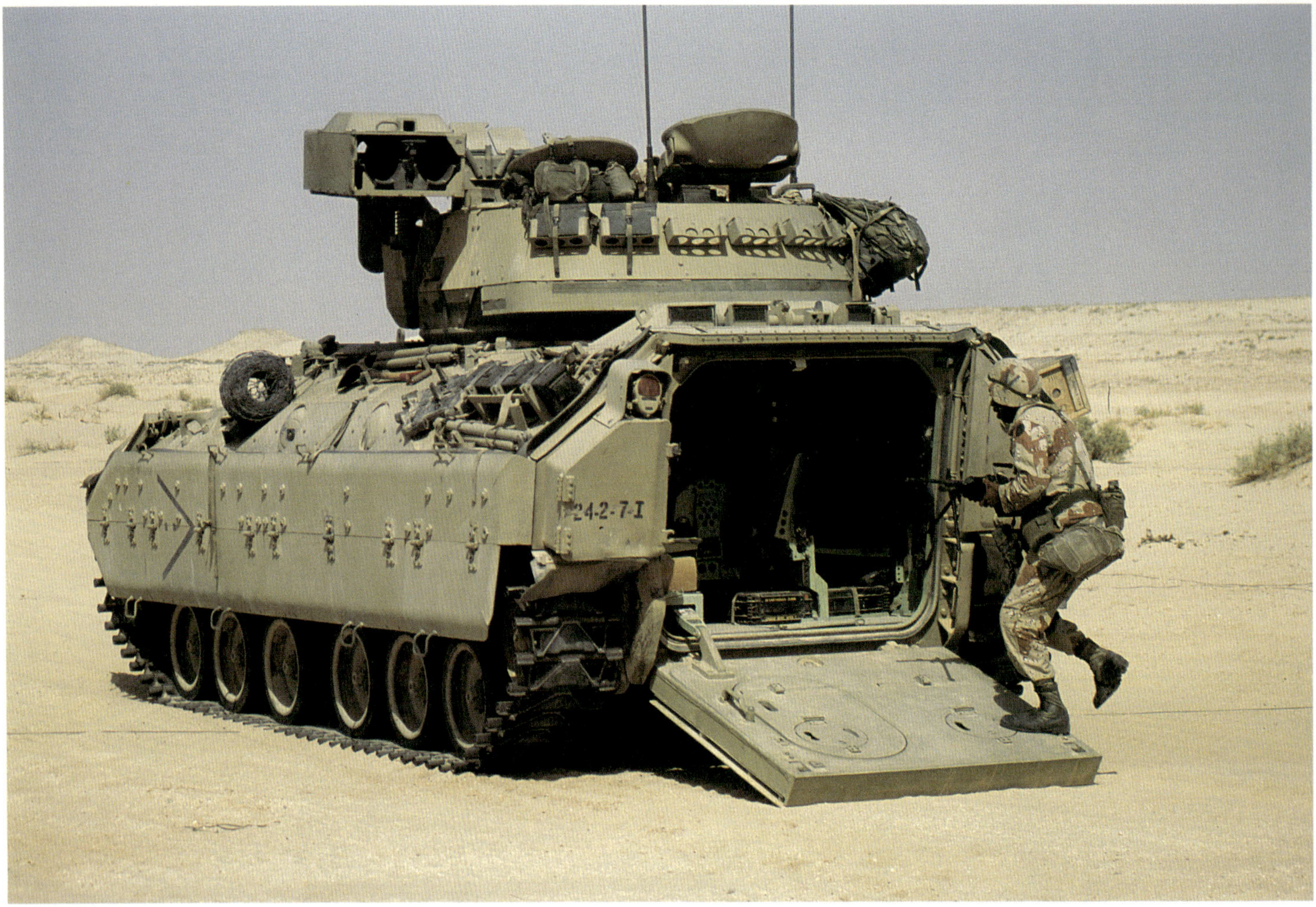

Soldier of the 24th Mechanized Infantry Division entering the rear compartment of an M2 Bradley during a training exercise in Saudi Arabia.

Both the M2 Infantry Fighting Vehicle (IFV) and M3 Cavalry Fighting Vehicle (CFV) have a two-man turret which mounts the 25mm automatic stabilized cannon, its primary armament, supported by the TOW anti-tank guided missile system, and the 7.62mm coaxial machine gun. The chain gun can fire both armor-piercing, discarding sabot and high-explosive ammunition.

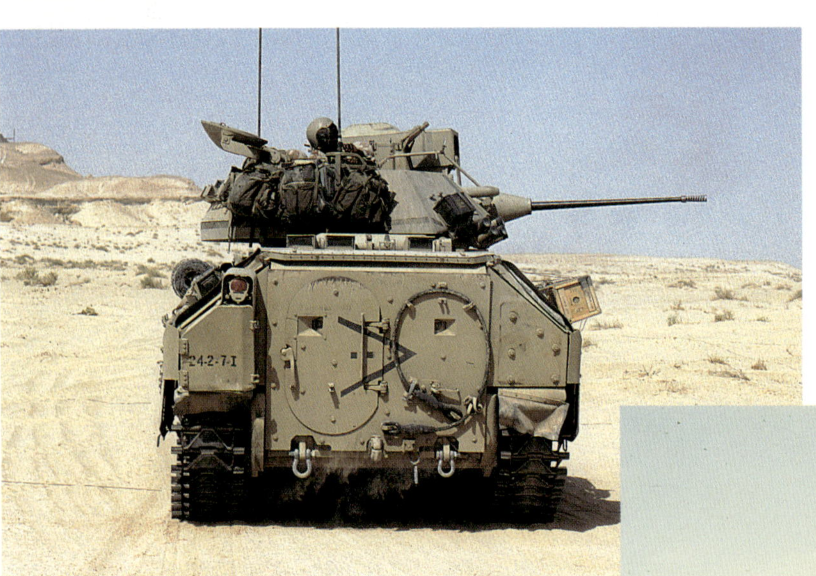

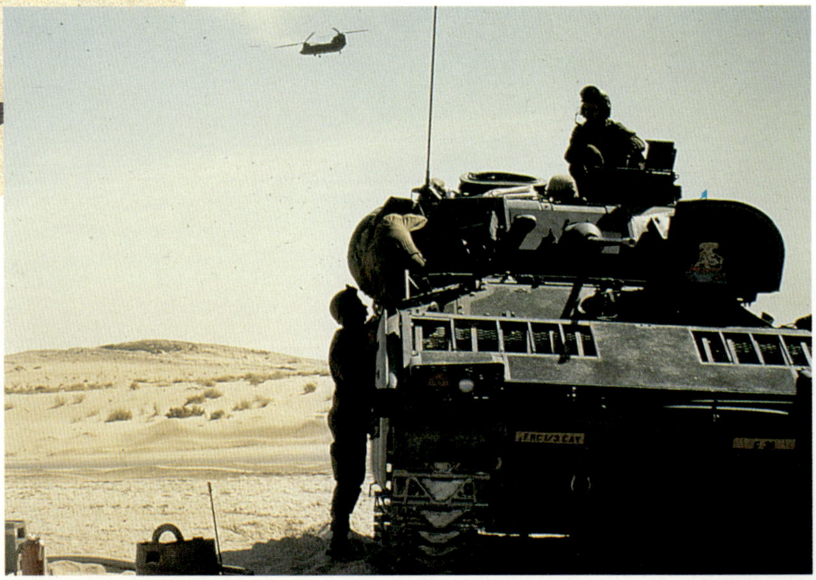

The early Bradleys deployed to Saudi Arabia were early model M2A1s and M3A1s. This Bradley has a Snoopy cartoon on the driver's hatch. (DoD)

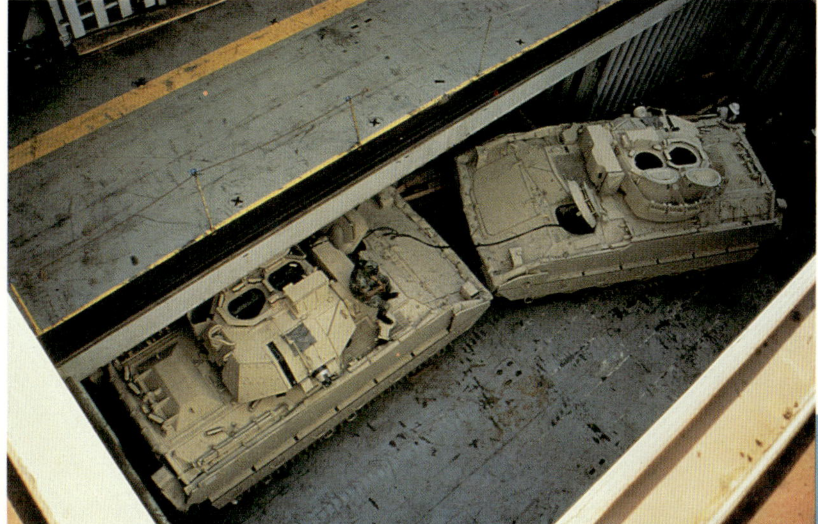

Later Bradleys deployed to Saudi Arabia were the new M2A2s and M3A2s. Shown is a pair of M3A2s waiting to be unloaded.(DoD)

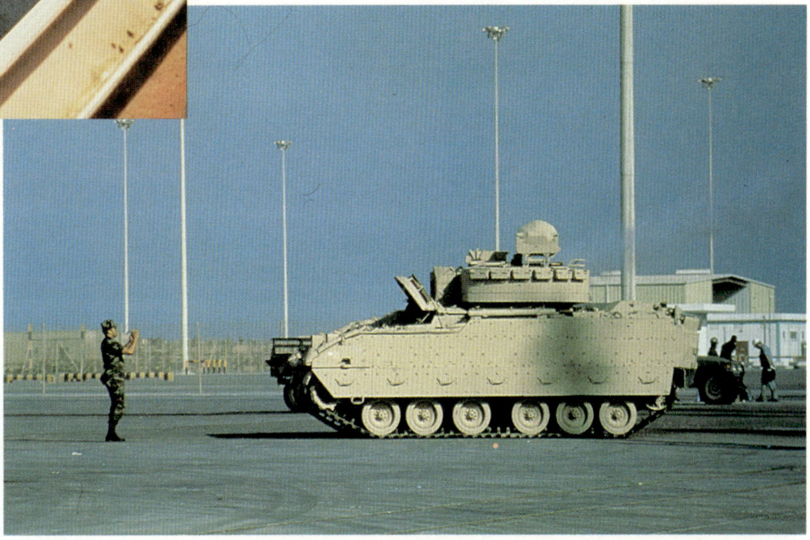

The M3A2 Bradley features two large steel side skirts running the full length of the hull on both sides of the vehicle. Additional armor plates were also fitted to the upper and lower front hull and to the turret. The M3A2 also boasted a larger engine, a stronger transmission and a heavier suspension system. (DoD)

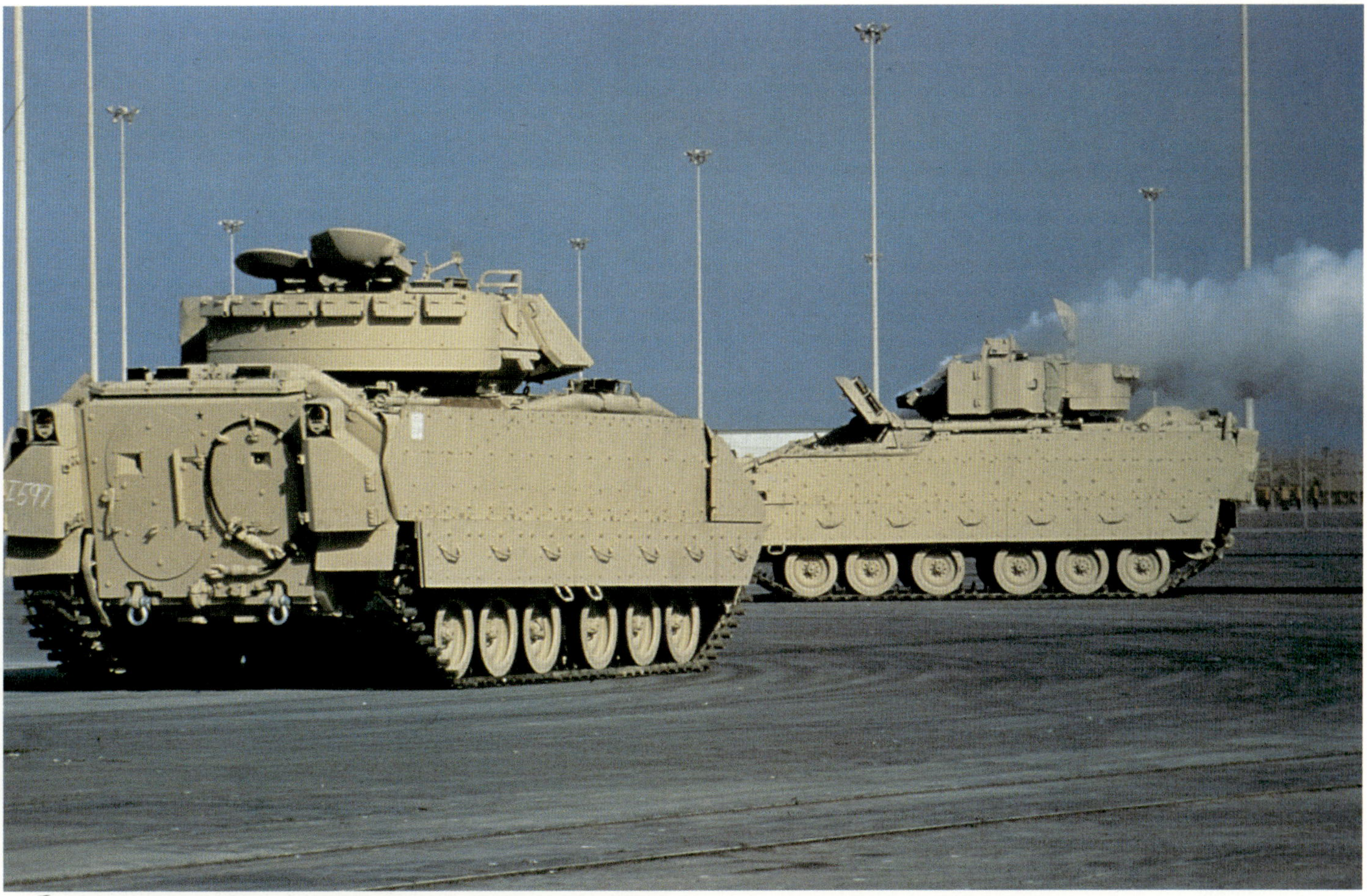

A pair of M3A2s minus their 25mm chain guns waiting to be transported to the front. Note the thickness of the new side skirts and the lifting handles. The vehicles were already painted with sand color before their arrival in Saudi Arabia.(DoD)

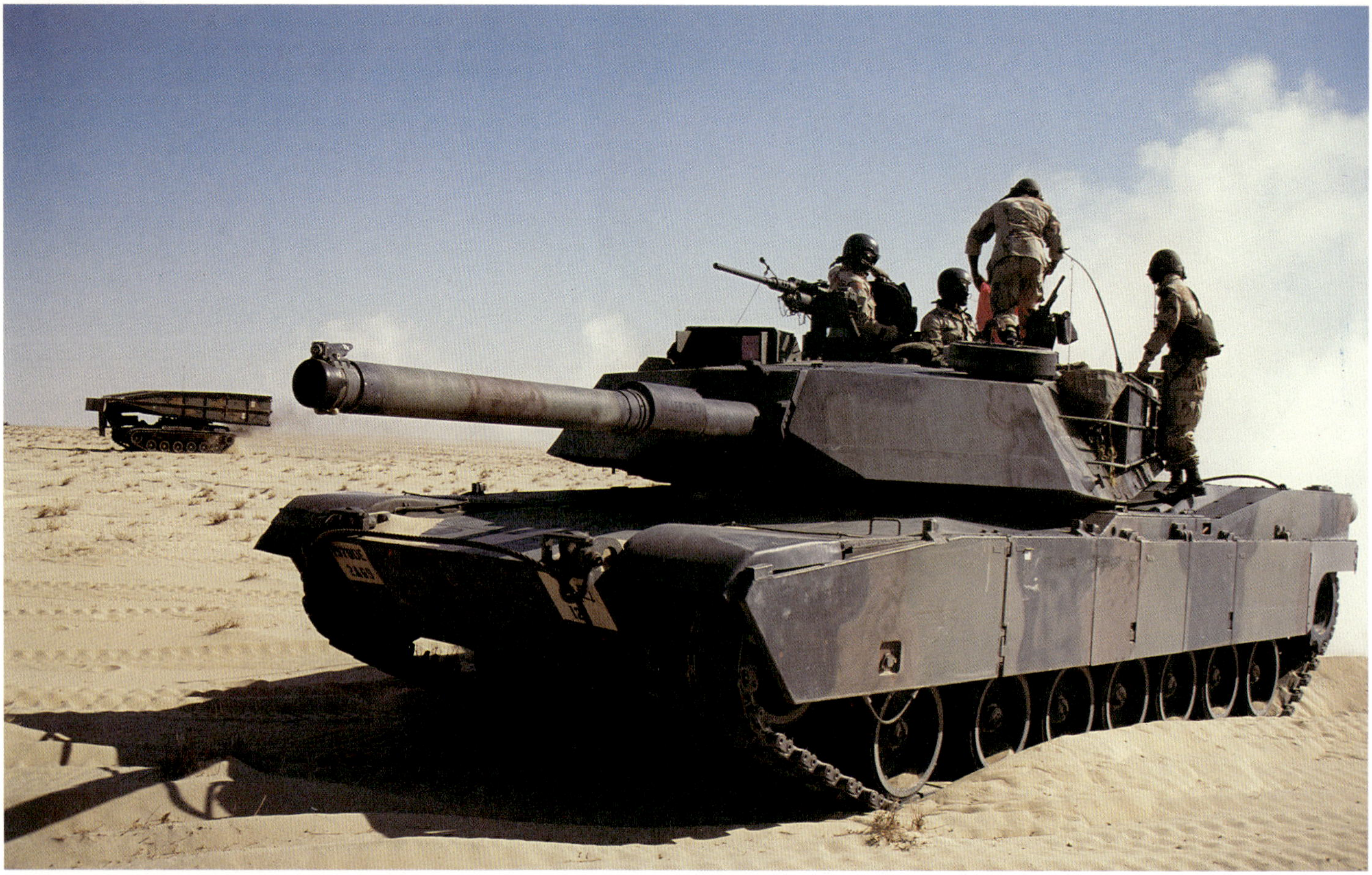

Among the first M1 tanks arrived in Saudi Arabia were the 105mm gun armed M1s of the 197th Mechanized Infantry Brigade. In the early stage of Operation Desert Shield, these M1s were the only vehicles that could pose a threat to the Iraqi T-72s.

Pictured is an M1 tank of the 24th Mechanized Infantry Division taking cover underneath a camouflage netting. If called into action it takes the crew only five minutes to fold the net and change position if need be.

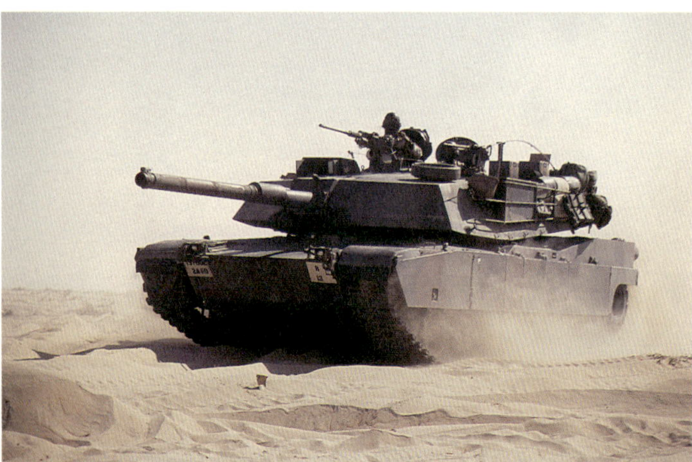

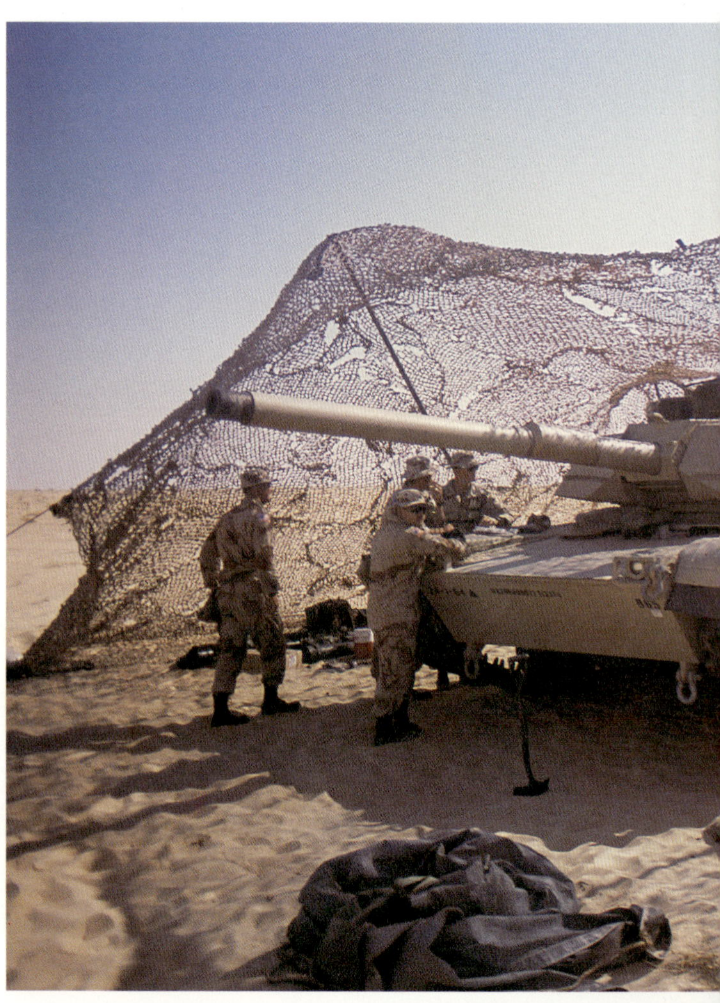

The M1 Abrams main battle tank is the Army's primary combat weapon system for closing with and destroying enemy forces using mobility, firepower, and shock action. Shown is an M1 of the 197th Mechanized Infantry brigade on maneuver in the Saudi desert shortly after its arrival. The tank is still in its NATO camouflage.

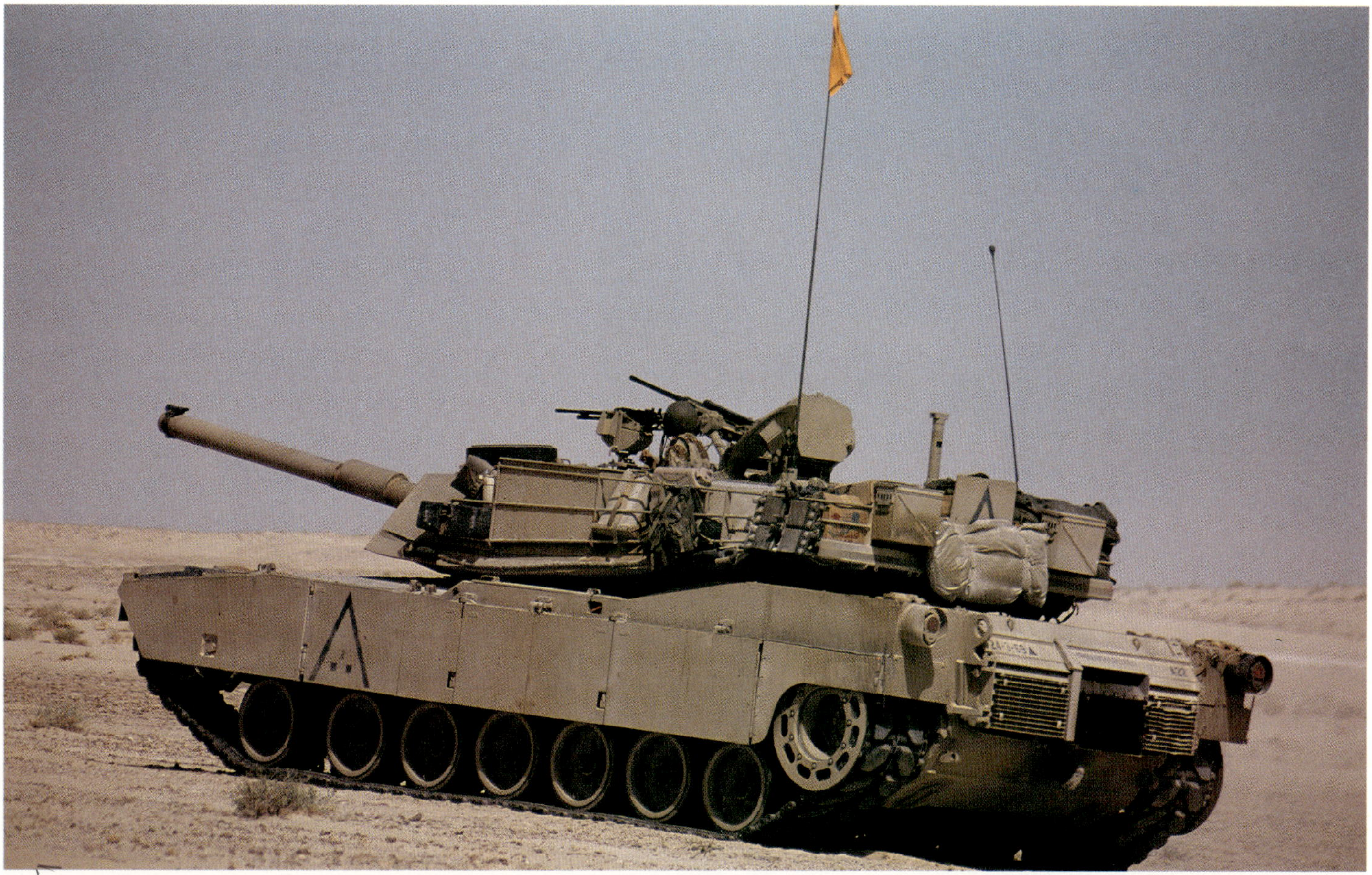

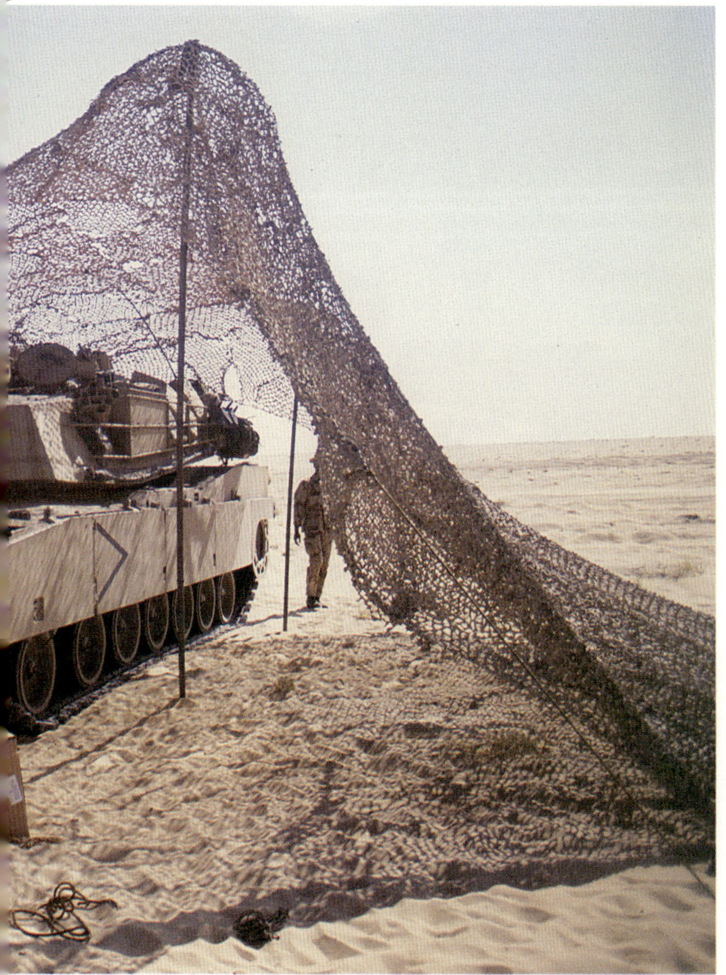

The M1 tanks of the 24th Mechanized Infantry Division are the early models armed with the 105mm rifled gun. Aside from the main gun, M1 is armed with a coaxial M240 7.62mm machine gun, a similar weapon on a flexible mount at the loader's hatch, and a M2HB .50 caliber machine gun at the commander's station.

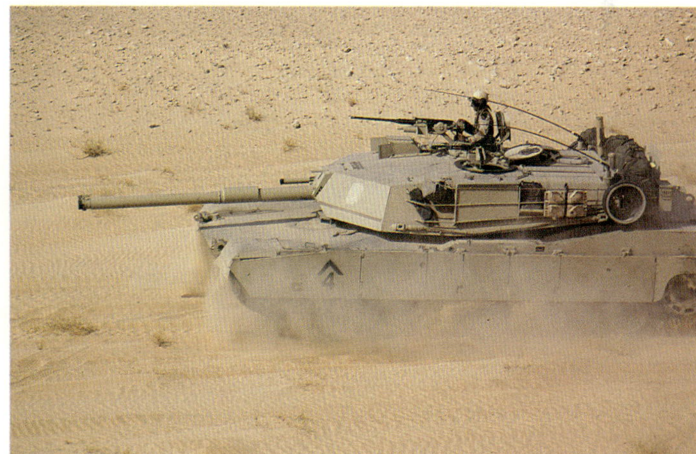

An M1 Abrams of the 1st Cavalry Division at speed. The driver is seated at the front of the vehicle. The commander and gunner are seated on the right of the turret and the loader on the left.

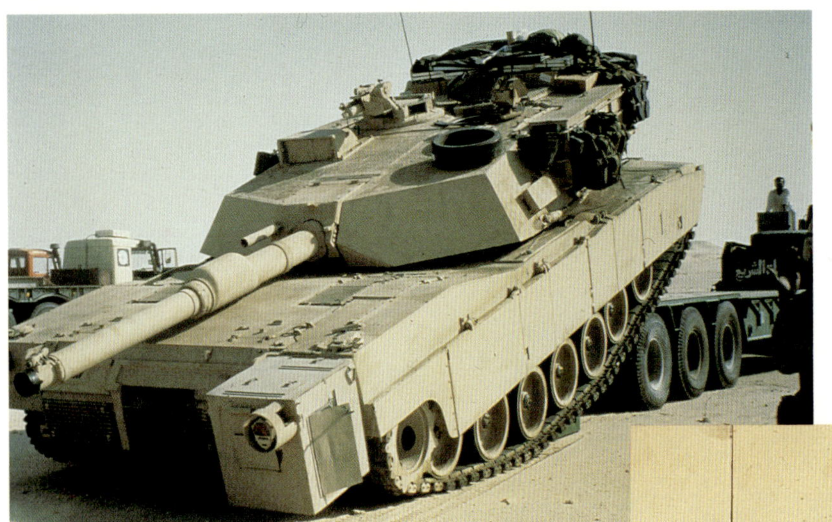

The Abrams starting to arrive Saudi Arabia in October 1990 were the newer M1A1s. This M1A1 being loaded onto a tank transporter is fitted with an externally mounted auxiliary power unit (APU).(DoD)

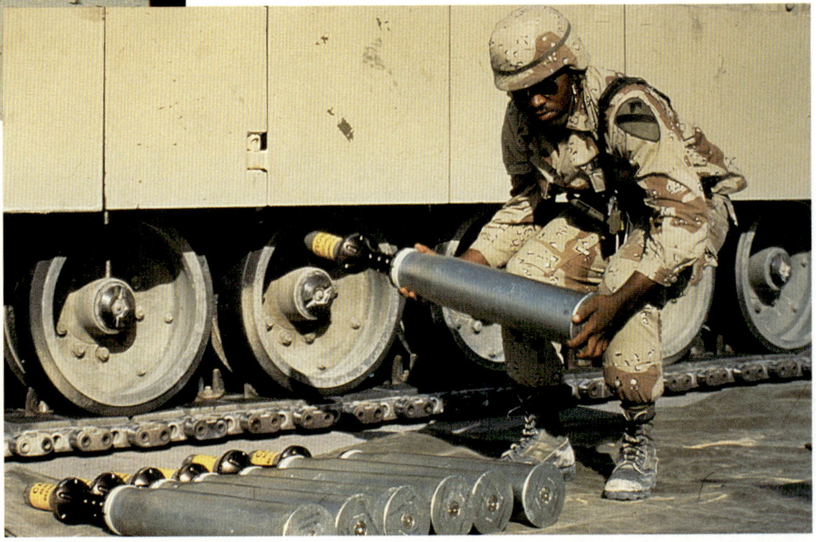

Unlike the 105mm gun mounted on earlier model M1 tanks which had six different types of ammunition available, the 120mm gun has had only two types of ammunition developed for it, a kinetic energy (KE) and a multi-purpose shaped-charge projectile High Explosive Anti-Tank (HEAT) round. Shown is a tanker of the 1st Cavalry Division picking up an KE round of 120mm (DoD)

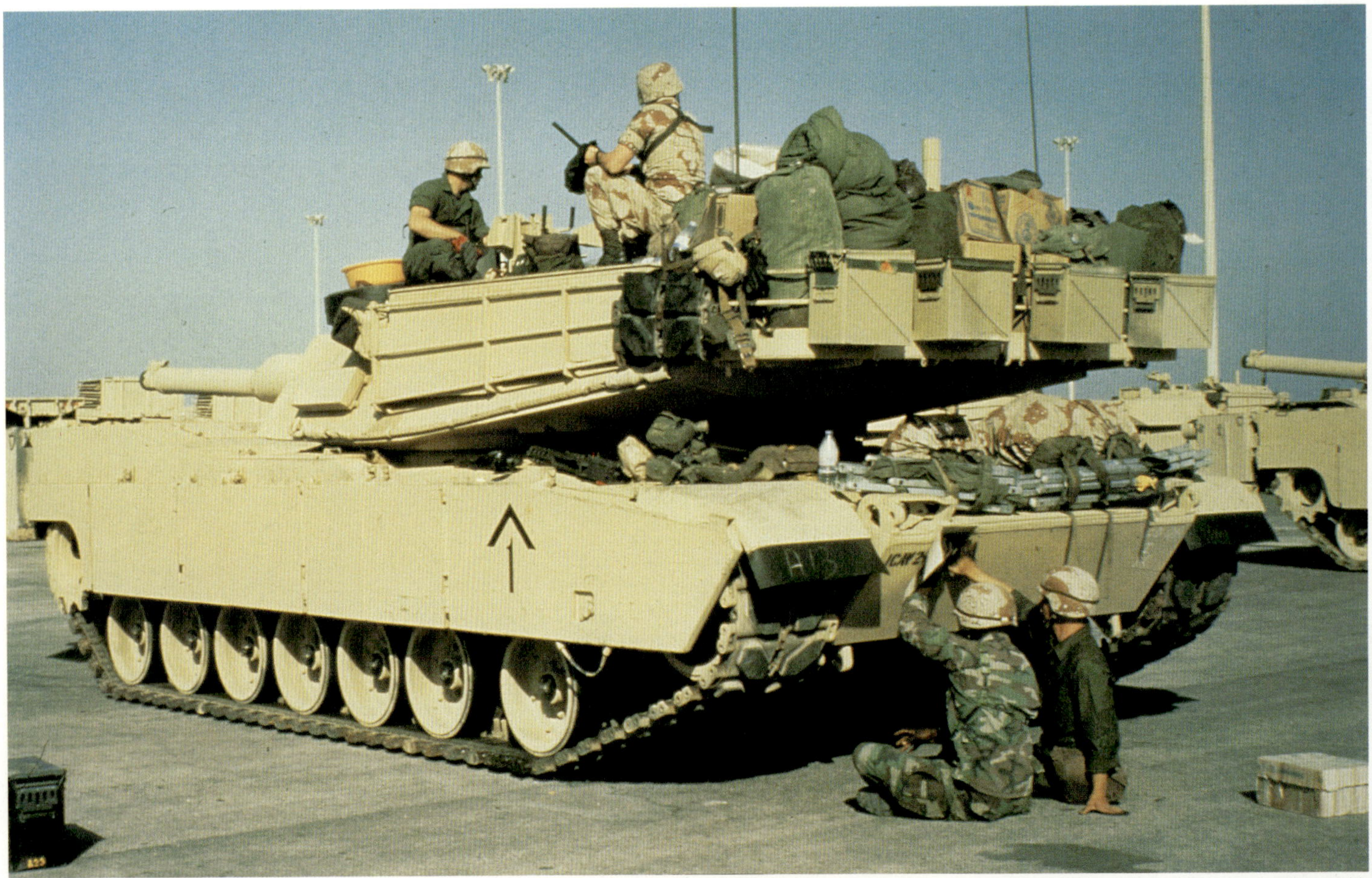

The crews of an M1A1 preparing their vehicle for field deployment while still on a Saudi dock. A larger turret bustle was fitted to the M1A1 tank, along with lengthened turret stowage boxes. Part of the reason for lengthening these turret stowage boxes was to accomodate the equipment normally stowed in the left sponsor box, which was deleted for the NBC overpressure system fitted to the M1A1 tank. (DoD)

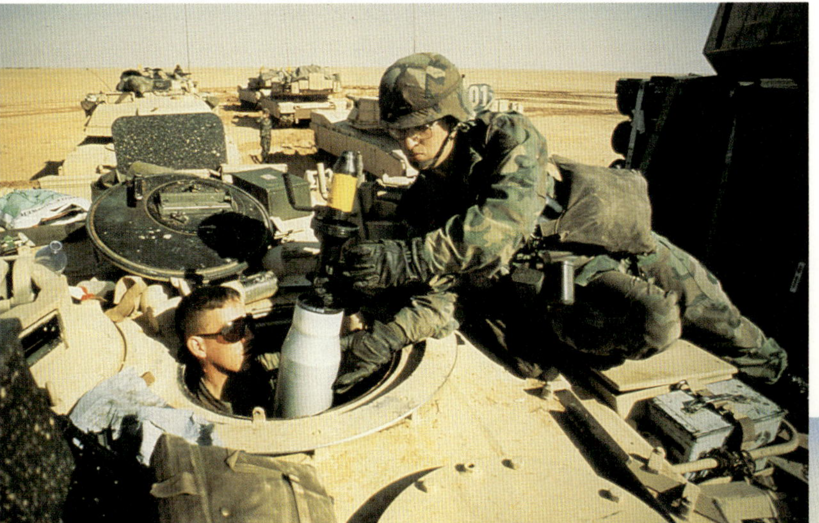

Two tankers busy loading their M1A1 tank with ammunition. In addition to the improved range and penentration performance, the 120mm gun had other advantages. Its fixed ammunition is slightly shorter than the 105mm rounds and used a partially combustable cartridge case. Only a small stub case and igniter tube remained after firing and it is ejected into a container. Thus the problem of hot cartridge cases on the turret basket floor was eliminated. (DoD)

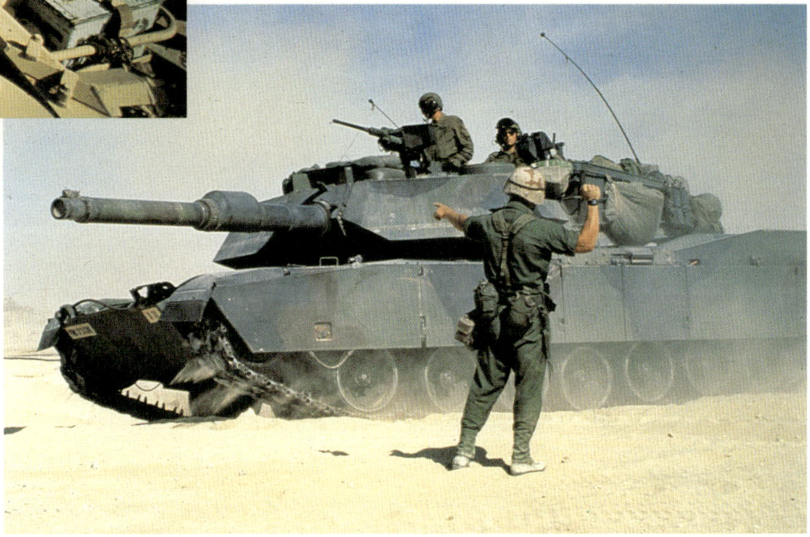

The larger 120mm gun breech on the M1A1 tank necessited the redesign of the tank commander's and loader's seats. The reconfigured turret bustle ammo stowage resulted in redesigned turret blo-off panels which are now in two pieces instead of three. The turret mantlet armor of the M1A1 tank also has been reconfigured to accomodate the larger 120mm gun tube. The M1A1 crosswind sensor was fitted with a hooded top to better channel ambient wind. (DoD)

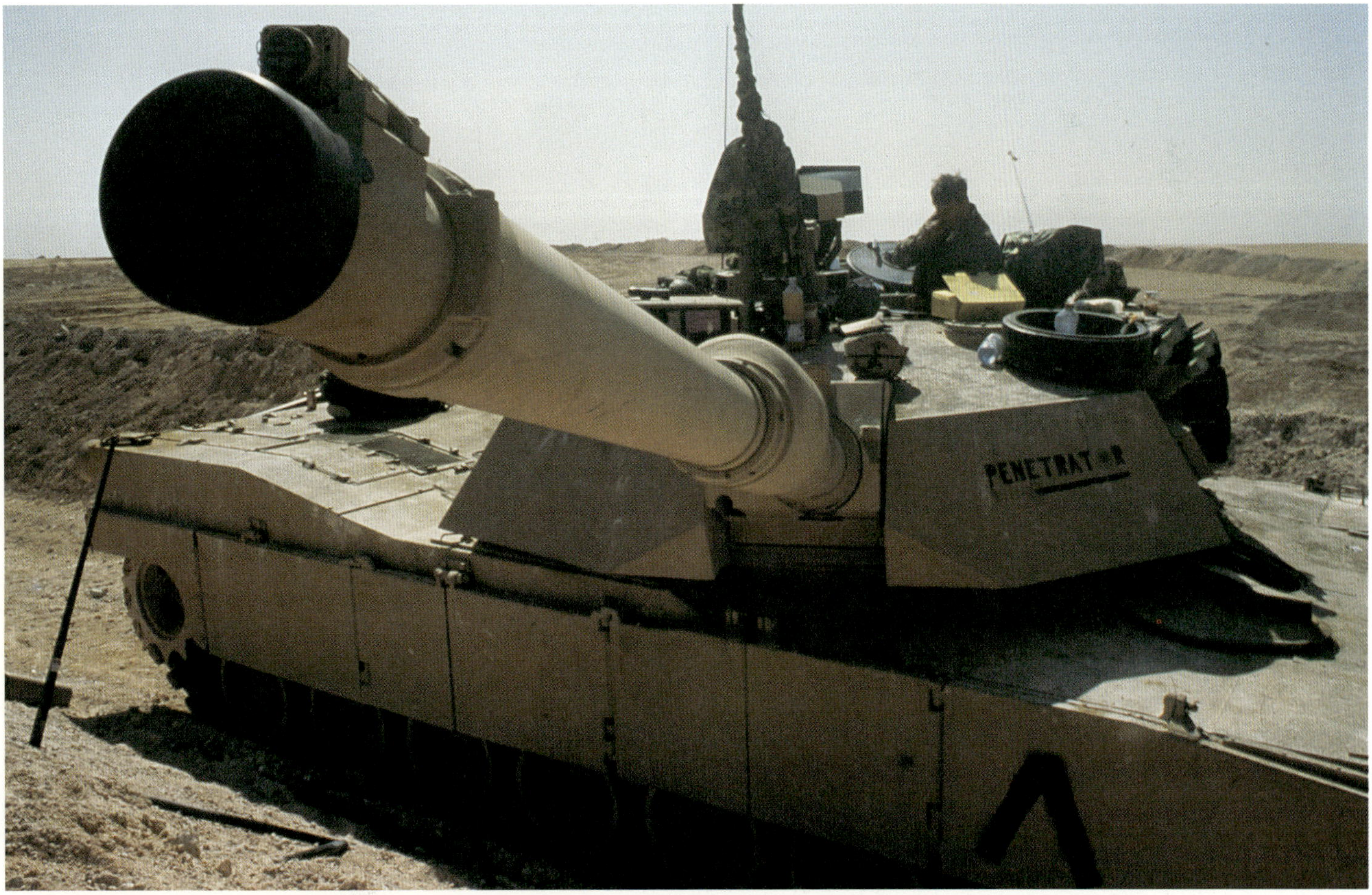

Another feature of the fire control system, the muzzle reference sensor (MRS), permits the gunner to measure and correct tube droop and bend through the computer to ensure an accurate boresight. Shown at the end of the gun tube of this M1A1 tank is the MRS.(DoD)

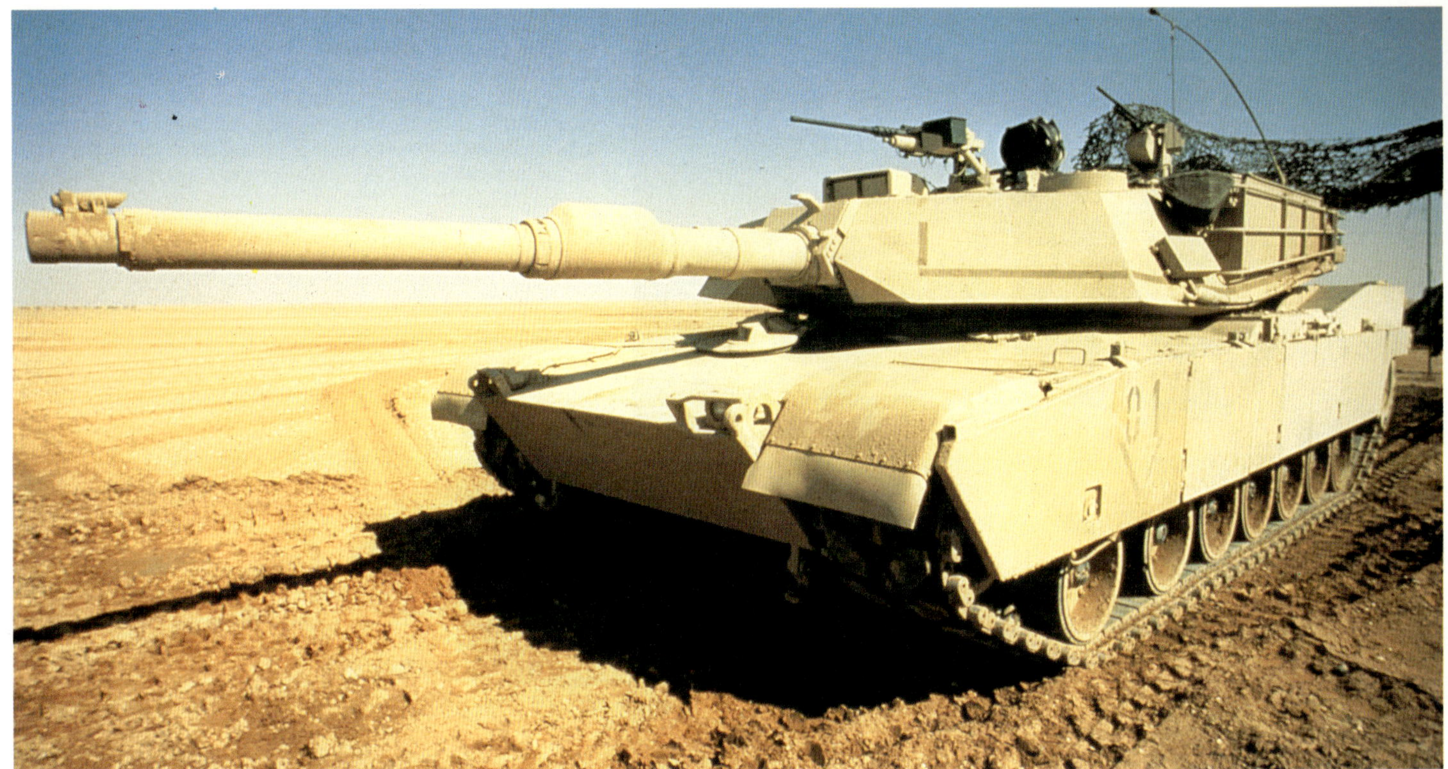

One of the highly classified modifications by the Army was the use of depleted uranium in the fabrication of armor plate for the M1A1 tank. This new armor greatly increases the penetration resistance of the M1A1 armor against kinetic energy rounds, something earlier composite armored M1 tanks were not as good at. With this major improvement in armor protection, the M1A1 tank is called M1A1 HA (Heavy Armor). Most of the M1A1 tanks to see action were equipped with the newer armor. (DoD)

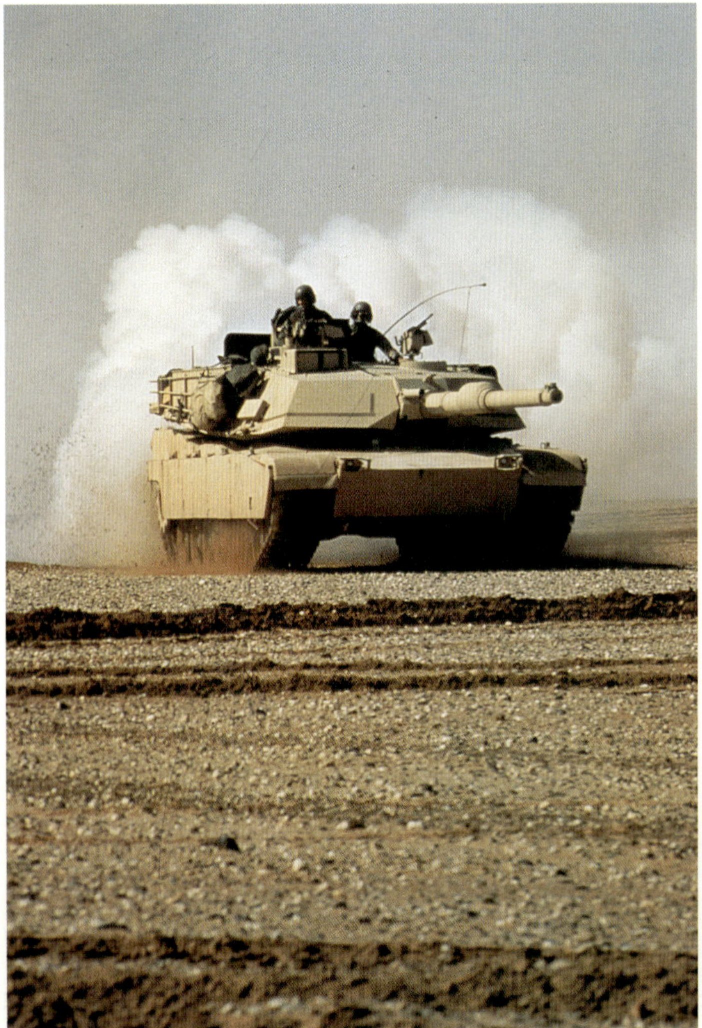

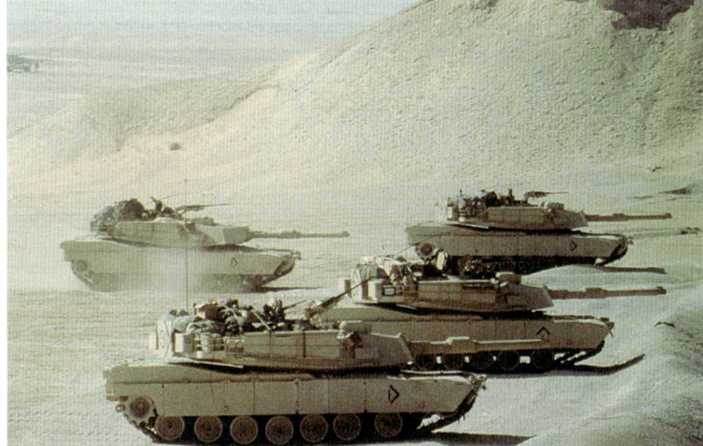

The M1A1 is equipped with an advanced onboard NBC protection system. This system allows the tank to operate in a contaminated environment without protective gear. (DoD)

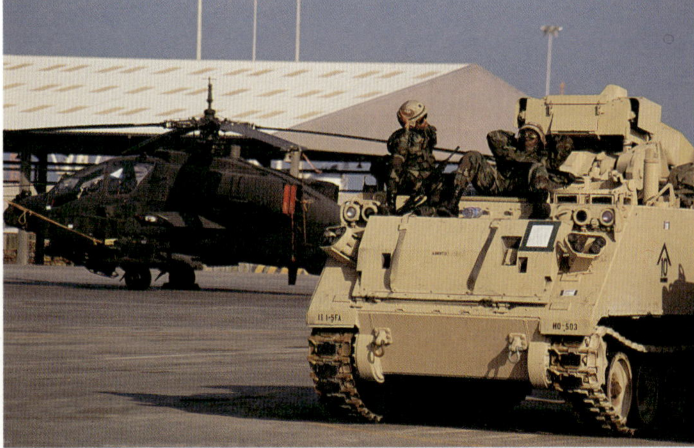

M901 "Hammerhead" of the 1st Mechanized Infantry Division "Big Red One" getting ready to be deployed to the west for the subsequent land battle. Behind it is an AH-64 Apache gunship.

The M1A1 tank has the ability to produce a heavy blanket of smoke for self-protection. (DoD)

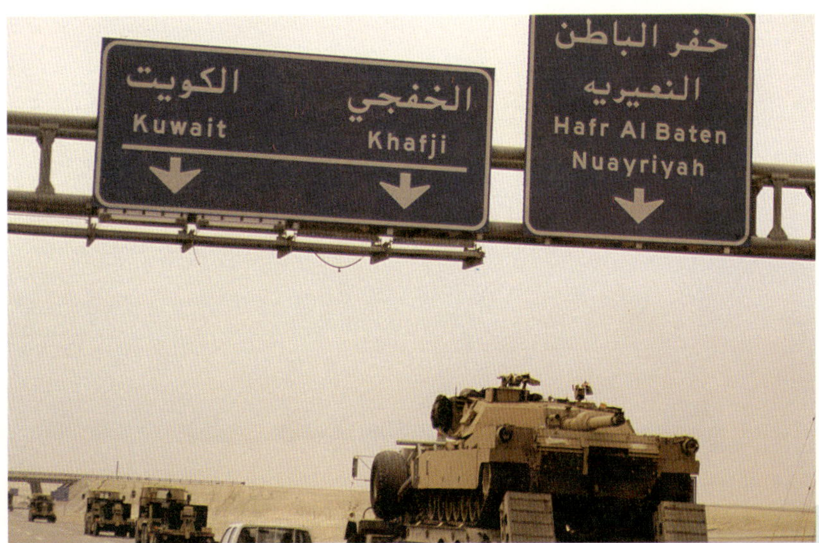

An M1A1 onboard a semi-trailer heading towards Hafr Al Baten, the staging point for the onslaught into Iraq.

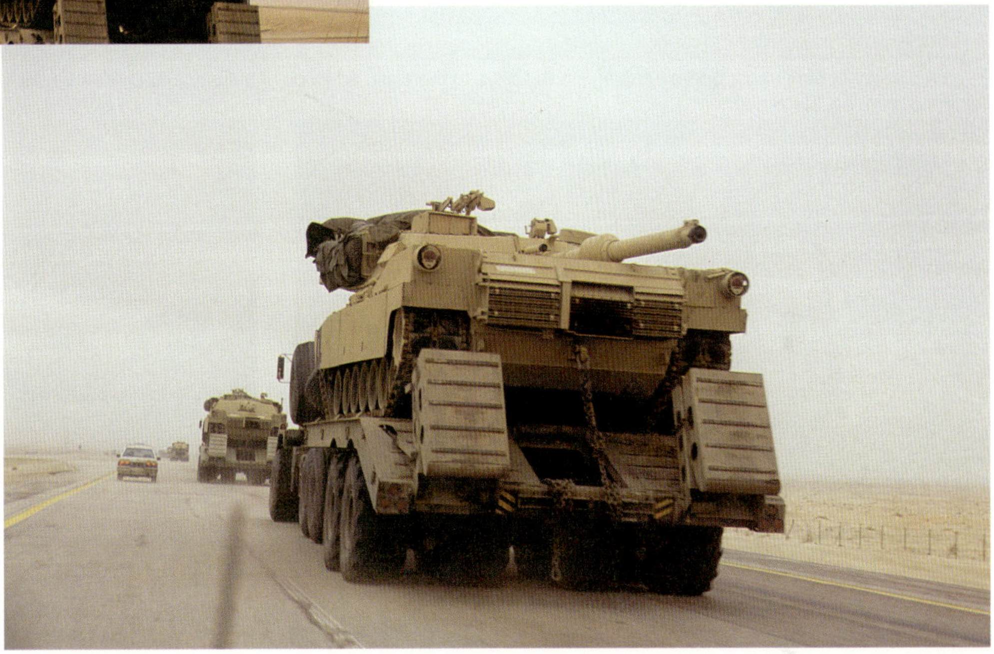

M1A1s of the 3rd Armored Division heading for the west. Saudi tank transporters provided the transportation. Most of the tracked vehicles were being transported to the front.

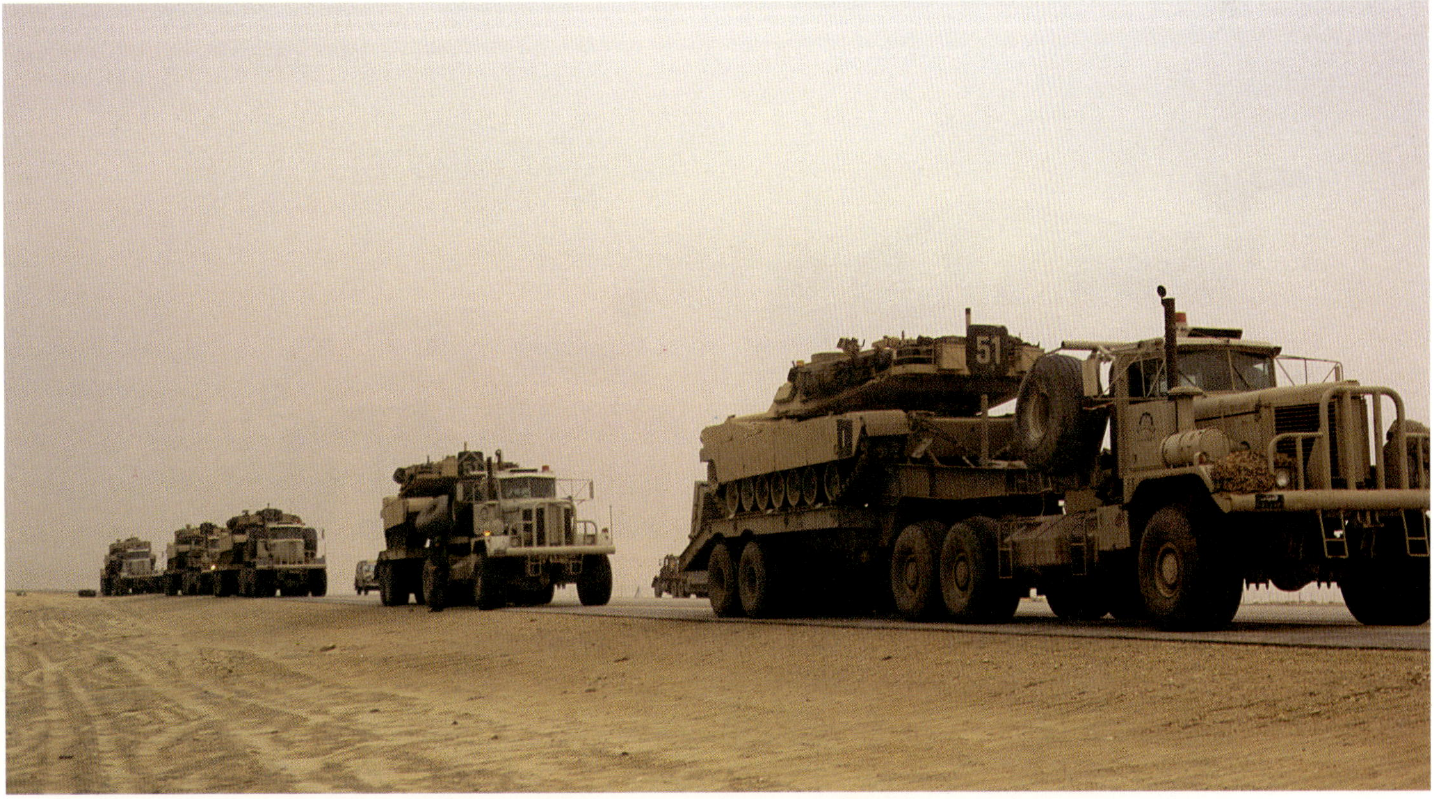

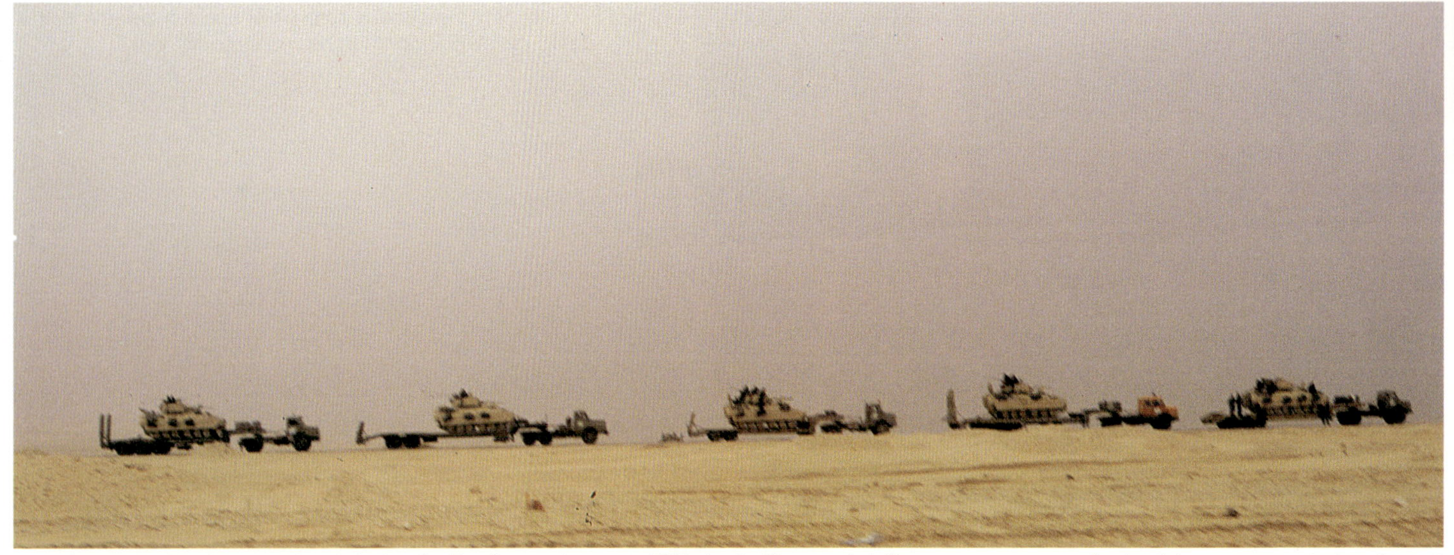

A convoy of tank transporters bringing the Bradleys to the west. All kinds of military and civilian tractors were used to haul the vast amount of equipment for the upcoming "Blitzkrieg".

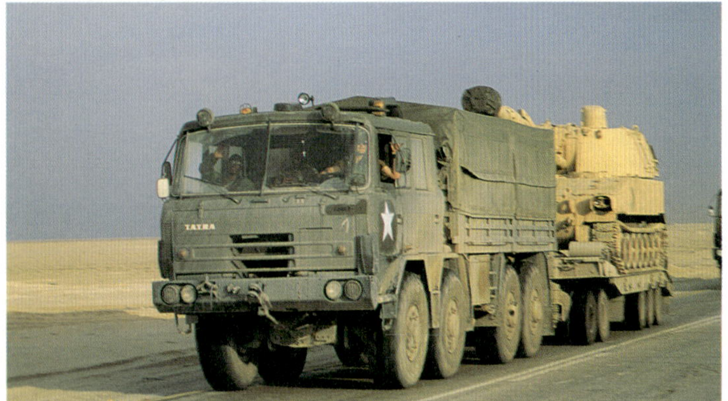

A Czechoslovakia-built Tatra T815 truck now employed by the U.S. Army towing a semi- trailer carrying an M109A1.

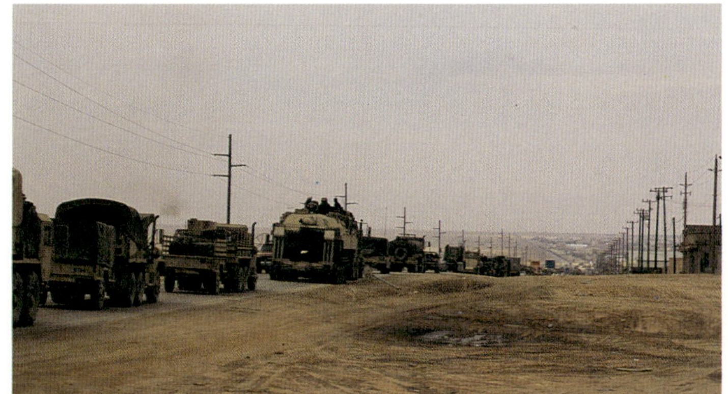

Units of the 1st Cavalry Division caught in a traffic jam at Hafr Al Baten.

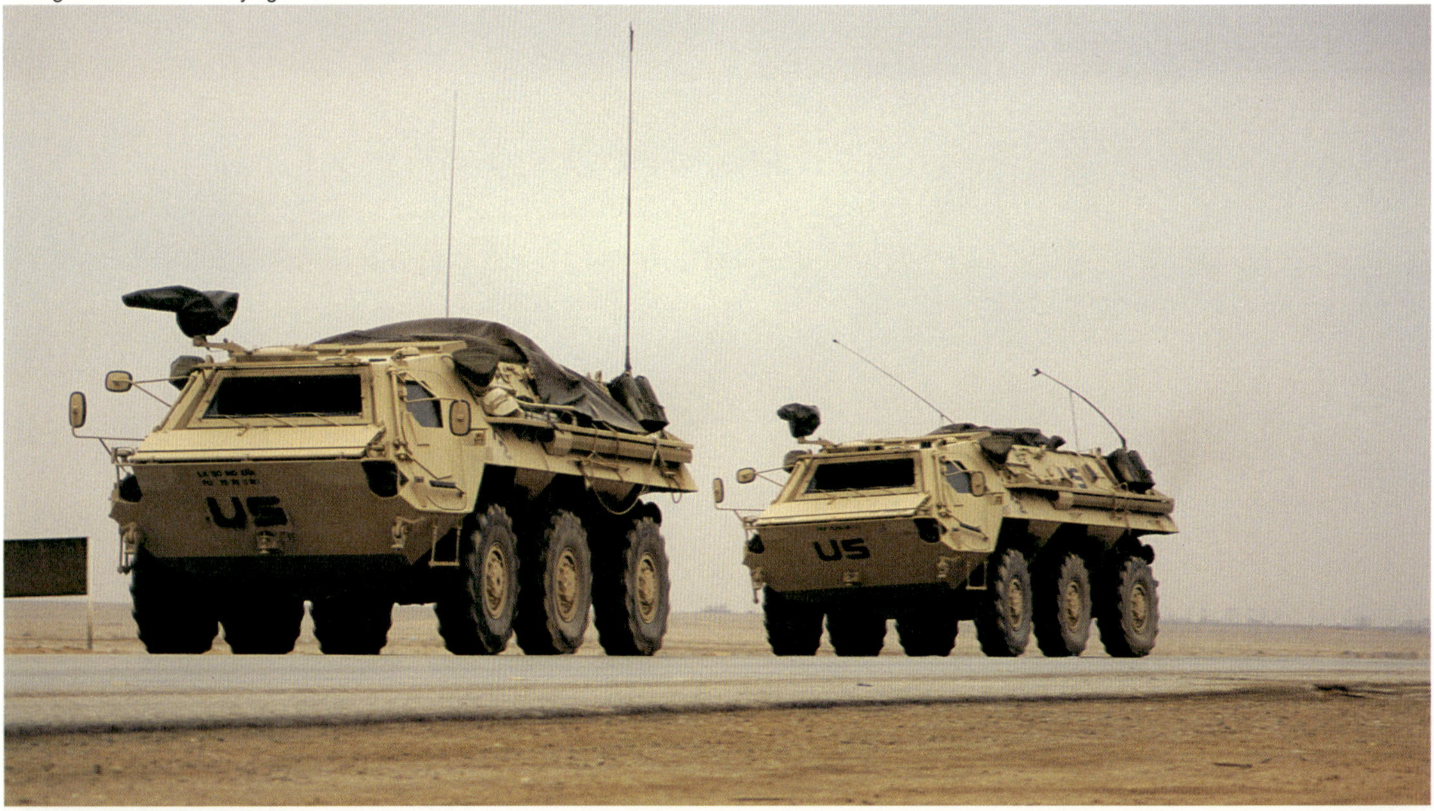

A couple of U.S. Army "Fox" NBC (Nuclear, Biological, and Chemical) Reconnaissance vehicles of the 3rd Infantry Division on a highway heading west. The Fox carries radiation and chemical agent detectors, sampling instruments and markers. All operations can be carried out inside the vehicle. The Fox is based on the German-designed "Fuch" NBC variant. The U.S. Army had only a few of these vehicles, but received 60 from the German government during the Desert Shield build-up.

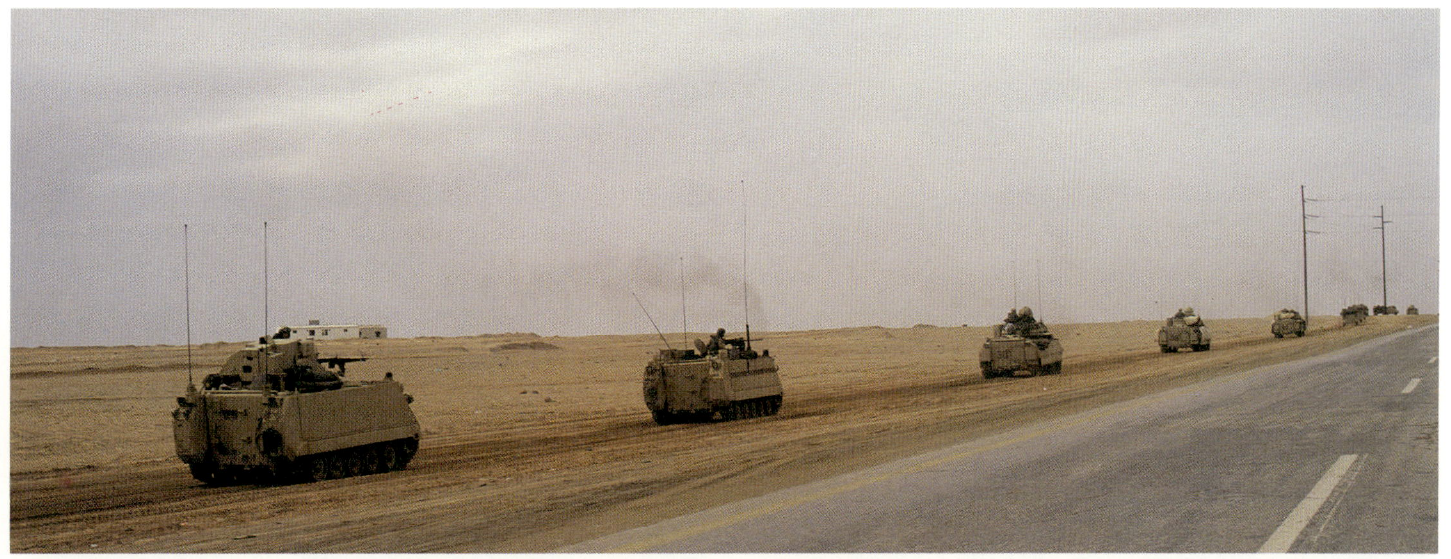

An anti-tank company of the 1st Cavalry on its way to its combat position near Hafr Al Baten.

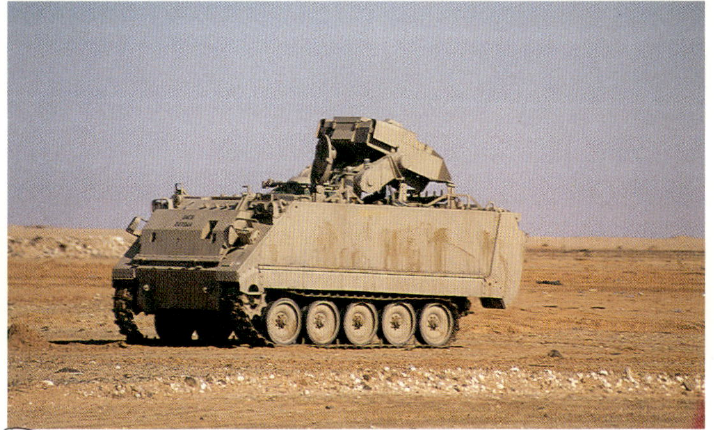

This M901 threw a track and has to wait for the recovery vehicle.

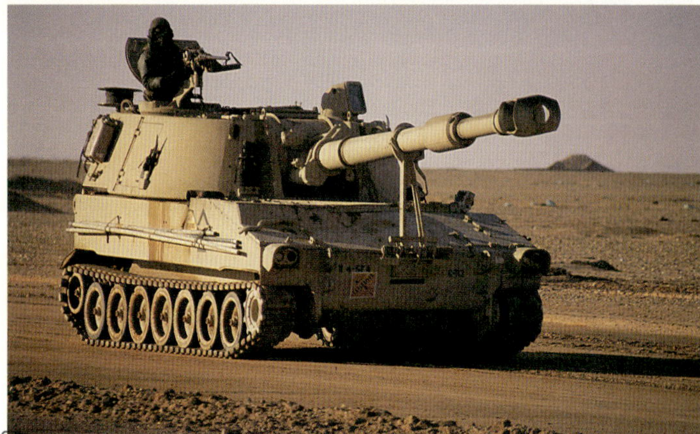

An M109A2 self-prolpelled gun of the 3/82 Field Artillery.

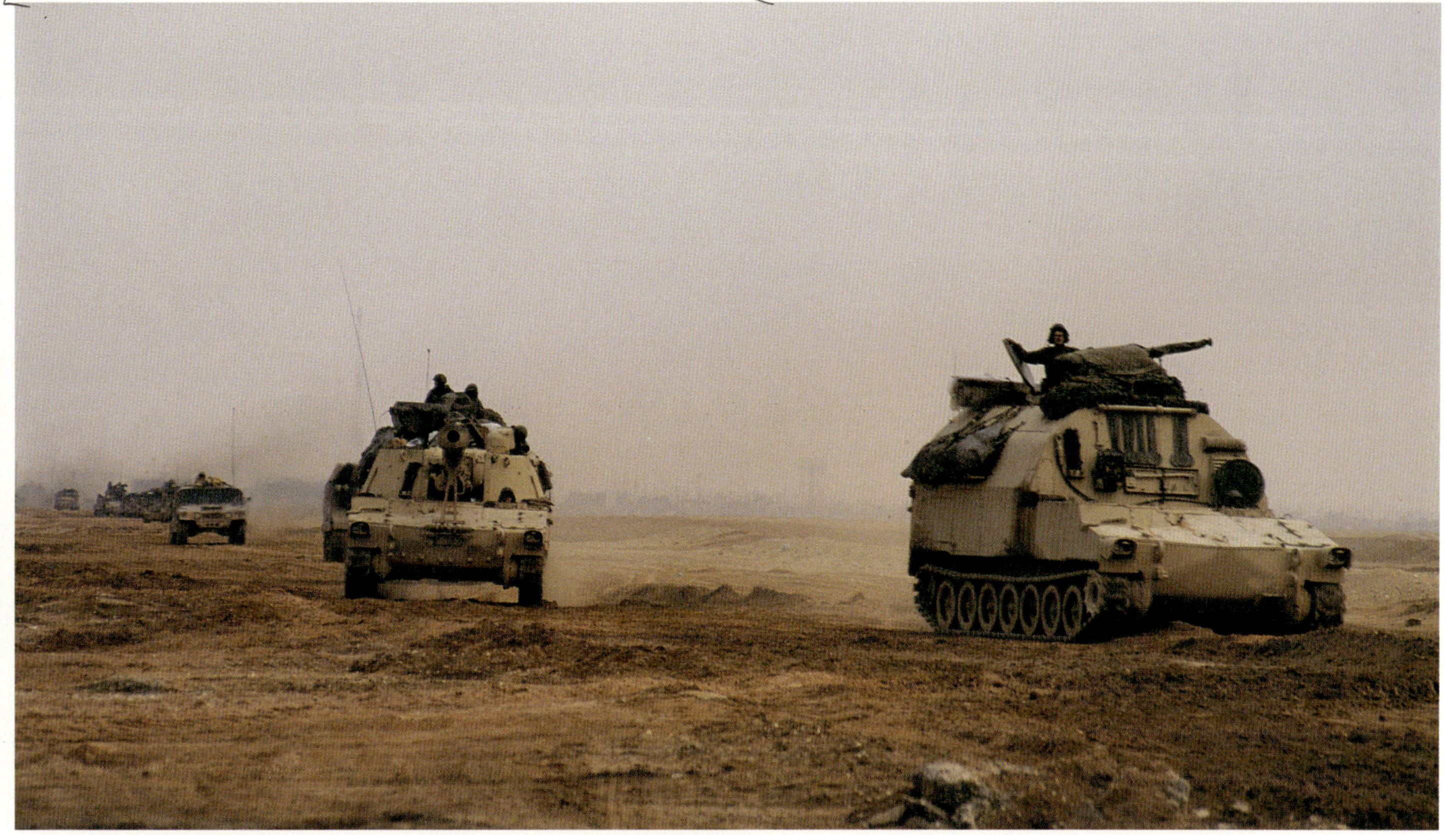

A battery of the 3/82 FA on the move. Leading the column is an M992 Feild Artillery Ammunition Support Vehicle. The M992 is based on the M109 chassis with the turret replaced by an enclosed superstructure housing 93 155mm projectiles, 99 propellant charges and 104 fuzes. The M992 is the basic ammunition resupply vehicle for the M109 self-propelled gun.

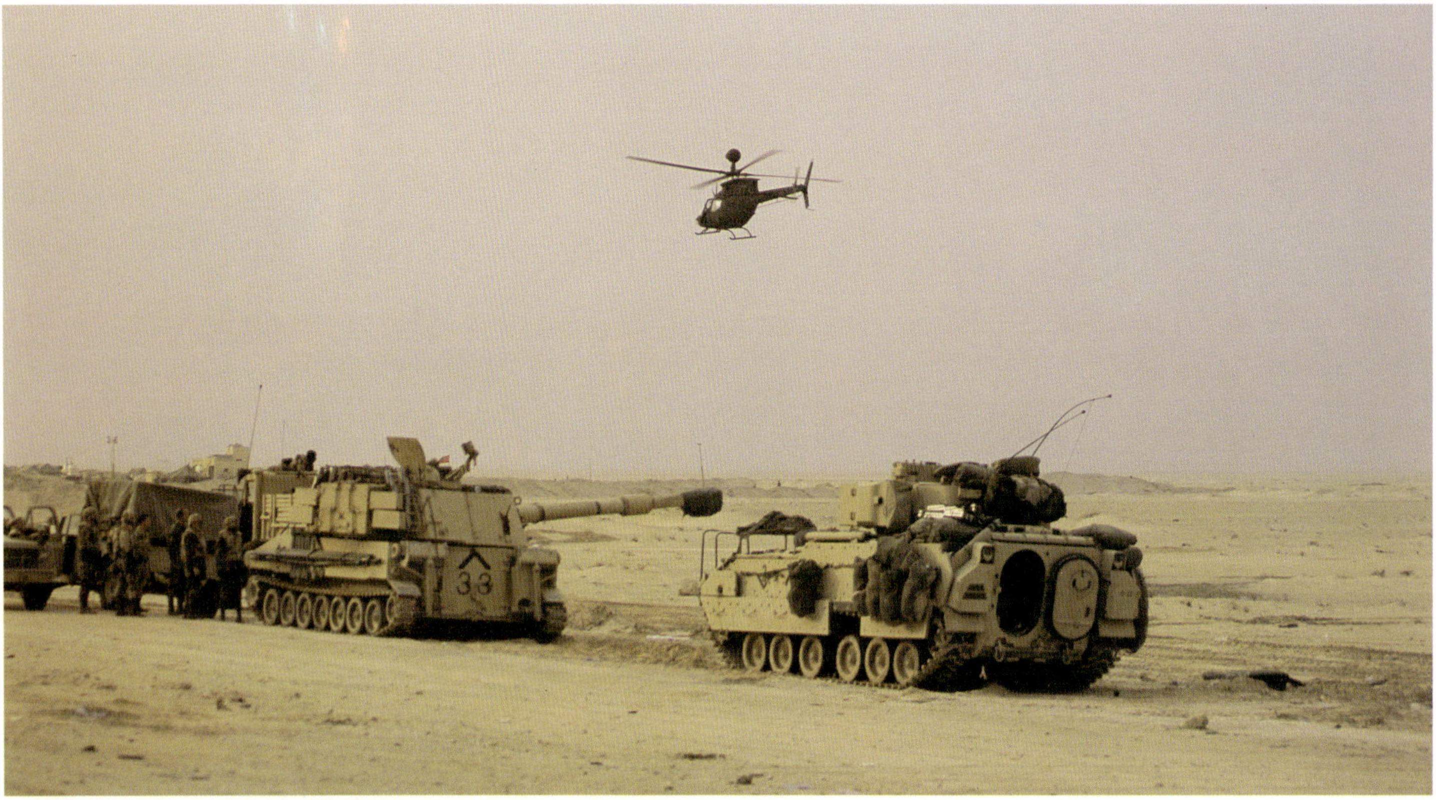

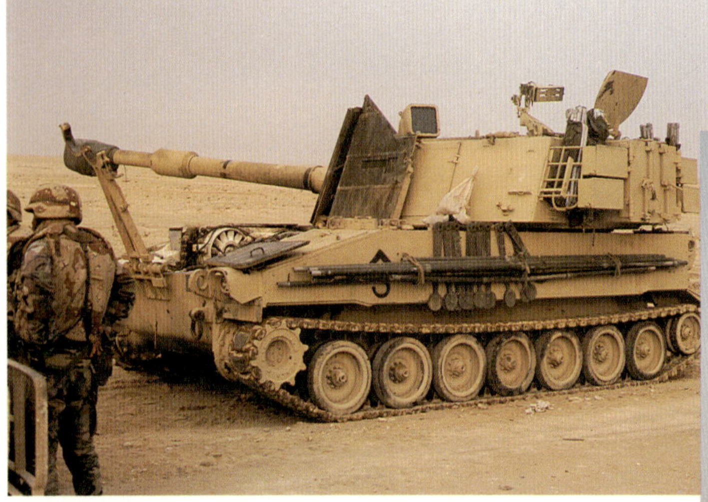

Another view of the disabled M109A2. Behind it is an up-armored Bradley. Flying above is the Kiowa scout helicopter.

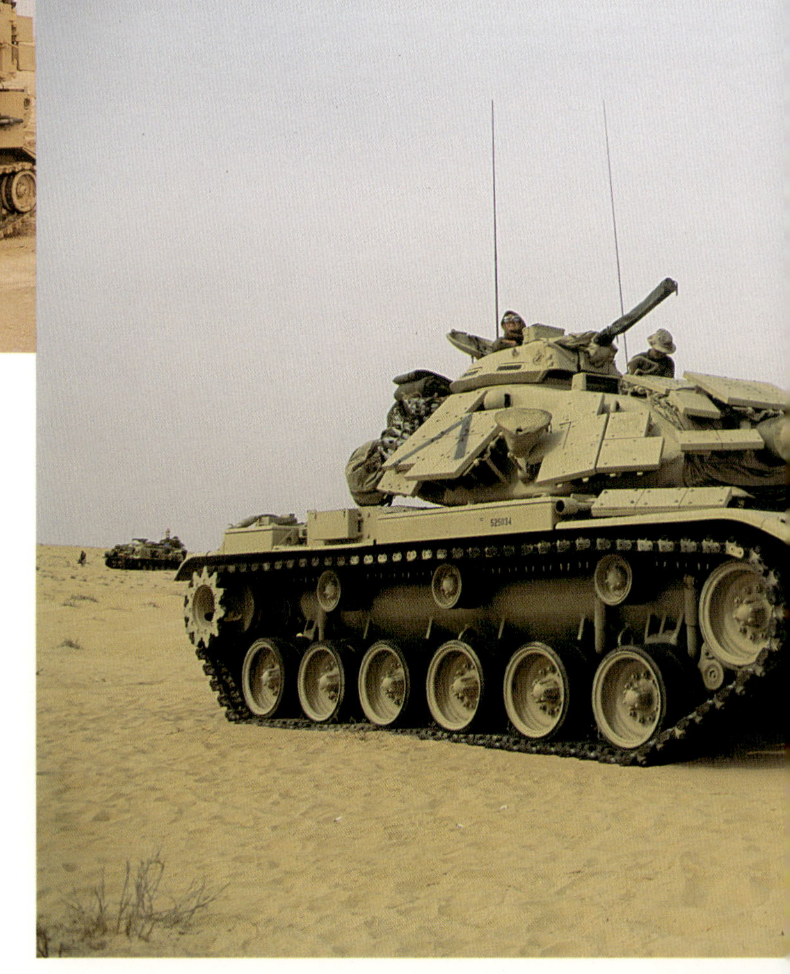

This M109A2 has an engine breakdown and is waiting for help.

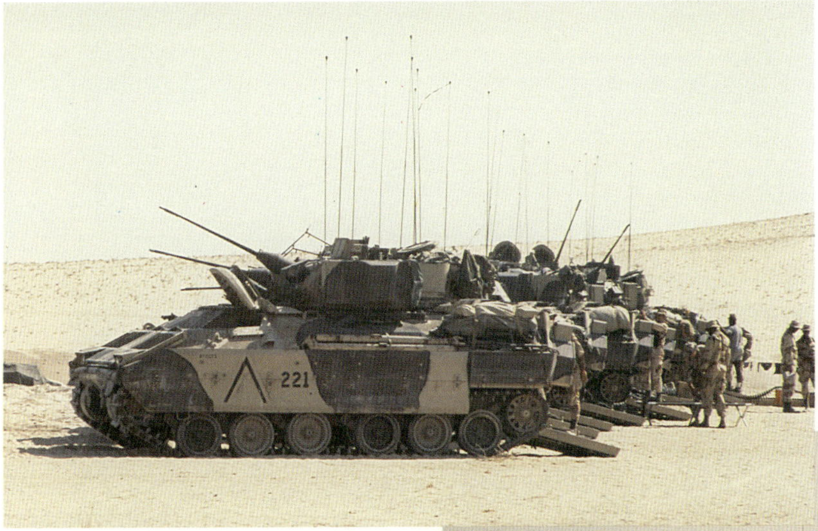

To the west, M2/M3 Bradley Fighting Vehicles and M1A1 Abrams are also preparing for the G-day.

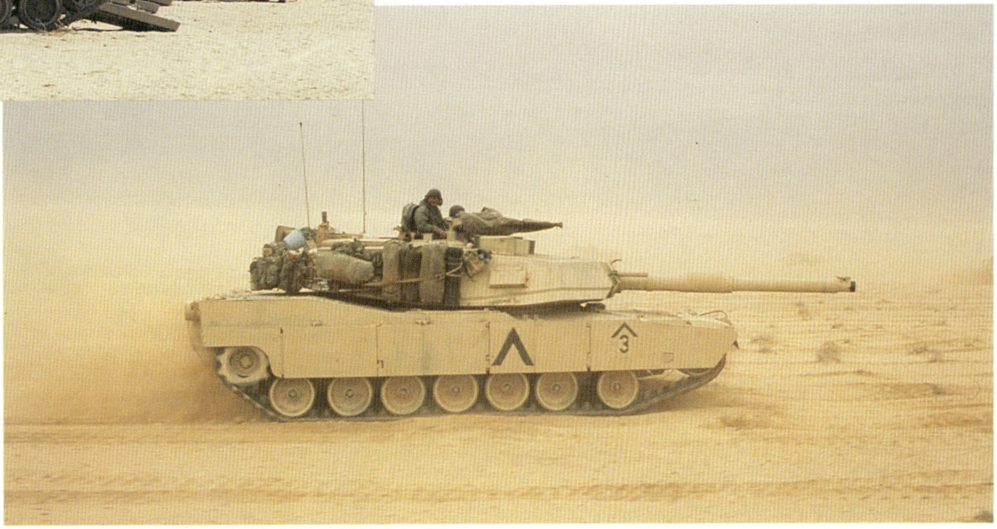

On the right flank, M60A1s of the Marine Corps fitted with reactive armor tiles are in position and ready for the onslaught into Southern Kuwait. The tanks are now painted with the inverted V invasion marking.

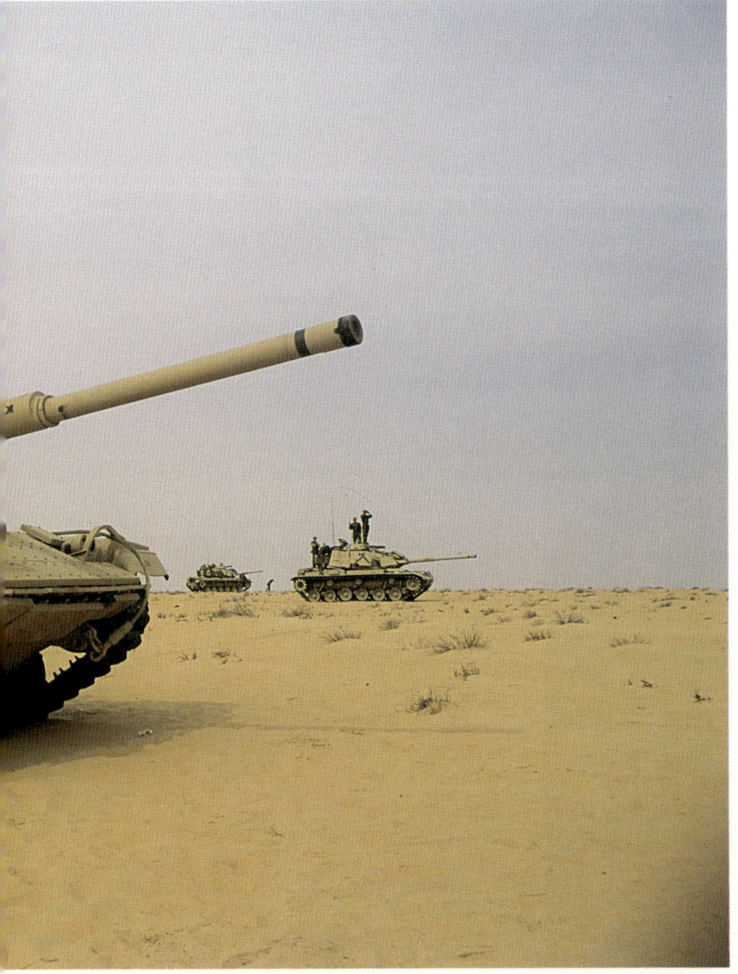

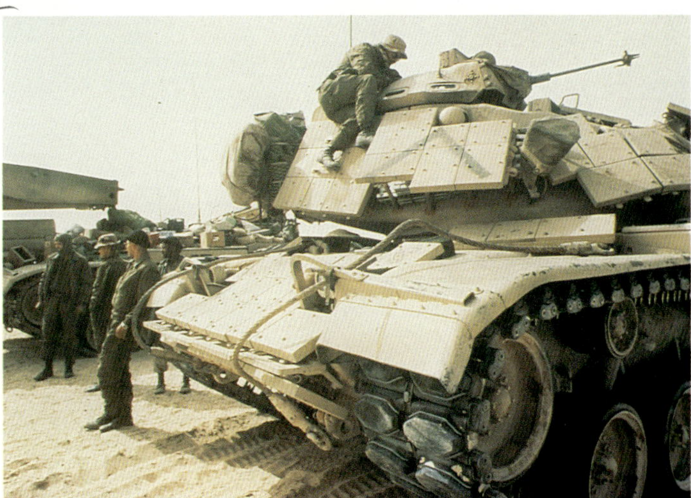

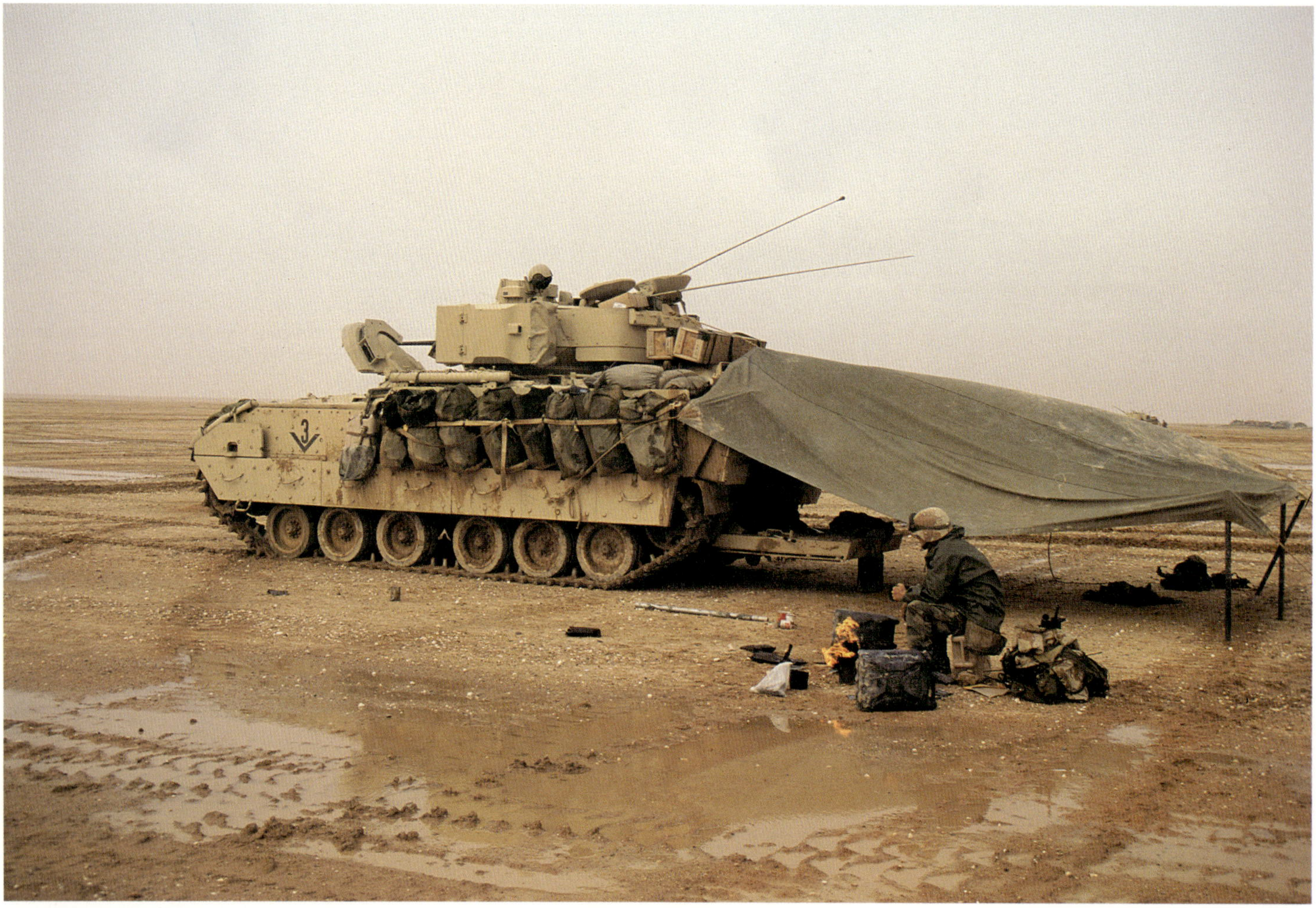

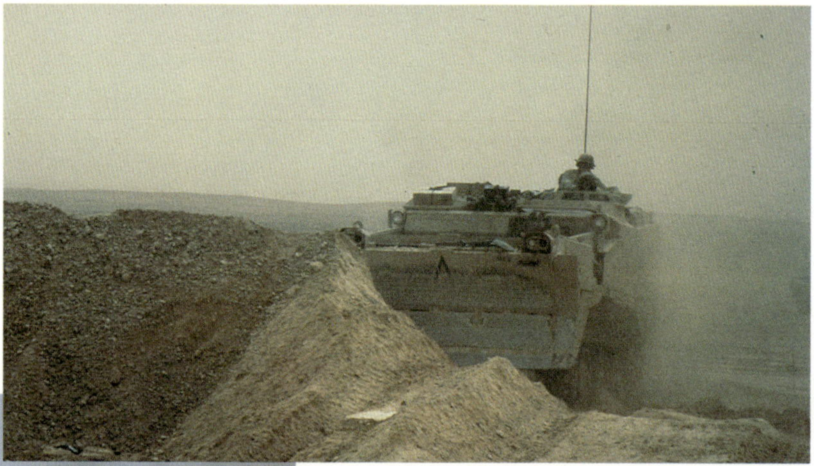

On G-day, February 24, 1991, the coalition forces launched the air-land offensive against Iraq, codenamed "Desert Sabre". Leading the assault were combat engineer vehicles. Here an M9 Armored Combat Earthmover of the 299th Engineer Battalion attached to the 24th Mechanized Infantry Division breaches a berm leading into Iraq.(DoD)

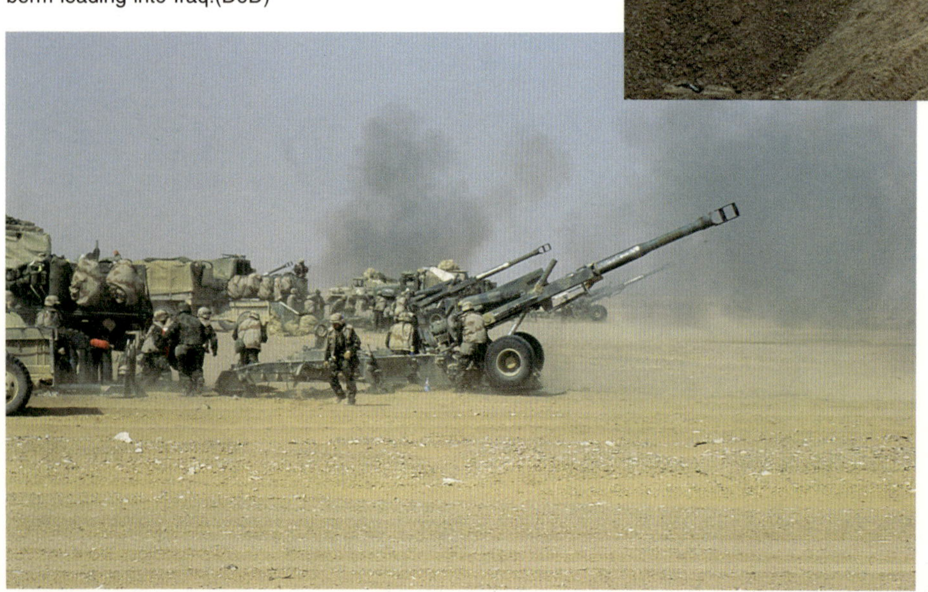

Allied forces quickly set up positions to pound the Iraqi Army with heavy artillery. Here, M198 howitzers of the XVIII Airborne Corps shelling Iraqi positions inside Iraq.

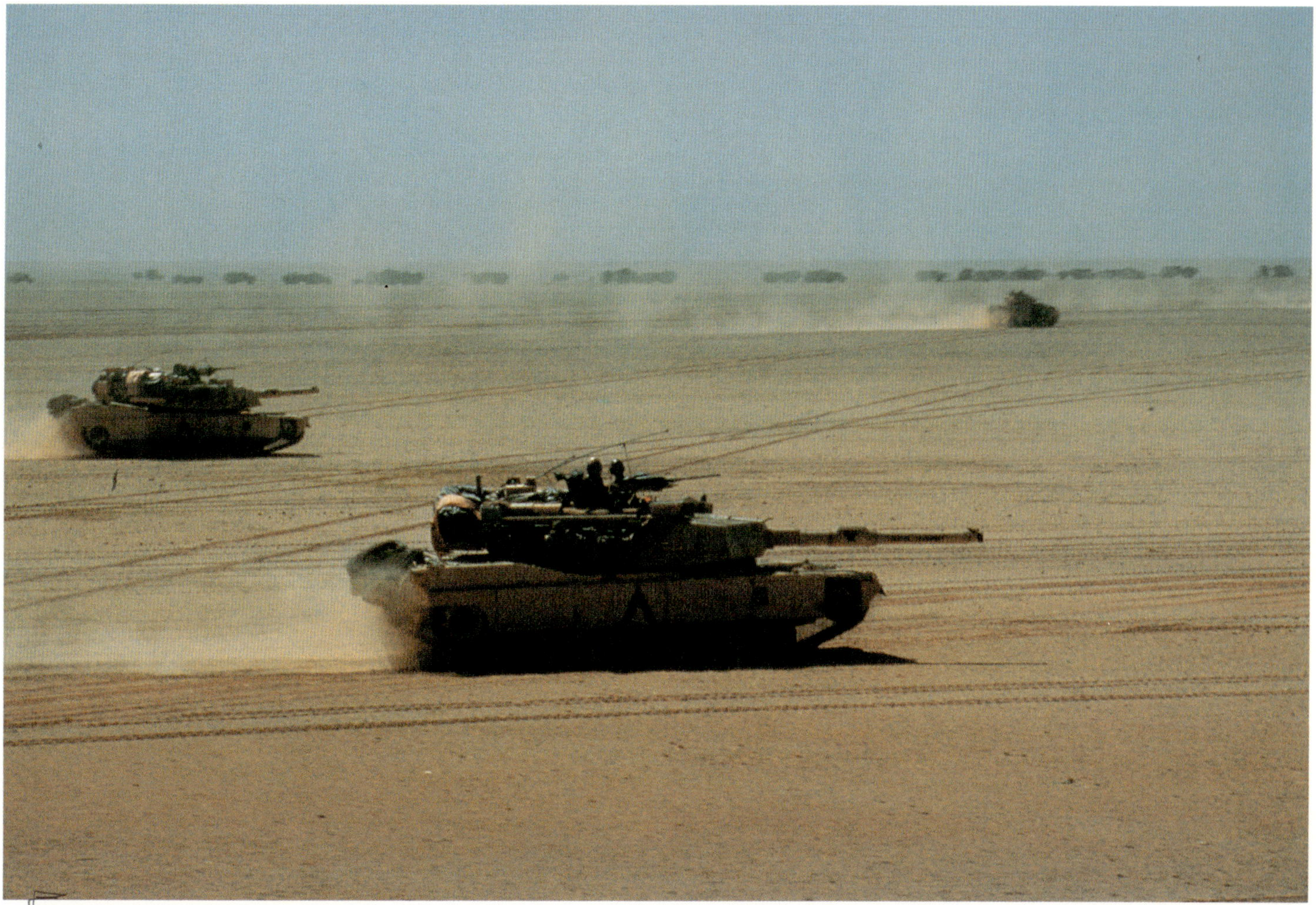

Spearheading the drive into Iraq were the M1A1 main battle tanks. During the ground war, the M1A1 HA tanks proved to be almost impervious to Iraqi tank fire, both from T-72 and T-55 tanks.(DoD)

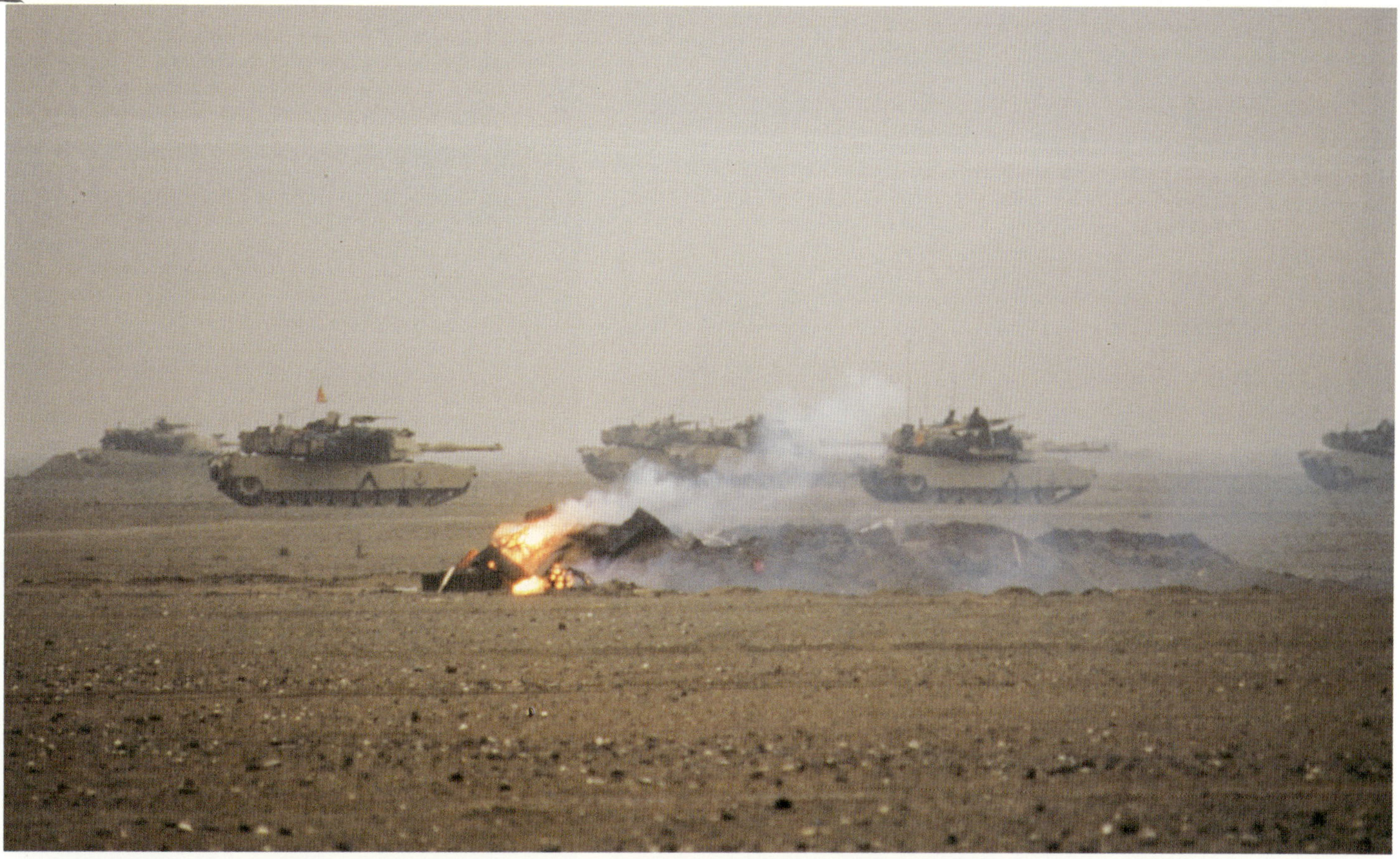

The thermal-imaging infrared systems on the M1A1 tank were far superior to the infrared and starlight scopes mounted on Iraqi tanks. The M1A1 tankers could pick up targets with their thermal-imaging sights even in sandstorms, or dense black smoke from oil-field fires.(DoD)

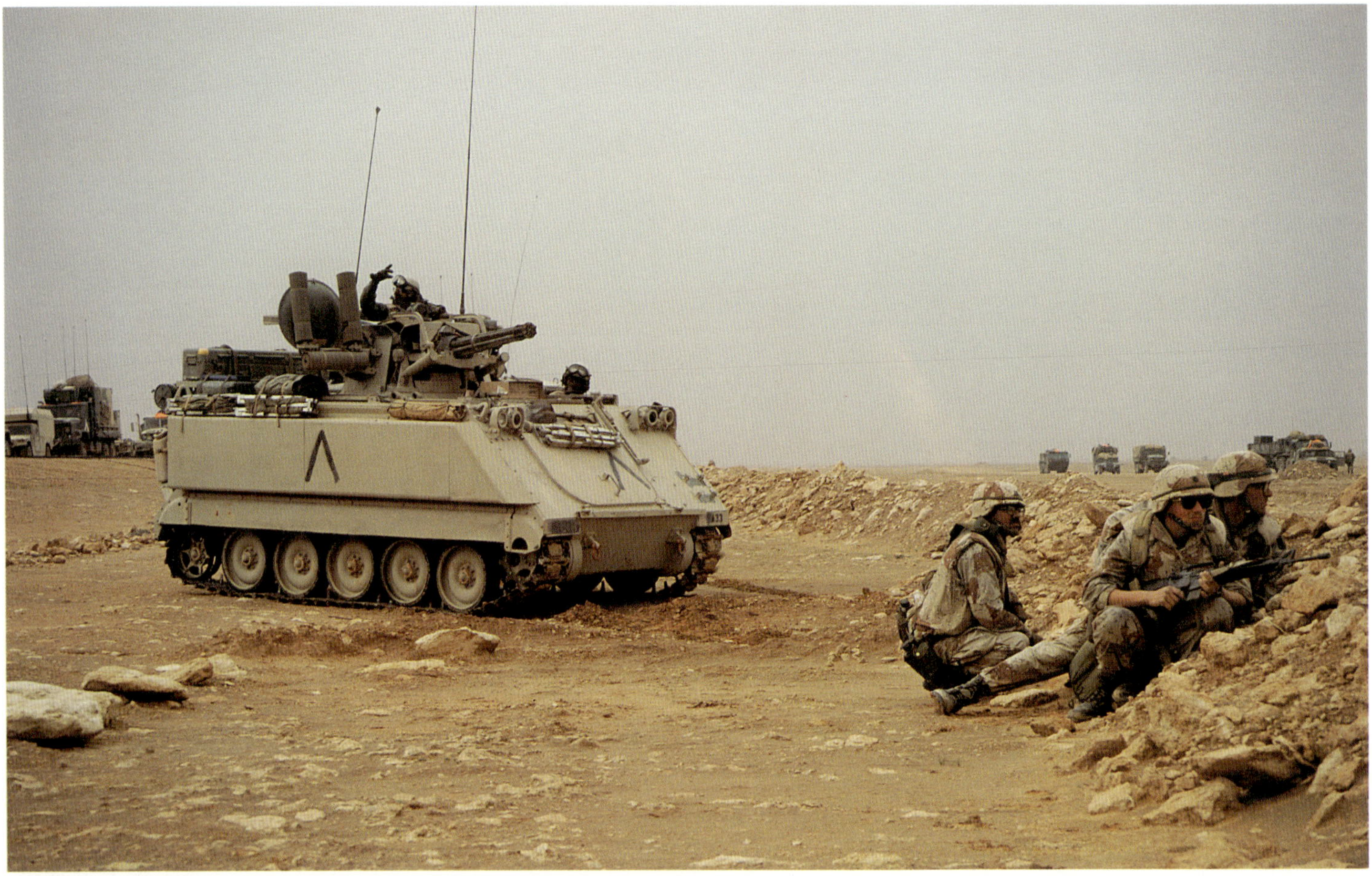

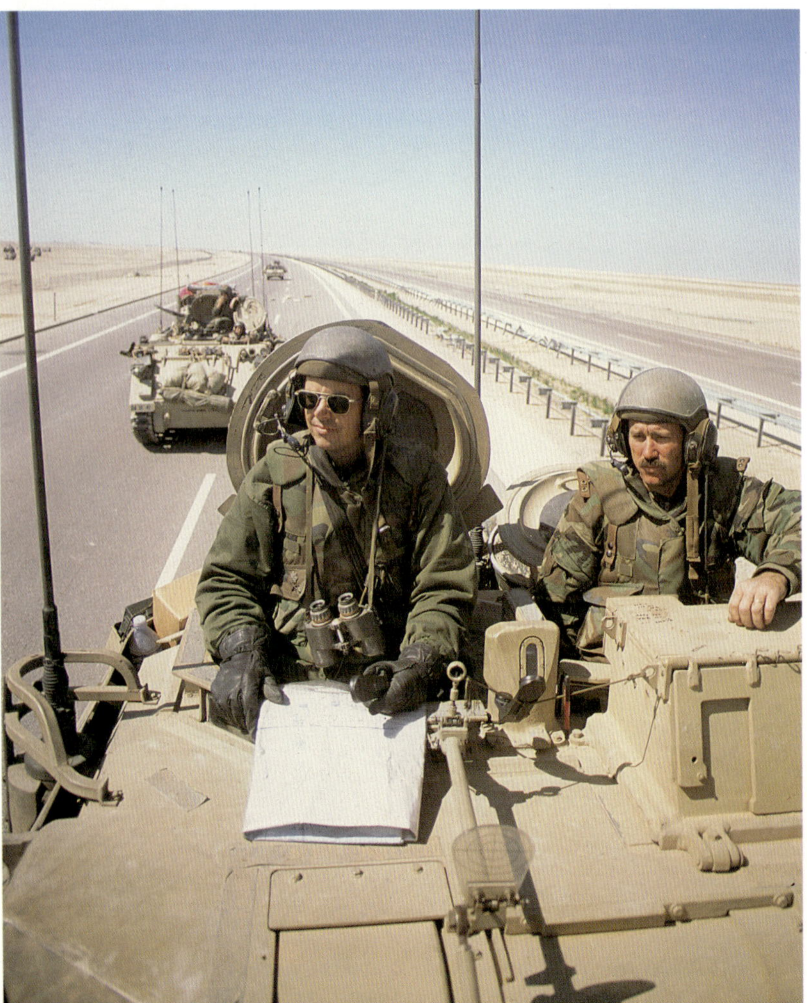

The M163 20mm Vulcan anti-aircraft gun proved to be also an effective infantry support weapon. Shown is an M163 providing fire-support for the paratroopers of the 82nd Airborne.

M2 Bradleys of the 24th Mechanized Infantry Division, nicknamed the "Victory Division", reached the Baghdad-Basra highway on February 28, 1991, isolated the KTO from reinforcement and cut-off the Iraqi Republican Guard units.

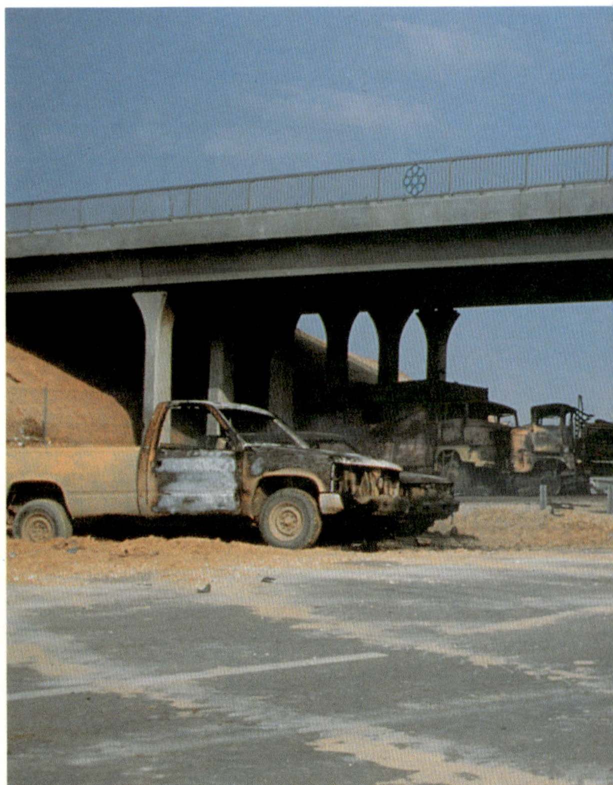

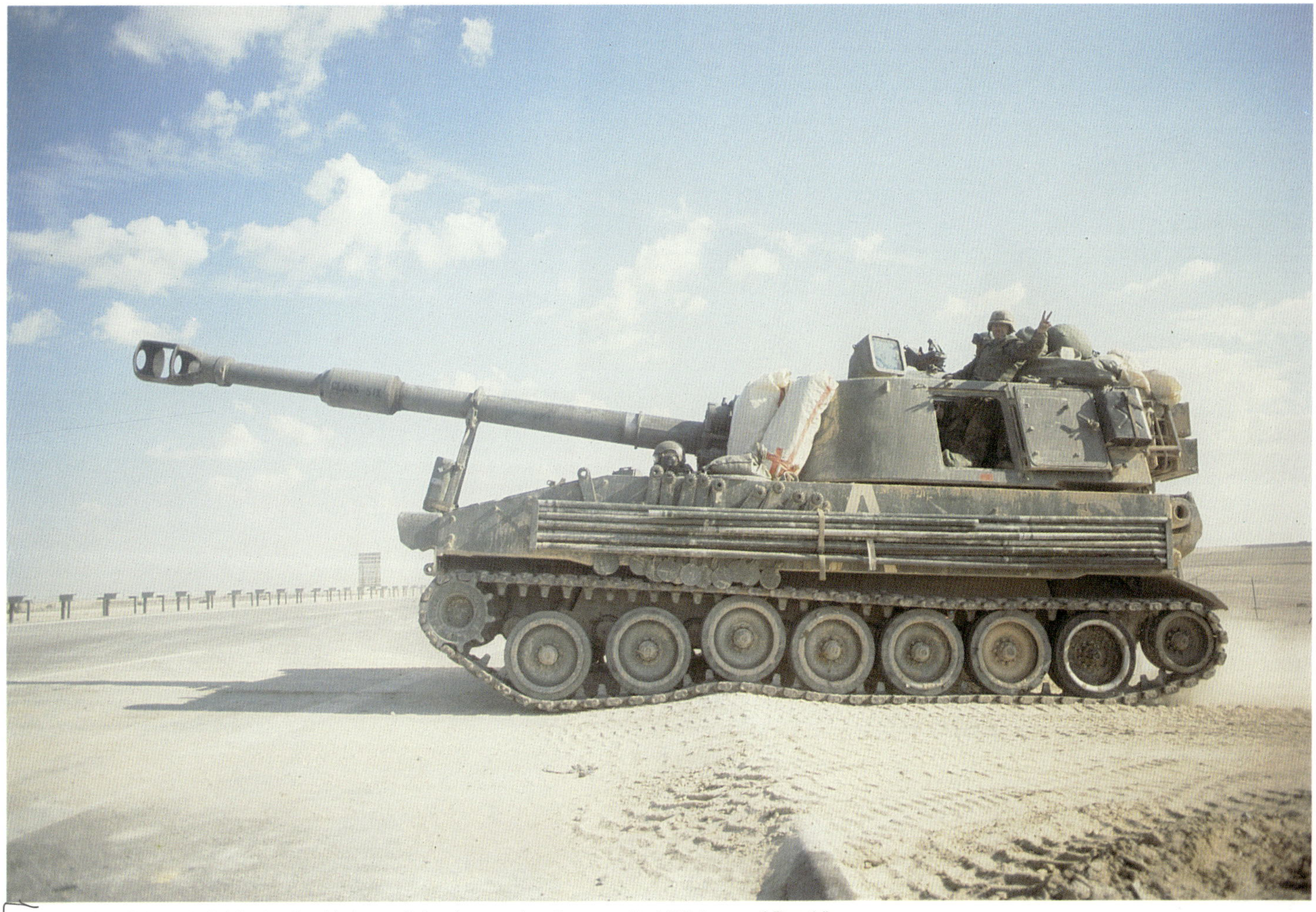

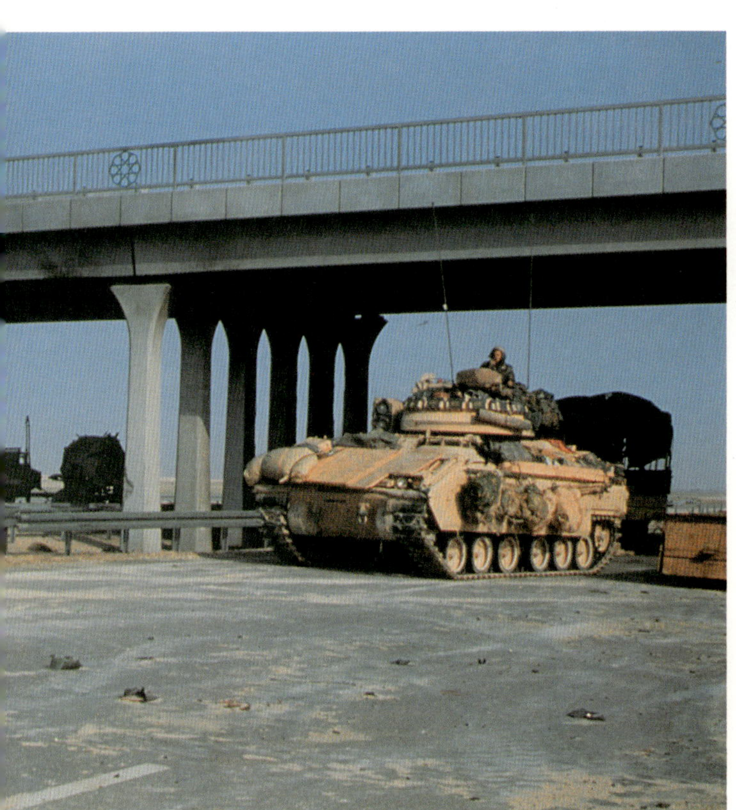

An M109A2 of the 197th Mechanized Infantry Brigade crossing the so-called "Highway of Death".

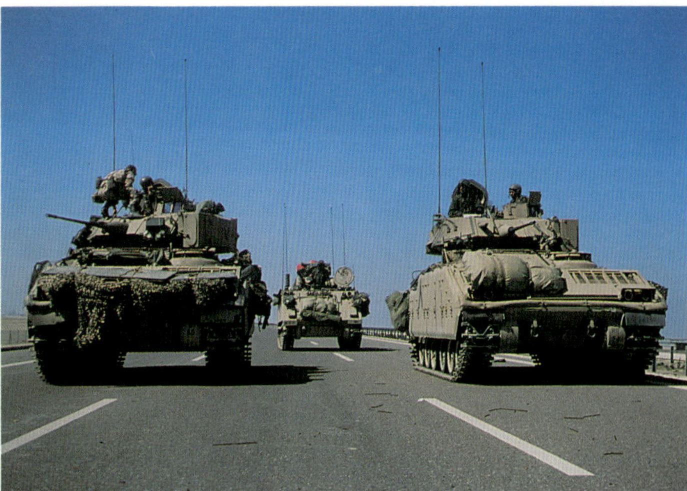

On February 28,1991 the 24th Mechanized Infantry Division still faced sporadic fire from Iraqi soldiers who didn't know that a cease-fire had been agreed upon. This was lack of communication on the part of the Iraqi soldiers.

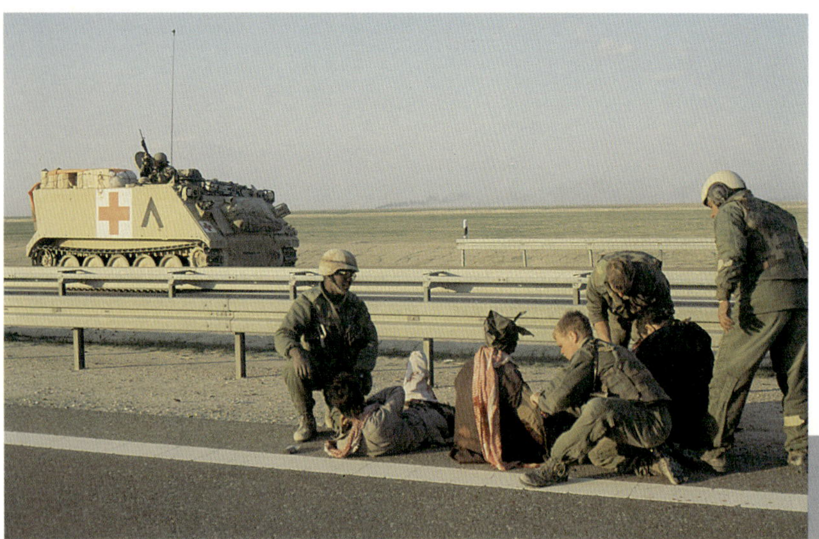

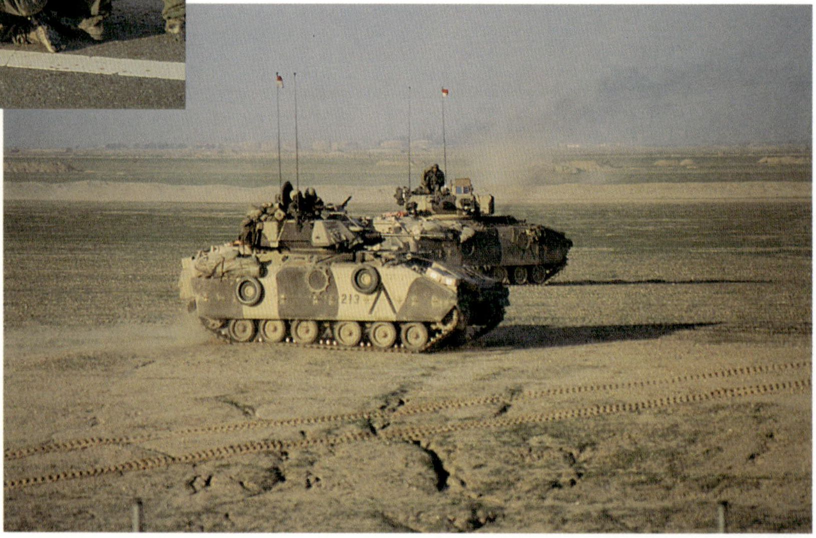

A pair of Bradleys of the 4th CAV 30km from Basra.

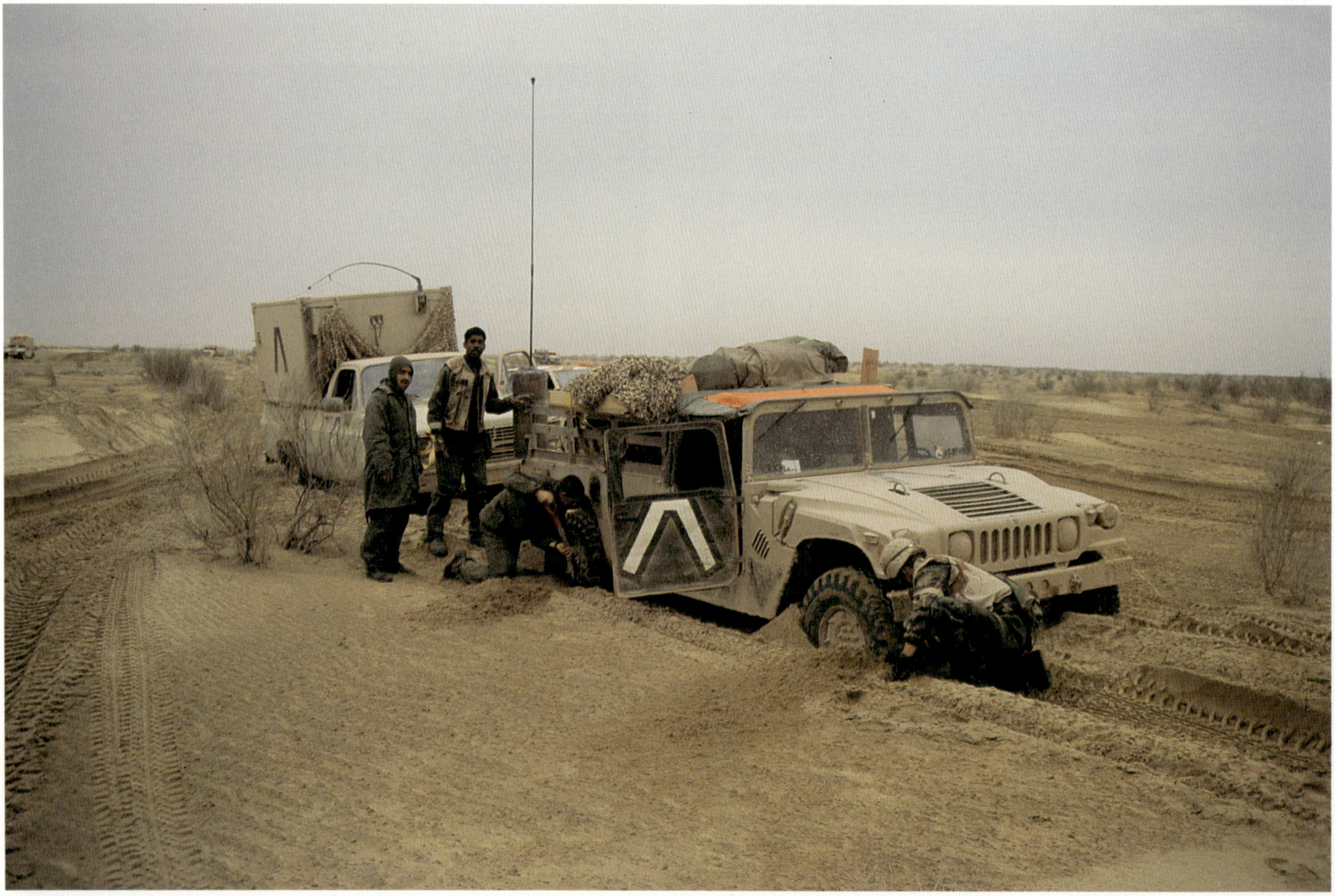

A HUMVEE of the 24th ID got stuck in the sand in the Shamya desert.

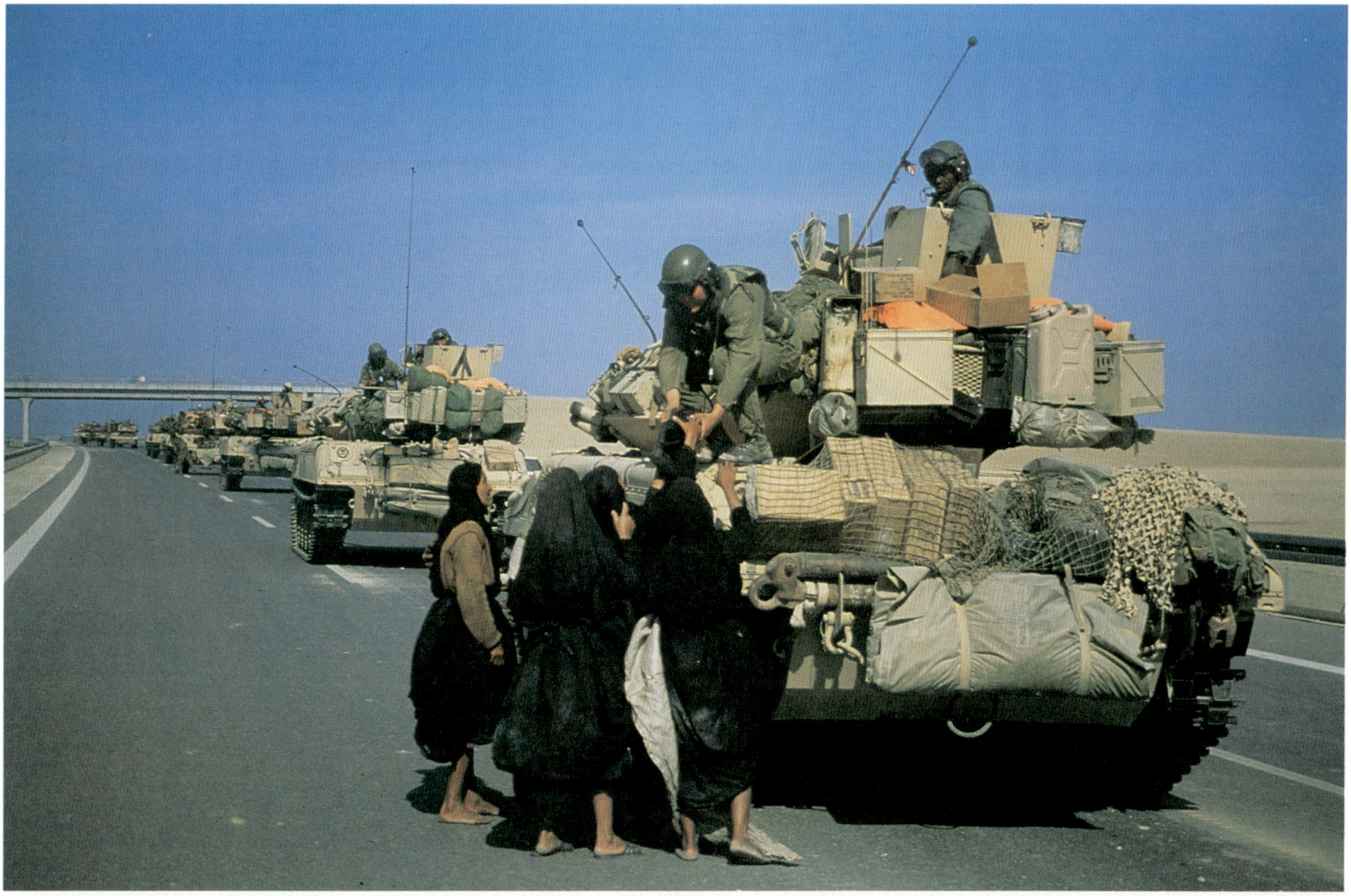

Iraqi civilians asking for food from the crew of an M551 Sheridan tank on March 2, 1991 near Basra.

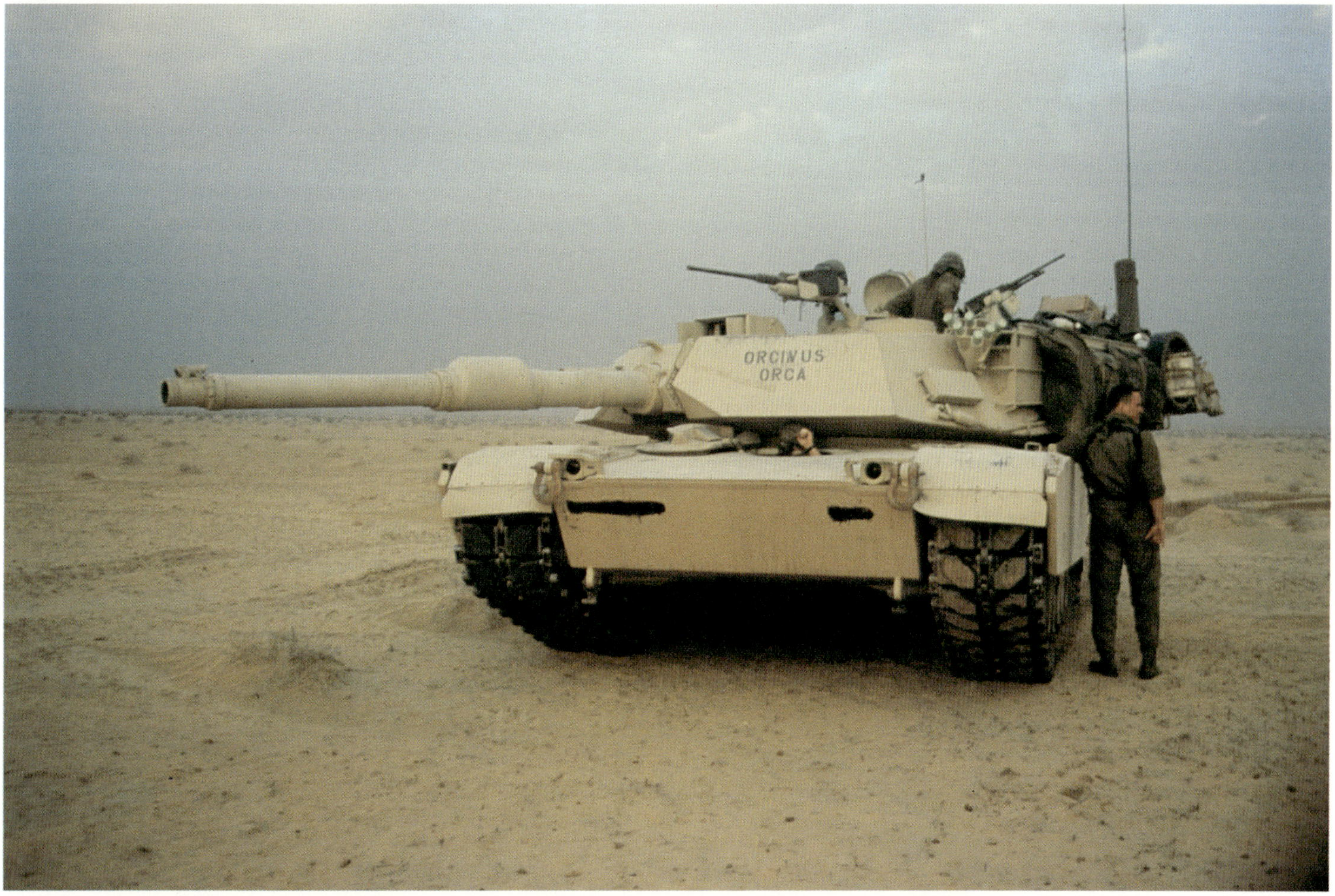

An M1A1 of the 3rd Armored Cavalry Regiment near Basra. Note the unit marking has been spray-painted over.

BRITISH ARMOR IN ACTION

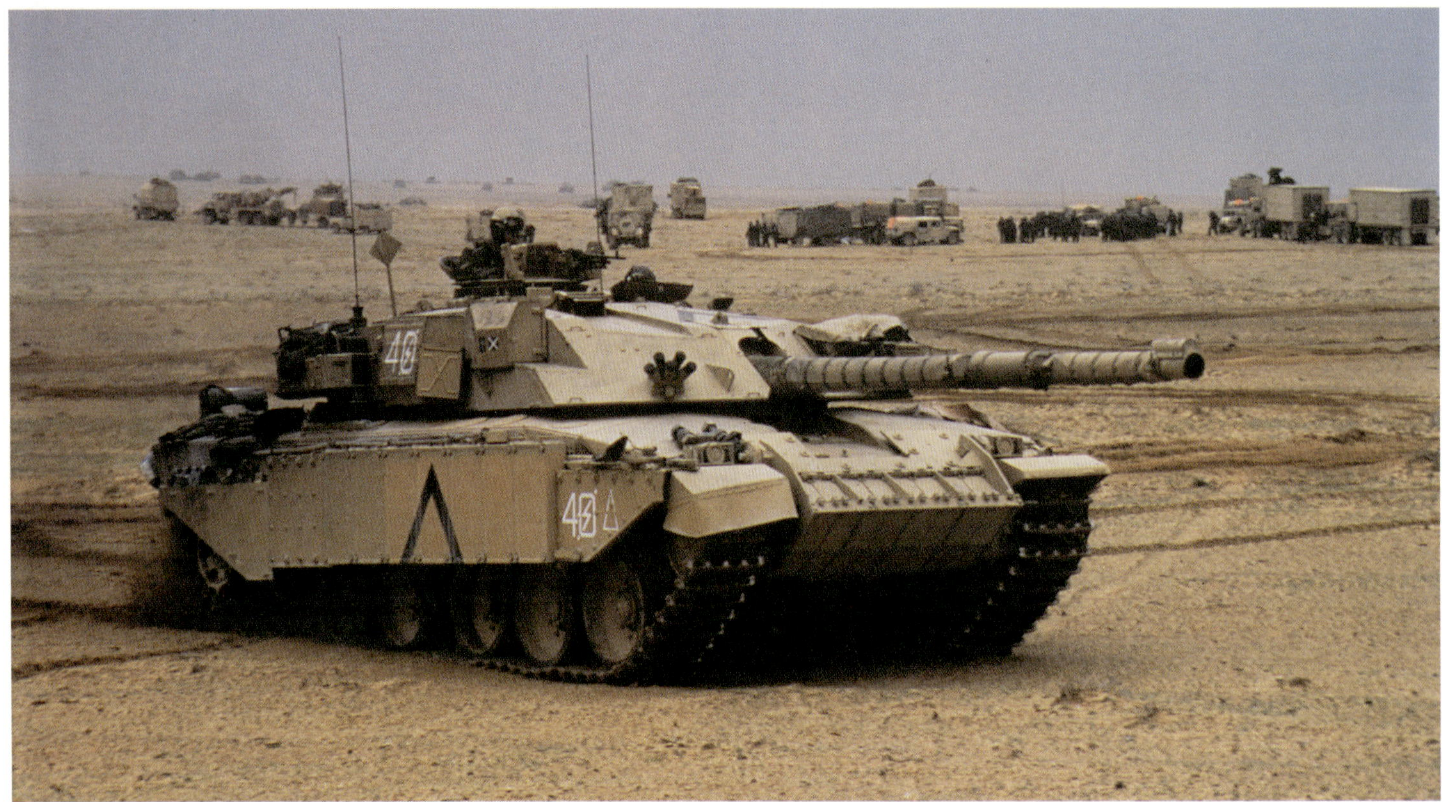

With the invasion of Kuwait by Iraq in August 1990, Great Britain quickly responded to President George Bush's call to arms.

In early September 1990, the entire garrison of the British Army of the Rhine (BAOR) was placed on alert. They quickly began to prepare their equipment for deployment to Saudi Arabia for Operation Granby.

The first unit selected to be sent to Saudi Arabia was the well known British 7th Armoured Brigade nicknamed the "Desert Rats". The soldiers quickly repainted their vehicles in sand color, and applied the red gerboa on their vehicles as a mascot.

In early October 1990, the British transport ship brought to Saudi soil the Challenger tanks of The Royal Scots Dragoon Guards. In the next few days, vehicles of the 7th Armoured Brigade started to arrive. The 7th Armoured Brigade was attached to the U.S. 1st Marine Expeditionary Force.

Then came the British 4th Armoured Brigade, some command elements, plus a number of infantry units. The two brigades formed the British 1st Armoured Division during Operation Granby.

On February 24, 1991, early in the afternoon, the British 1st Armoured Division entered into Iraq, following the U.S. Army's 1st Infantry Division (nicknamed "the Big Red One"), which had driven a breach in the highly overrated Saddam defensive line.

The 16th/5th Queen's Royal Lancers was the first unit to engage in combat. Assisted by British Army helicopters, they destroyed 4 Iraqi tanks and 7 armored personnel carriers.

The two British armored brigades advanced on two separate paths northeast into Iraq. By the evening of the 24th, The Royal Scots Dragoon Guards Battle Group began an attack against an Iraqi army communication center which was protected by two companies and a number of tanks. The British infantrymen, using grenades and small arms, captured 60 Iraqi prisoners. The Iraqi tanks were destroyed by the 120mm guns of the Challengers.

Once in Iraq, the British swung east and raced towards Kuwait, securing the flank of the U.S. VII Corps in the process. In a night battle, the 1st Armoured Division destroyed a large number of Iraqi T-62 tanks and armored fighting vehicles. No Challenger tanks were lost to Iraqi fire.

However, on the 27th, nine British soldiers were killed when two Warrior armored personnel carriers were hit mistakenly by an American A-10 tank-killer.

By Thursday, February 28, 1992 the British units of the 1st Armoured Division reached the main highway into Kuwait city, 10 minutes before the cease-fire was arranged.

During the land campaign, the 1st Armoured Division had traveled almost 300 miles across Iraq into Kuwait. In the process they inflicted heavy damage to three Iraqi Army divisions, destroying 150 tanks and capturing thousands of prisoners of war.

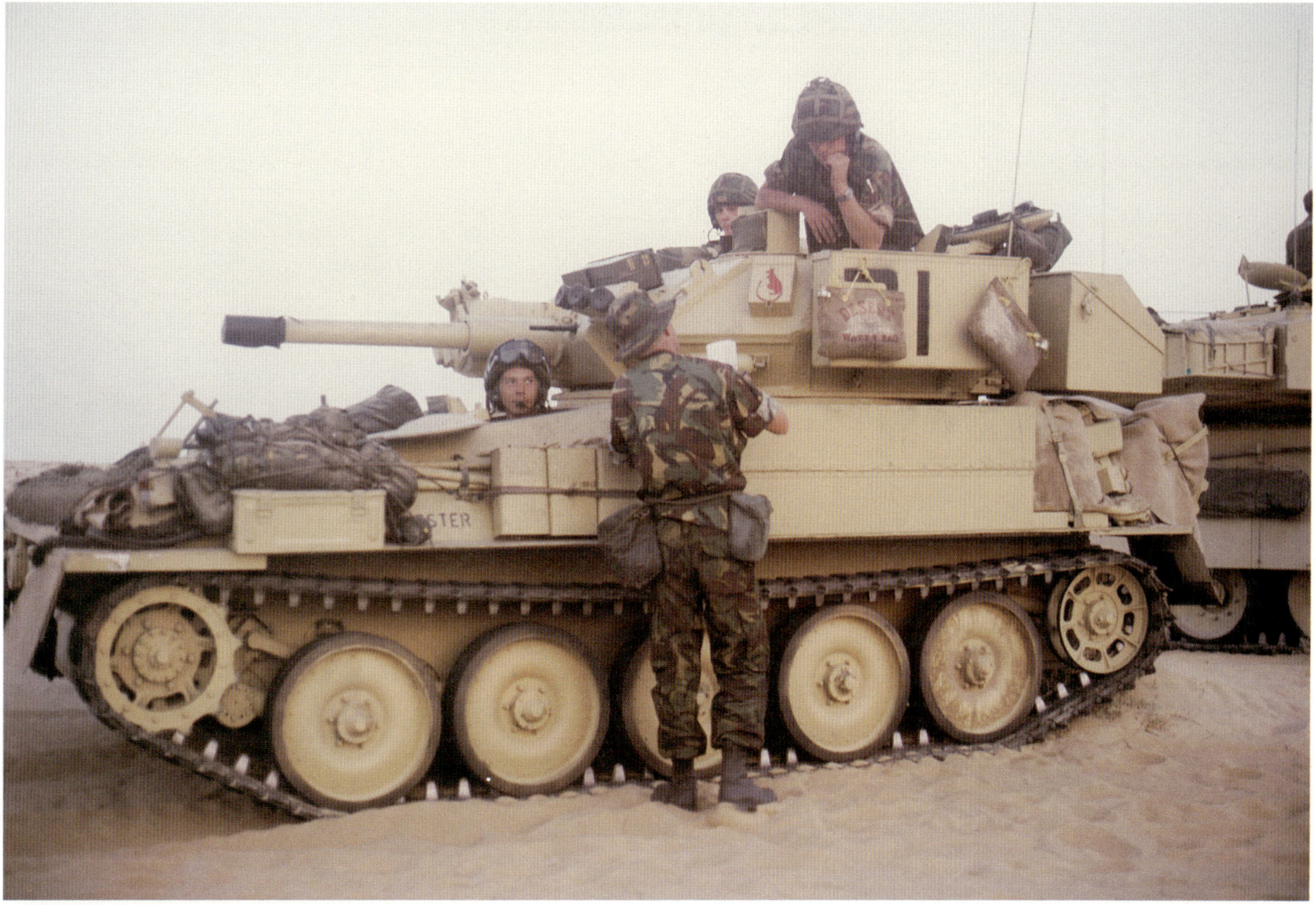

A Scorpion of the 16th/5th The Queen's Royal Lancers. The Scorpion reconnaissance vehicle is one of the fastest tracked vehicles in the world. It is armed with a 76mm gun and one 7.62mm machine gun.

An old Ferret scout car of the 2nd Field Regt. RA being cleaned up after a mission. The Ferret is used mainly in the scout and reconnaissance role. It has a maximun road speed of 90km/hr and a range of 300km.

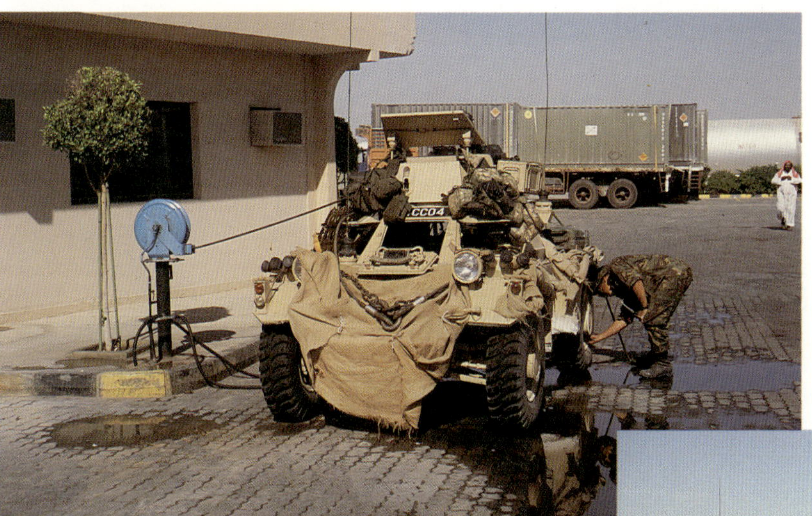

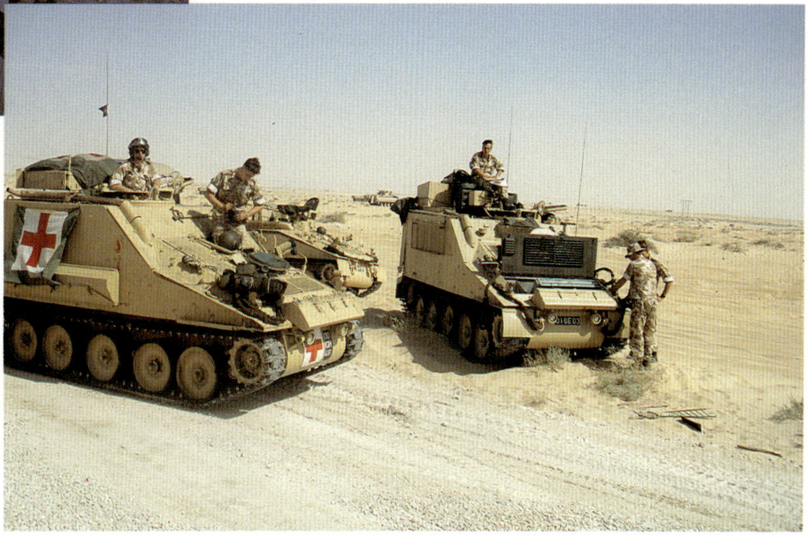

A Samaritan armored ambulance and a Sultan armored command post. Both vehicles sport the "red gerboa" of the 7th Armored Brigade.

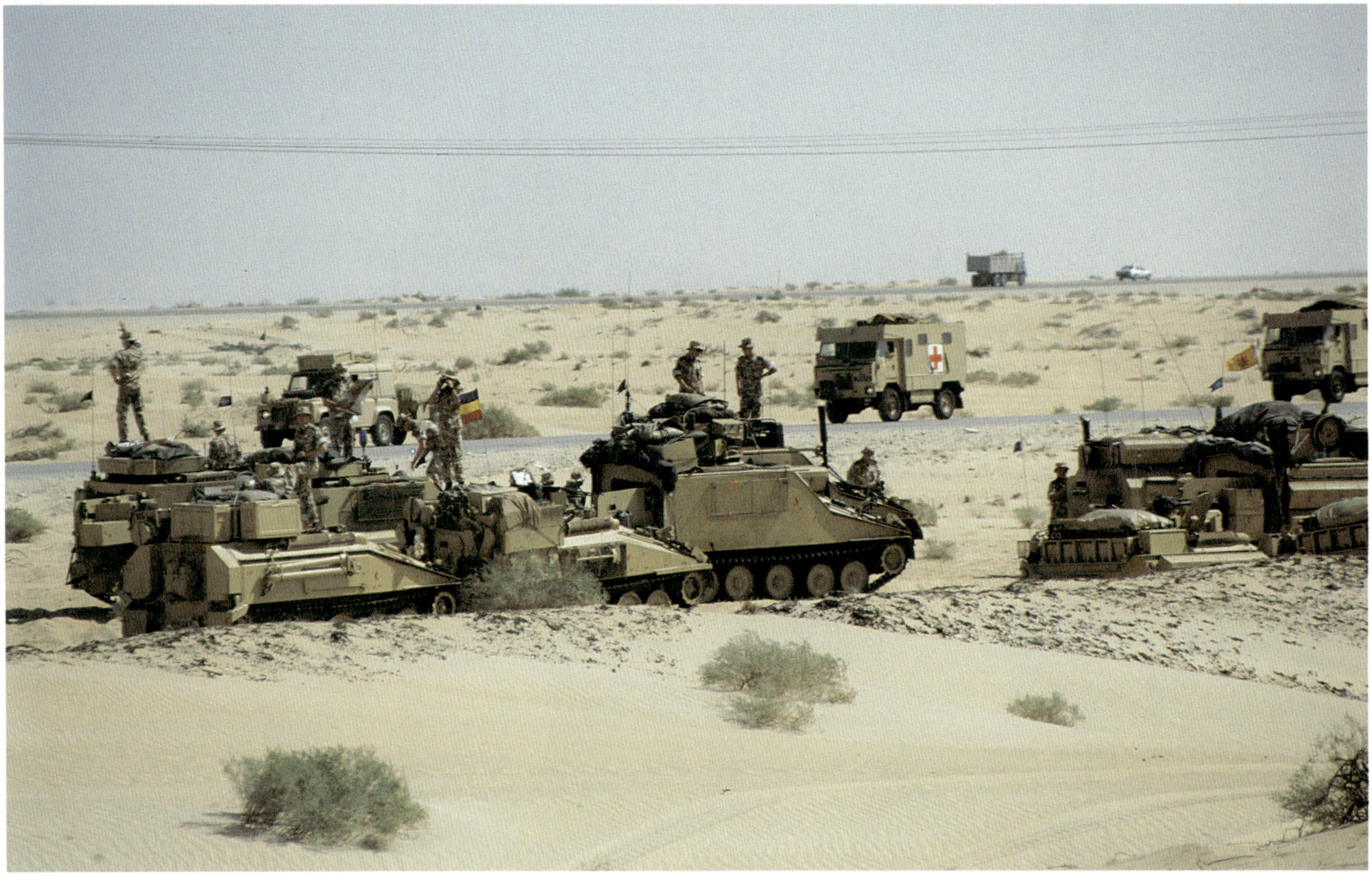

▲ Shown are various vehicles of the 21st Engineer Regt. RE, including Samson armored recovery vehicles and Sultan armored command post.

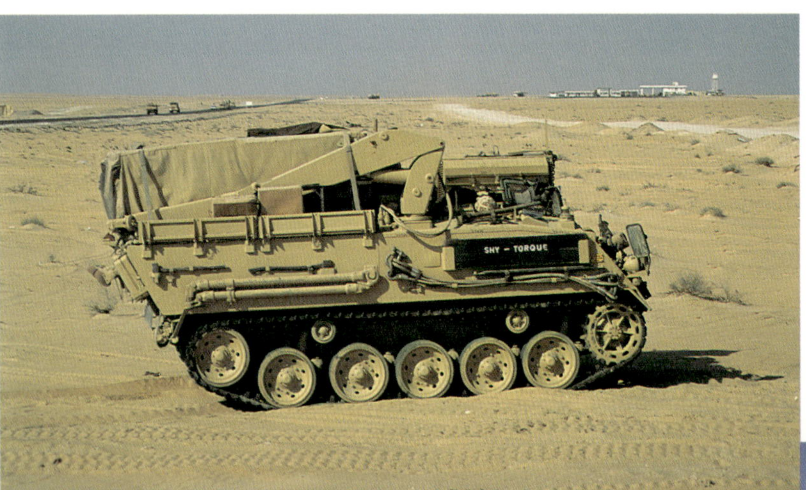

◄ Many variants of the FV432 continue to serve the British Army in combat support service jobs. Pictured is a recovery version of the FV432 that belongs to the 21st Royal Engineer Regt.

▼ An old FV432 Trojan being used as an ambulance. First produced in 1963, it is now being replaced in the role of armored personnel carrier by the Warrior.

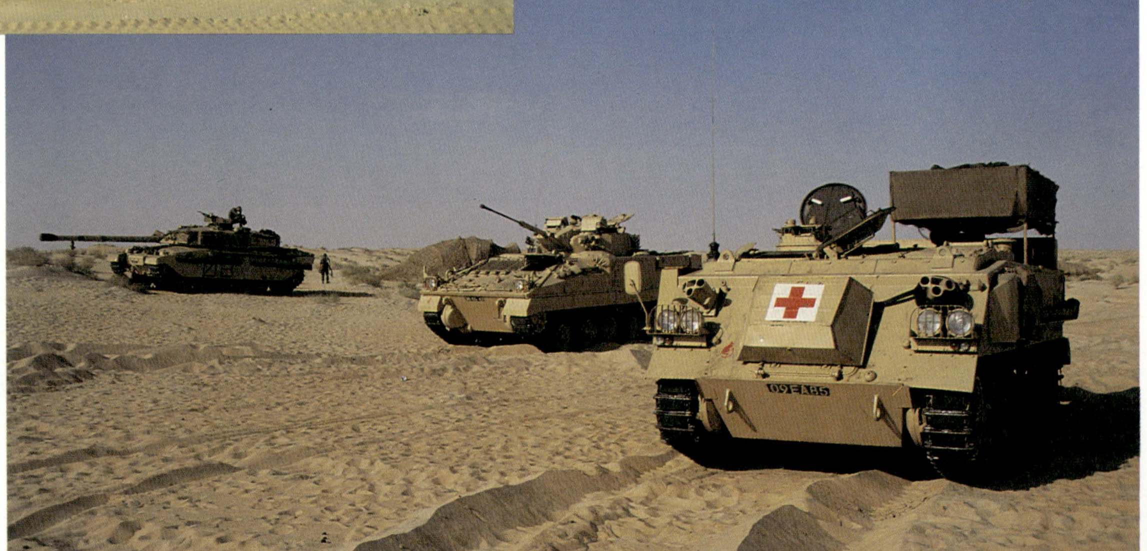

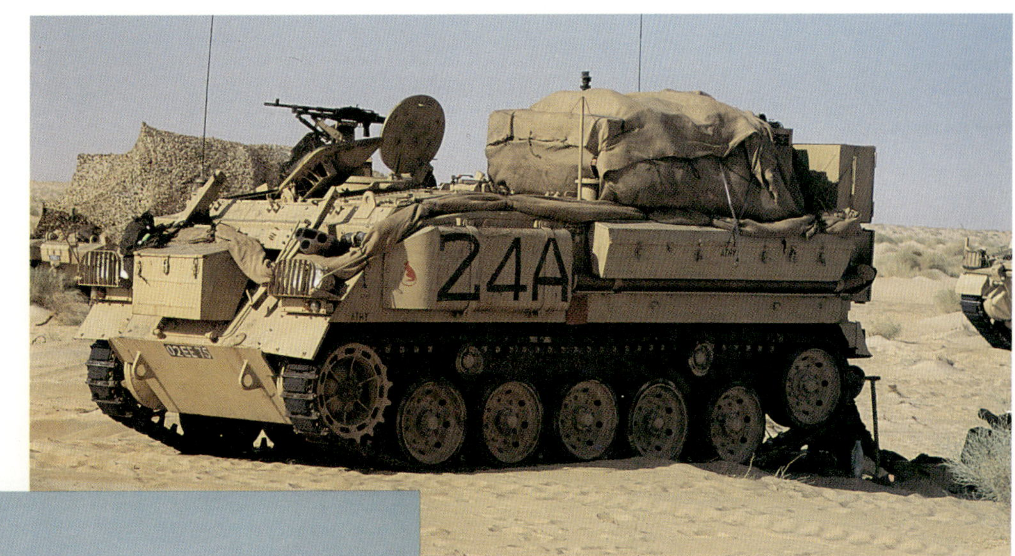

A Royal Engineers FV432 with cargo on its back.

The Royal Engineers employ many specialist vehicles, one of them is the CET (Combat Engineer Tractor). The CET is ideal for filling trenches prepared by the Iraqis.

A bridge-layer that belongs to the 32nd Armored Engineer Regt. RE, a part of the divisional unit.

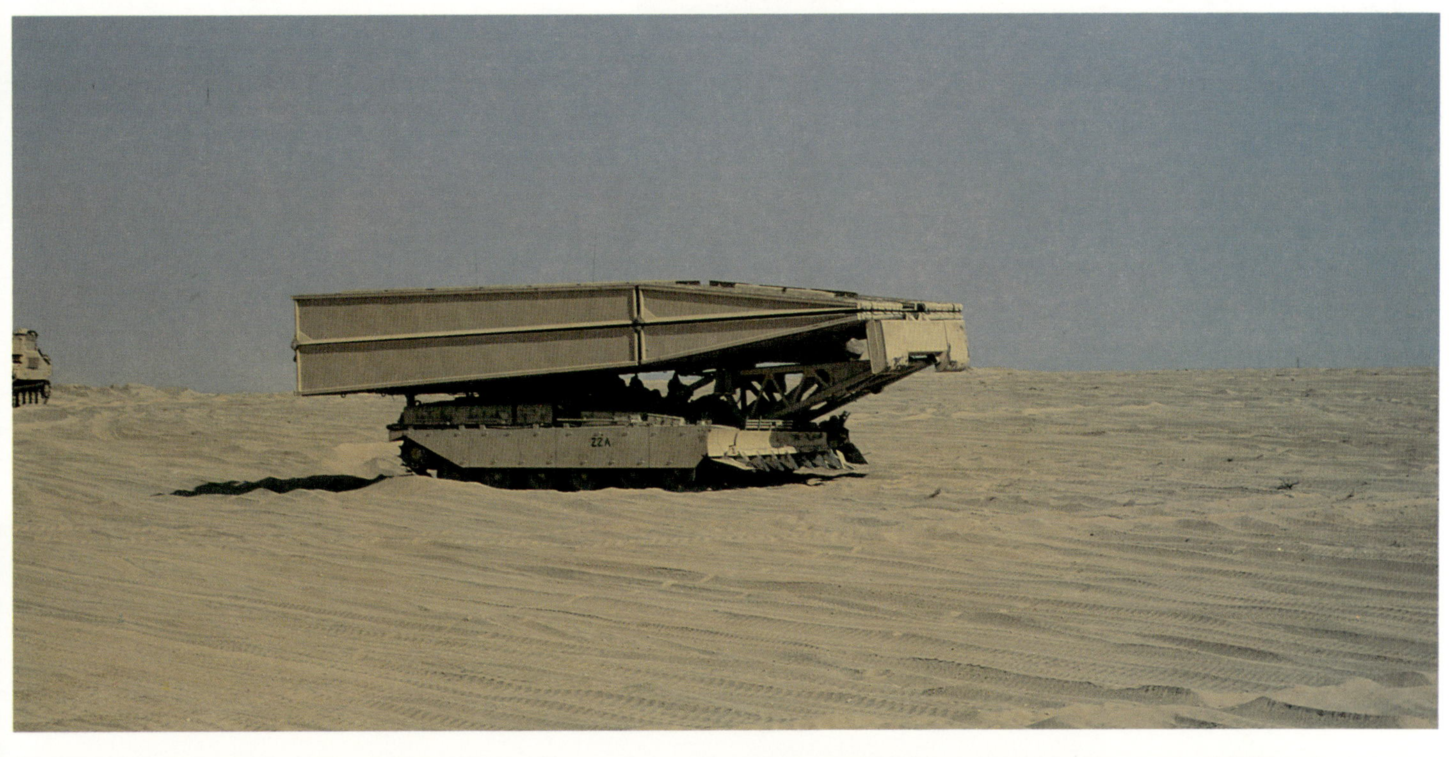

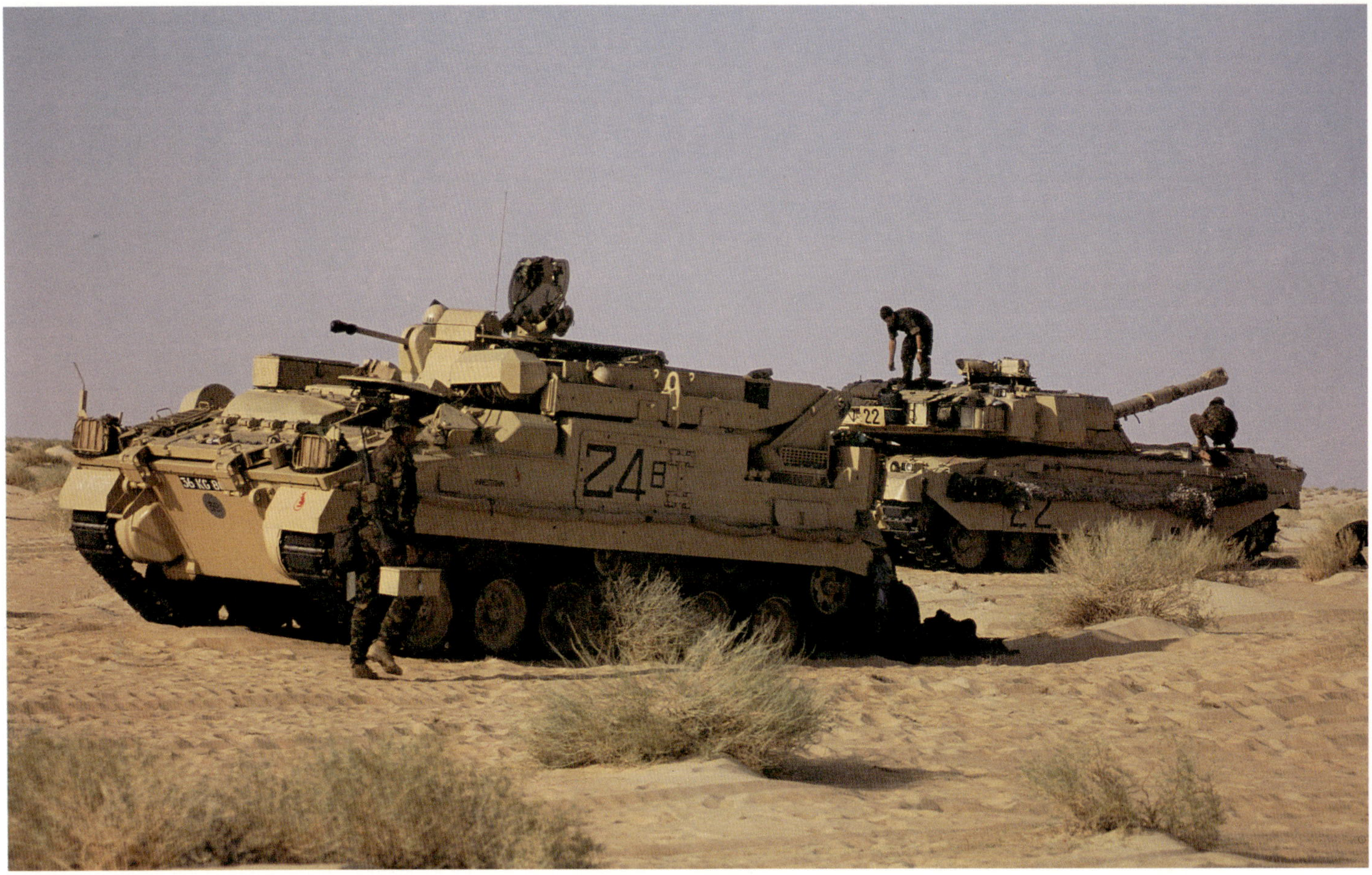

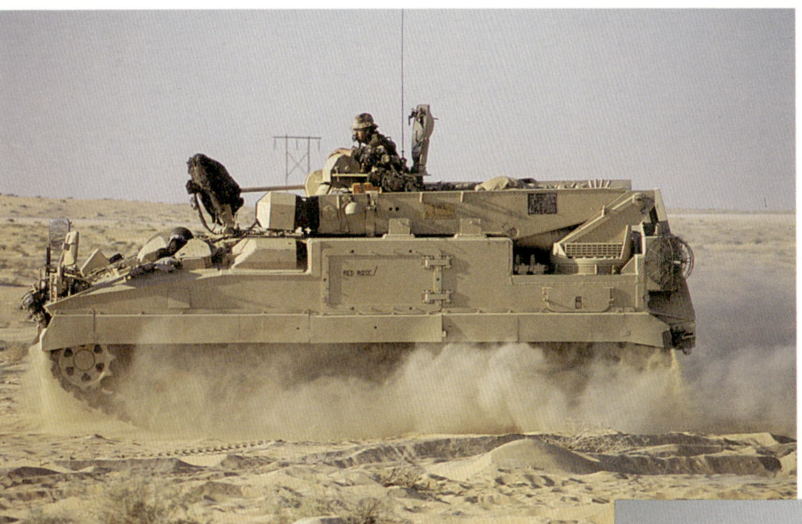

The MRVR has a one-man turret armed with a 7.62mm machine gun for self defense. This vehicle is attached to the Queen's Royal Irish Hussars.

The Warrior Repair and Recovery Vehicle (MRVR) has a crew of five consisting of the commander, driver, gunner and two fitters. The vehicle is equipped with a hydraulically operated crane and winch.

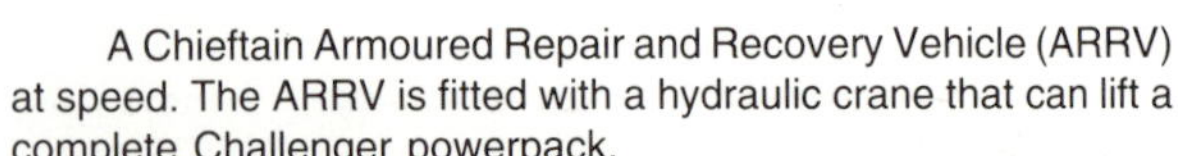

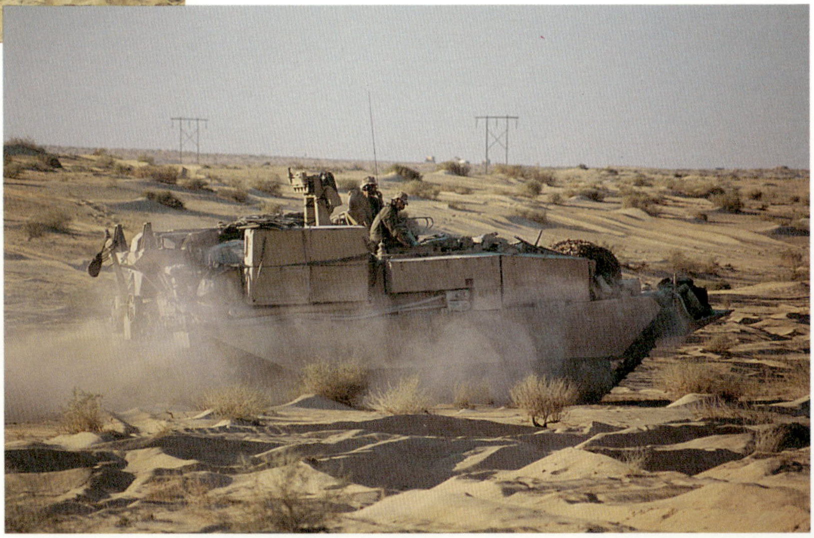

A Chieftain Armoured Repair and Recovery Vehicle (ARRV) at speed. The ARRV is fitted with a hydraulic crane that can lift a complete Challenger powerpack.

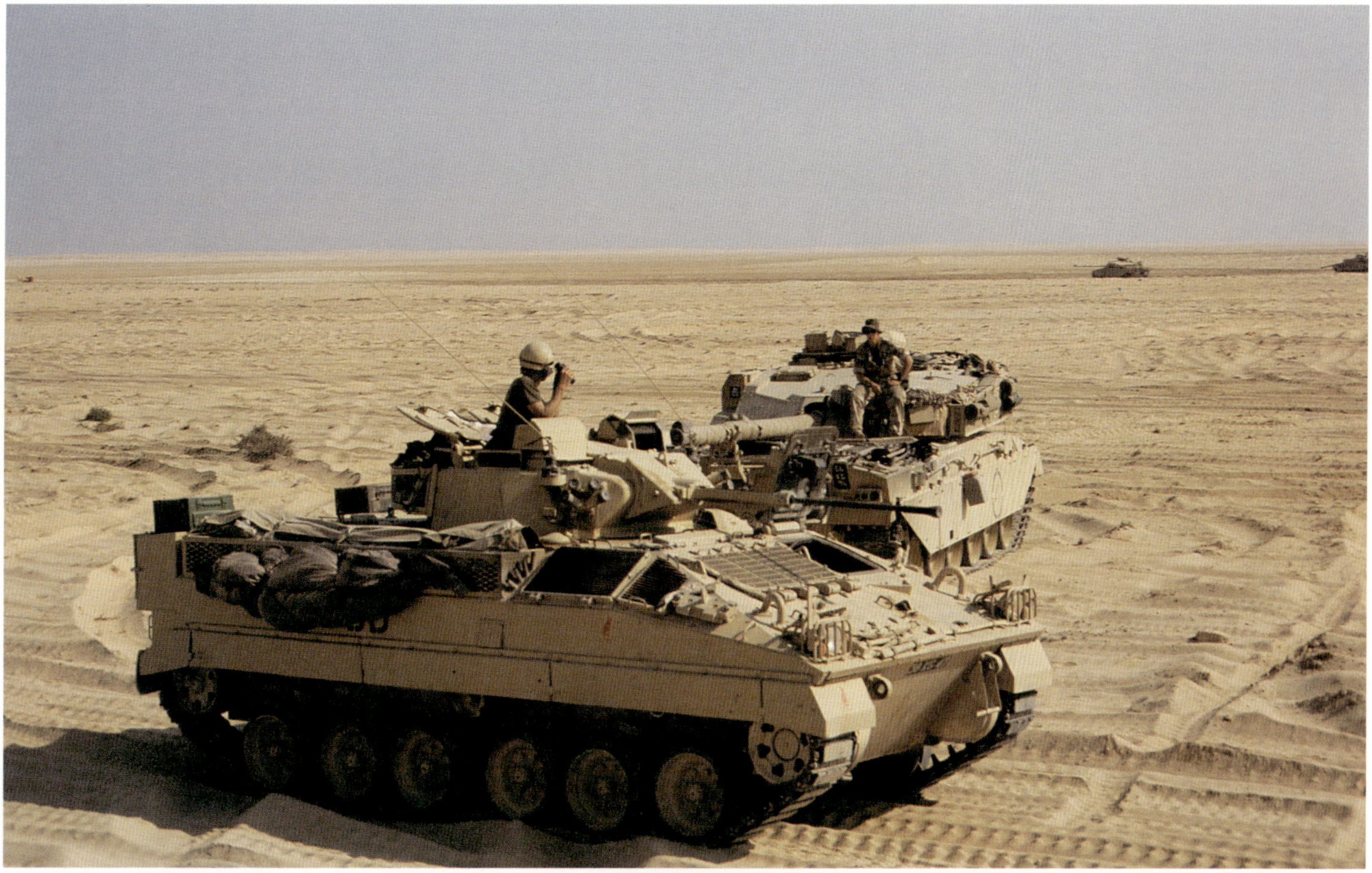

A Warrior of the 7th Armored Brigade, the Desert Rats. It is armed with the British-built Rarden 30mm cannon and a coaxial 7.62mm machine gun.

The Warrior Mechanized Combat Vehicle has a three man crew, and carries seven infantrymen in its rear compartment. This vehicle belongs to the 1st Bn. The Staffordshire Regt. (The Prince of Wales's).

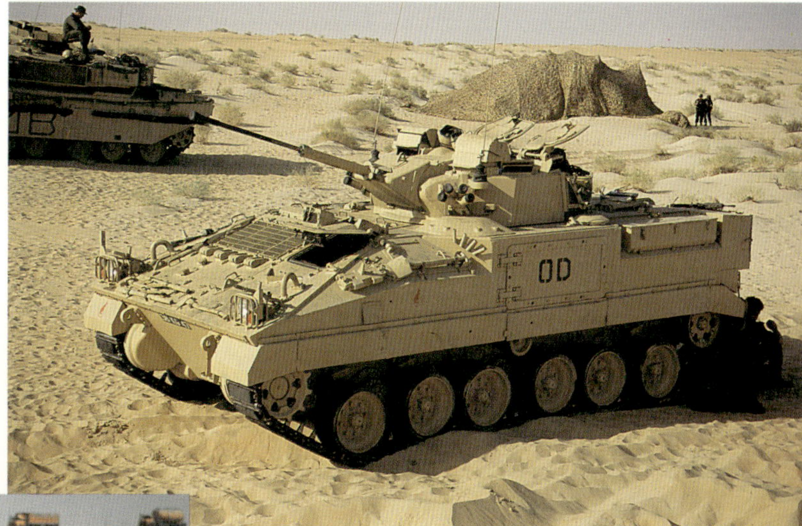

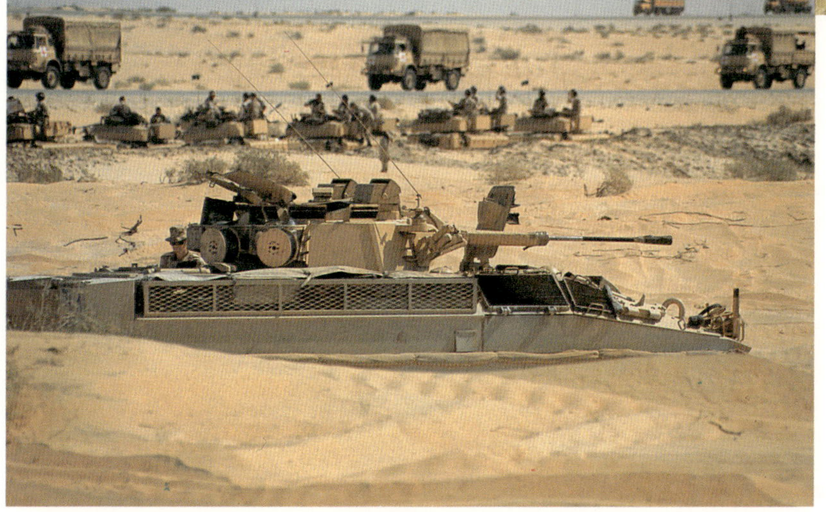

A Warrior positioned in a defensive position. On the background is a row of Scorpions.

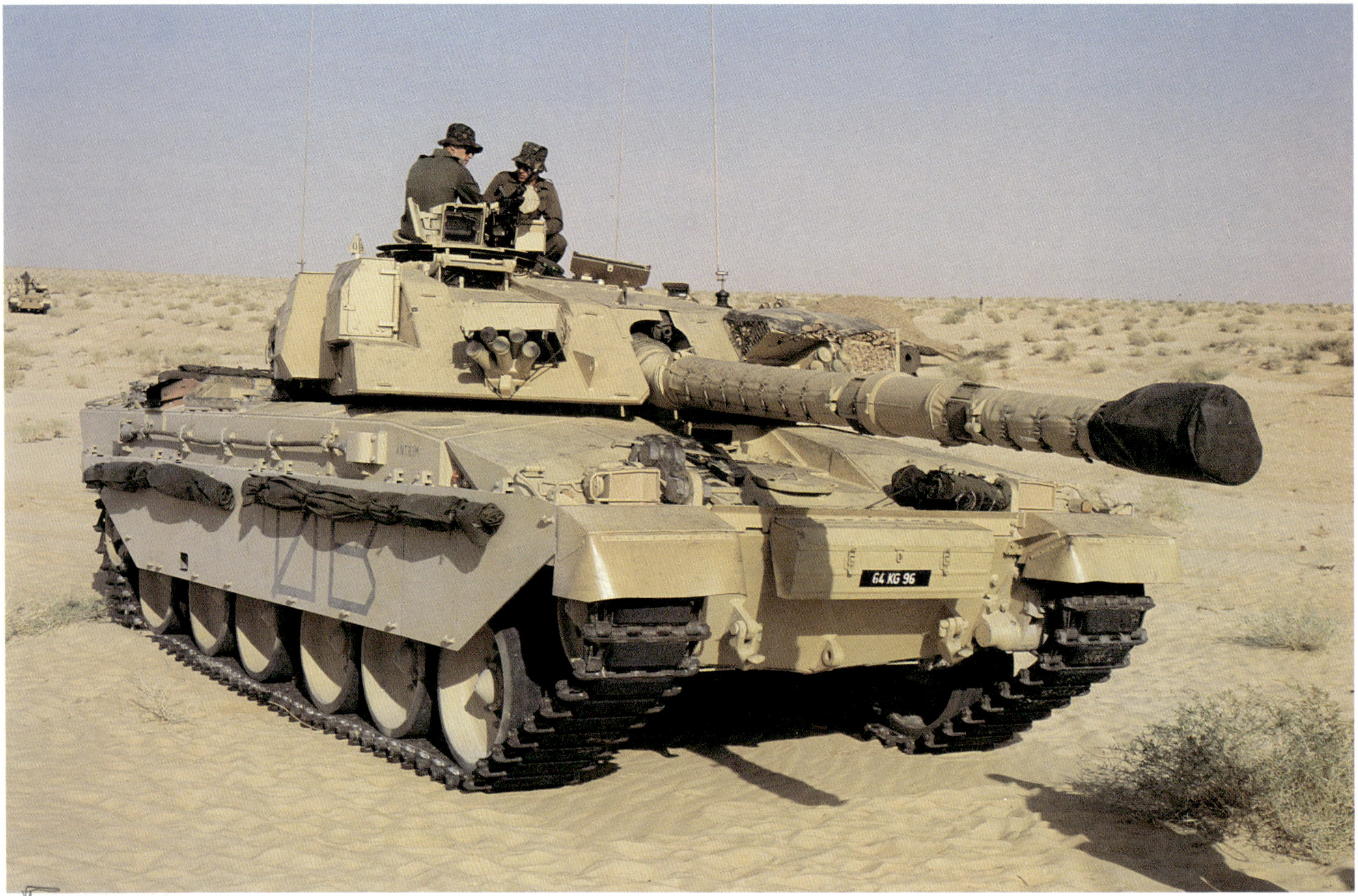

A Challenger of The Queen's Royal Irish Hussars deployed to Saudi Arabia. The QRIH has 60 Challenger MBTs and belongs to the famed 7th Armoured Brigade under the command of Brig. P. Cordingley.

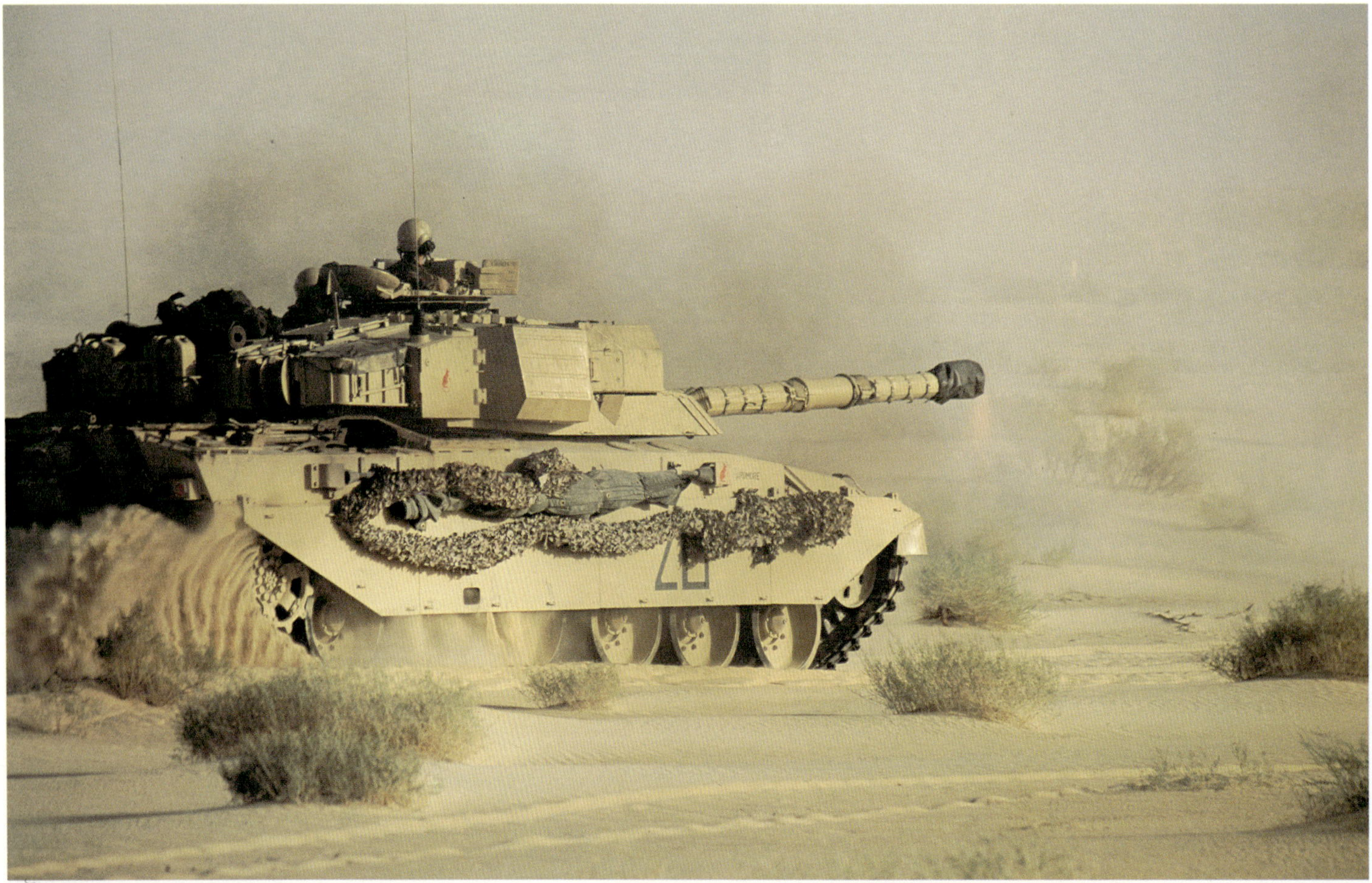

The Challenger has a crew of four. It is powered by a Perkins Engines, Condor 12V 1200 diesel, giving it a top speed of 56km/hr.

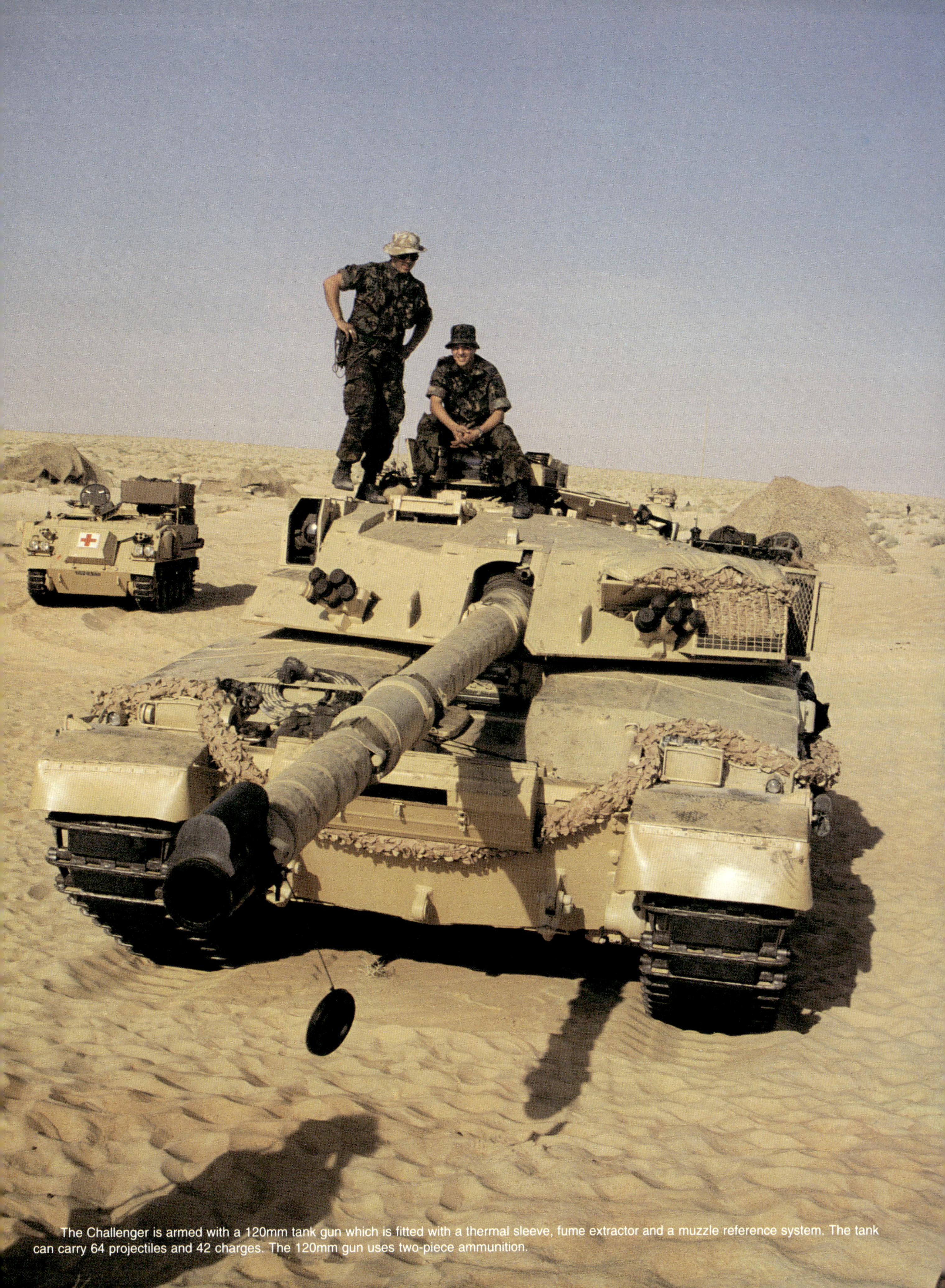

The Challenger is armed with a 120mm tank gun which is fitted with a thermal sleeve, fume extractor and a muzzle reference system. The tank can carry 64 projectiles and 42 charges. The 120mm gun uses two-piece ammunition.

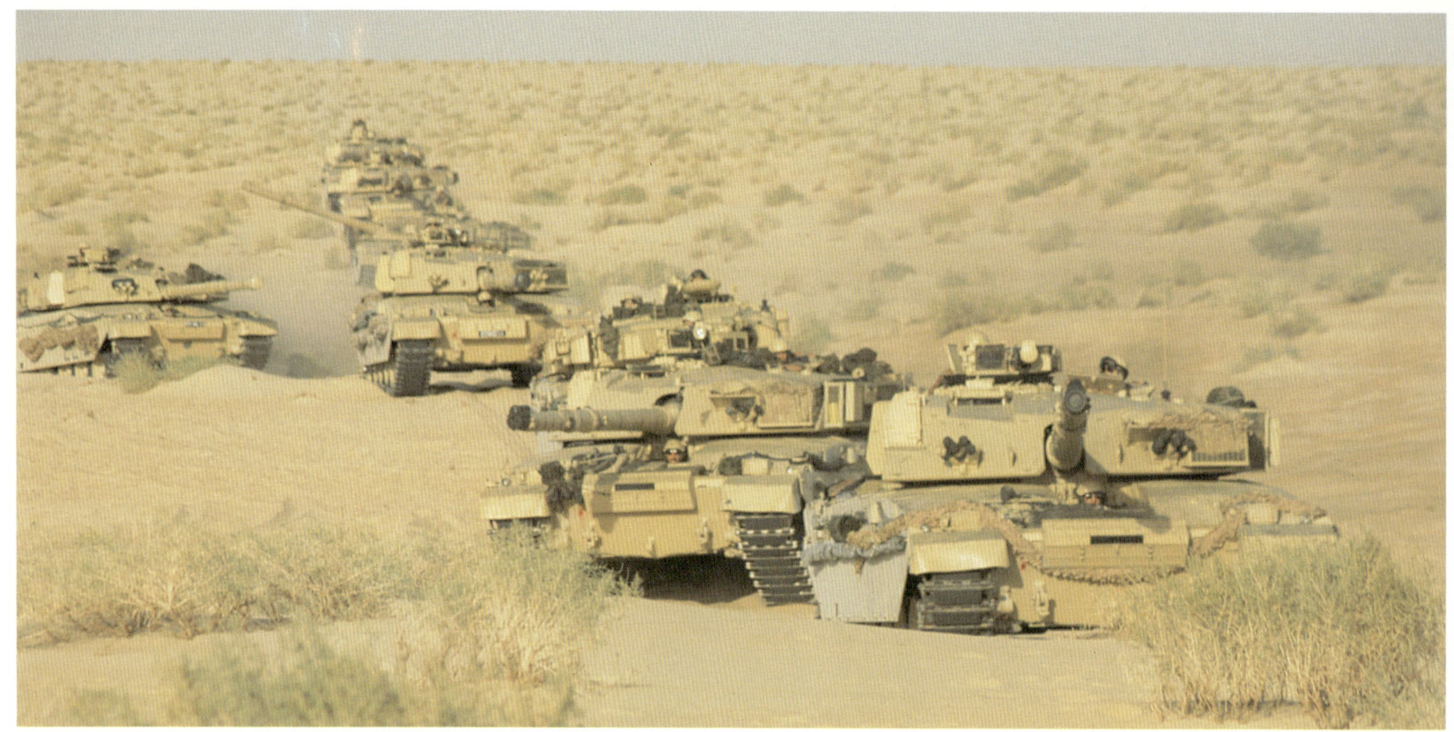

A column of QRIH Challengers on maneuver in the Saudi desert.

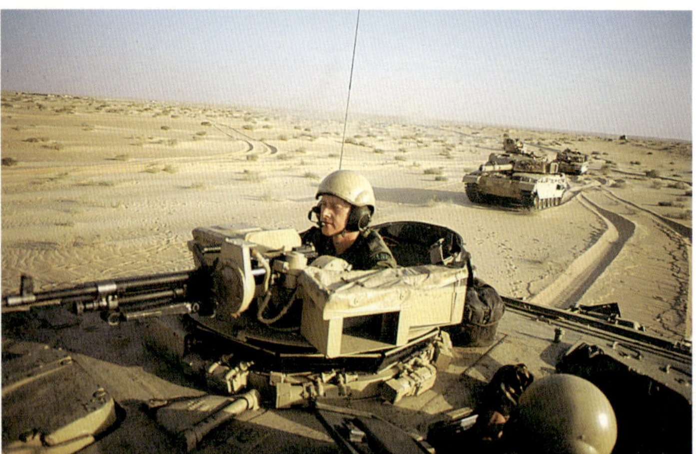

The commander of the Challenger is seated on the right side of the turret. He is provided with a cupola which has nine periscopes for all-round observation, plus a day sight or an image intensification system. The cupola is also fitted with a 7.62mm machine gun.

The turret and hull of the Challenger is protected by Chobham armor. It is fitted with a hydro-pneumatic suspension system which gives the vehicle increased mobility across difficult terrain.

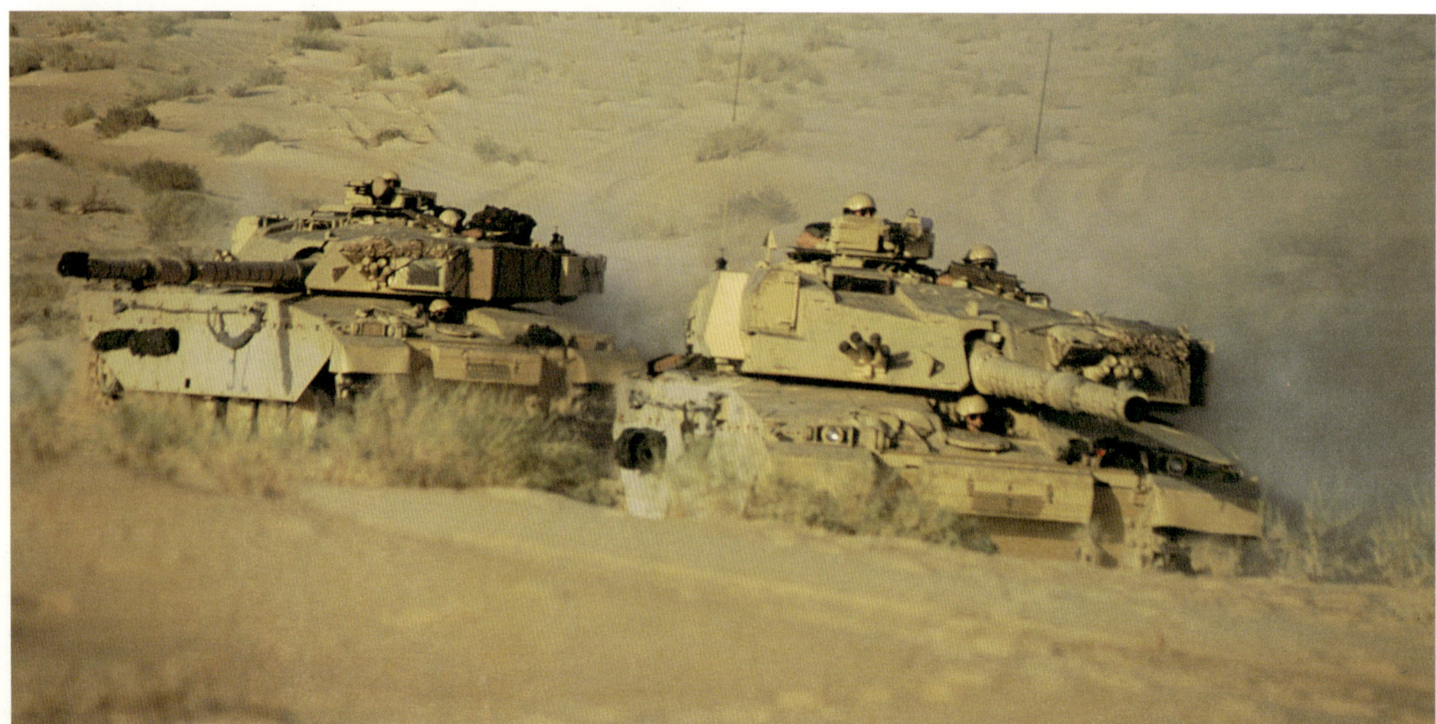

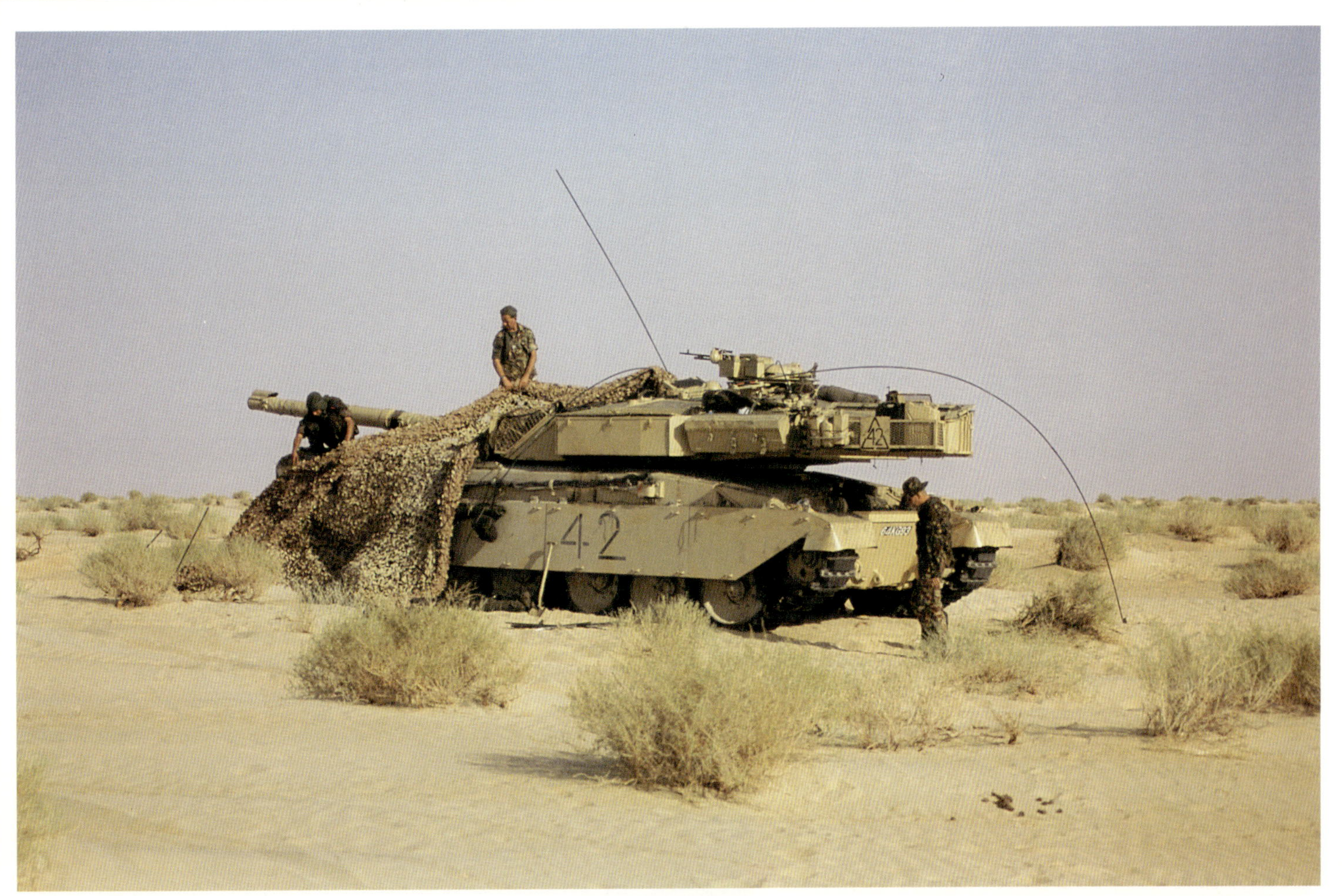

The 7th Armoured Brigade has 120 Challengers, 60 from The Royal Scots Dragoon Guards and 60 from The Queen's Royal Irish Hussars. The 4th Armoured Brigade has 43 Challengers from the 14th/20th King's Hussars. Altogether the 1st Armoured Division has 163 Challengers deployed for Operation Granby.

The British 1st Armoured Division on the move. Just prior to G-Day, the division moved into position to cover the right flank of the U.S. VII Corps.(DoD)

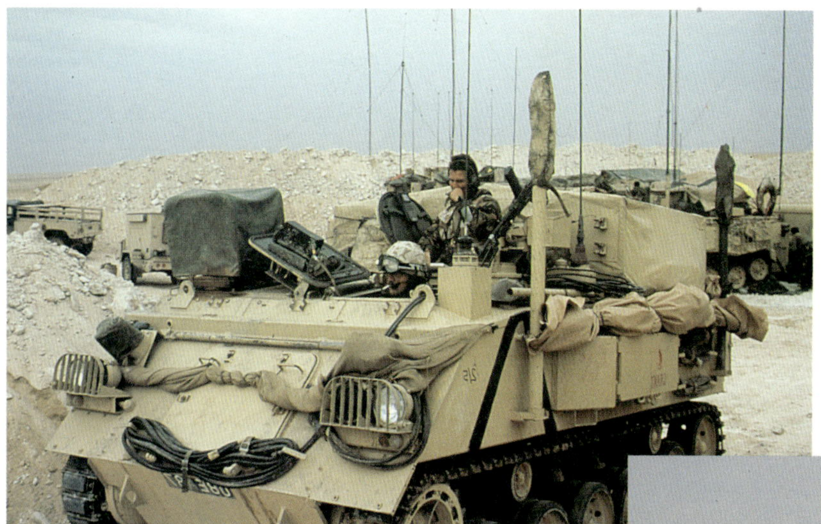

The command post version of FV432 in southern Iraq. This version is fitted internally with mapboards and additional communications equipment.

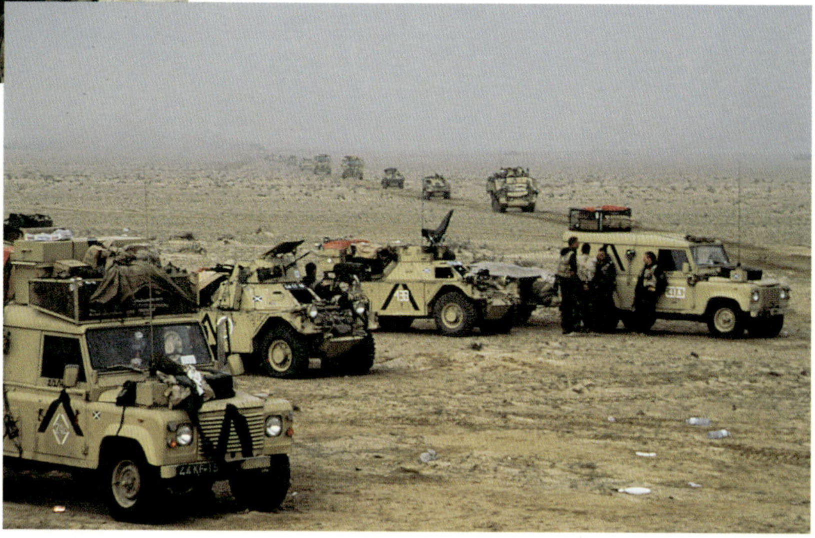

Ferrets and Land Rovers in invasion markings, the inverted V. (DoD)

An Allied command center with FV432s and M577s. Note the number of antennas and erected tents. (DoD)

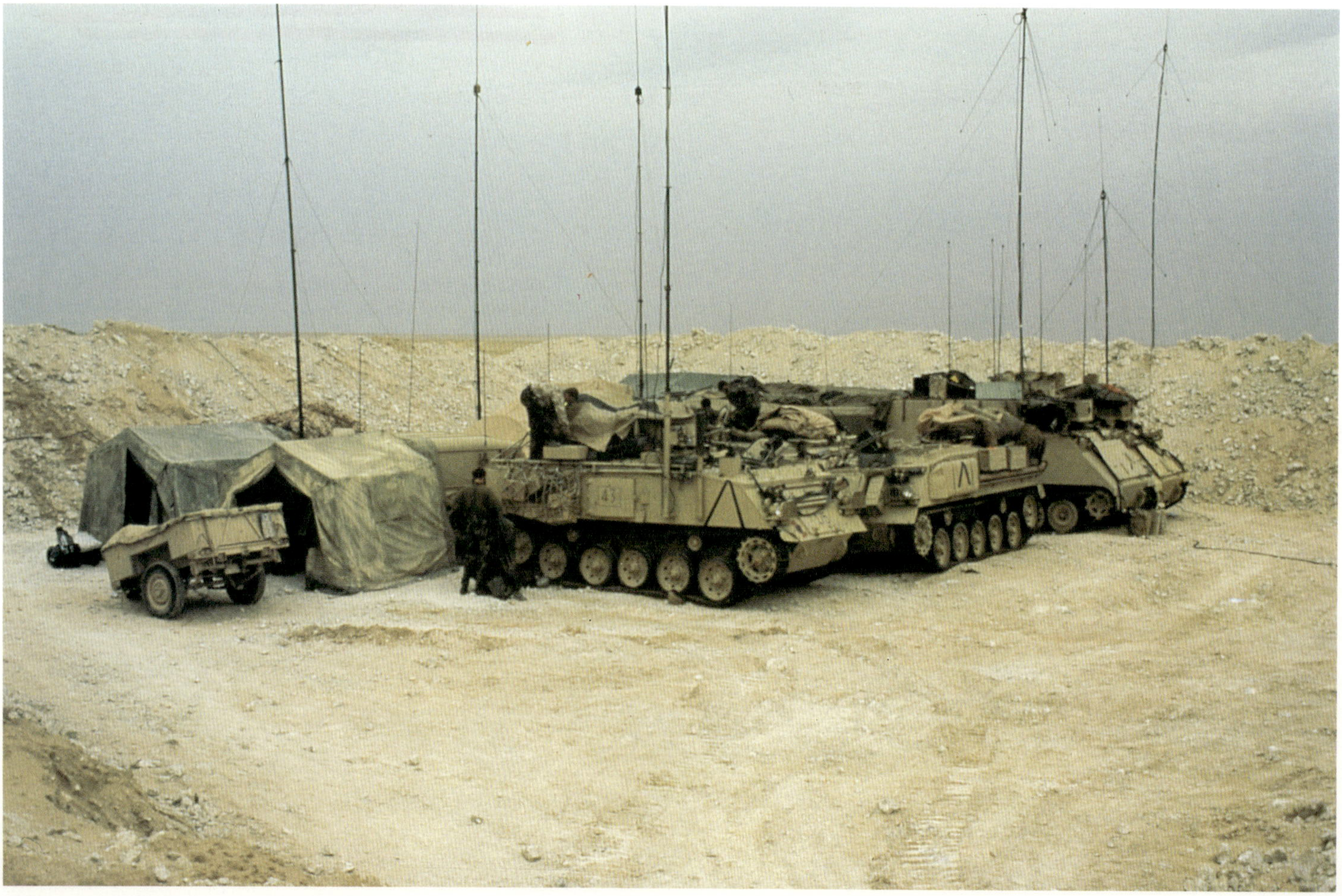

Samaritan is the armored ambulance version of the Scorpion. It can carry four stretcher cases and a medical orderly in a fully NBC protected environment. It is followed by an FV432, also with red crescent and invasion markings.(DoD)

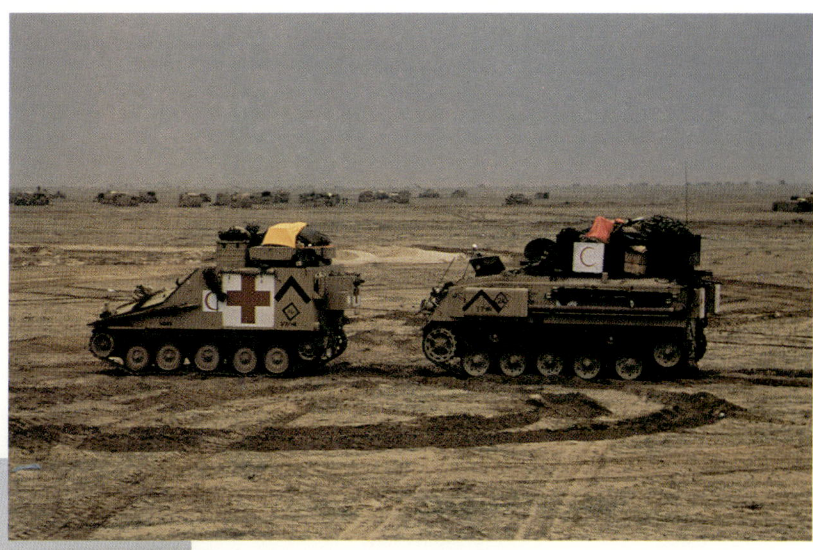

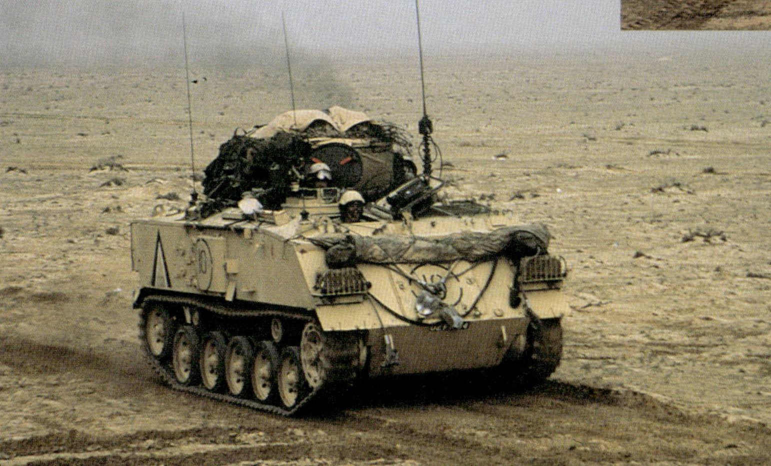

An FV432 on its way to the front. This vehicle has the red gerboa marking on the side. (DoD)

FV432s and M548 with Red Cross and red crescent markings. A lot of vehicles were converted into ambulances, as high casualty rate was expected. (DoD)

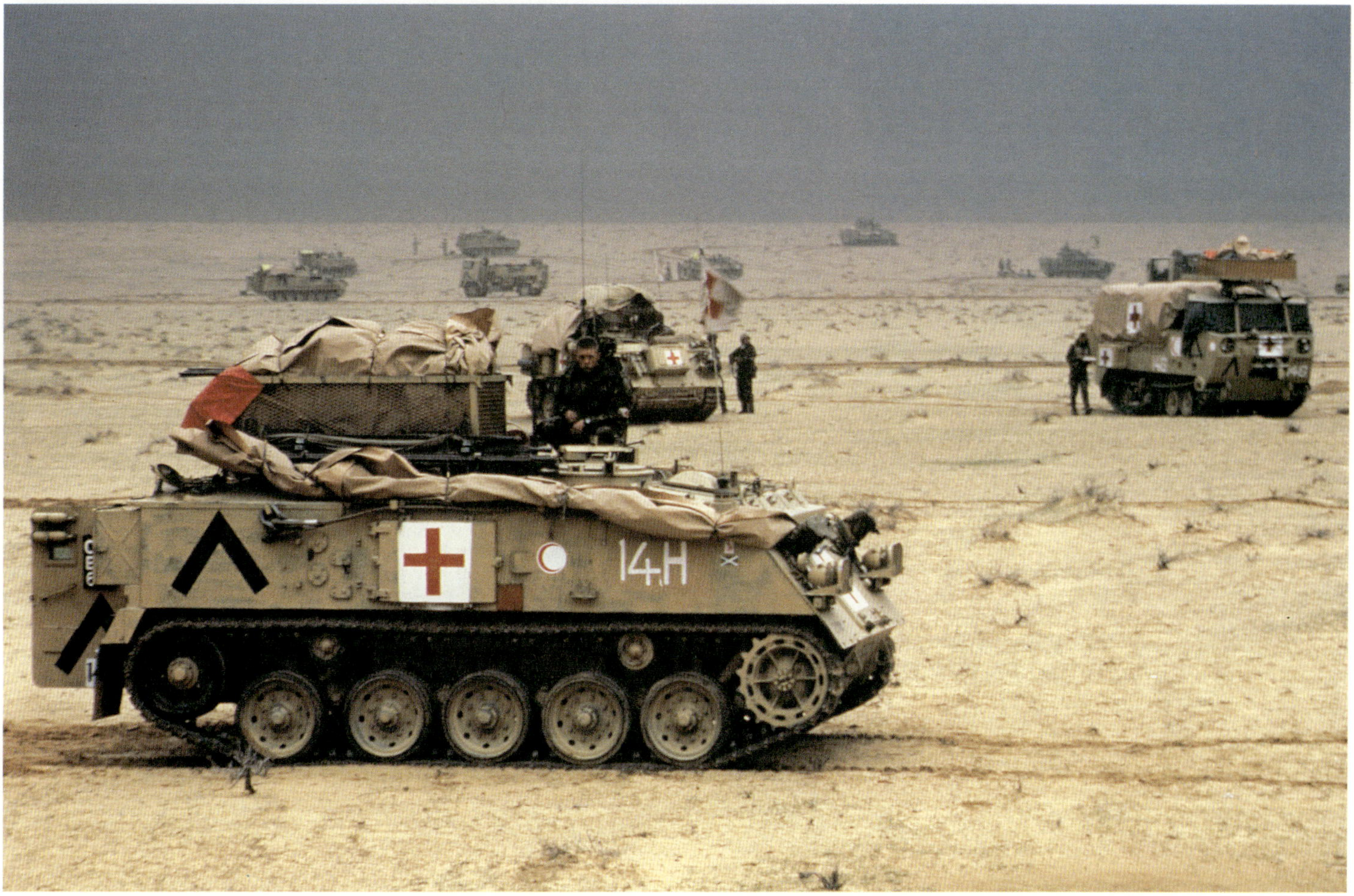

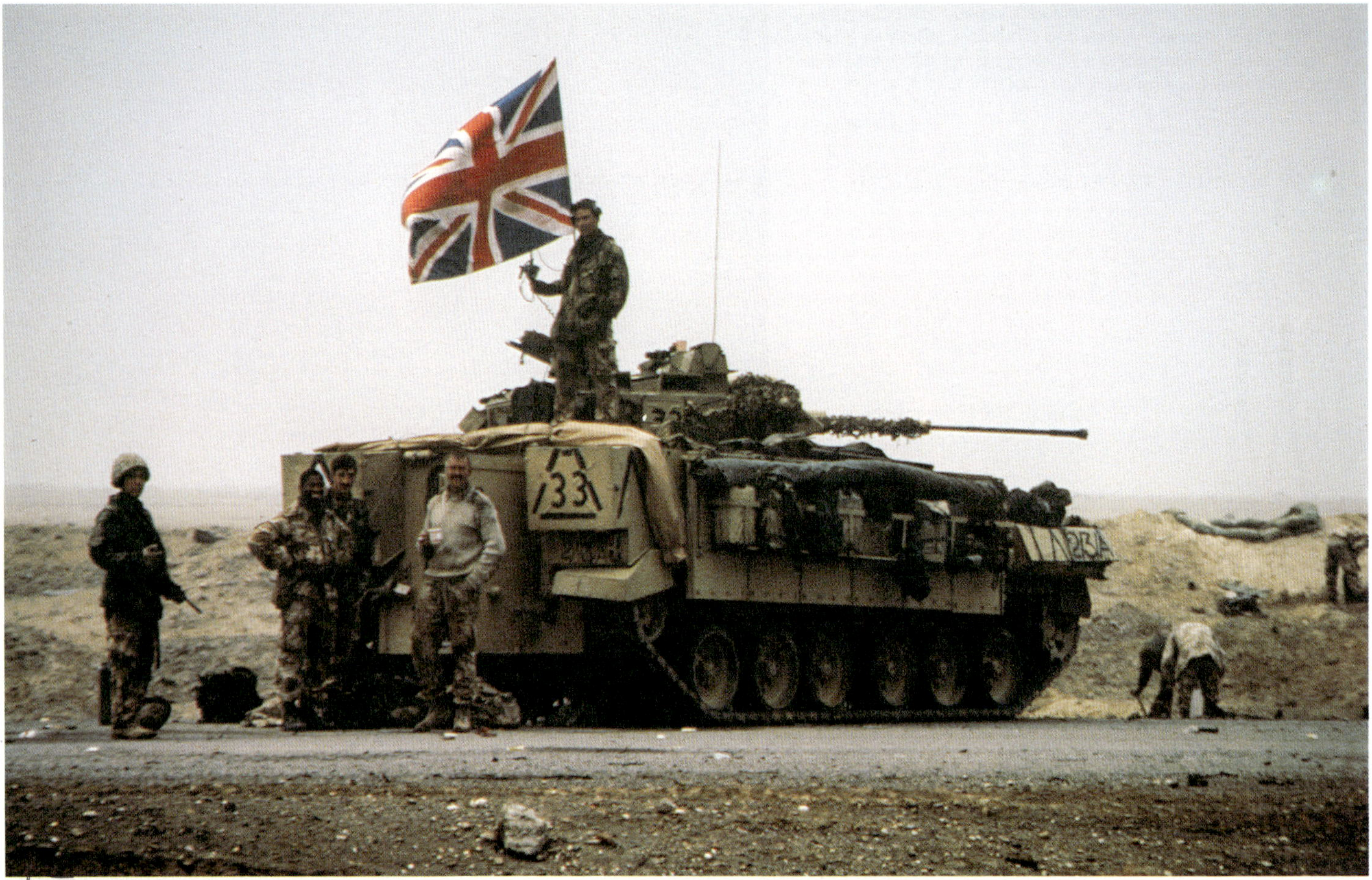

An up-armored Warrior with the Union Jack. The crew is taking a break during the thrust into Iraq.(DoD)

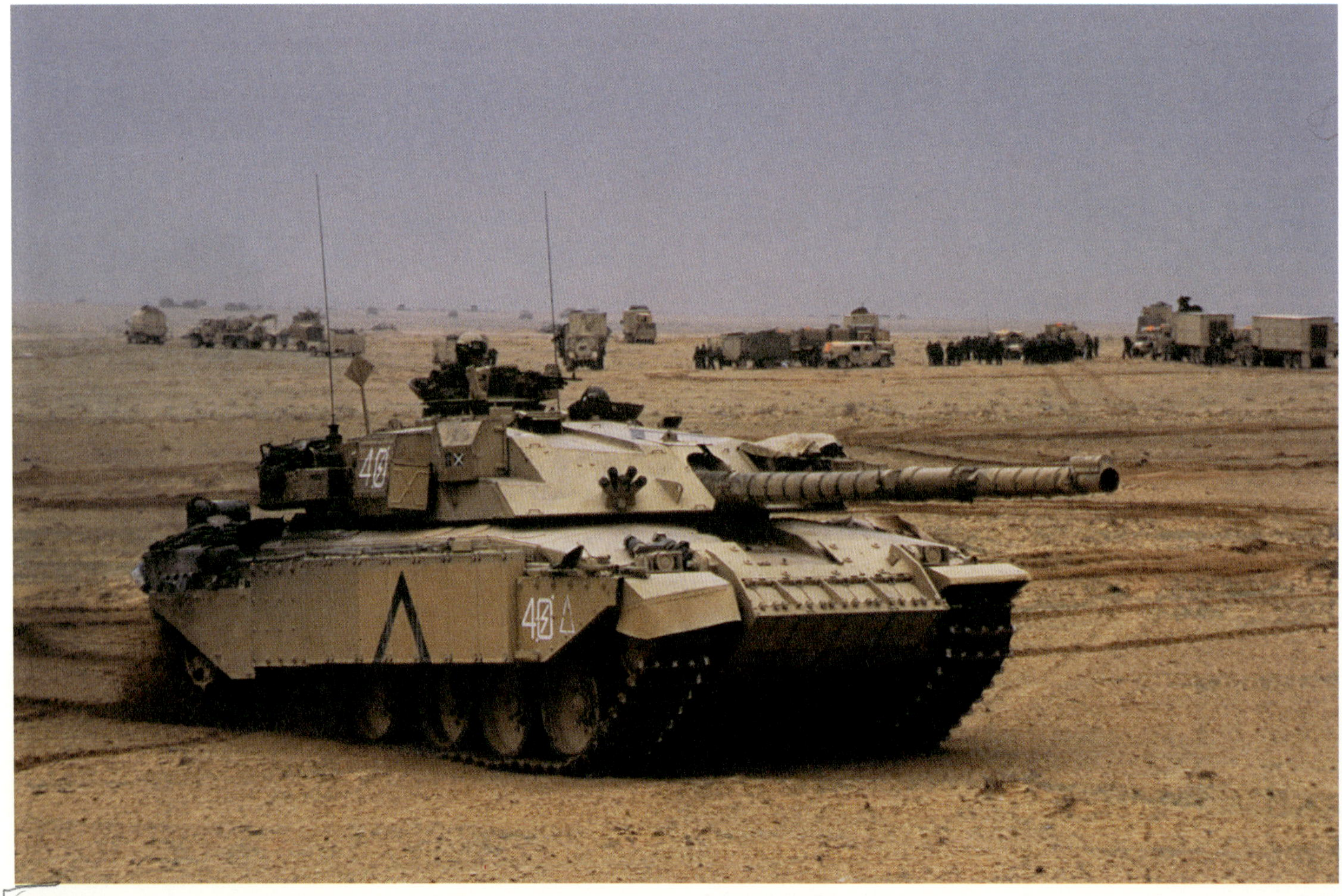

The Challengers were upgraded with full side and frontal armor just prior to the big push. (DoD)

FRENCH ARMOR IN ACTION

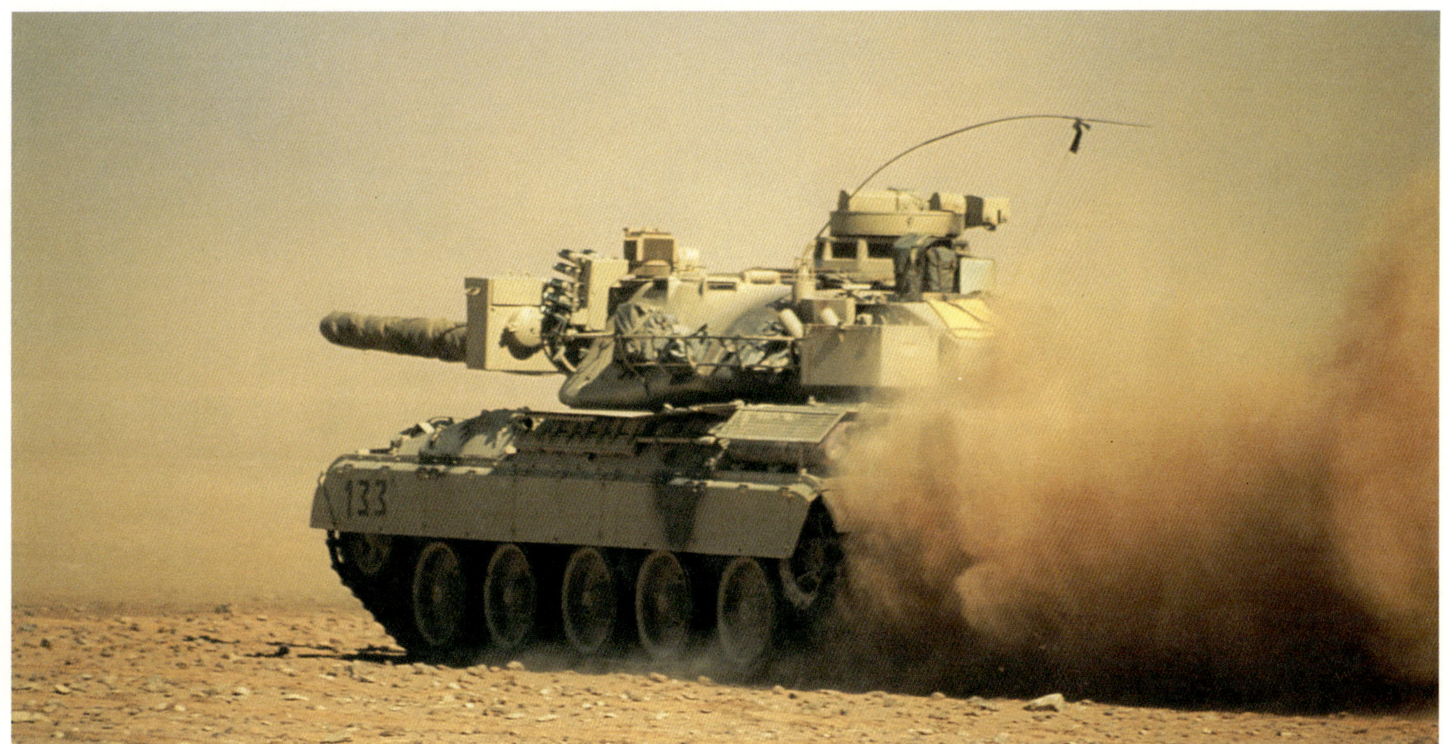

After the invasion of Kuwait by Iraq, the French government did not immediately send troops and equipment to support "Operation Desert Shield", although France did vote in the United Nations to support economic sanctions against Iraq.

However, in mid-September 1990, a unit of Iraqi soldiers forced opened the gates of the French Embassy in Kuwait City. During the incident four embassy employees were wounded. To counter this provocation, the French government decided to send troops to Saudi Arabia. This was the beginning of "Operation Daguet".

The first French units deployed to Saudi Arabia were taken from the Rapid Deployment Force. These troops and their equipment arrived at the Saudi port of Yanbu. They were positioned at Hafr Al Baten with the headquarter in King Khalid Military City.

The French 6th Light Armored Division was later assigned to a position code-named Miramar. Built-up continued by reinforcements from France which included the French Foreign Legion units. Other units sent included additional combat forces, plus engineering, anti-aircraft, helicopters, and logistic elements.

The 6th Light Armored Division had only AMX-10RC armored cars, though a potent weapon system, suffered a lack of firepower as offered by main battle tanks. January 1991 saw the arrival of 40 tropicalized AMX-30B2 tanks and more AMX-10RCs, as well as 155mm TRF-1 guns and more troops to beef up the French forces.

The French forces were placed under the command of the U.S. XVIII Corps (Airborne). They were assigned the left flank of the coalition forces, the objective was to capture the important communication crossroads and air base of Al Salman deep inside Iraq.

On February 22, 1991, the French forces received order to take the cliff which marked the Iraqi-Saudi border. With the quick capture of the cliff, the French quickly sent out two separate armored columns through the Iraqi border. One column was supported by M551 tanks of the U.S. 82nd Airborne Division, plus a unit of the 325th Airborne Infantry backing up the MLRS. The two armored columns were in position for the coming ground campaign.

Beginning early on February 24, 1991, the French and American forces began their attack after a massive artillery barrage. Shortly afterwards, Iraqi soldiers began to surrender in large numbers. By the afternoon, the French forces had overrun an Iraqi strong point on the road leading to the Al Salman air base. This strong point Rochambeau was defended by two Iraqi infantry battalions, plus dug-in T-55 tanks and backed up by artillery pieces. The Iraqis gave up after little resistance. On February 26, at first light, the French forces entered both the town of Al Salman and the air base without a fight. By the evening, the French forces ended their advance and took up defensive positions.

During their three day advance into Iraq, the French forces destroyed the Iraqi 45th Infantry Division and took 3,077 prisoners. They also captured a large number of a small arms, tanks and armored vehicles.

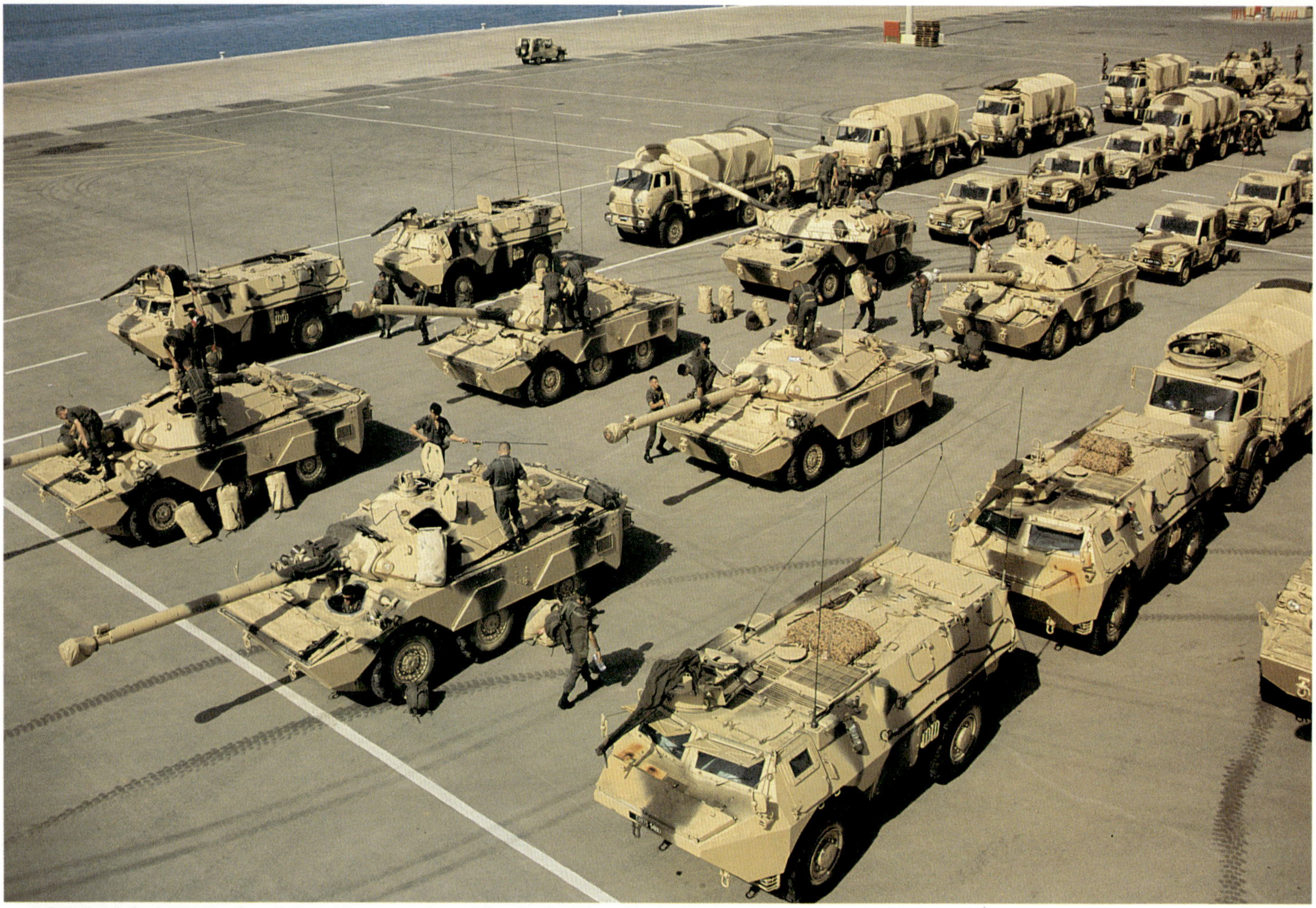

Ready to depart to the Saudi desert is a squadron of the 1st Spahis at Yanbu Harbor. Pictured are the VAB (4x4) armored personnel carriers, AMX-10RC reconnaissance vehicles, and various soft skin vehicles.

Shown are French-built AMX-10RC reconnaissance vehicles being unloaded from the cargo ship Girolata in Saudi Arabia.

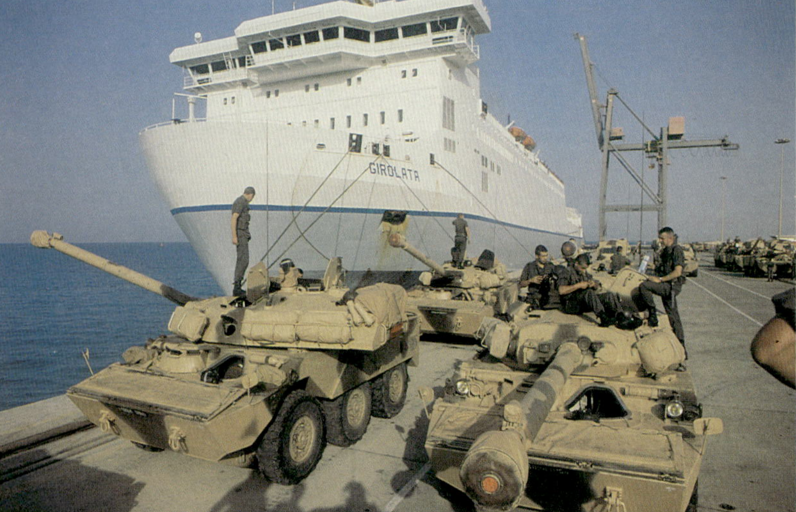

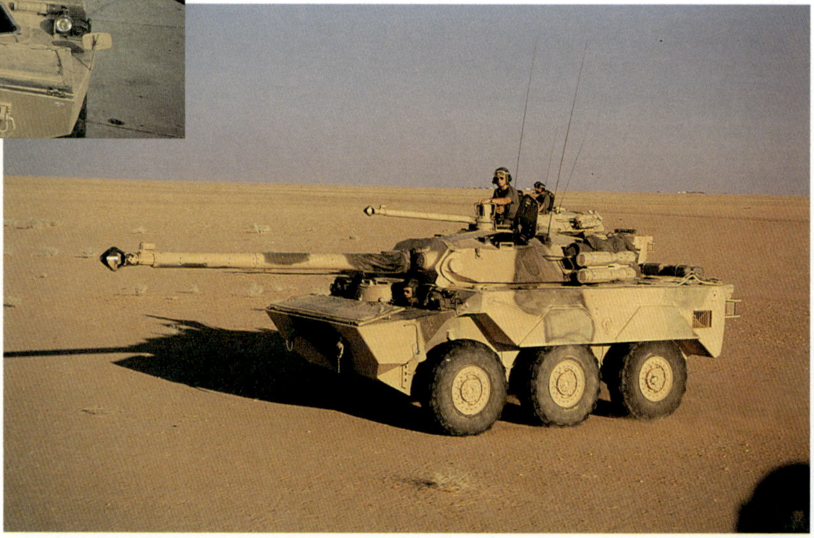

AMX-10RC of the 1st REC, a Foreign Legion unit with combat experience in Chad and Lebanon. The AMX-10RC is a 6x6 wheeled reconnaissance vehicle armed with a turret-mounted 105mm gun.

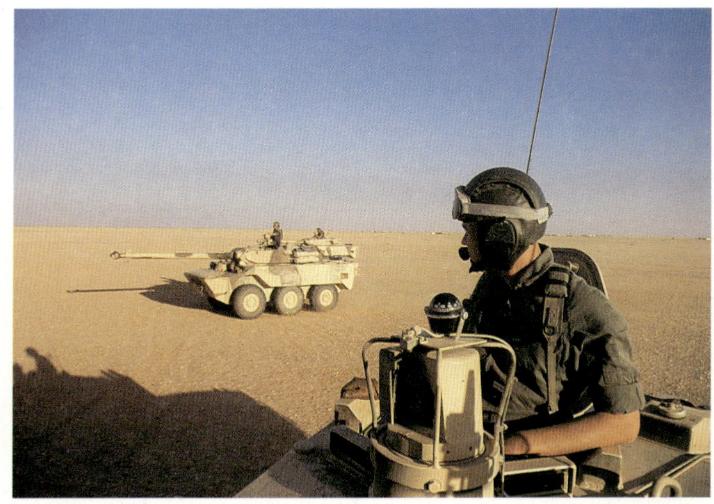

The AMX-10RC has an all-welded aluminium hull and turret which provides its crew from protection against small arms fire and artillery shell splinters. It has a maximum road speed of 85km/hr.

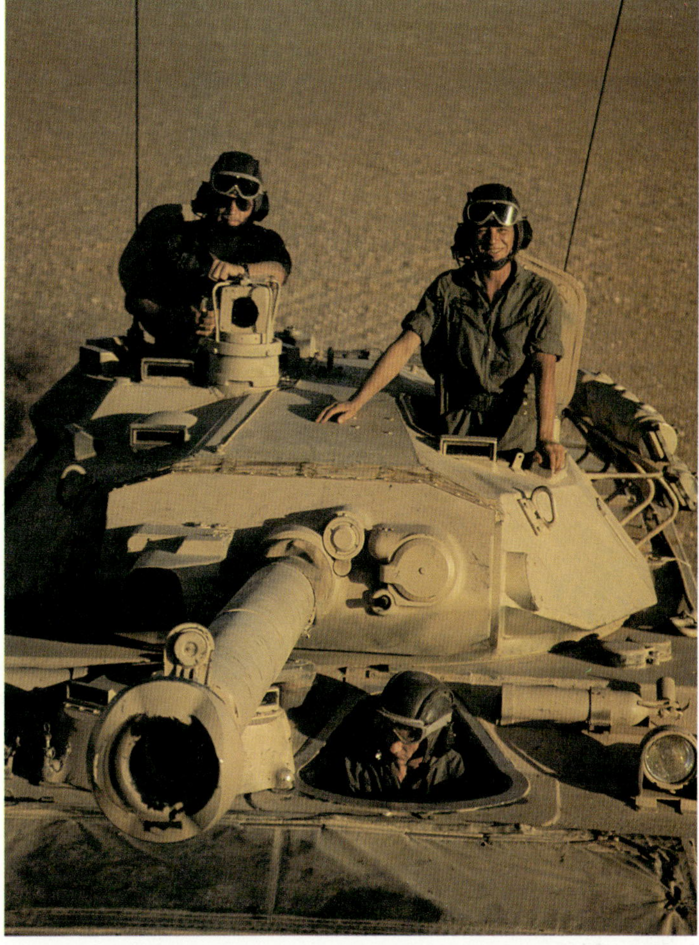

The turret of the AMX-10RC carries the commander, gunner, and loader who also acts as the radio operator. The commander has six periscopes for all-round observation plus a M389 telescope which has 360 degrees of rotation which enables the commander to observe the target regardless of the position of the turret.

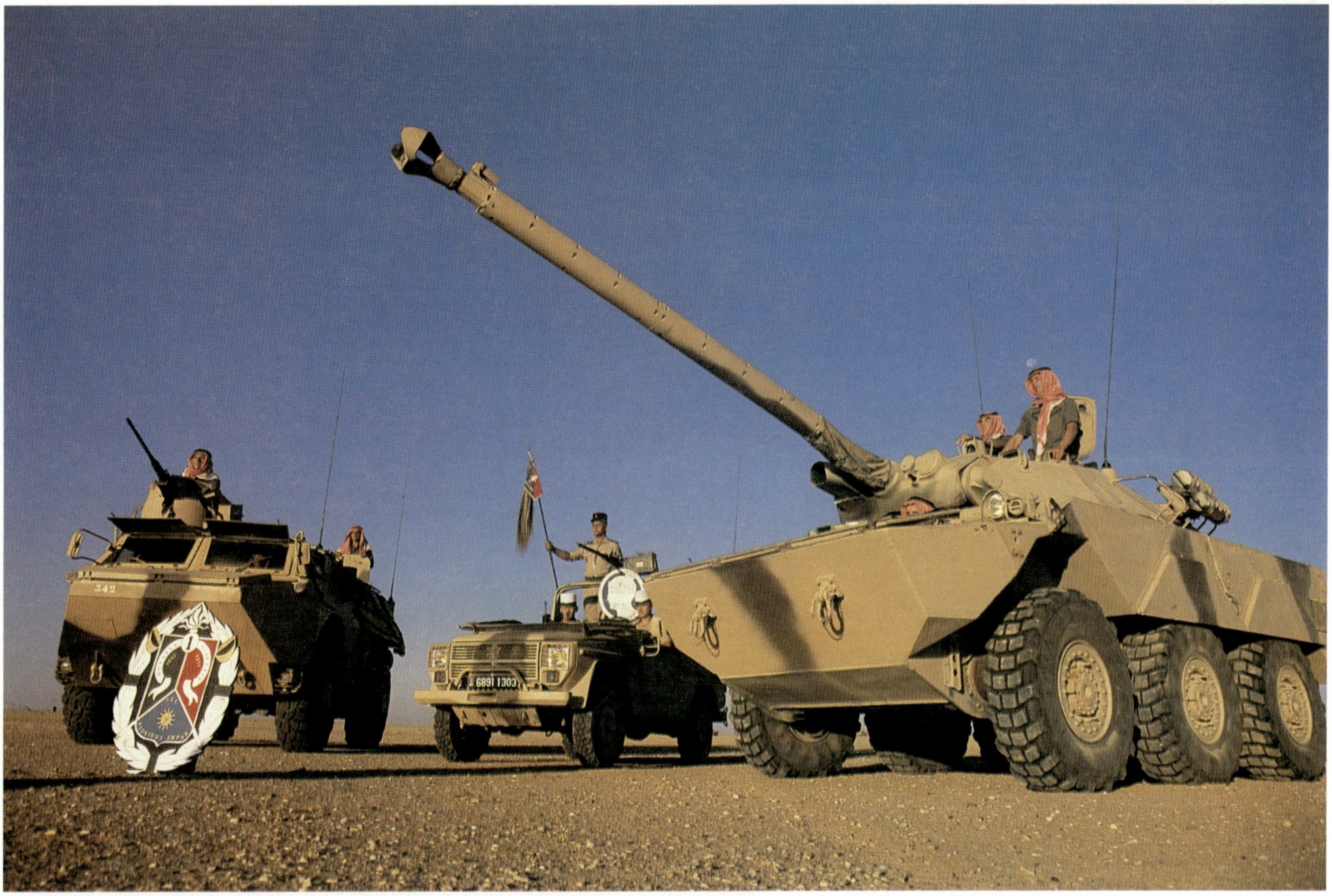

A traditional souvenir photo-taking of the 1st REC in the Saudi desert.

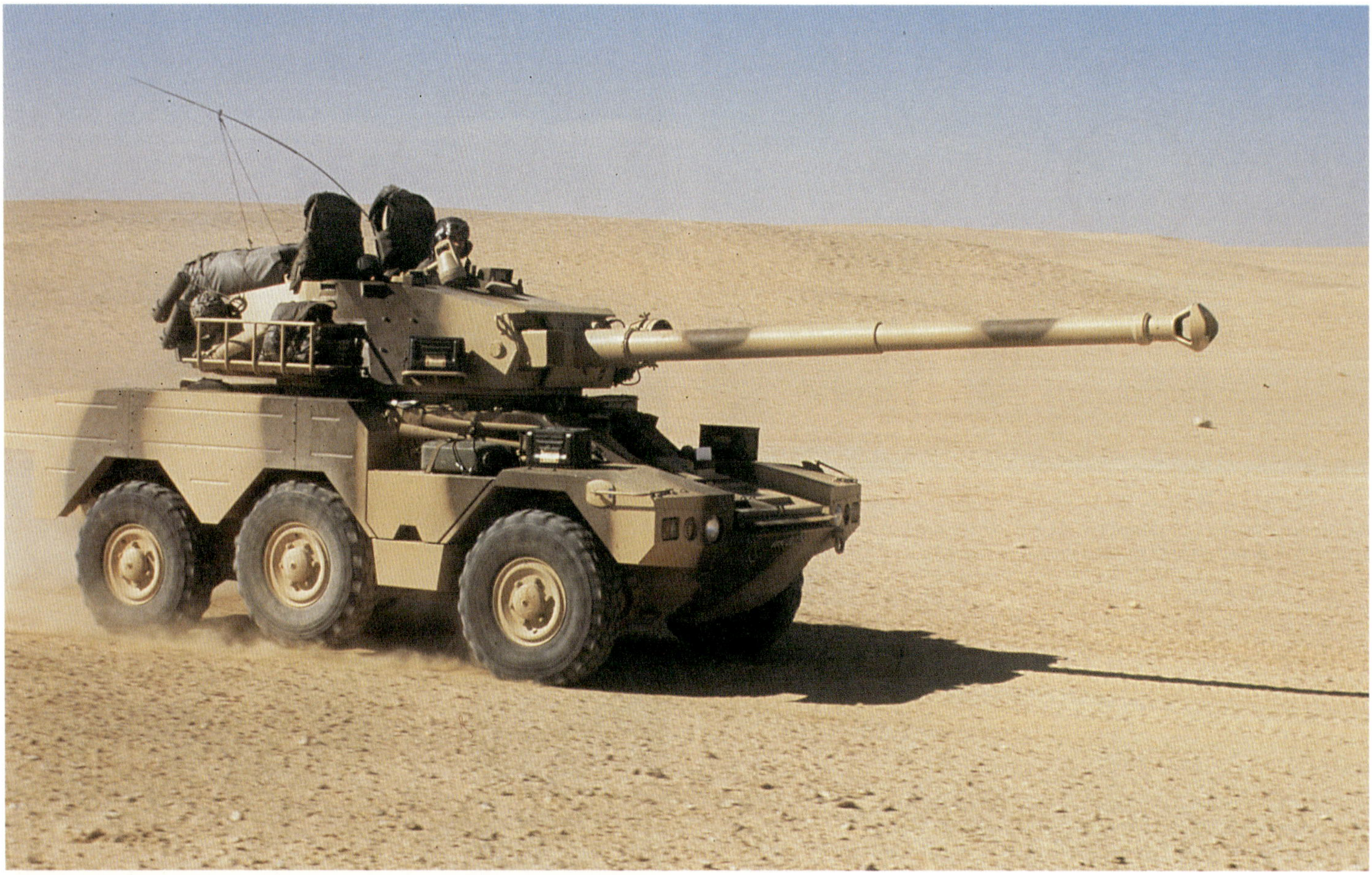

Pictured is a Panhard ERC 90 (6x6) armored car. Twelve of these vehicles were deployed to Saudi Arabia with the 1st RHP.

The Renault VAB armored personnel carrier is the standard vehicle of the French motorized infantry units. It is fully amphibious, being propelled in the water by two water jets located at the rear of the vehicle. (DoD)

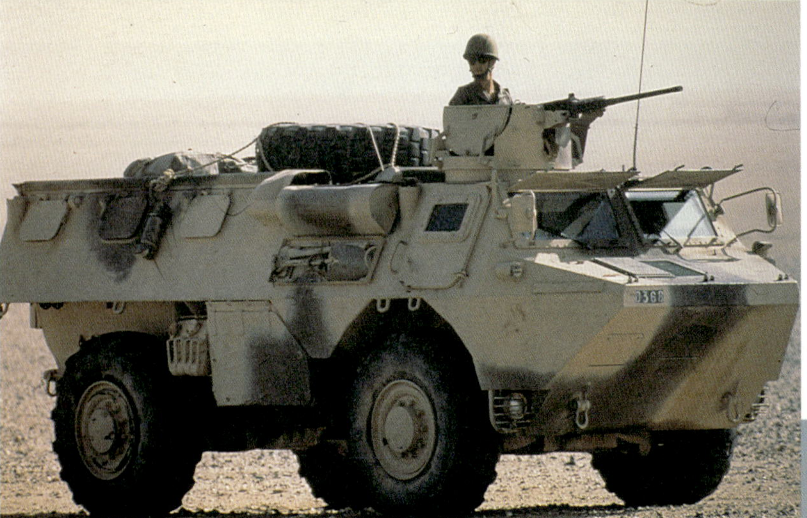

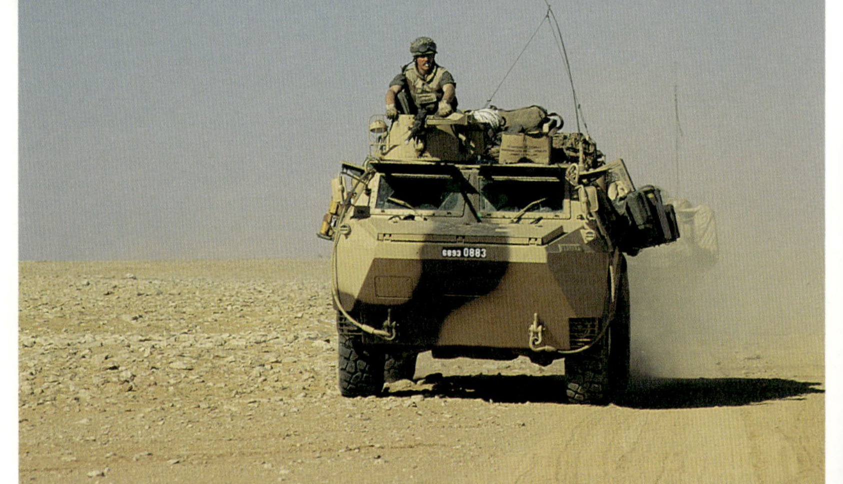

The VAB can be configured for a wide variety of military roles including anti-tank, 120mm mortar carrier vehicle, and twin 20mm anti-aircraft guns. This VAB belongs to 2nd REI.

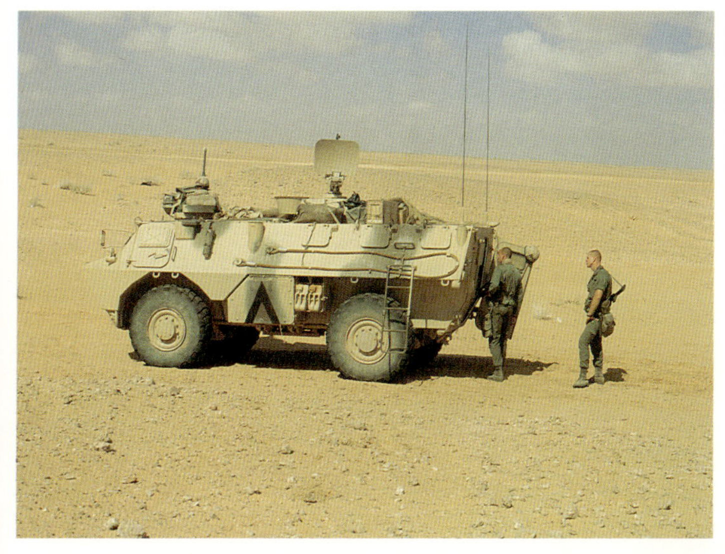

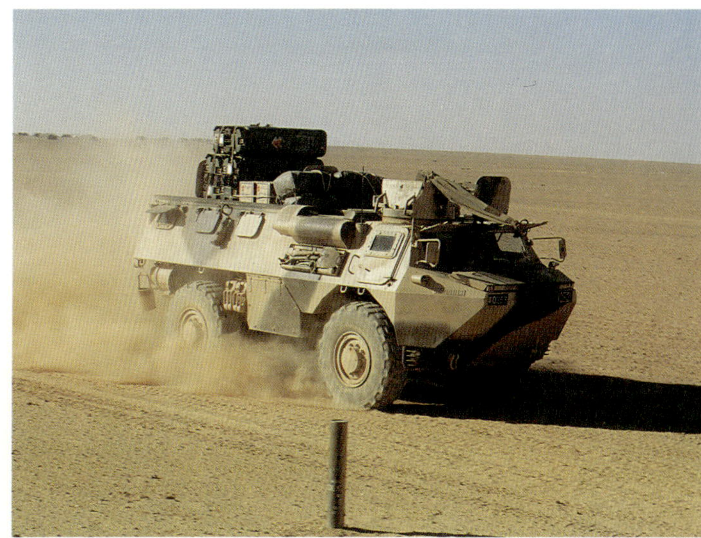

▲ Shown is a VAB fitted with a Ratac artillery radar system. The roof-mounted Doppler radar has a 20km range and the generating set is installed on the right side of the hull.

▲▶ Each VAB infantry unit has four combat companies, one command, company, one instruction company, and one support company. The support company has two or three anti-tank platoons with Milan AT missiles. Shown is a VAB with Milan missiles stacked on the roof.

▶ VAB ambulances of the 3rd RIMA. The VAB Sanitaire can carry four stretcher or 10 seated patients. It is fitted with an air conditioning system.

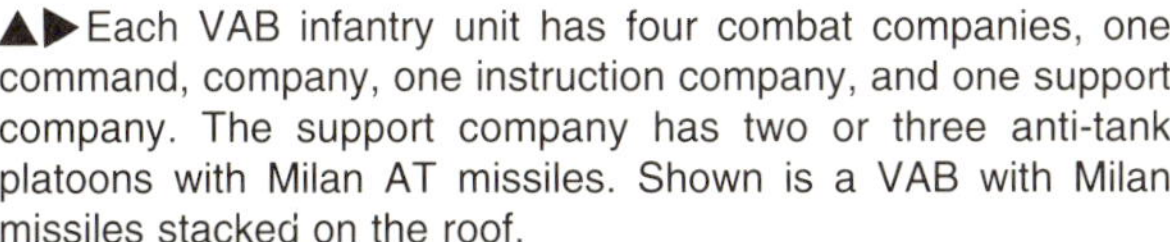

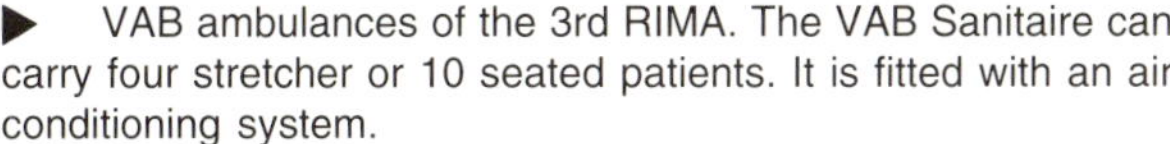

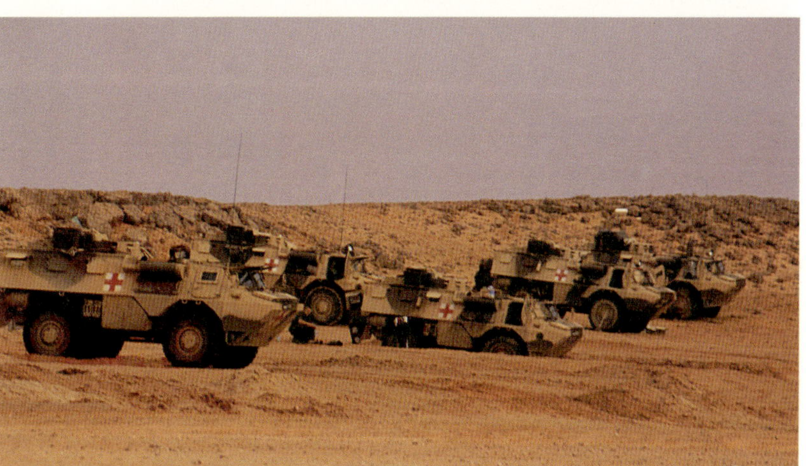

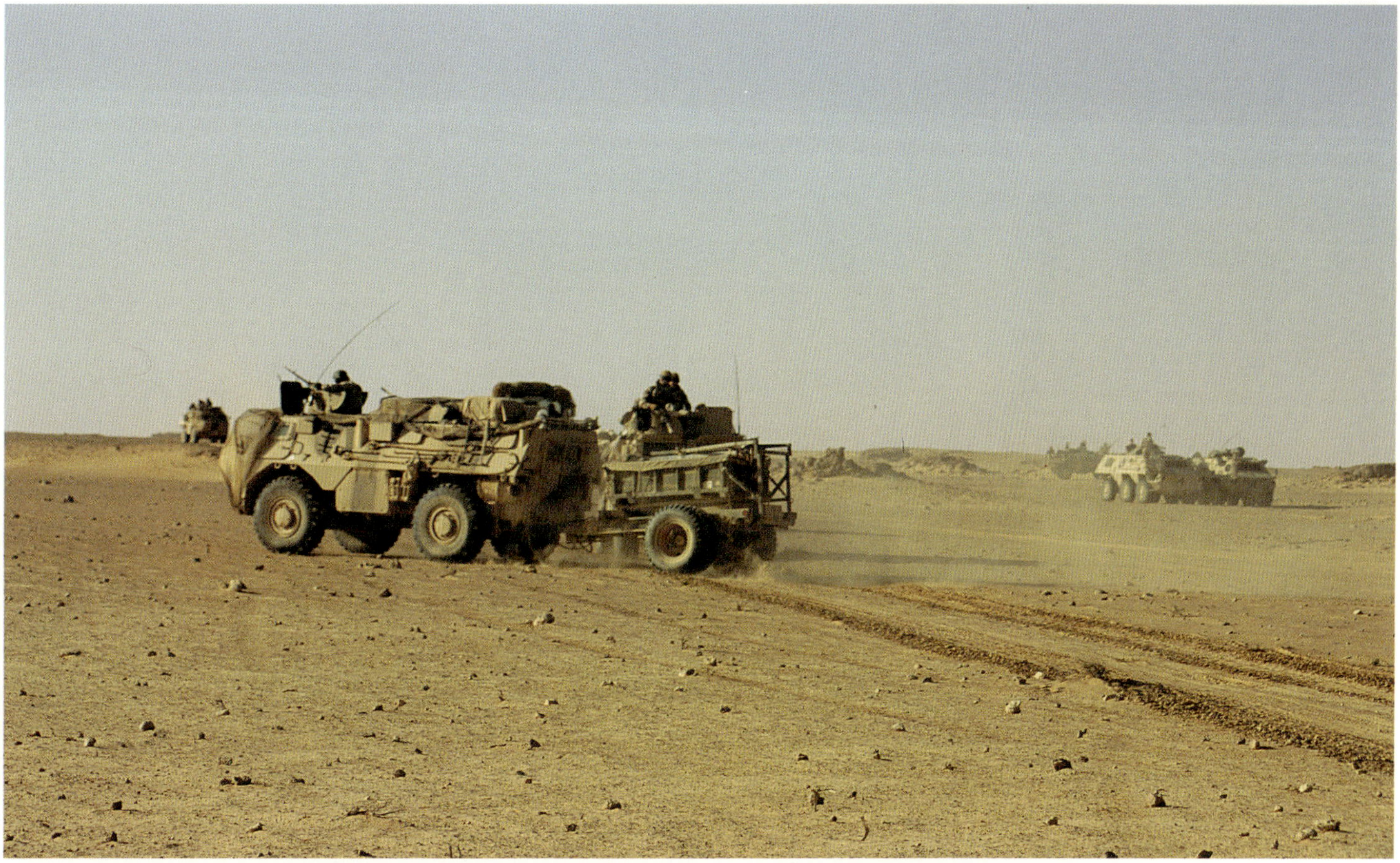

Pictured is a VAB engineer vehicle of the 6th REG towing a U.S. Mine Clearing Line Charge (MICLIC) trailer.

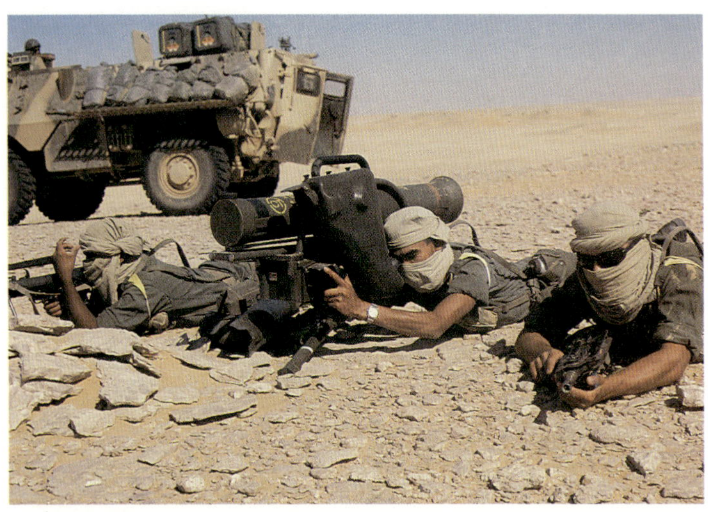

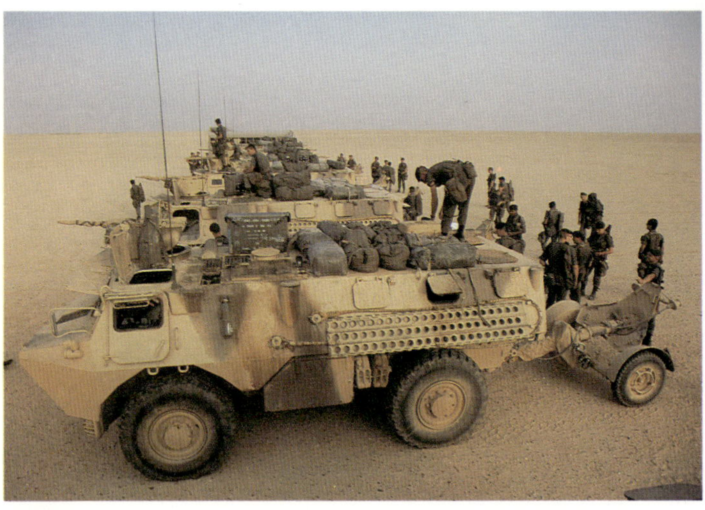

▲◄ A Milan equipped anti-tank unit of the 2nd REI takes up firing position at Hafr-Al Baten. The VAB in the background is their carrier.

▲ A line-up of the VTM 120 Mortar Towing Vehicles. The VTM 120 is a version of VAB that tows a Thomson-Brandt 120mm mortar. The VTM 120 has a crew of six, a TLi 52A turret at the front and carries 70 mortar round.

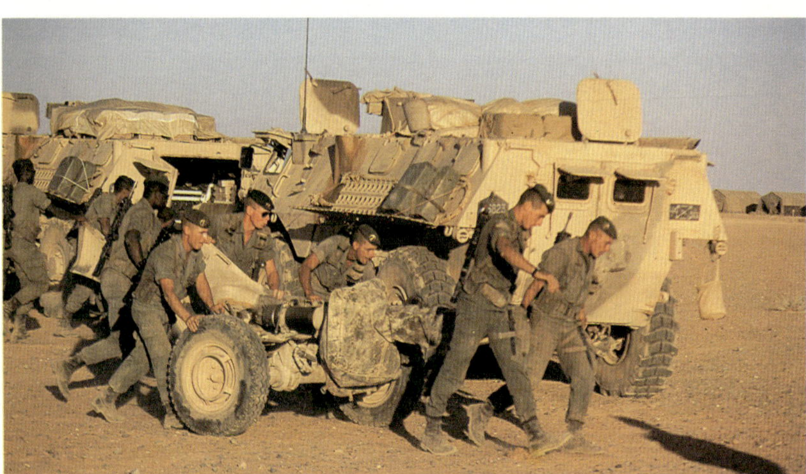

◄ A group of Legionnaire moving the Thomson-Brandt 120mm mortar into position. The VTM 120 behind them is the tractor.

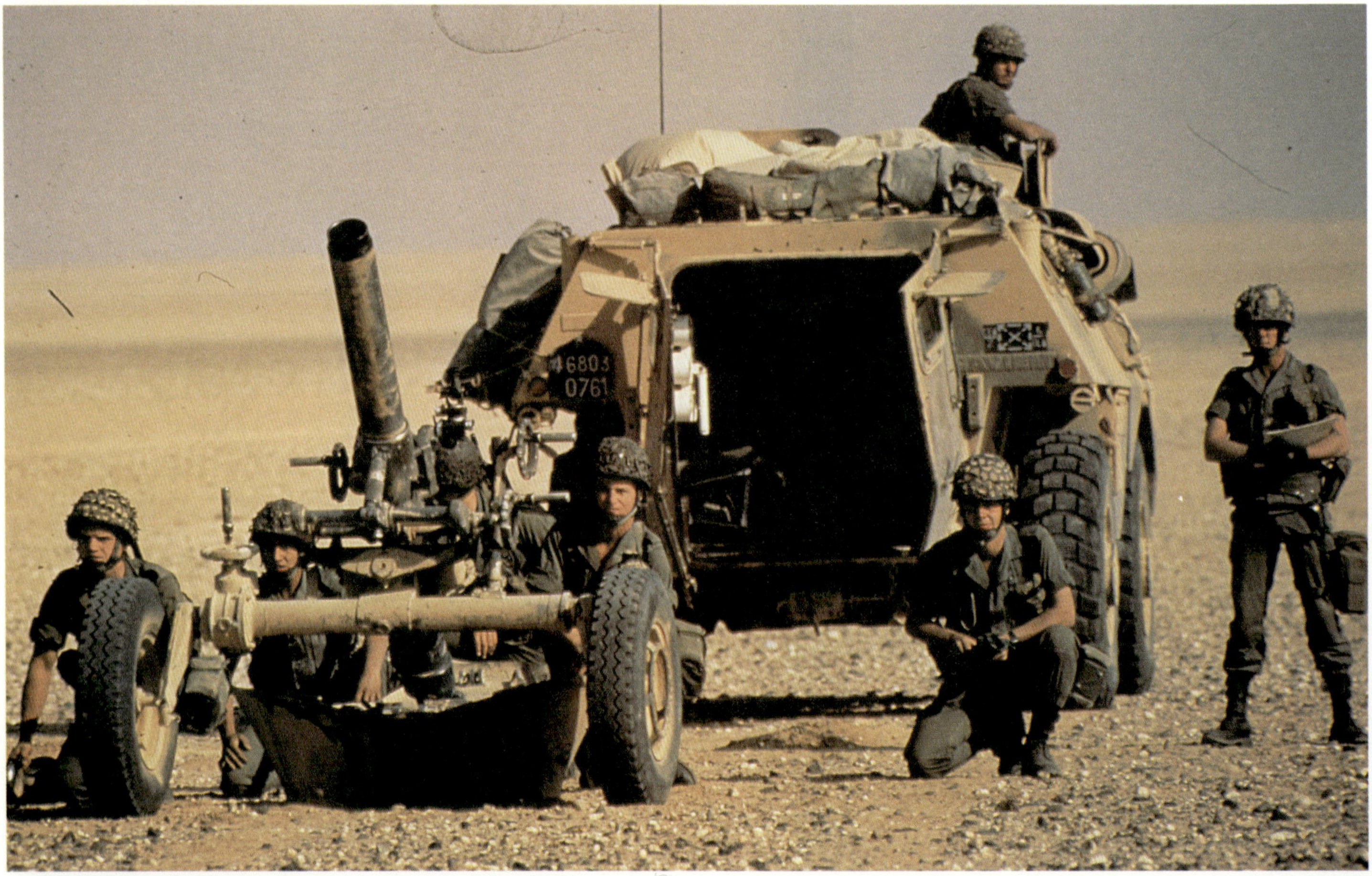

A Thomson-Brandt 120mm mortar unit is ready for action. (DoD)

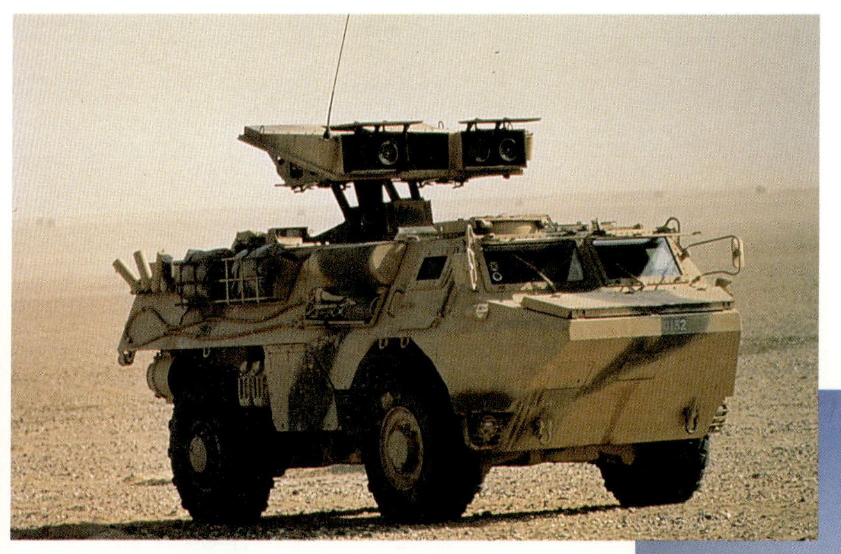

The VAB HOT is basically a VAB which has been turned into an anti-tank vehicle. With their HOT missiles they are able to destroy a tank at 4,000 meters. The launcher can be retracted into the hull, and has four ready to launcher HOT missiles. A further eight missiles can be carried in the vehicle. (DoD)

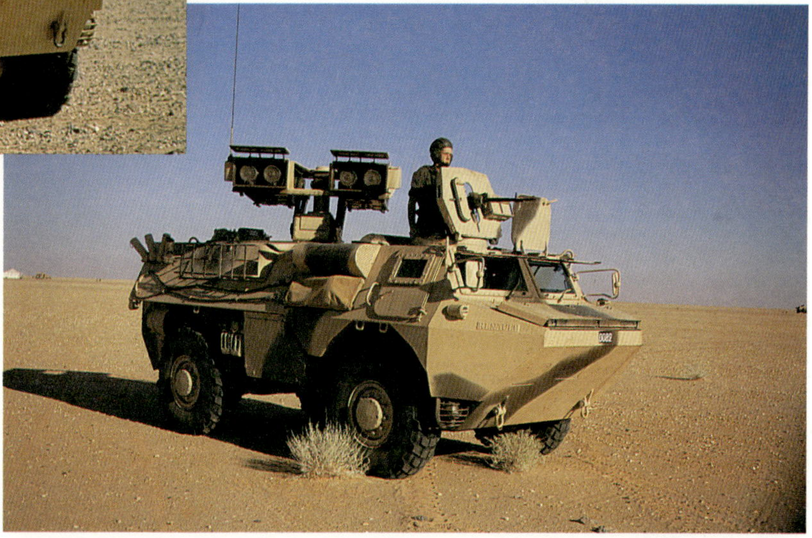

A VAB HOT of the 4th squadron of the 1st REC. Each Cavalry Regiment has a squadron of 12 vehicles.

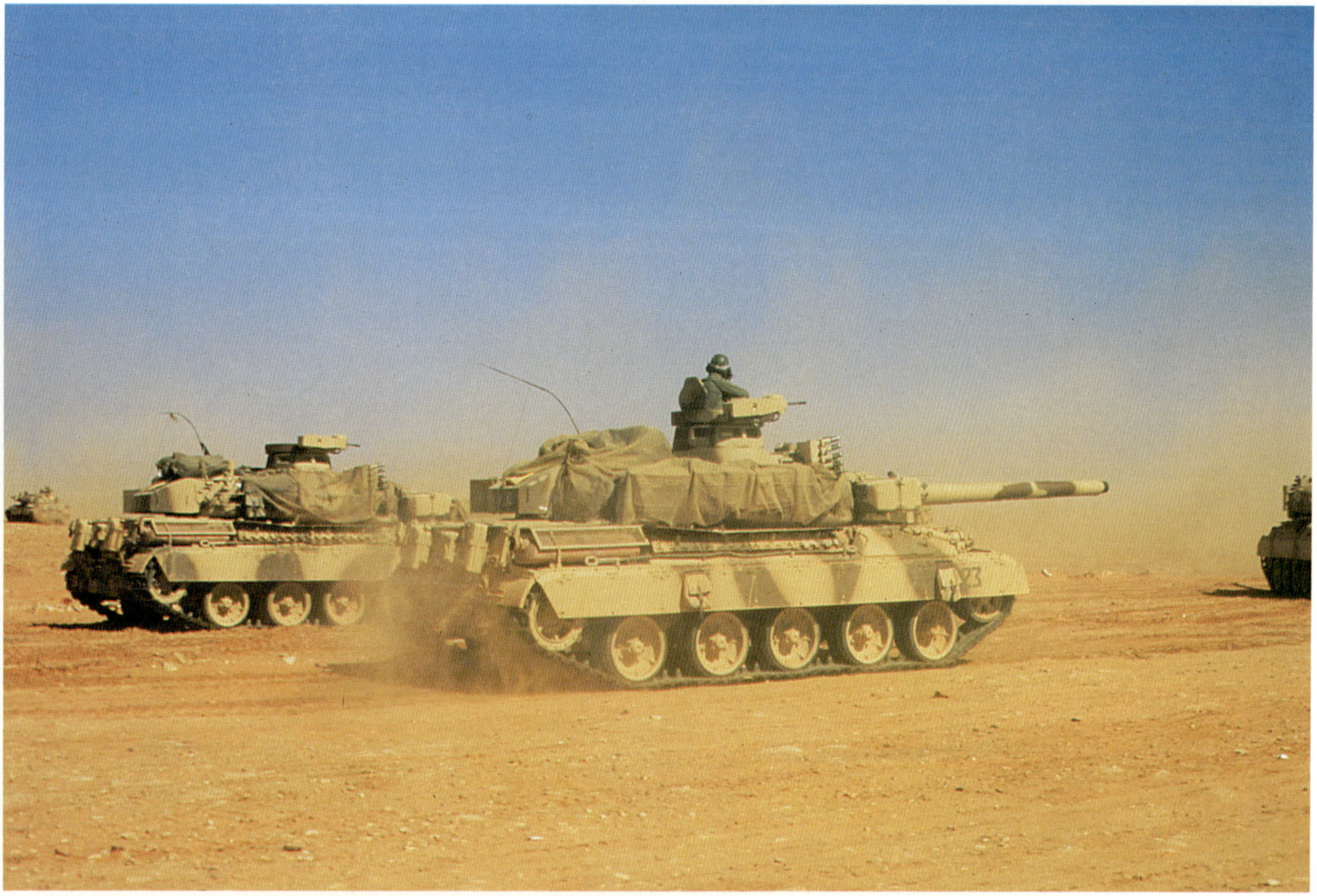

In early January 1991, 40 French Army AMX-30B2 main battle tanks of the 4th Dragoons arrived in the Saudi desert. These tanks were needed to beef-up the French ground forces in case of strong Iraqi resistance.

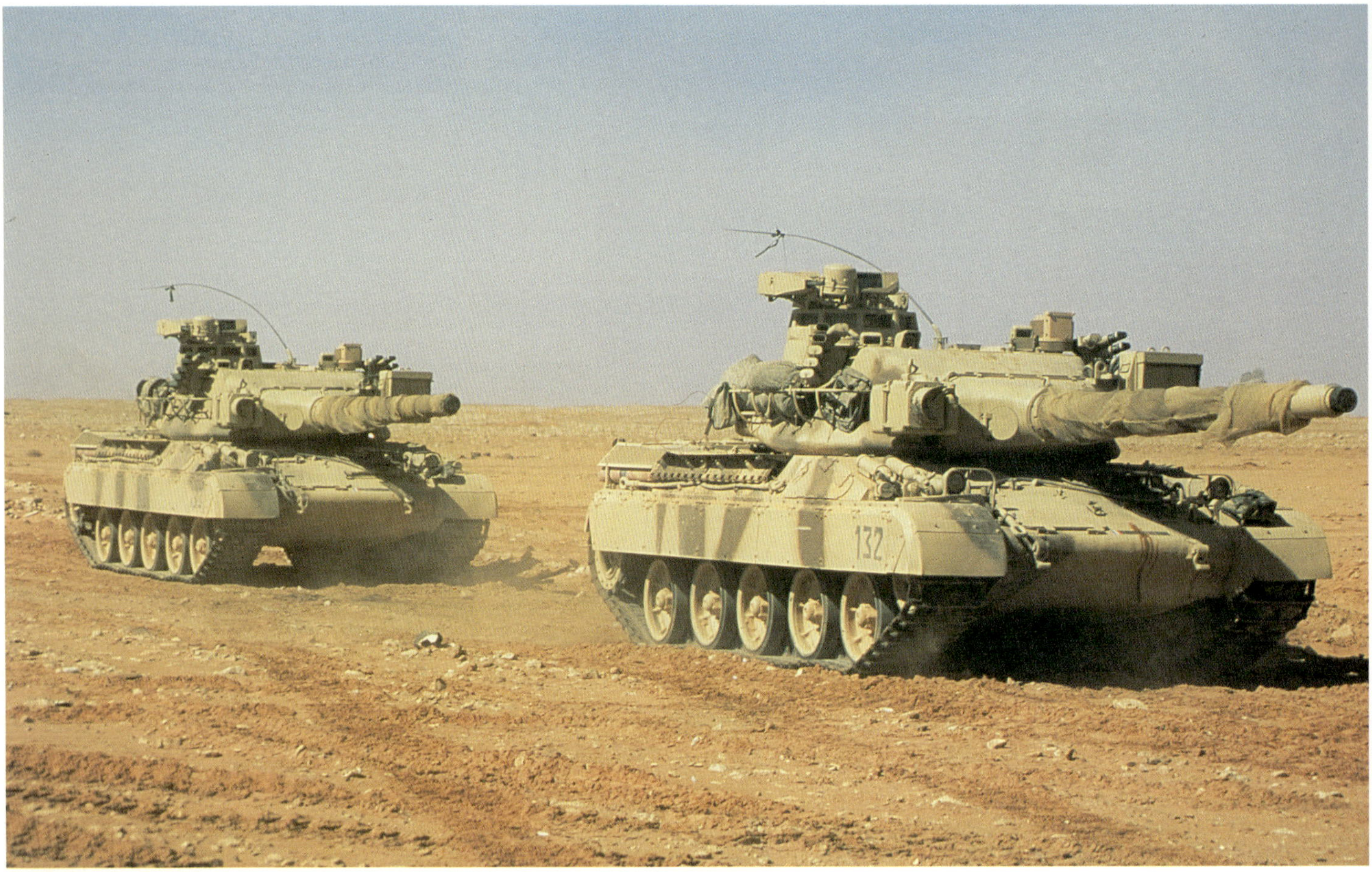

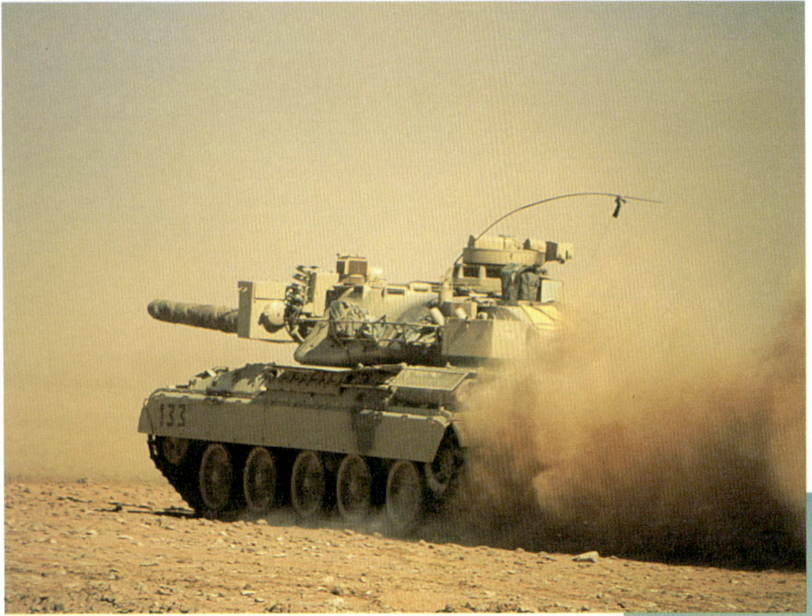

The AMX-30B2 is specially prepared for the desert. Modifications included sand filters, side armor plates and smoke launchers. The AMX-30B2 is armed with a 105mm gun with an integrated fire control system based on a laser rangefinder and a night-vision camera.

During the ground war, the 4th Dragoons fought alongside the 2nd Brigade of the U.S. 82nd Airborne. On two occasions, the AMX-30B2s charged and destroyed Iraqi T-55s and T-59s.

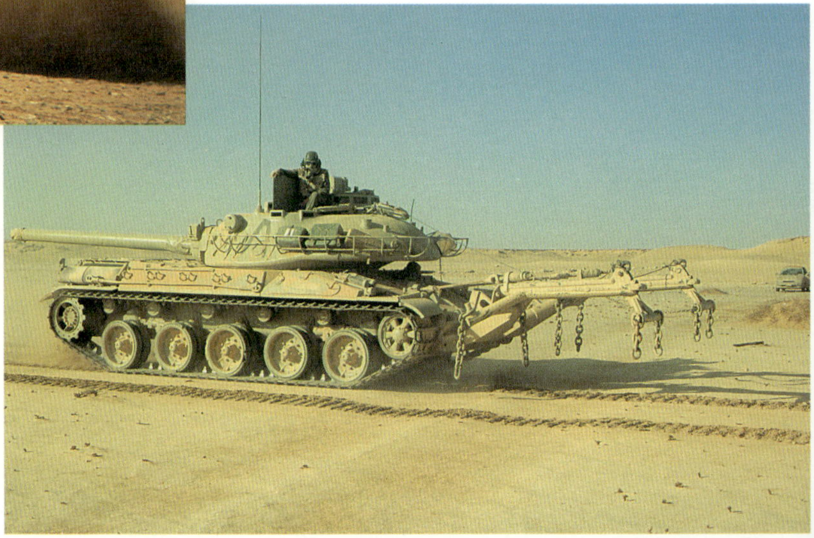

Shown is one of the strangest vehicles used by the French forces in Operation Daguet. An old AMX-30 has been fitted with a Soviet-built KMT mine-roller that came from the ex-East German Army and was donated by the German government for the French war effort.

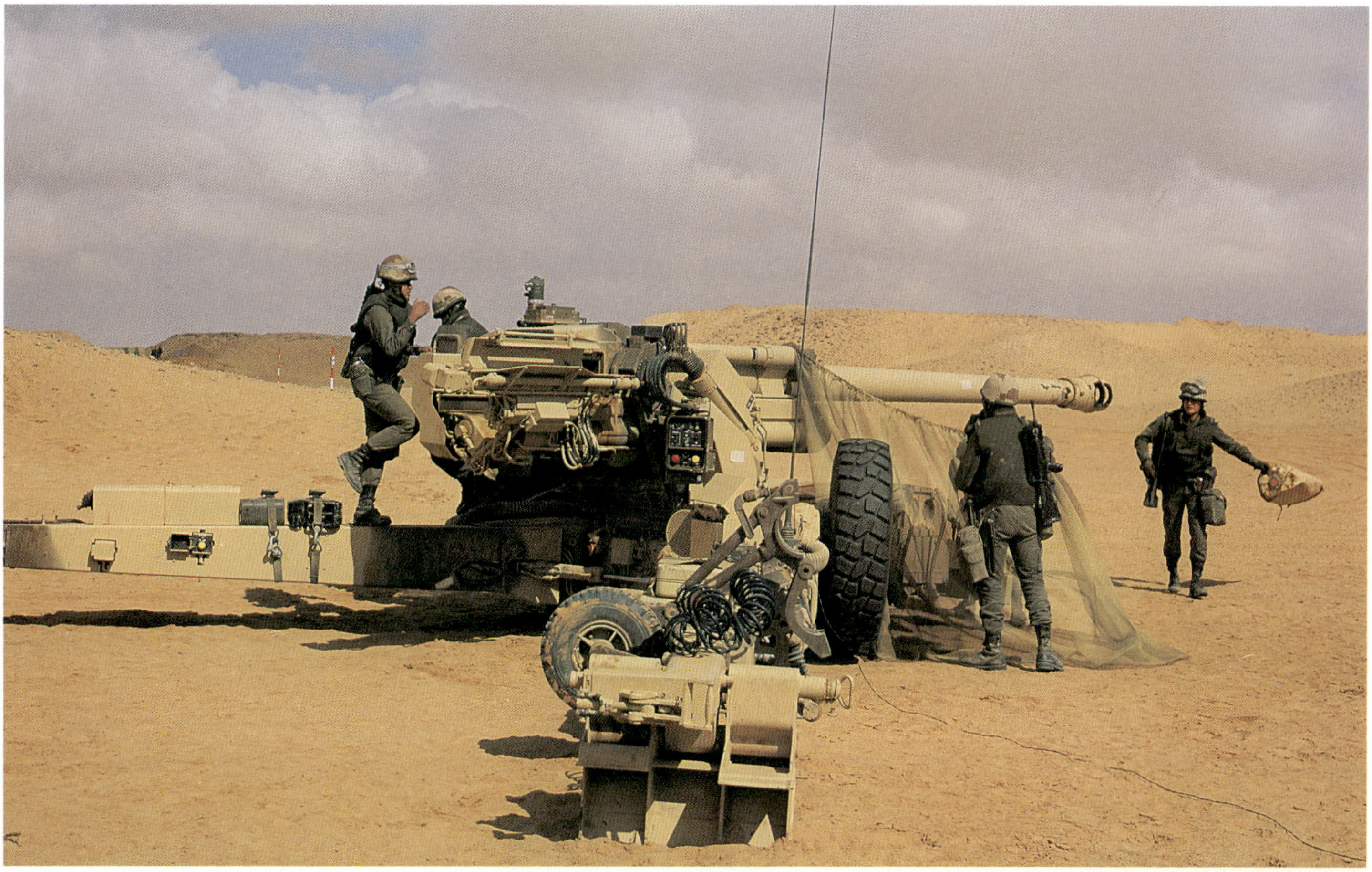

The TRF-1 155mm towed gun has a double-baffle muzzle brake and can fire a variety of shells. It has a range of 24,000 meters. When travelling, the barrel can be swung through 180 degrees and secured in position over the trails.

TRF-1 of the 11th RAMa ready to fire. The French gunners were assisted by the new ATILA system just fielded by the French military. The ATILA is basically a computerized command and control system that allows French gunners to optimize the utilization of their available firepower against enemy targets. The system is fitted to the VAB vehicles.

Pictured is a TRM-10,000 Renault truck towing the TRF-1 155mm gun of the 11th RAMa. The TRM-10,000 truck carriers a crew of eight for the TRF-1 plus 48 rounds of ammunition.

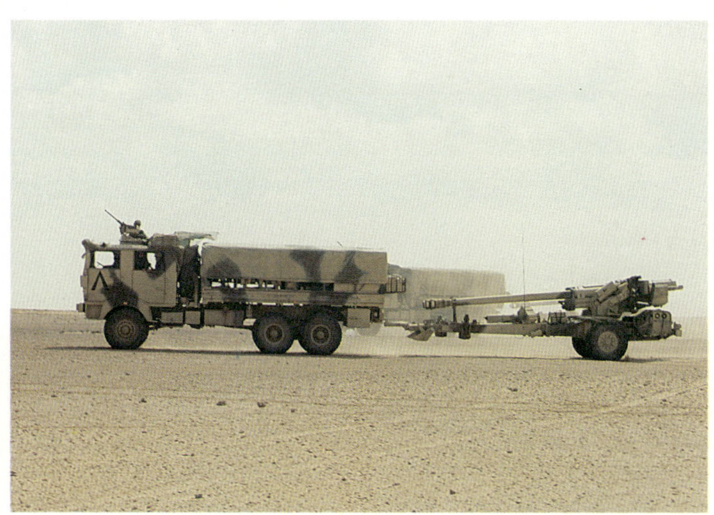

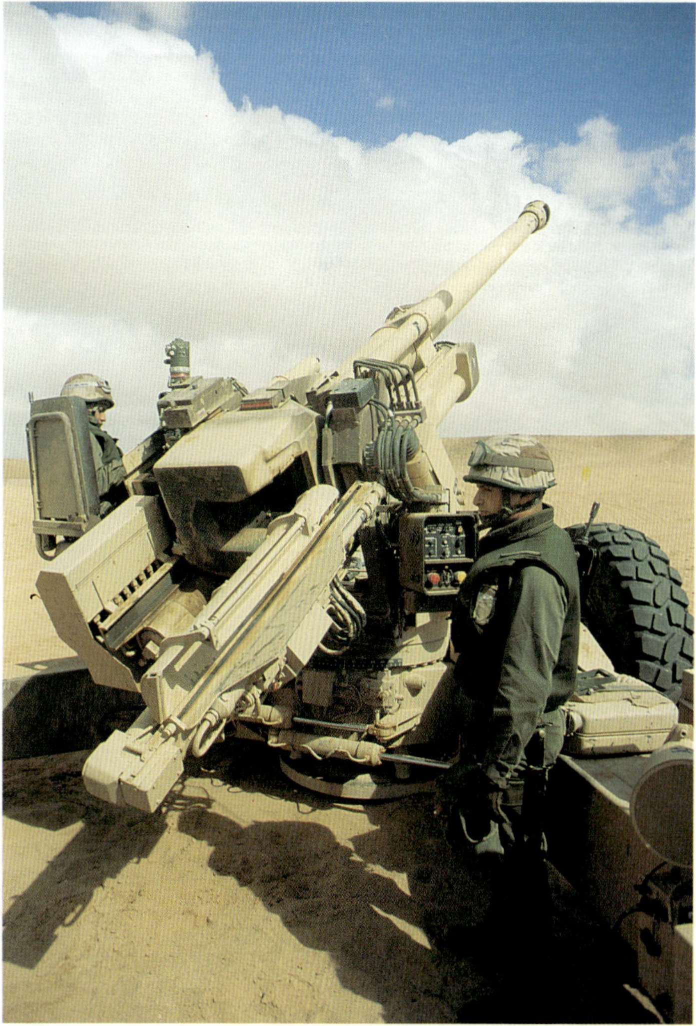

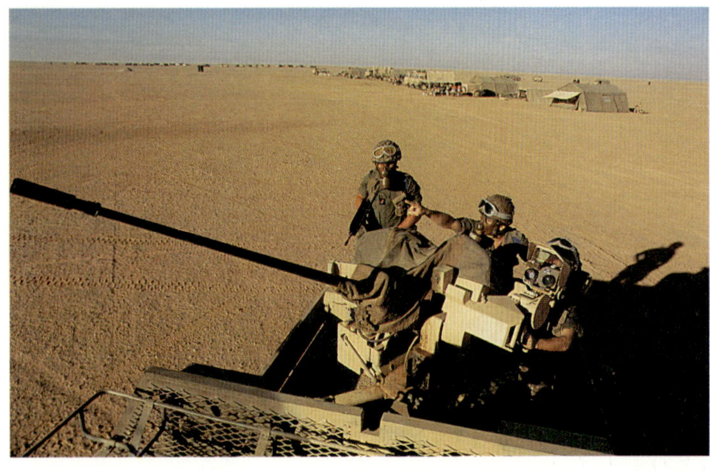

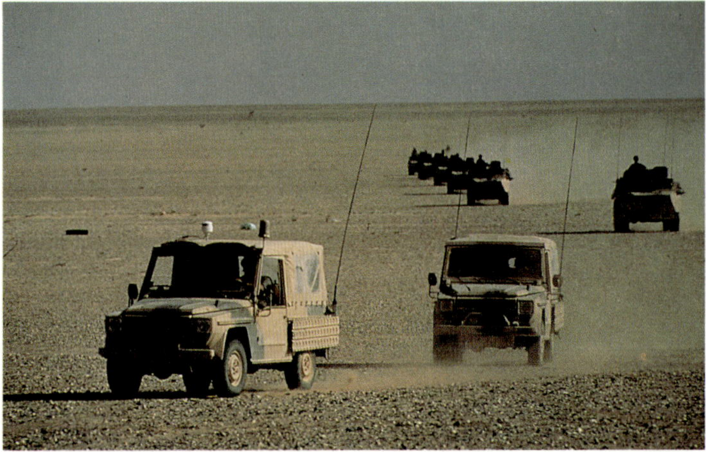

▲   A 20mm gun mounted on a truck. The gunners of 21st RIMa are wearing gas masks.

▲▶ A column of French vehicles moving into position just prior to G-day. (DoD)

▶   VABs being deployed to the Saudi-Iraqi border, the vehicles are loaded with personal equipments.

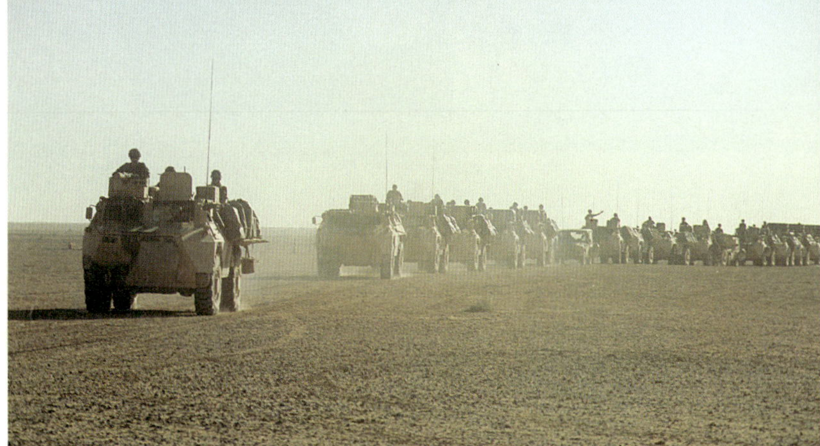

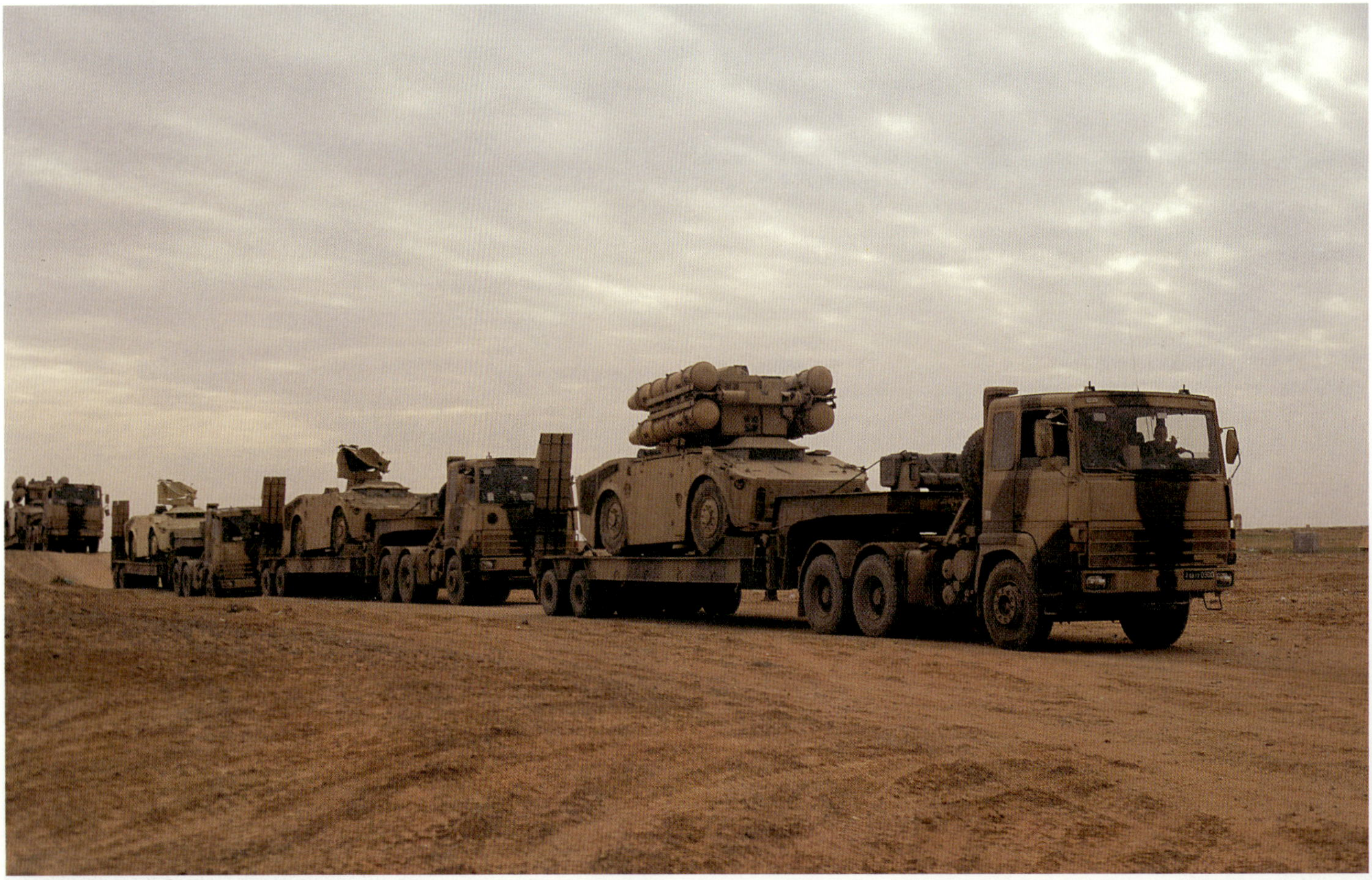

The French military deployed to Saudi Arabia one battery of Crotale all-weather surface-to-air missile system to protect their headquarter units. Shown is the Crotale system moving to the Saudi-Iraqi border.

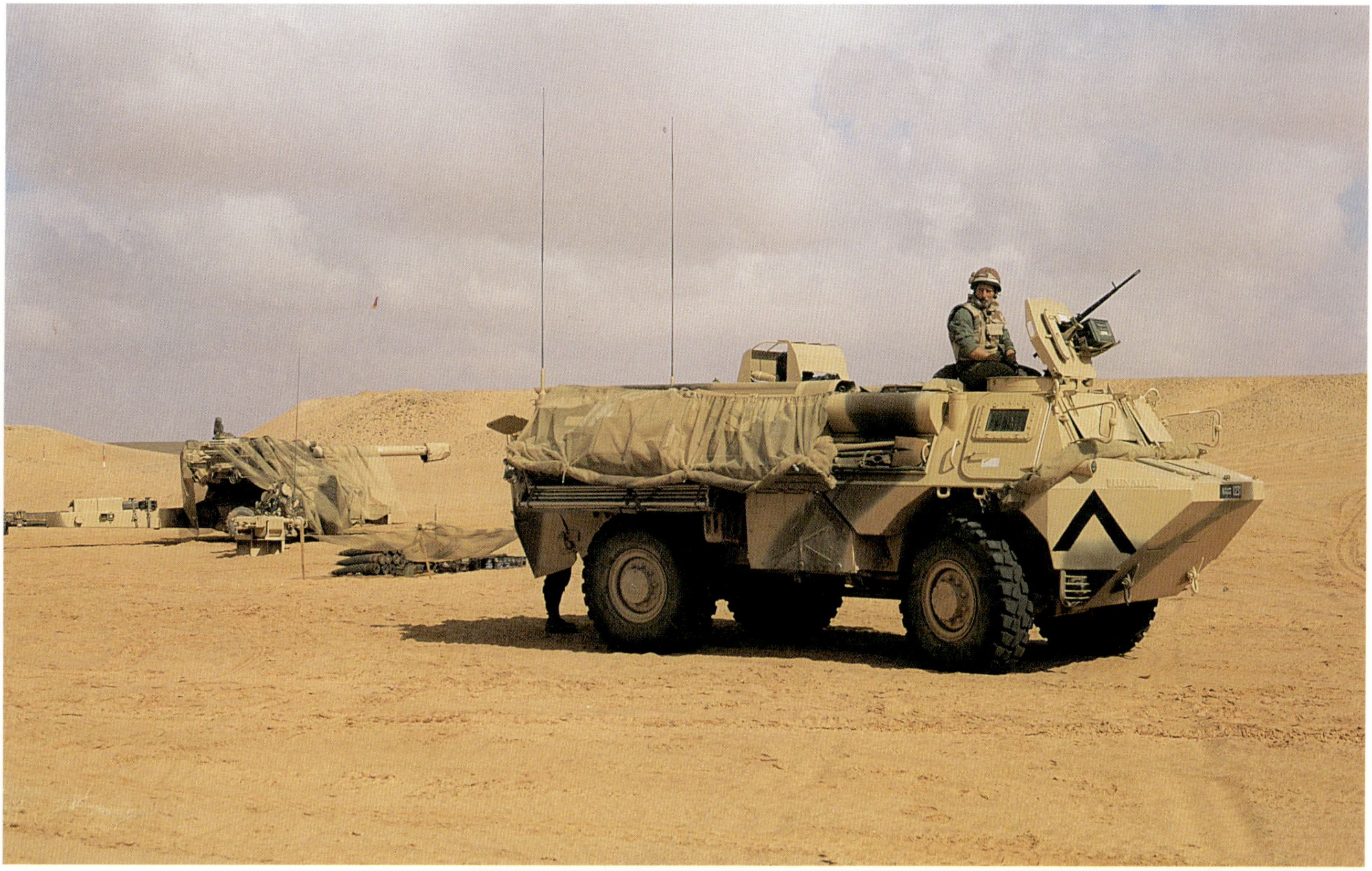

Pictured is a command post version of the VAB armored personnel carrier, the workhorse of the French military. In the background is a 155mm TRF-1.

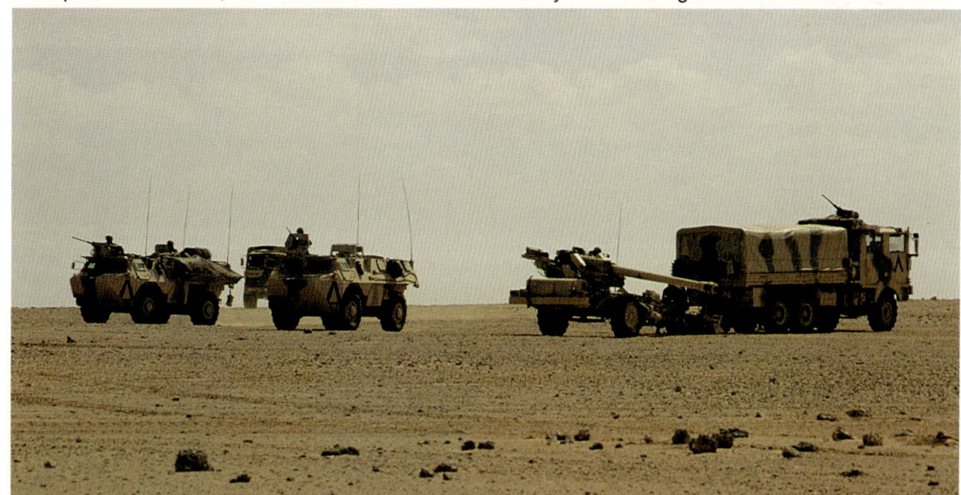

Renault TRM-10,000 truck towing the TRF-1 gun with two VABs. All are painted the inverted V invasion marking.

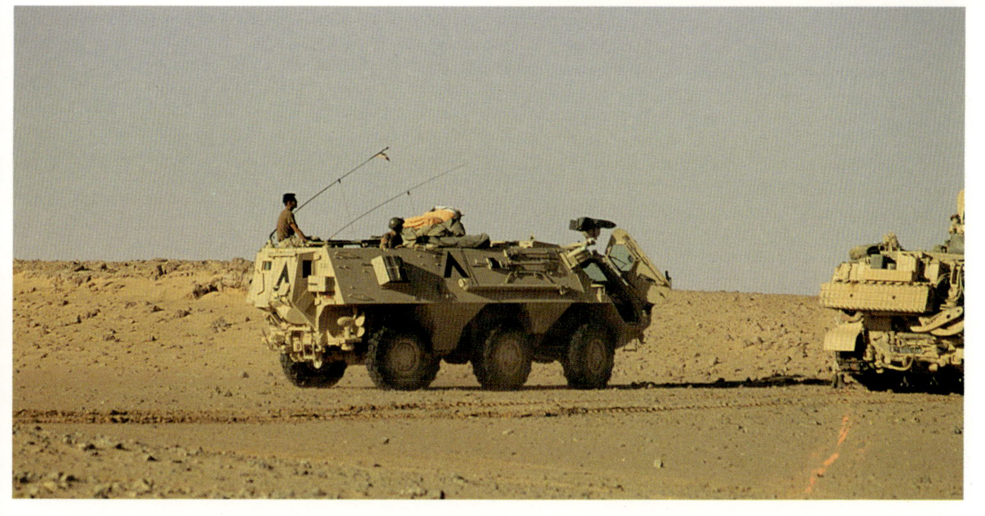

A German-designed and built U.S. Army Fuchs Nuclear, Biological, Chemical Reconnaissance System Vehicle belonging to the 3rd Infantry Division chemical company. This vehicle was assigned to the French forces during Operation Daguet.

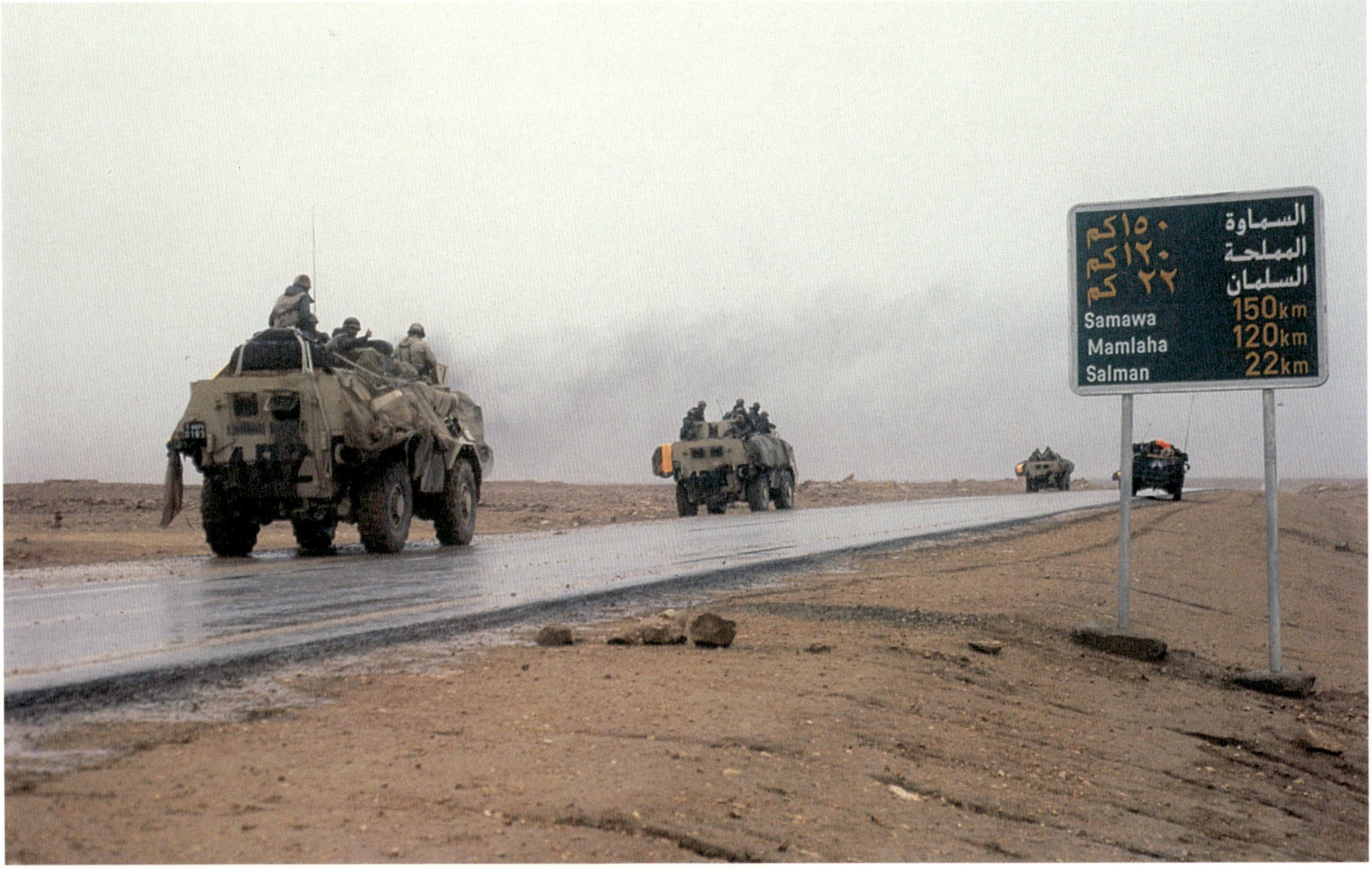

VABs of the 3rd RIMa just 22km away from Al Salman, the main objective. The vehicles are caught in a sand storm.

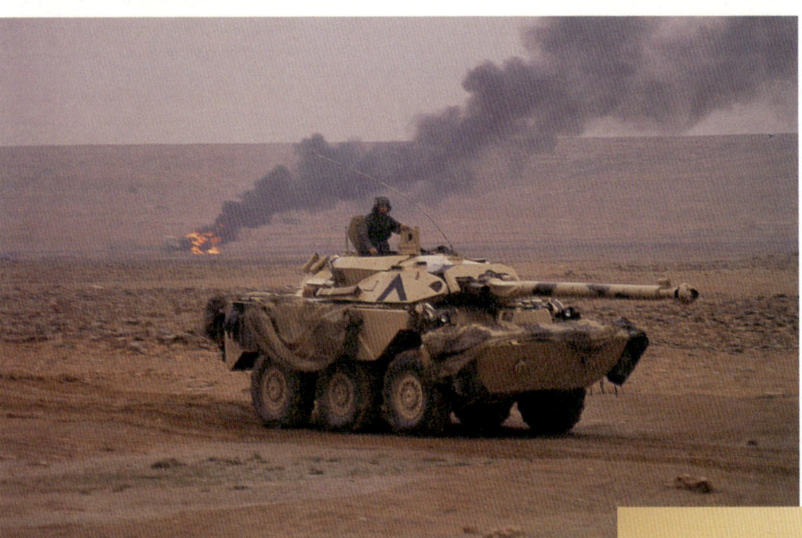

On the way to Al Salman, an AMX-10RC guarding the 3rd RIMa passes by a burning Iraqi truck.

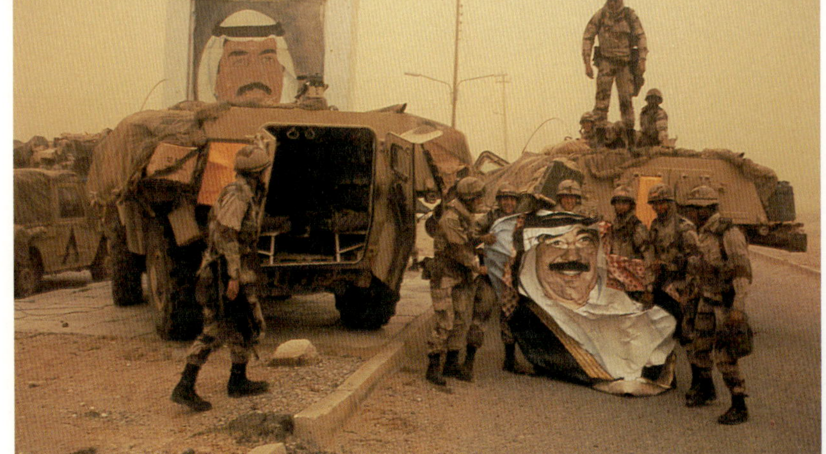

French Marines of the 3rd RIMa in Al Salman posing for a souvenir photo while holding the picture of Saddam Hussein.

ARAB COALITION ARMOR IN ACTION

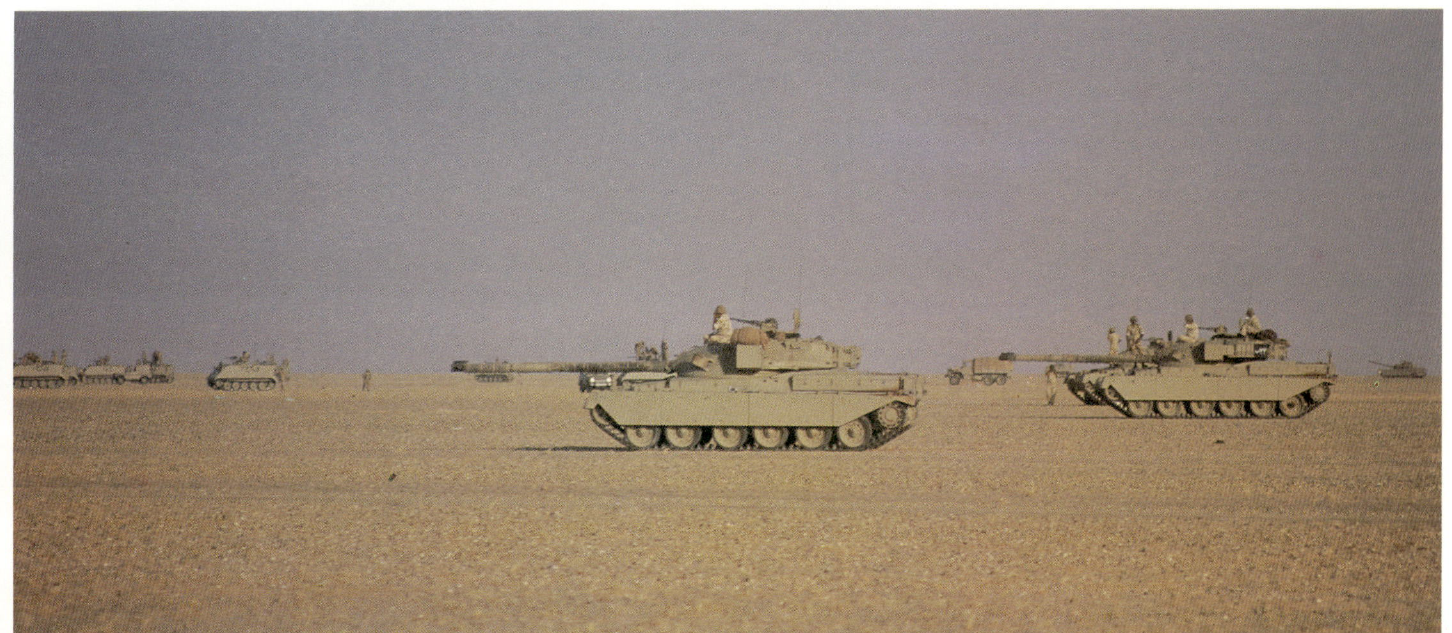

The Saudi ground forces, under the command of Prince Sultan ben Abdul Aziz, consist of about 75,000 soldiers and roughly 550 tanks. The Saudi Army is comprised of two armored brigades, four mechanized brigades, one wheeled infantry brigade and one airborne brigade. There are three Royal Guard battalions.

Backing up the Saudi Army is the Saudi Arabian National Guard, equipped with only Cadillac Gage V-150 armored cars. In contrast, the Saudi Army is equipped with a combination of both American-built M60A3 and French-built AMX-30 tanks and armored personnel carriers.

The Saudi forces first saw action when nine brigades of Iraq's 5th Mechanized Division attacked the Saudi border town of Khafji at the end of January 1991. After several days of bitter fighting, Saudi troops, backed up by Qatari troops and U.S. Marines, retook the town.

During the ground compaign, the Saudi Army attacked through Southern Kuwait with the U.S. Marines and Egyptain Army.

Egypt's contribution to the United Nations coalition force includes two of its best divisions, the 3rd Mechanized Division and the 4th Armored Division. Commanded by Major General Salah Mohammed Atia Halabi, these units were equipped with 450 M60A3 tanks, 600 M113A2 armored personnel carriers, and M109 self-propelled guns.

On February 26, 1991 Egyptian troops launched a frontal assault on the dug-in defensive positions of the Iraqi 26th Infantry Division in southwest Kuwait. The Iraqi obstacle belt consisted of a high sand berm followed by a large anti-tank dich, backed-up by barbed wire and mines and overwatched by dug-in tanks. The Egyptain forces damaged a number of M60A3 tanks while crossing the Iraqi minefields, but other than some isolated pockets of resistance, most Iraqi soldiers were more interested in surrendering than fighting.

After crossing the Iraqi defensive positions, the Egyptian forces quickly drove into Kuwait, where they captured a large ex-Kuwaiti army base being used by the Iraqi military. After that, the Egyptians turned to the east and headed towards Kuwait City. With the quick collapse of the Iraqi forces, the Egyptian forces were just entering the suburbs of Kuwait City when the cease-fire was called by President Bush.

The Egyptians did suffer high causalty rate. 35 soldiers were killed when two of their M113s were destroyed, one by an anti-tank mine and the other by a direct hit from an Iraqi anti-tank rocket.

Syria had also sent troops to support the coalition forces. Besides one airborne brigade, the Syrians deployed their 9th Armored Division equipped with T-72 and T-62 tanks and BMP armored personnel carriers. All together, Syria sent almost 16,000 soldiers and 250 tanks. They fought alongside the Egyptian forces during the ground campaign.

The remnants of Kuwait's military ground forces, which numbered over 20,000 before the Iraq invasion, were based in north-eastern Saudi Arabia. The Kuwaiti Army-in-exile had three brigades and a number of Chieftain and M-84 tanks.

The Kuwaitis were trained by U.S. Special Forces and other specialists both in clearing minefields and urban warfare. Fortunately, the block-to-block streetfighting in Kuwait City never happened.

Qatar sent in two battalions of troops to Saudi Arabia. One of which was equipped with AMX-30 tanks and VAB HOT vehicles. During the retaking of Khafji, the Qatari troops fought bravely, losing two of their AMX-30 tanks but in exchange they destroyed a number of Iraqi tanks

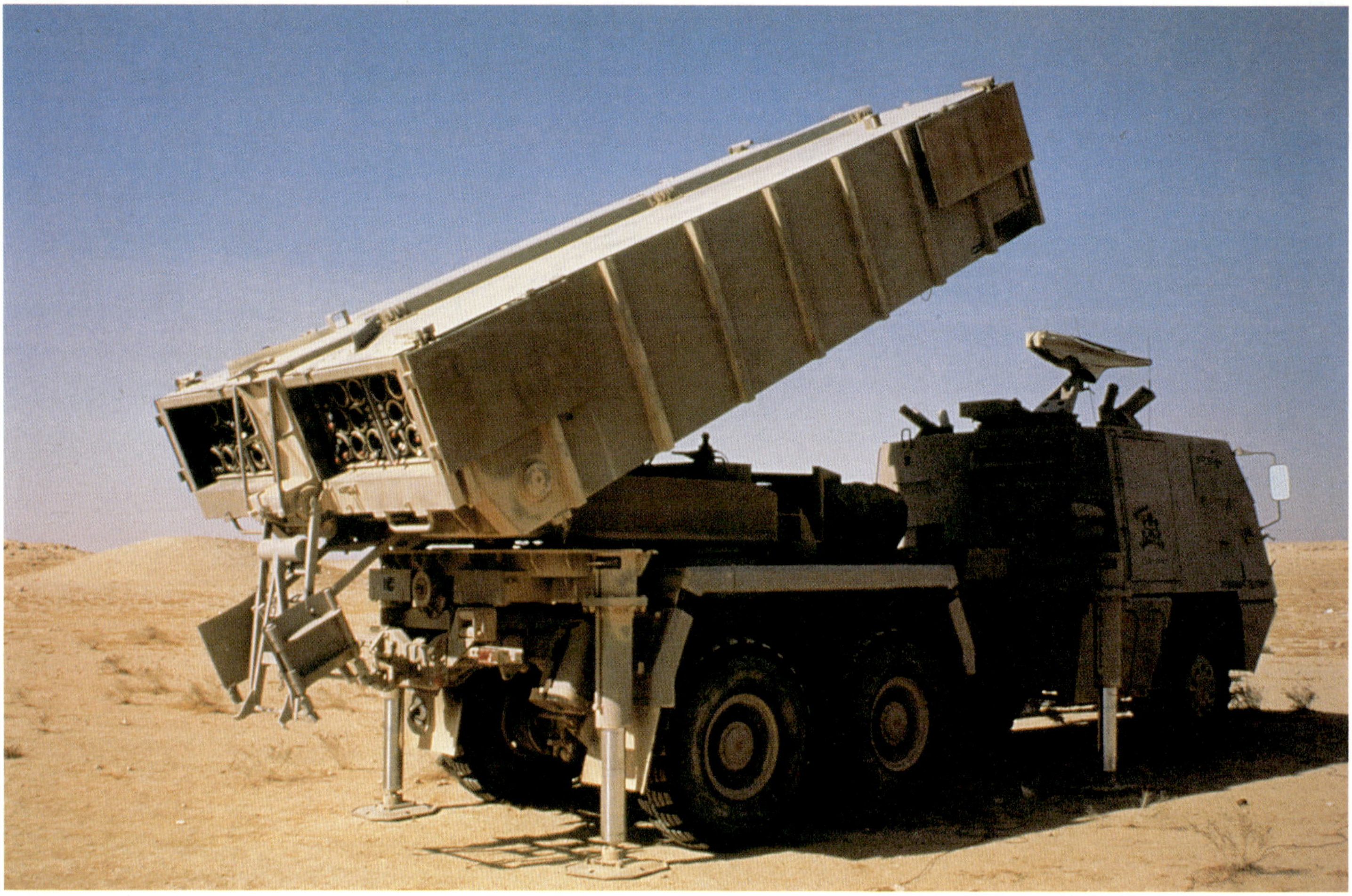

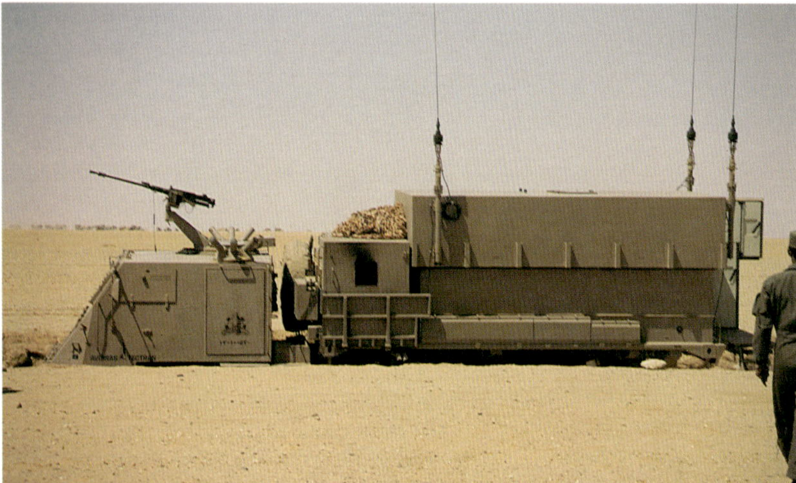

▲ Shown is a Saudi Army Artillery Saturation Rocket System (ASTROS). Used by both the Iraqi and Saudi armies, the ASTROS is a multiple rocket launcher vehicle designed and built in Brazil.(DoD)

◄ Pictured is the command and control vehicle of the ASTROS battery.

◄▼ The launcher can fire different types of rockets, the Avibras SS-30 with 32 rounds per launcher, SS-40 with 16 rounds per launcher, and SS-60 with four rounds per launcher. Shown is the SS-30 with 127mm rockets having a maximun range of 30km. The rockets are effective against both infantry and armored vehicles.

▼ The ASTROS system consists of the launching vehicles, ammunition resupply vehicles, a command and control vehicle, a radar vehicle and several workshop vehicles. All the vehicles are based on the Brazilian-built Tectran 6x6 truck chassis.

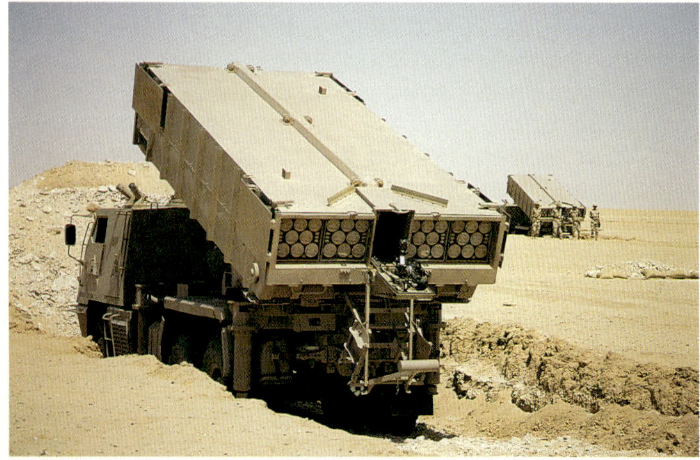

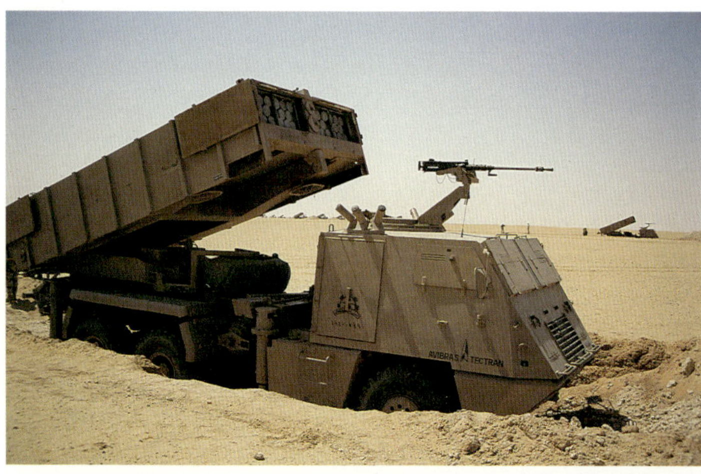

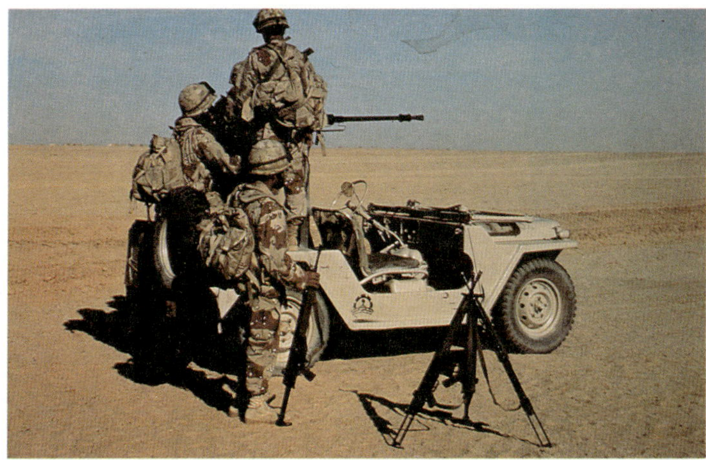

Another Saudi jeep, this time armed with a .50 cal heavy machine gun.(DoD)

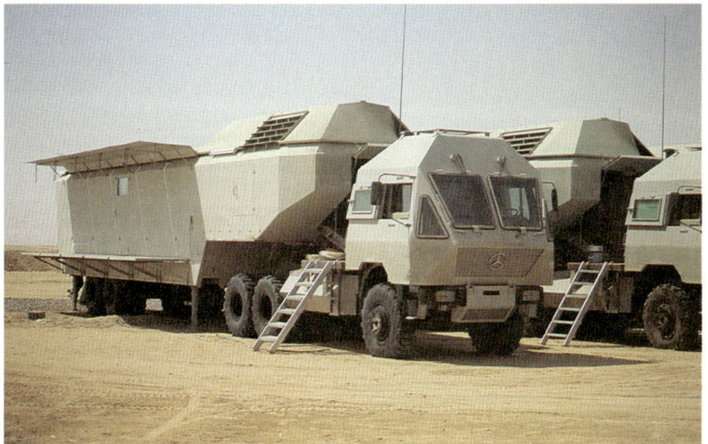

An ultra modern Saudi Army Mercedes-Benz mobile field hospital.

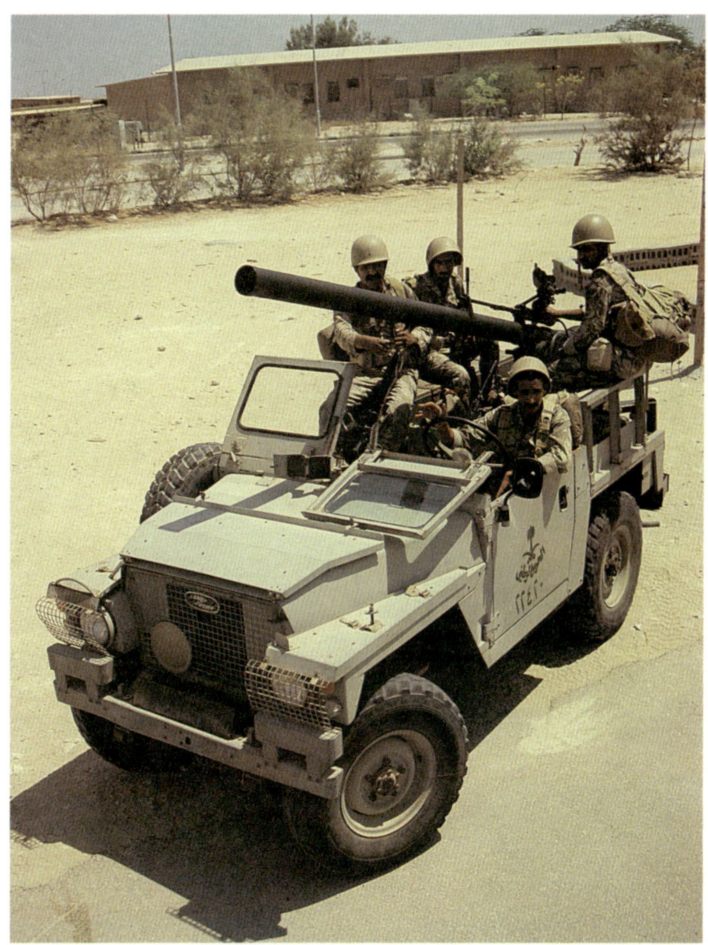

A Saudi jeep armed with a 106mm recoilless rifle. It belongs to the Saudi National Guard.

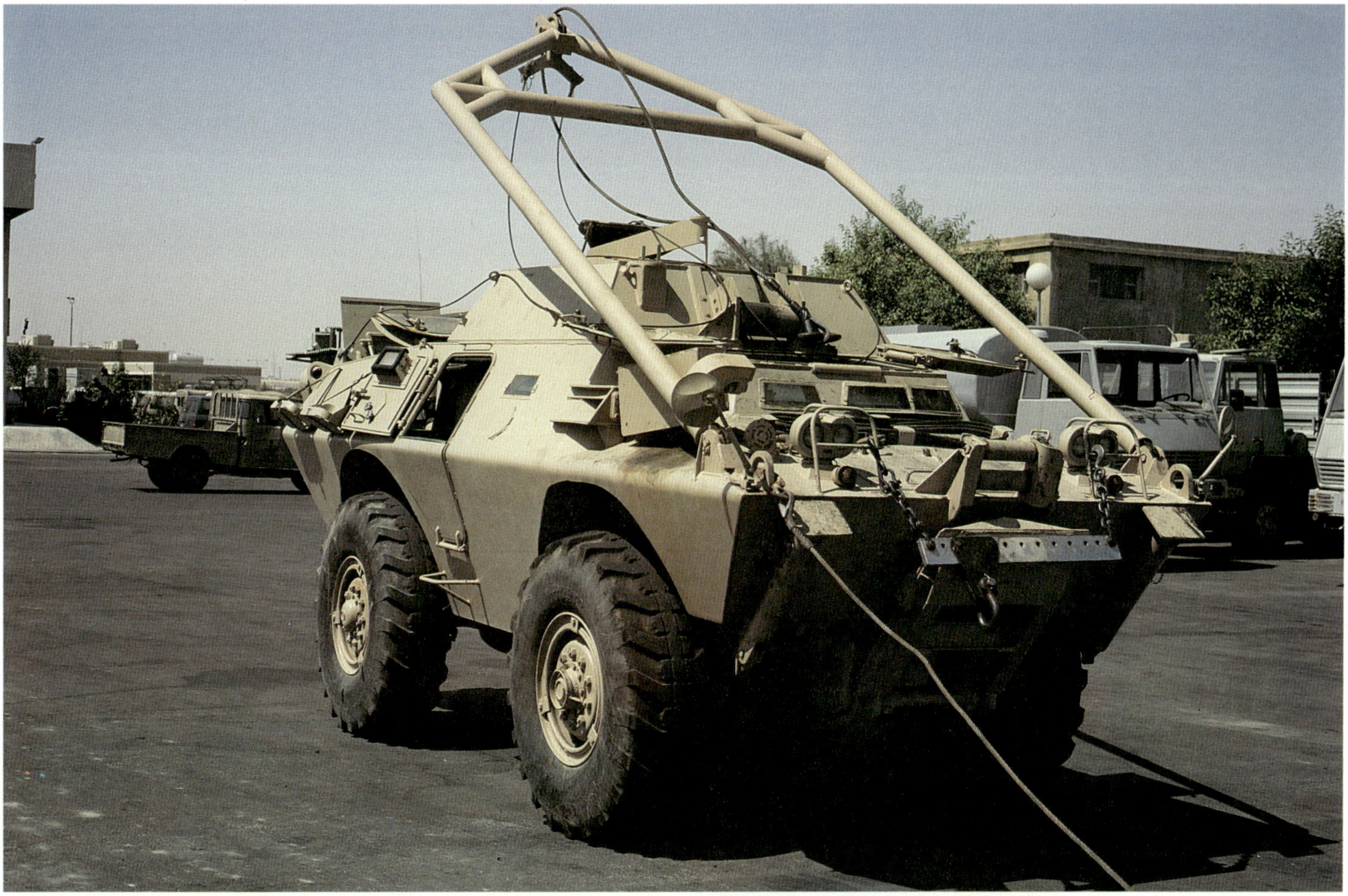

A Saudi National Guard Cadillac Gage Commando Recovery Vehicle fitted with a heavy-duty winch.

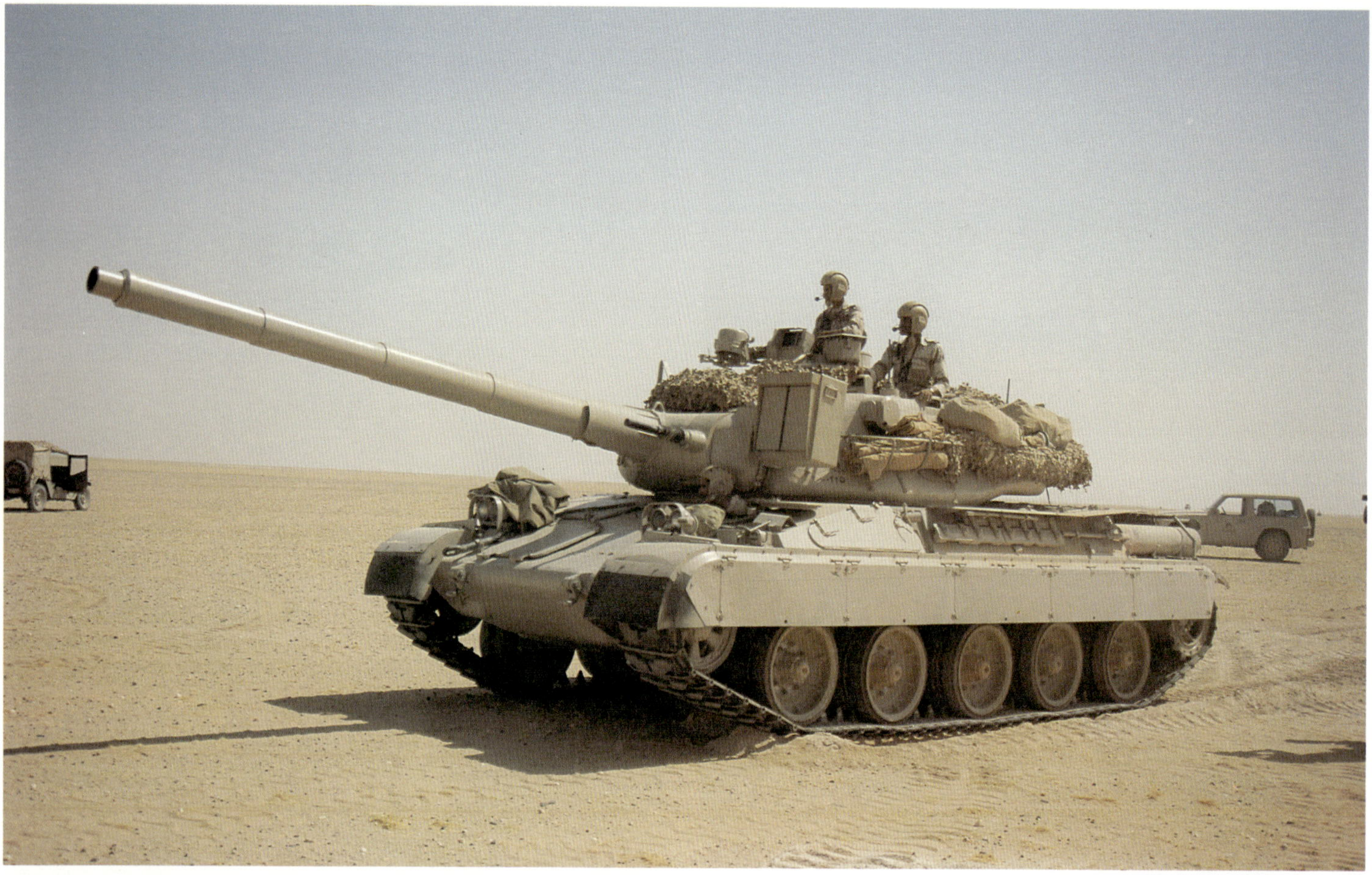

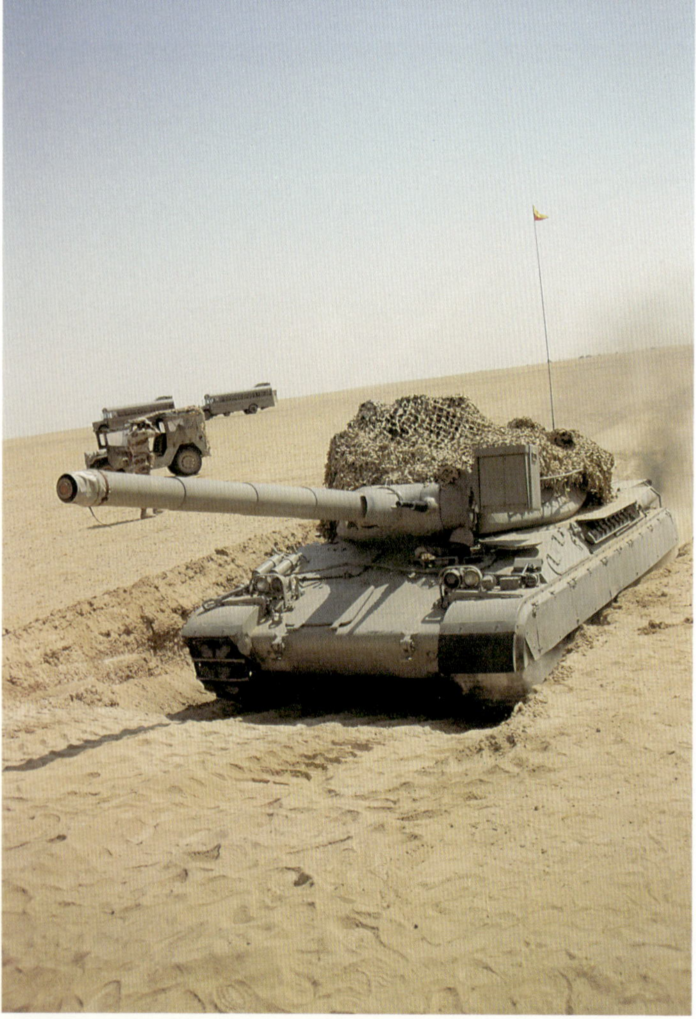

The Saudi Army has 290 AMX-30S main battle tanks in service.

AMX-30S of the Saudi 20th Brigade well-entrenched in Hafr Al Baten area.

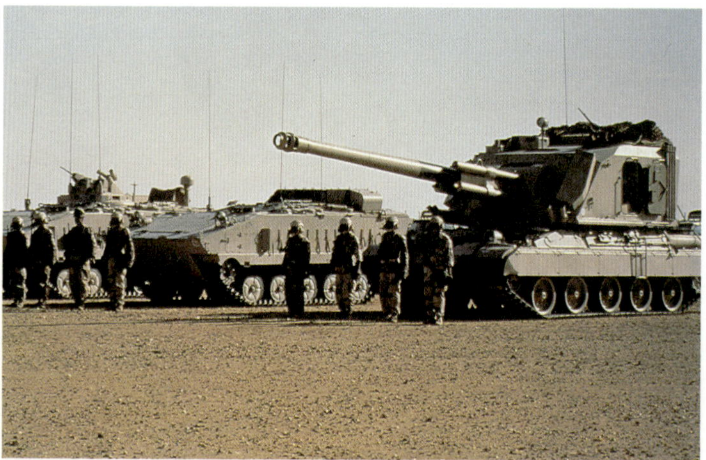

The French-built 155mm GCT self-propelled gun is in service with both Iraq and Saudi Arabia. the 155mm GCT utilizes the AMX-30 chassis and fitted with a turret armed with a 155mm gun and an automatic loader. It has a crew of four. Shown is a Saudi 155mm GCT, an AMX-10PC command vehicle and an AMX-10 SAO artillery observation vehicle. (DoD)

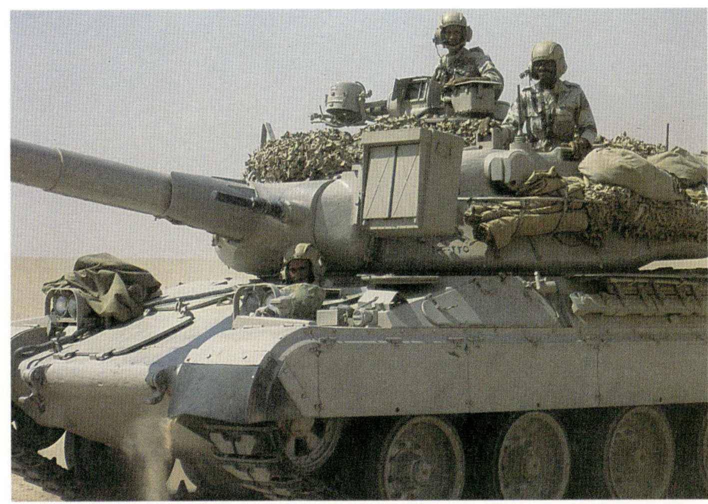

The AMX-30S is a tropicalized version modified to meet Saudi requirements which include the fitting of sand shields, a reduction in the ratios of the vehicle's gearbox to limit the speed, and the fitting with a special day/night sight combined with a laser rangefinder.

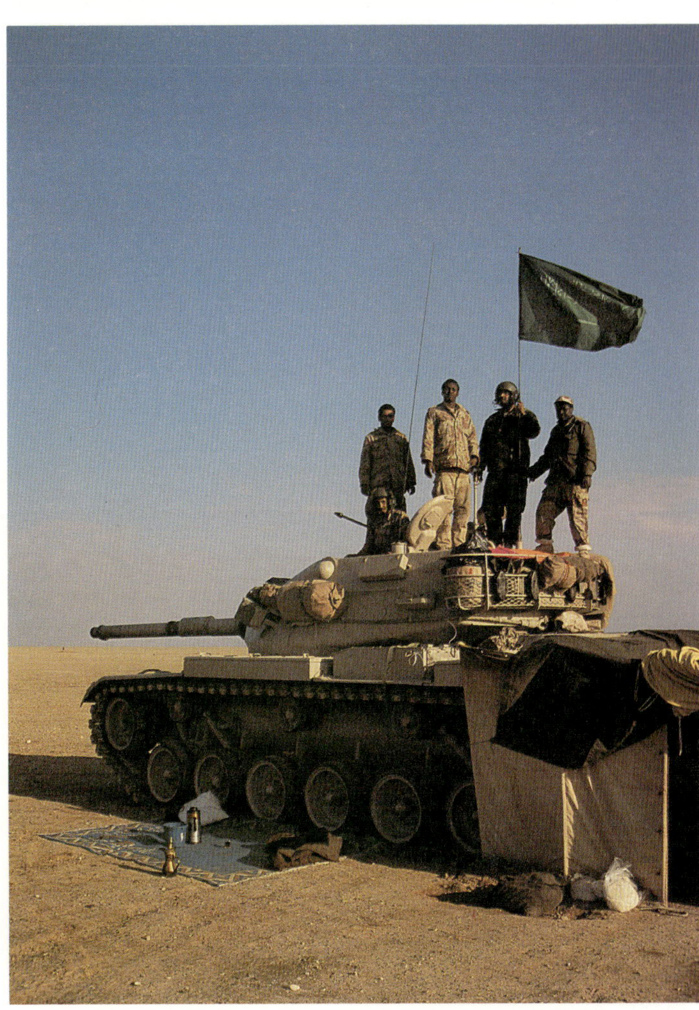

An M60A3 of the Saudi 4th Merchanized Brigade. Saudi Arabia has 258 M60A3s in service

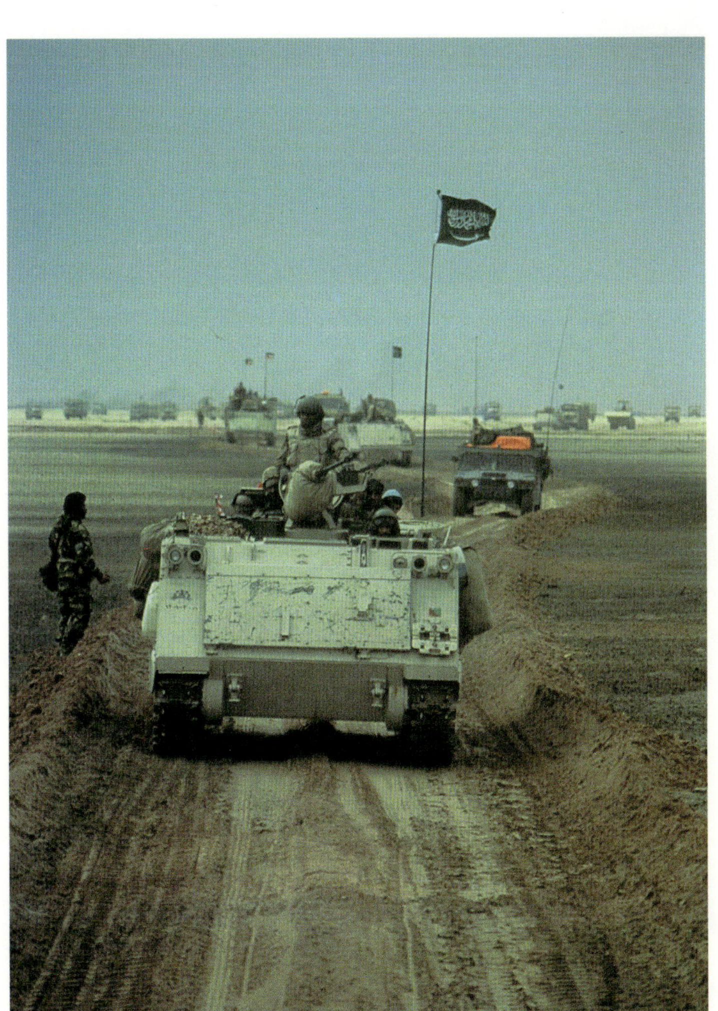

A Saudi M113 on its way to Kuwait City. It is leading a column of Saudi and Kuwaiti M113s and American HMMWV. (DoD)

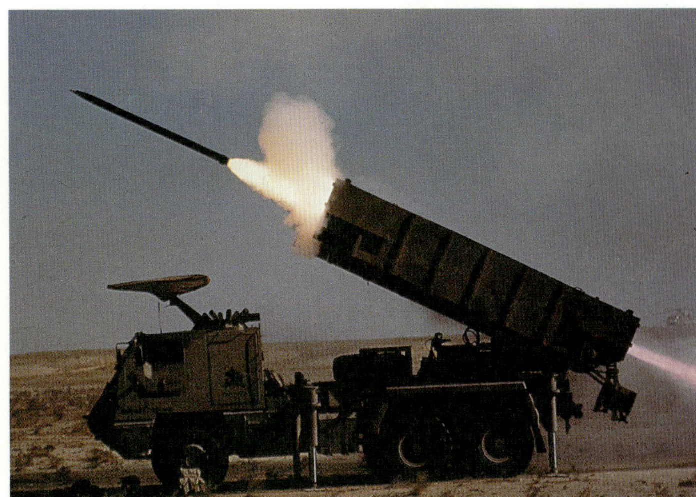

Saudi ASTROS launcher vehicle firing rockets into Iraqi positions in preparation for the assault to free Kuwait. (DoD)

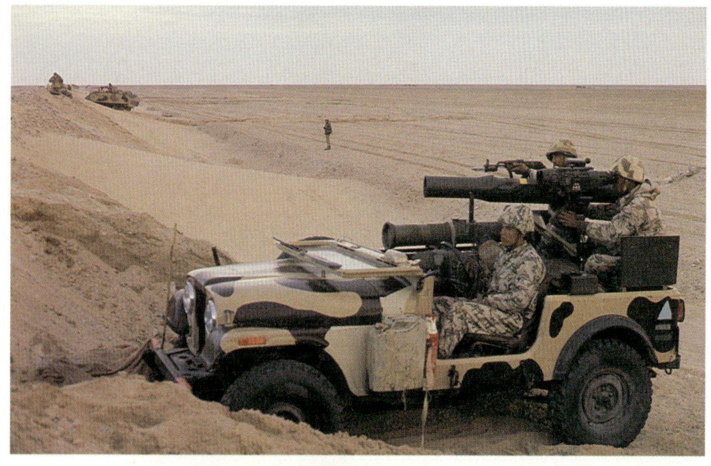

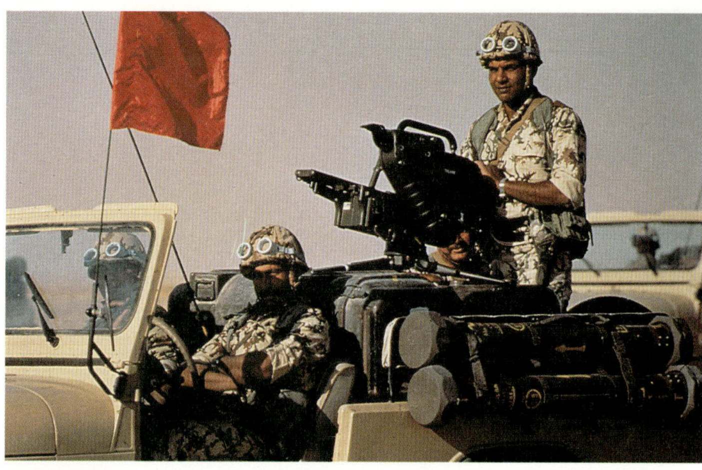

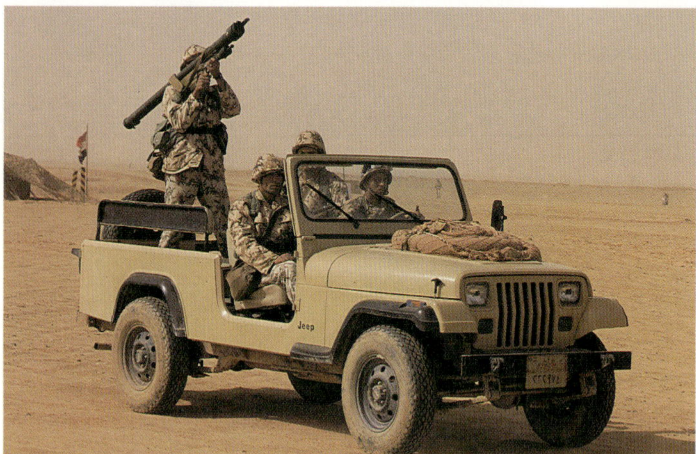

Using Licence-built copies of American designed Jeeps, Egyptian Special Forces have mounted both MILAN and TOW anti-tank missiles on these vehicles.

Egyptian Special Forces Jeep with portable SA-7 anti-aircraft missile.

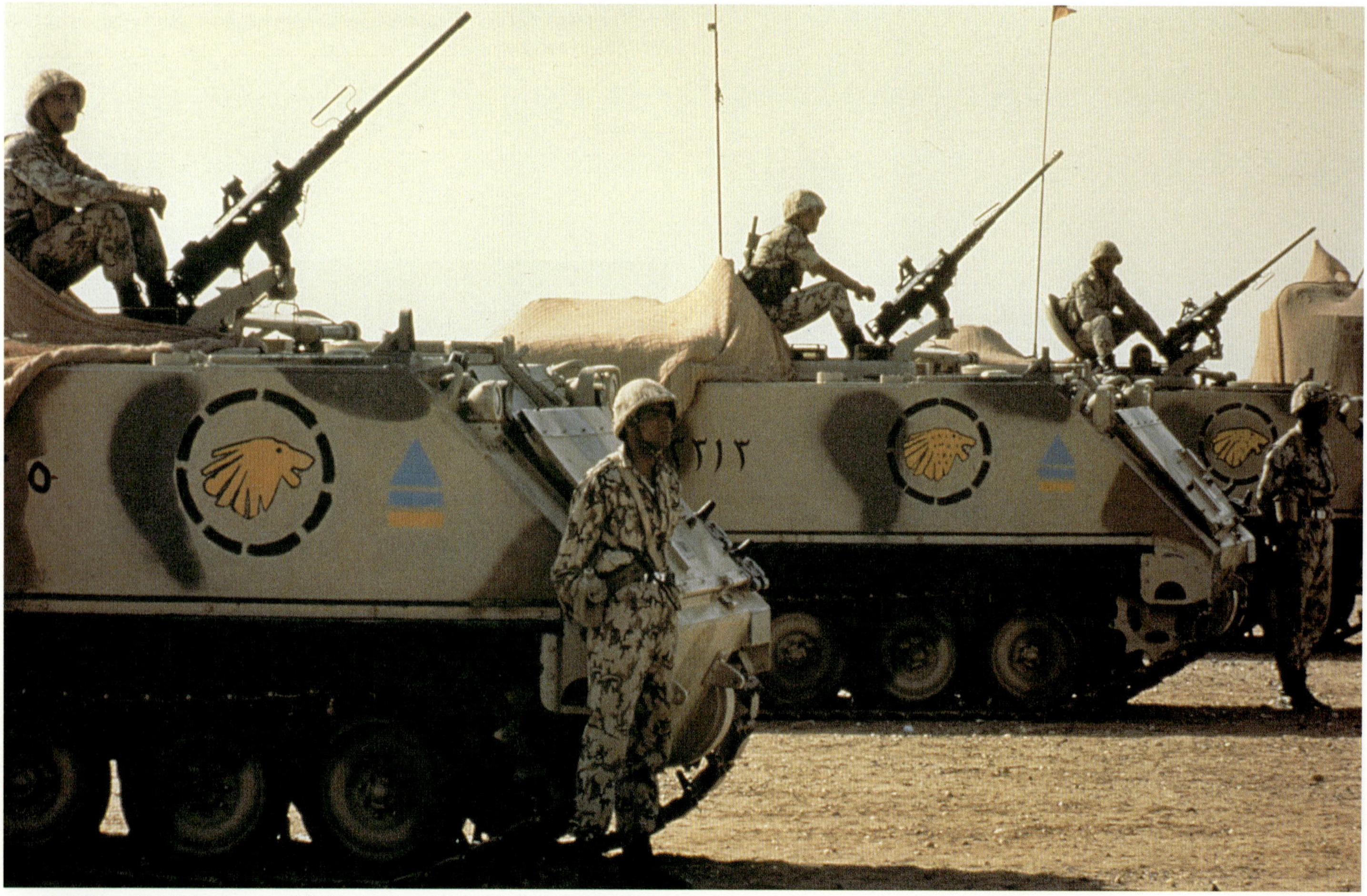

The Egyptian Army has modified a number of American-built M113A2 armored personnel carriers to carry Soviet designed weapon systems, such as mortars and anti-aircraft gun and missiles. (DoD)

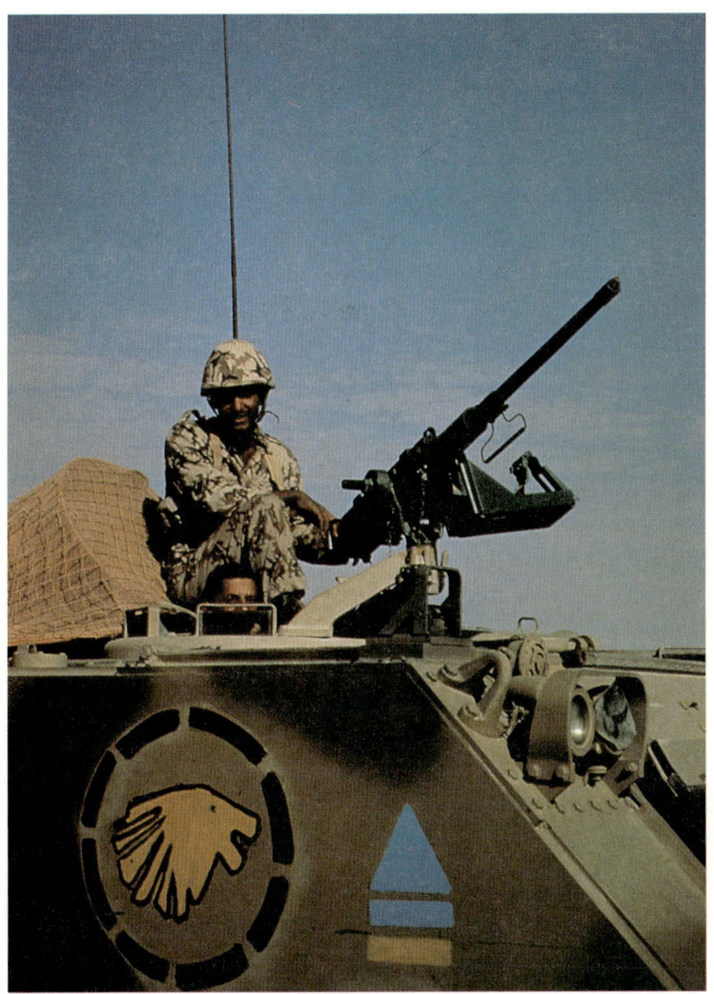

The typical M113A2 APC used by the Egyptian Army is armed only with a .50 caliber machine gun, pintle-mounted on the forward part of the commander's cupola. (DoD)

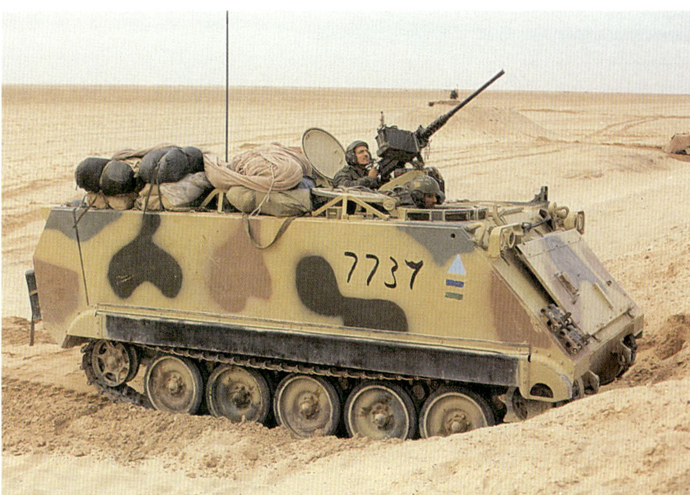

Shown is an Egyptian Army M113A2 APC of the 3rd Mechanized Division. The Blue triangle with the bars underneath it is the 3rd Division's sign.

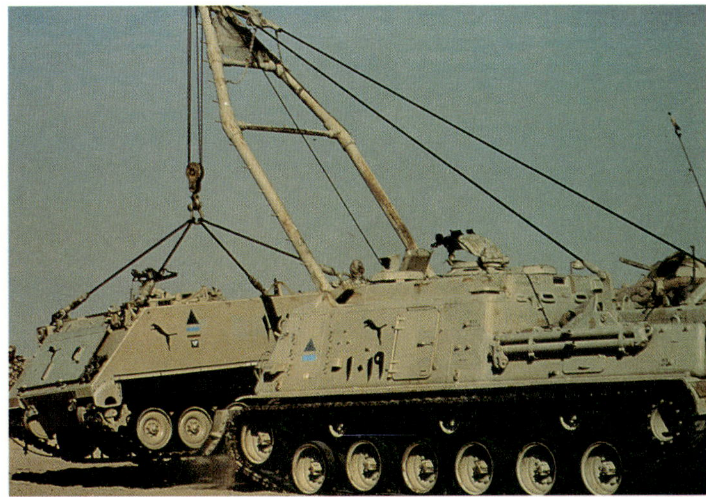

An Egyptian M88 armored recovery vehicle lifting an M113A2. Note the black puma marking. This unit was the spearhead of the Egyptian's assault into Kuwait. (DoD)

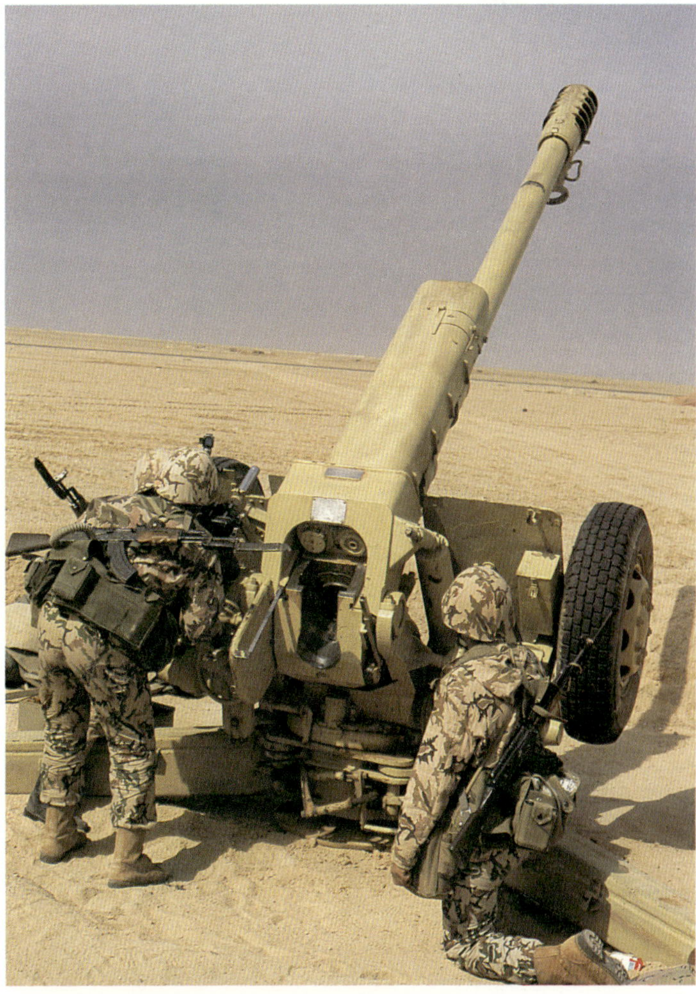

The Soviet-built D-30 122mm howitzer can be recognized by its unique three-trail carriage, the conspicuous box-like shield for recoil-recuperator mechanism mounted above the gun tube, the multi-baffle muzzle brake, and the small protective shield fitted between the wheels. This D-30 belongs to the Egyptian 4th Armored Division deployed near Al Ruky.

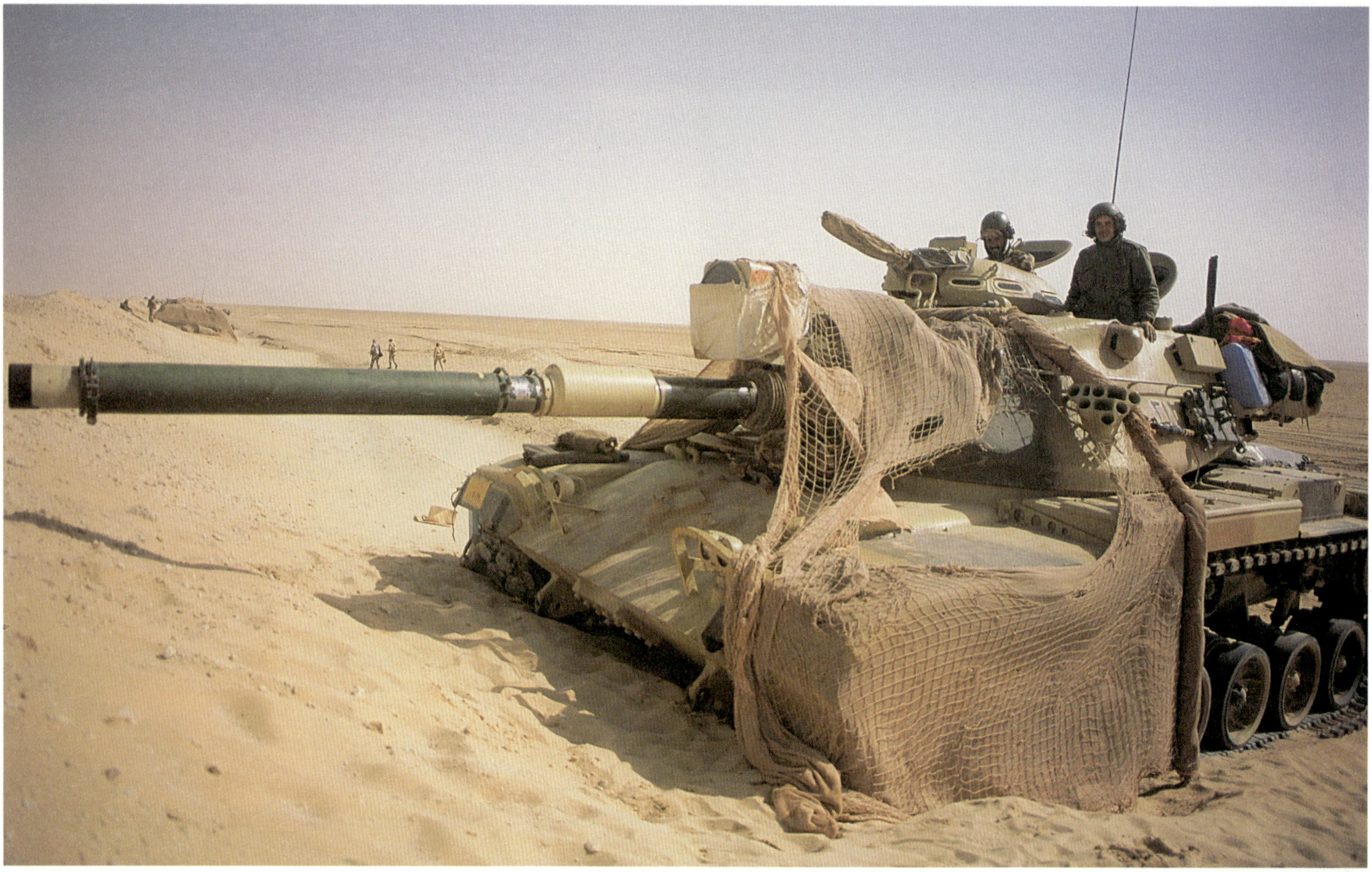

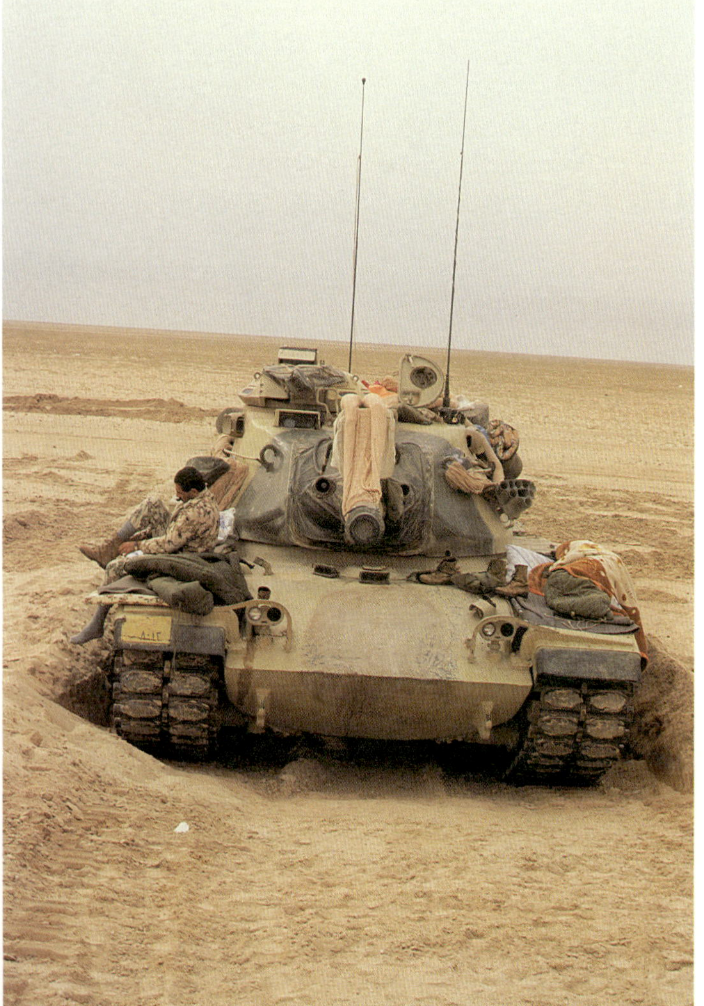

The Egyptian Army has a fleet of American-built M60A3 tanks totaling about 753 vehicles. These tanks were provided at no cost by the U.S. Government because of the poor condition they were in.

An M60A3 of the Egyptian 3rd Mechanized Division entrenched on the sand berms which marked the border between Kuwait and Saudi Arabia.

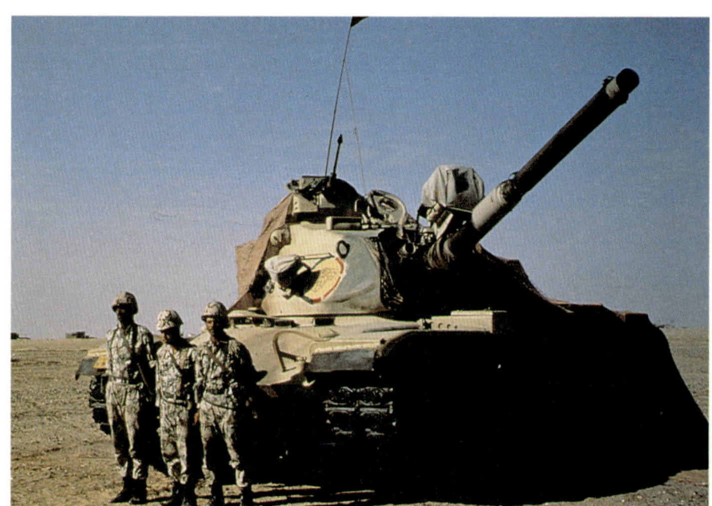

The M60A3 tank is basically a product-improved M60A1 tank with an add-on stabilization system, product-improved engine, and an updated fire-control system. The M60A3 has a crew of four and is armed with a 105mm gun. (DoD)

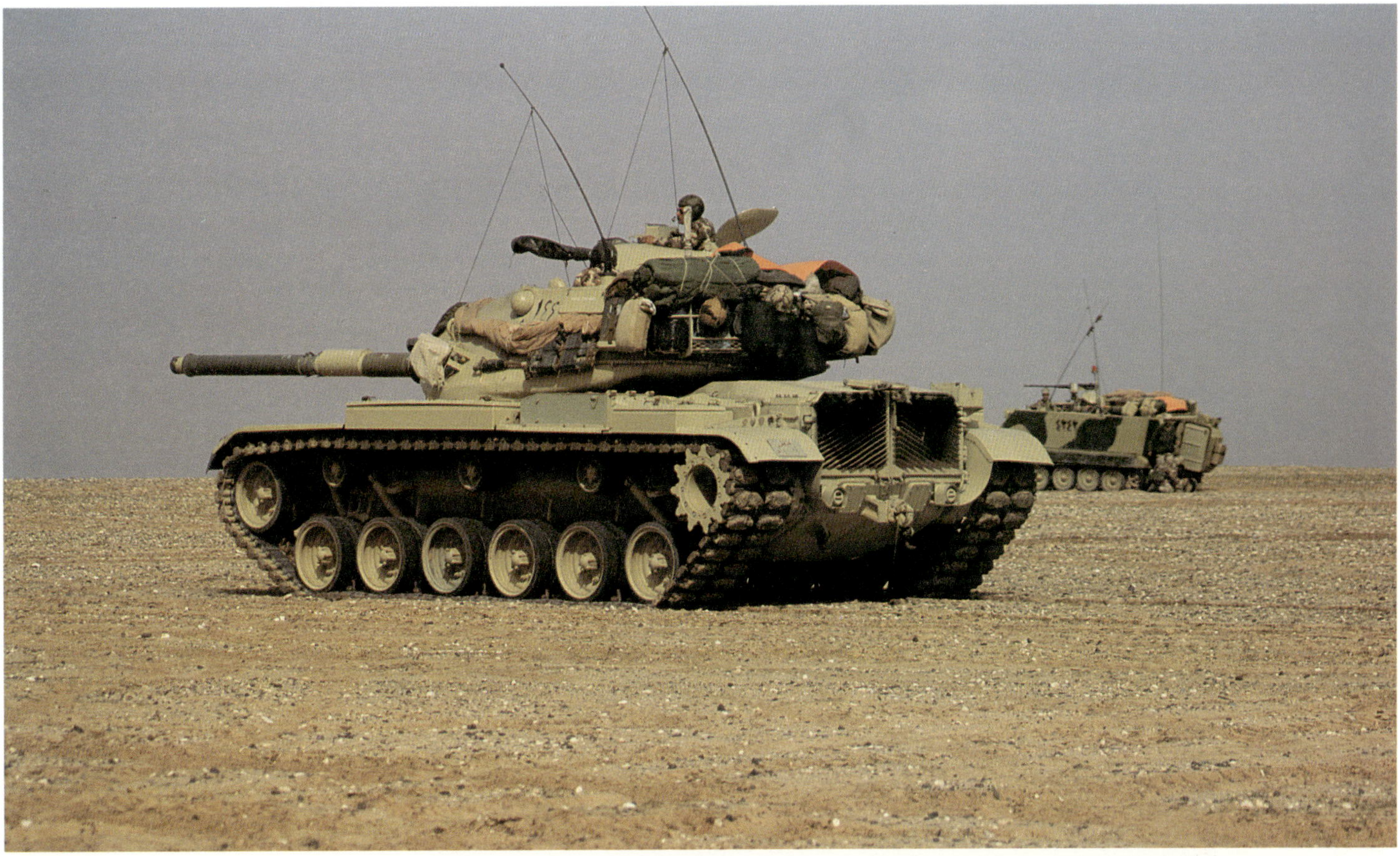

▲ The M60A3 tanks used by the Egyptian Army carry 63 rounds of ammunition. The M60A3 tank is of older generation, and the Egyptian Army is building a tank plant to make license-built copies of the American M1A1 tank. Shown is an M60A3 of the 4th Armored Division near Al Ruky.

▼▶ Egyptian Army M109A2 155mm self-propelled guns. The M109A2 has a crew of six, a commander, a gunner, three ammunition members and a driver. Egypt has 164 M109A2s in service. (DoD)

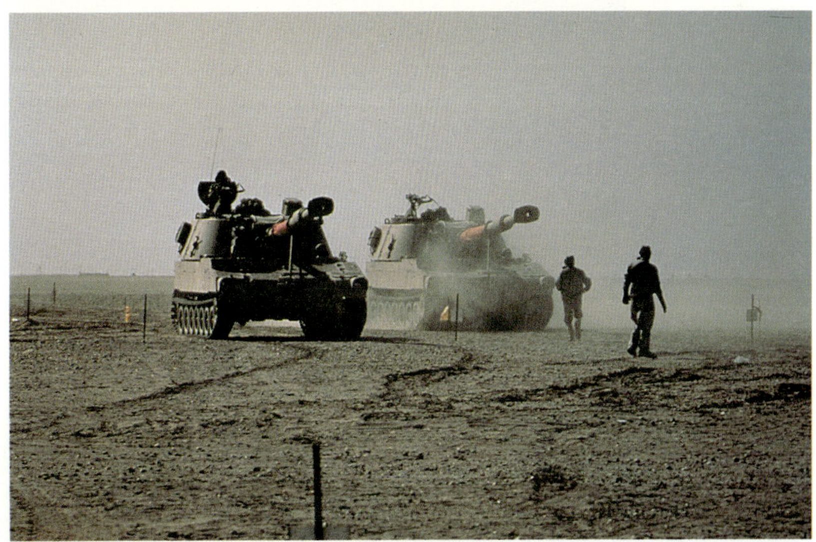

▶ Egyptian M109A2s of the 3rd Mechanized Division moving through a minefield. The Egyptian armor launched a frontal assault through fortified Iraqi positions in south-western Kuwait. (DoD)

▼ An Egyptian M60A3 with the powerpack lifted up by an M88. (DoD)

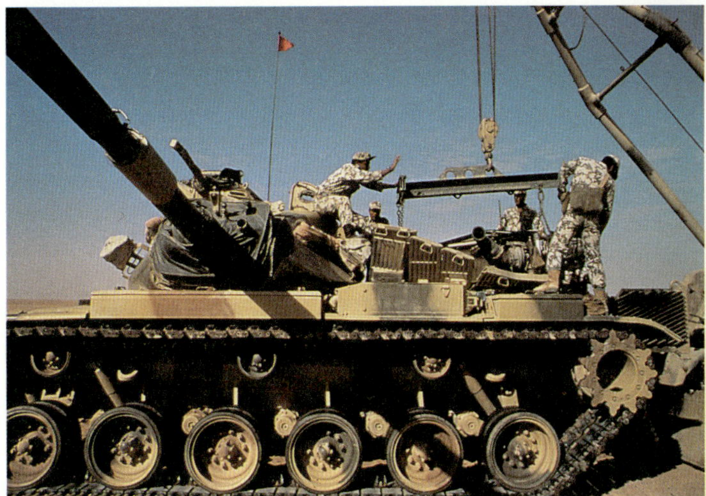

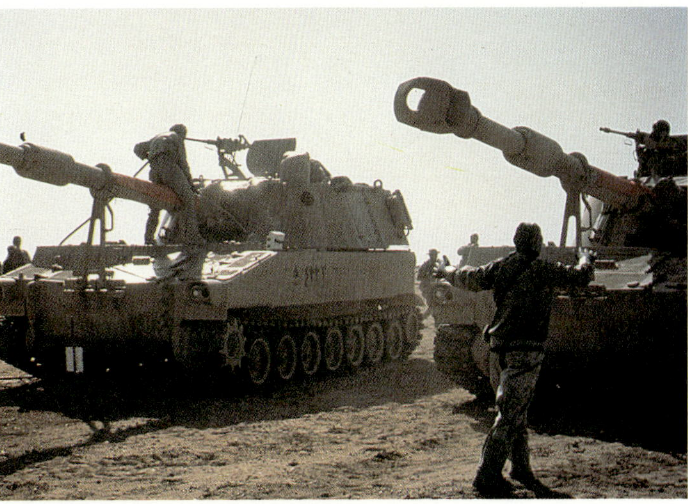

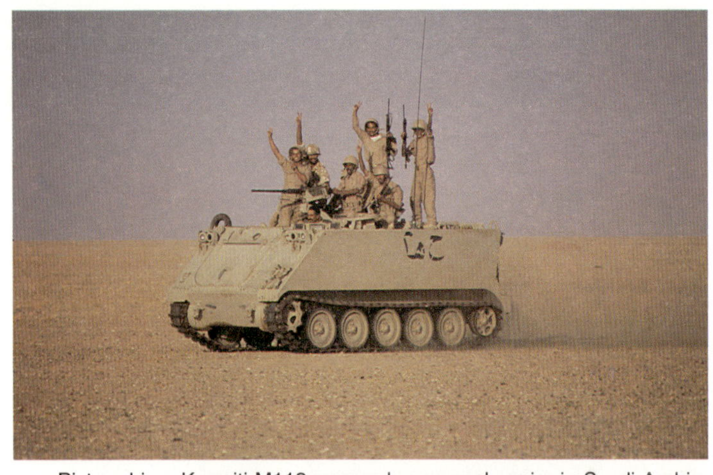

Pictured is a Kuwaiti M113 armored personnel carrier in Saudi Arabia. The Kuwaiti soldiers are apparently in high spirit.

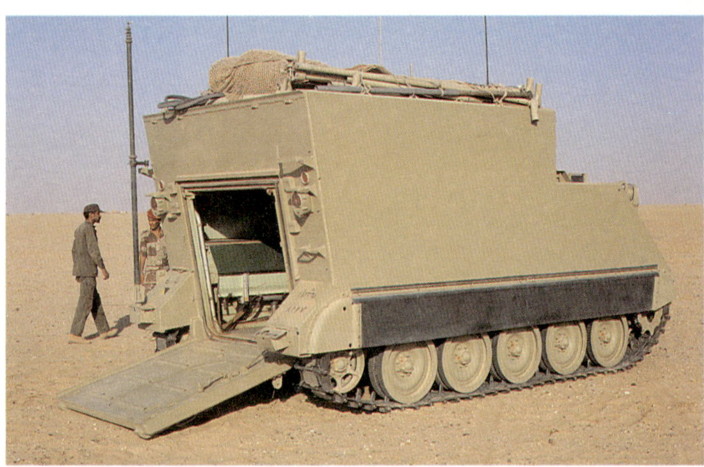

A Kuwaiti Army M577 command post vehicle.

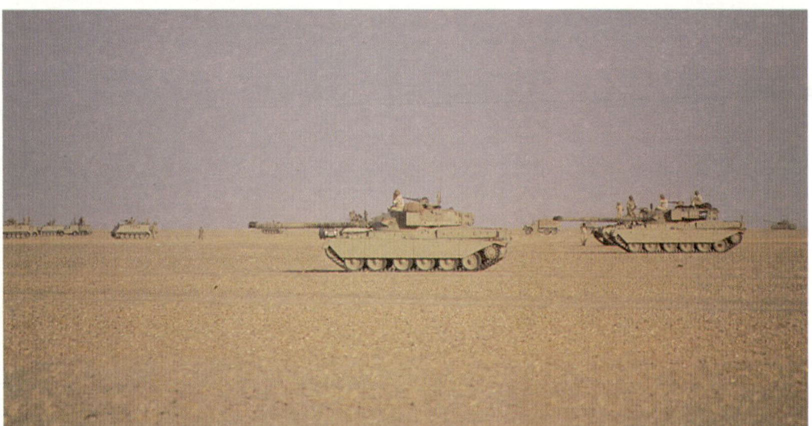

Chieftains and M113s of the Free Kuwait Brigade, in preparation to liberate their homeland.

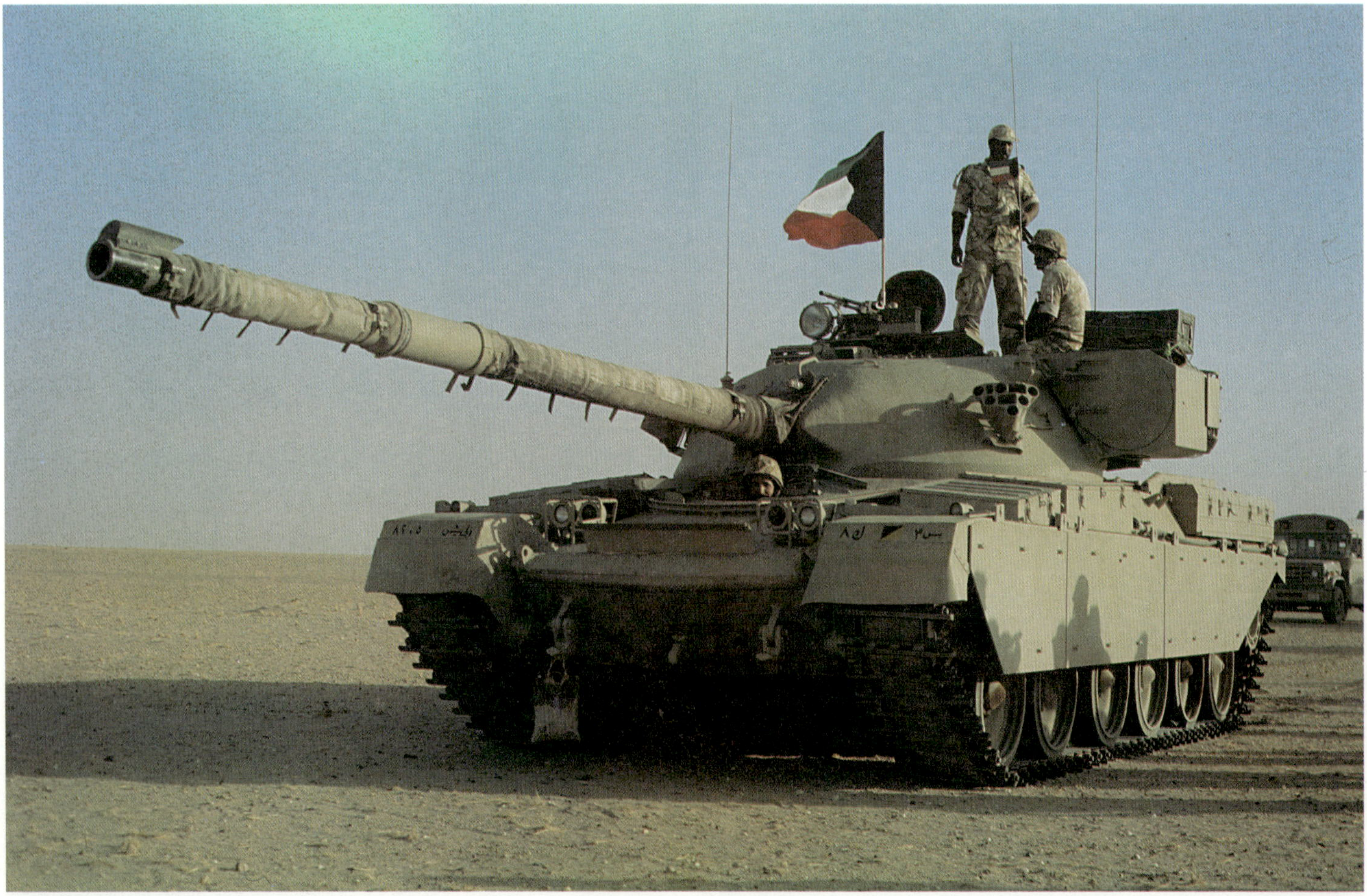

Armed with British-made Chieftain main battle tanks, the Kuwaiti Army fled to Saudi Arabia with only 22 of their 80 Chieftain tanks. Before retreating into Saudi Arabia, the Kuwaiti Chieftains did manage to destroy some Iraqi tanks, including the T-72.

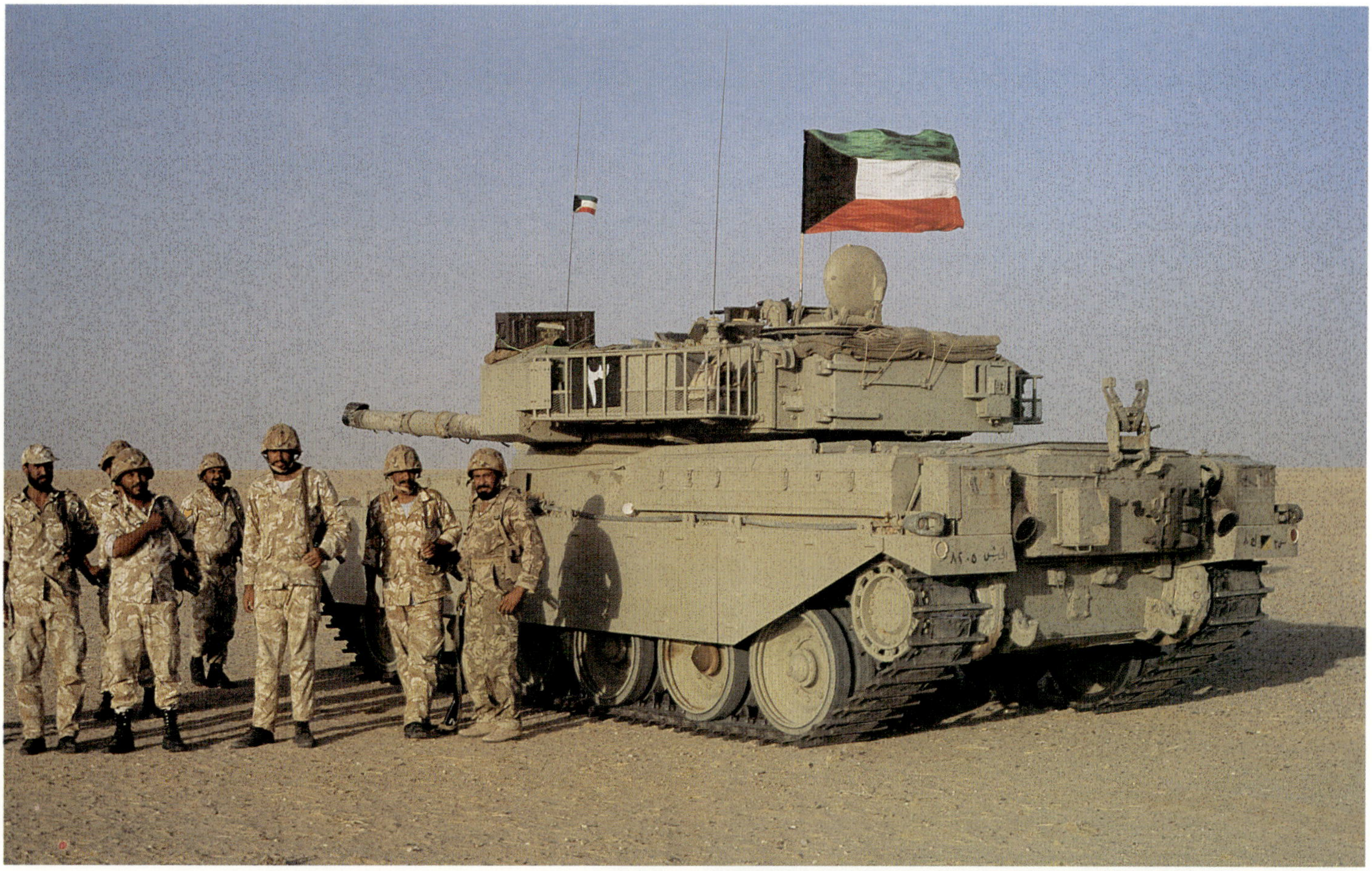

The main armament of the Chieftain tank is a 120mm gun which has a fume extractor, a muzzle reference system, and a thermal sleeve,. Pictured is a Chieftain of the Free Kuwait Brigade.

The Kuwaiti M-84 differs from the Soviet T-72 in the computerized fire control system and a mast mounted sensor on the forward part of the turret roof. Like the T-72, it is fitted with day/night vision equipment and NBC system

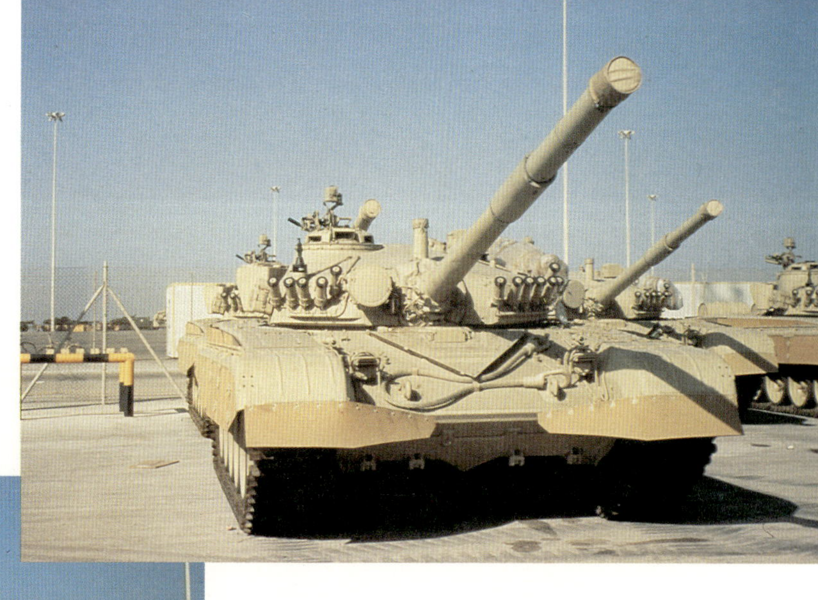

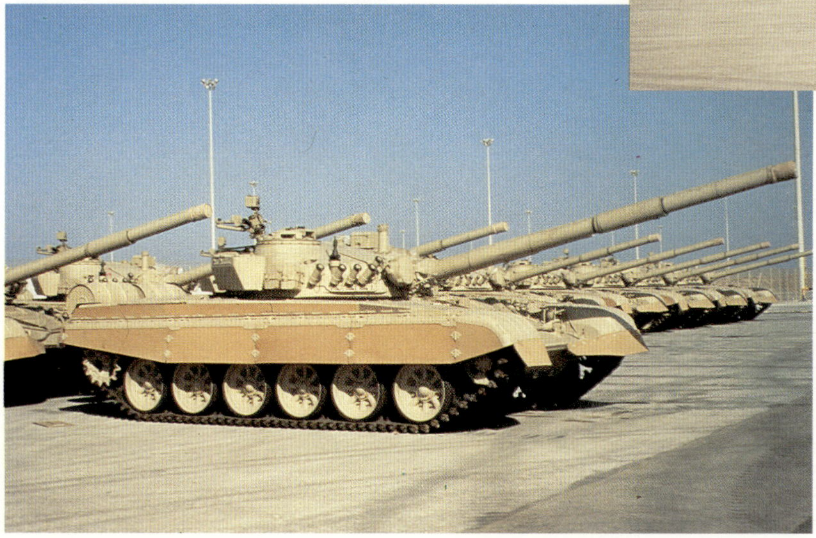

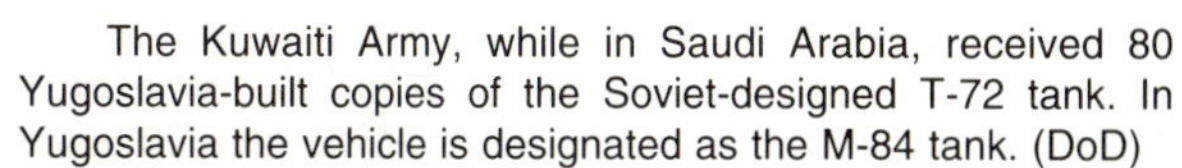

The Kuwaiti Army, while in Saudi Arabia, received 80 Yugoslavia-built copies of the Soviet-designed T-72 tank. In Yugoslavia the vehicle is designated as the M-84 tank. (DoD)

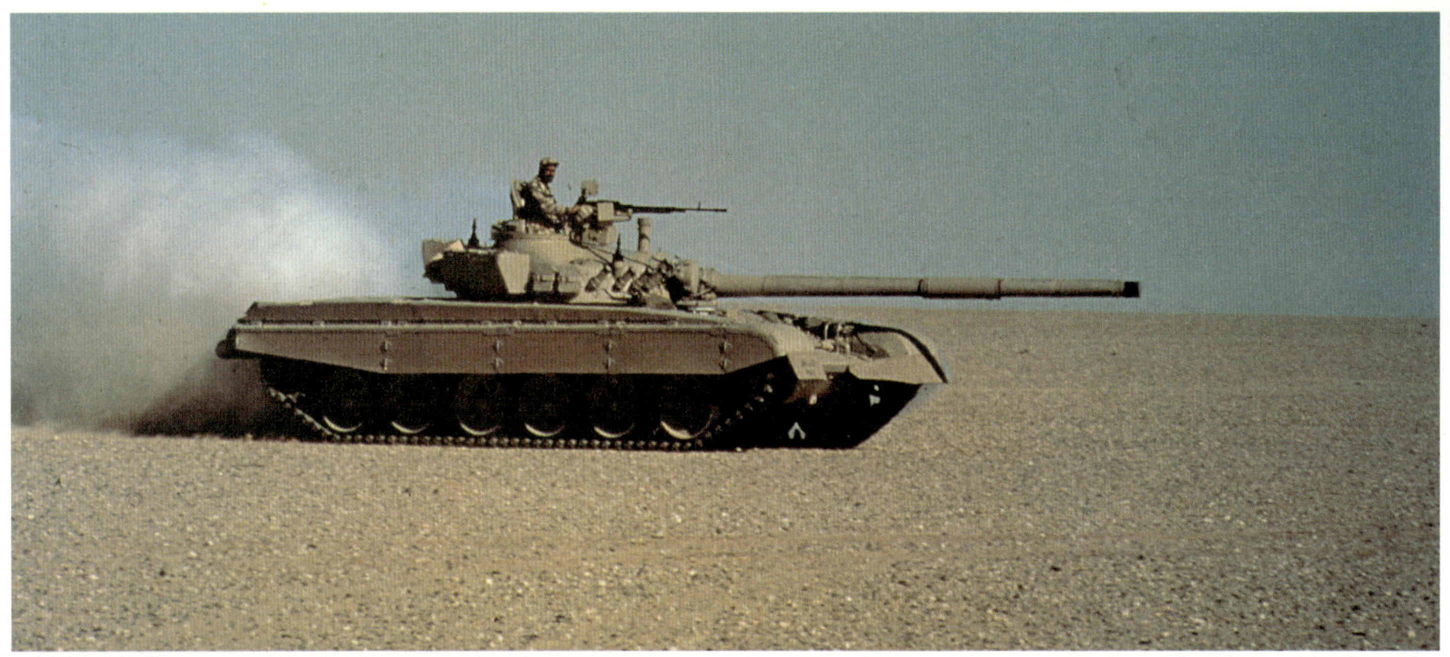

A Kuwaiti M-84 at speed. The M-84 is armed with a 125mm smoothbore gun with a 7.62mm PKT machine gun mounted coaxially. A 12.7mm NSVT machine gun is mounted on the commander's cupola for air defense. (DoD)

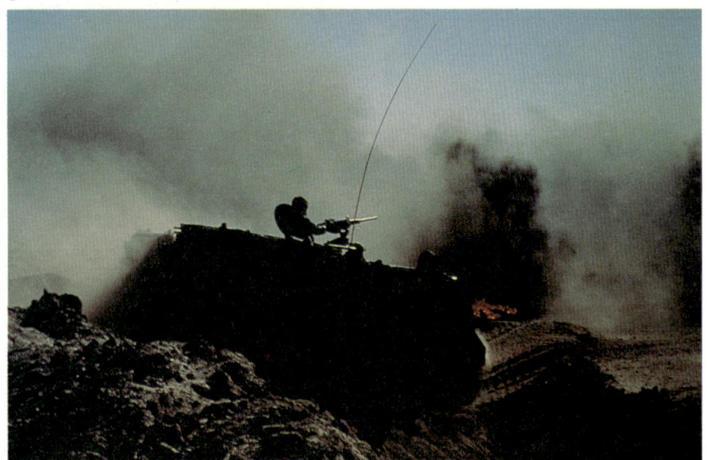

A Kuwaiti M113 crossing an anti-tank ditch built by the Iraqis. Little resistance was met during the drive into Kuwait. (DoD)

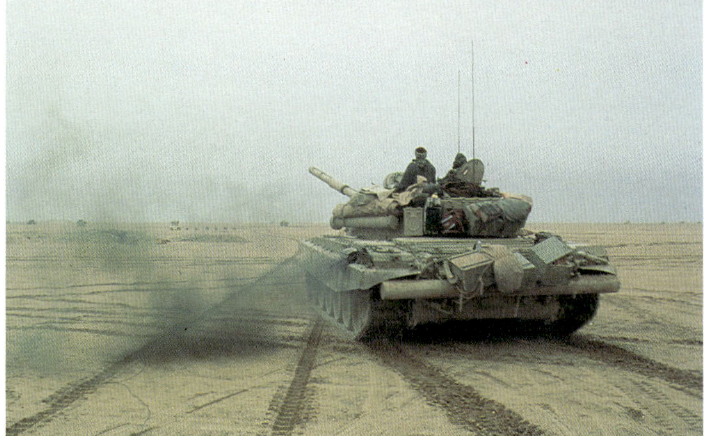

M-84 of the Free Kuwait Brigade on its way to liberate its homeland.(DoD)

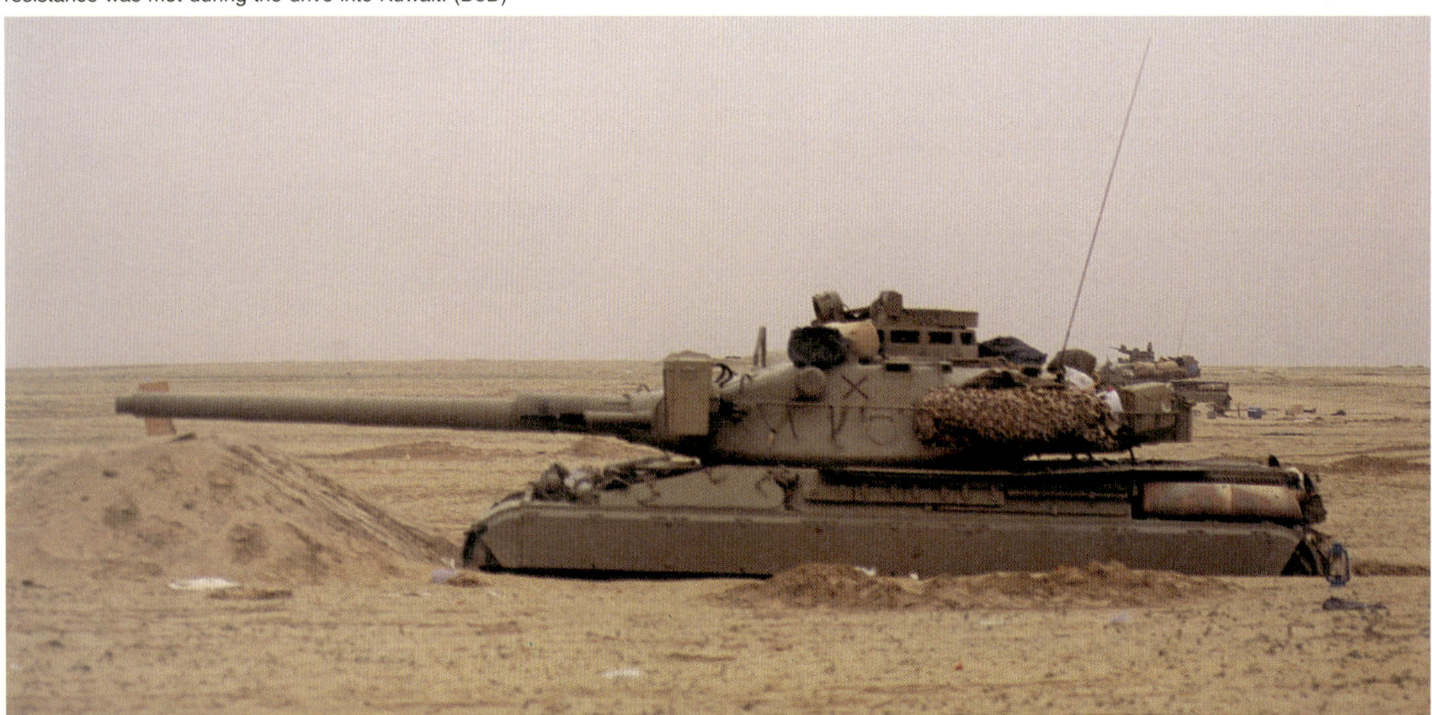

A Qatari Army AMX-30 tank stuck in a ditch south of the Saudi town Khafji, four days before the Battle of Khafji began.

IRAQI ARMOR IN DEFEAT

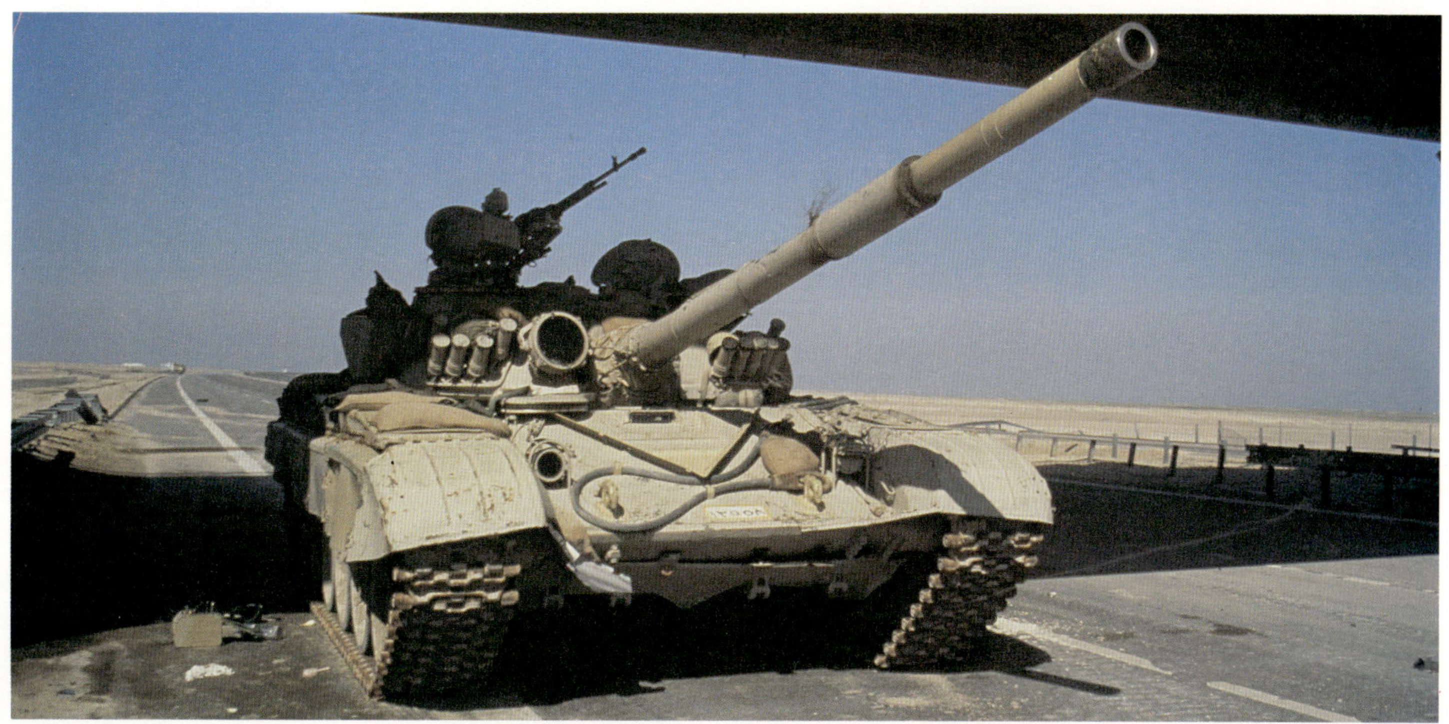

In the morning hours of August 2, 1990 the Iraqi military began a combined arms, multi-service invasion of the small country of Kuwait. The attack was spear-headed by the Republican Guard, which took only 10 hours to cover the distance from the Iraqi border to Kuwait City. The Republican Guard consisted of eight divisions (120,000 men) of the most loyal troops in the Iraqi Army. Armed with the best equipment, the Republican Guard had been battle-tested in the eight year war with Iran, which ended in a stalemate in 1988.

The Iraqi military machine consisted of about 1 million men. Raised by conscription, every young Iraqi has to serve his time. Prior to the invasion of Kuwait, the Iraqi Army was organized into seven corps with 7 armored/mechanized divisions, 40 infantry divisions and 20 commando brigades; plus the Republican Guard's 3 armored/mechanized divisions, 4 infantry divisions, and 1 special forces division. Shortly after the "Operation Desert Shield" build-up, the Iraqi Army formed a number of new divisions and corps made up of reserve formations. According to a number of sources, the Iraqi Army had around 4,280 tanks before the Gulf War broke out. While the number of tanks is impressive on paper, most of Iraq's tank fleet consisted of older generation Soviet-built tanks such as T-54/T-55s, T-62s, and Chinese-built Type T-59/T-69s. The Iraqis had modified a number of their Soviet-designed and built T-55 tanks with very thick multi-layer add-on armor kits. They had even modified a few of their T-55s with a 125mm gun.

The most modern tank in Iraqi Army service were around 500 Soviet-designed T-72 tanks armed with a 125mm gun. The Iraqis had both exported version from the Soviet Union and the Warsaw Pact countries of Poland and Czechoslovakia. They had also in service a small number of T-72M tanks nicknamed the "Lion of Babylon". These vehicles were assembled in Iraq using both Soviet and Iraqi components.

Iraq's mechanized infantry and tank units also fielded a fleet of 2,870 armored personnel carriers. Most of them were older generation Soviet and Warsaw Pact built vehicles, such as BTR-50/60/152, MT-LB and OT-62/64. The newer BMP-1s and BMP-2s would mainly be found in the Republican Guard units. The most visible armored personnel carriers seen in the early stages of the war were the Chinese-made YW531 vehicles. A large number of these vehicles were destroyed or abandoned during the battle over the Saudi town of Khafji.

Backing up this large inventory of armored personnel carriers were a number of Brazilian made EE-11 armored cars and various types of armored vehicles.

While the Iraqi military was feared because of its large number of artillery pieces, only 500 were self-propelled guns and 200 were multiple rocket launchers; the rest 2,400 pieces being towed guns.

Due to the air supremacy of the coalition forces, the entreched Iraqi tanks and armored vehicles were sitting ducks for the allied anti-tank helicopters and planes. While large numbers of Iraqi tanks and armored vehicles were being destroyed by allied air power, many were simply abandoned by their demoralized crew. Though a few put up a fight, they were no match against the firepower of the allied tanks. A rough estimate put Iraq's losses at 3,700 tanks, 2,400 armored vehicles and 2,600 artillery pieces destroyed.

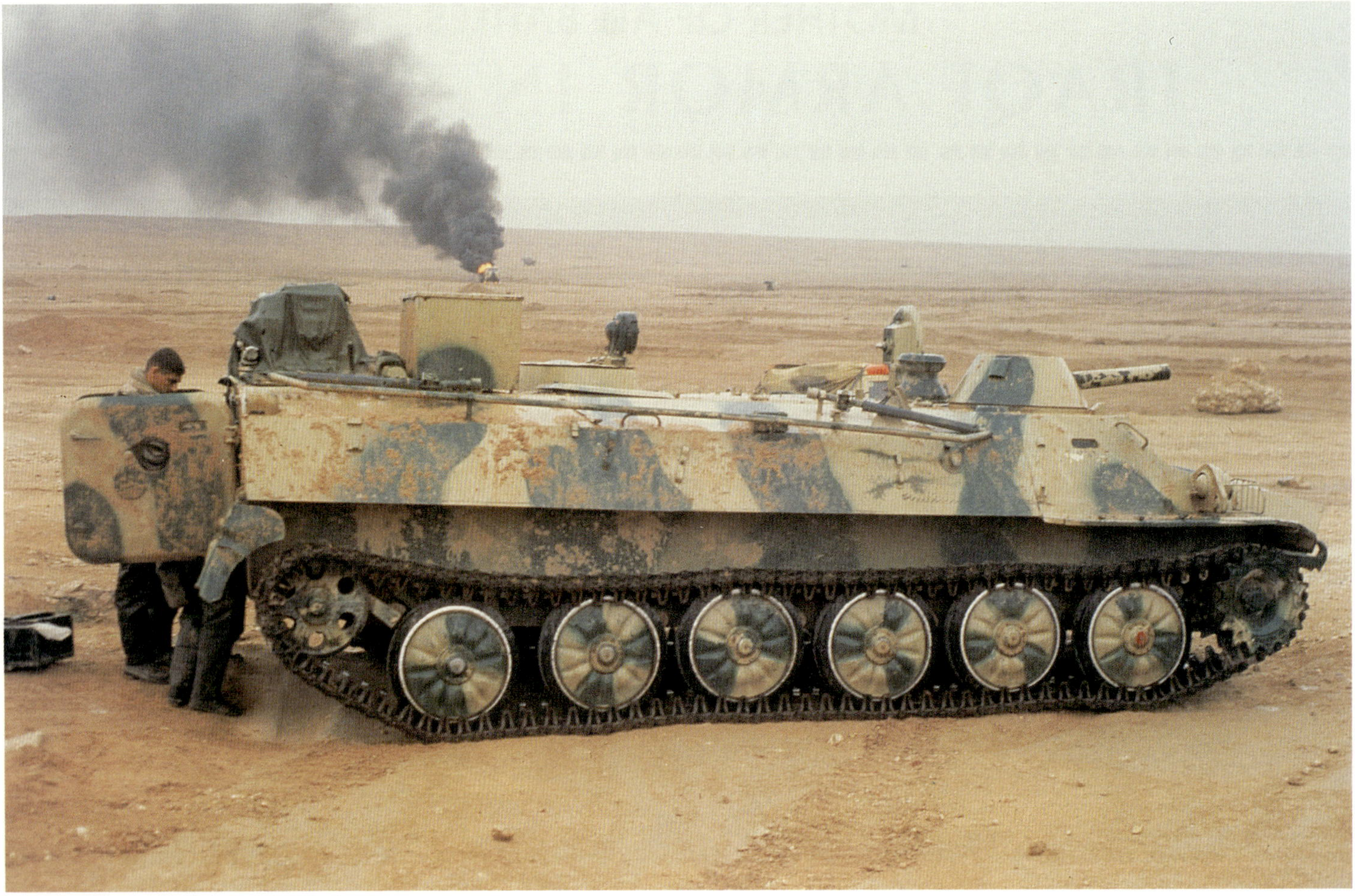

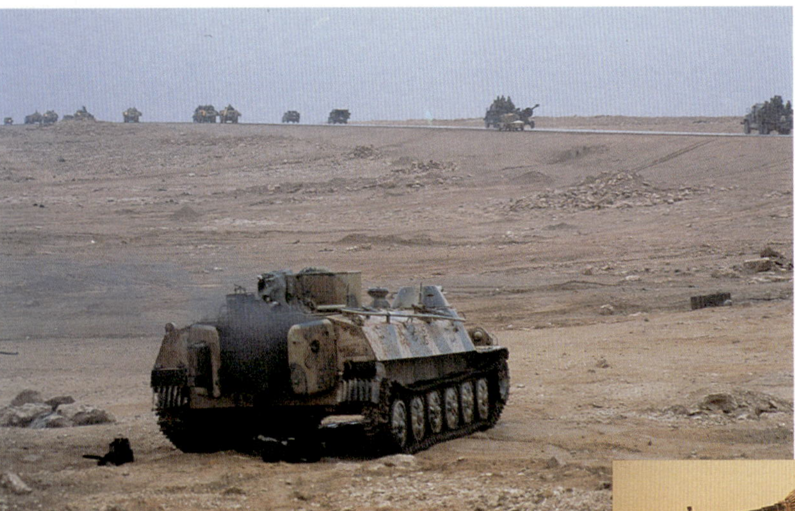

A destroyed Iraqi MT-LB being examined by French soldiers. A large number of these multi-purpose tracked vehicles were in service with the Iraqi Army.

An Iraqi MT-LB of the 45th Infantry Division destroyed by the French south of Al Salman. In the background can be seen the VABs and HMMWVs and towed artillery of U.S. XVIII Airborne Corps.

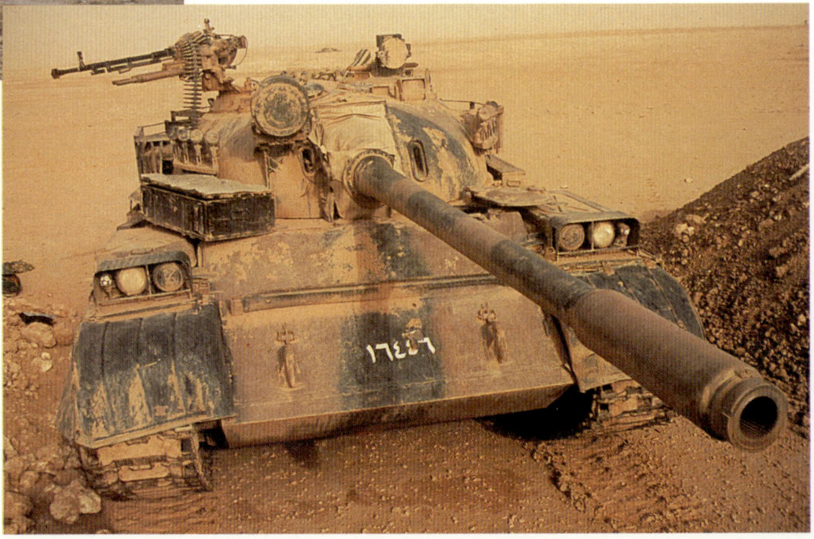

A Type 69 Chinese-built tank of the 45th Infantry Division captured intact by the French forces.

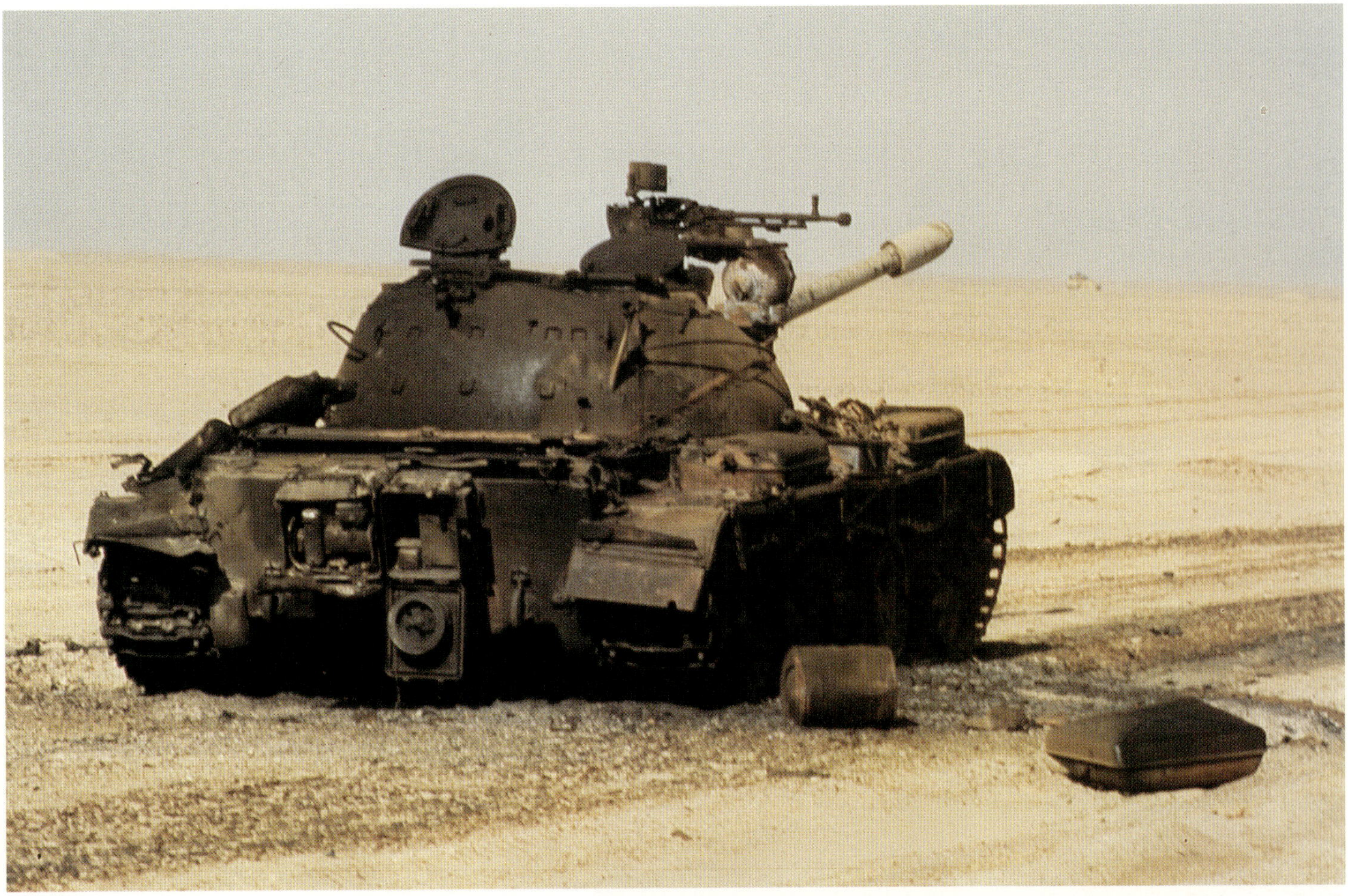

A knocked out Iraqi T-54/T-55 tank sitting still in the desert. Iraq had plenty of T-54s and T-55s in different variants. (DoD)

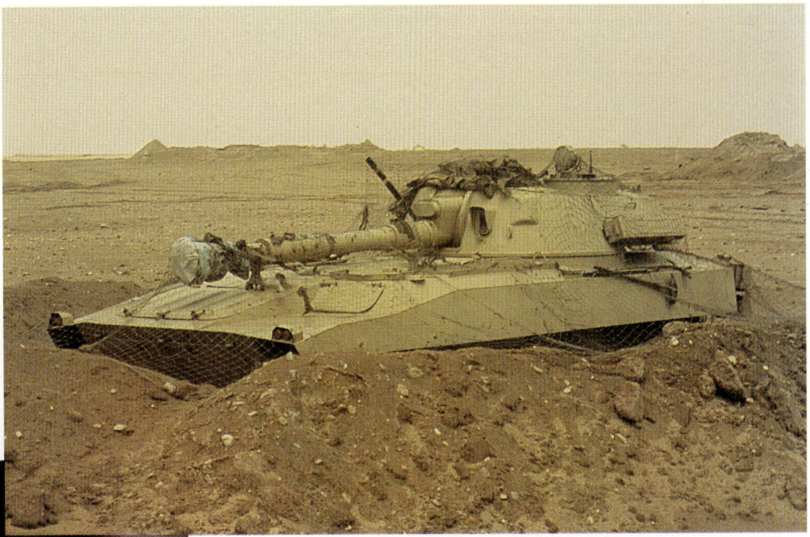

An abandoned 2S1 122mm self-propelled gun, also known as SO-122 or Gvozdika (Carnation). The 122mm gun is a modified version of the D-30 towed howitzer.

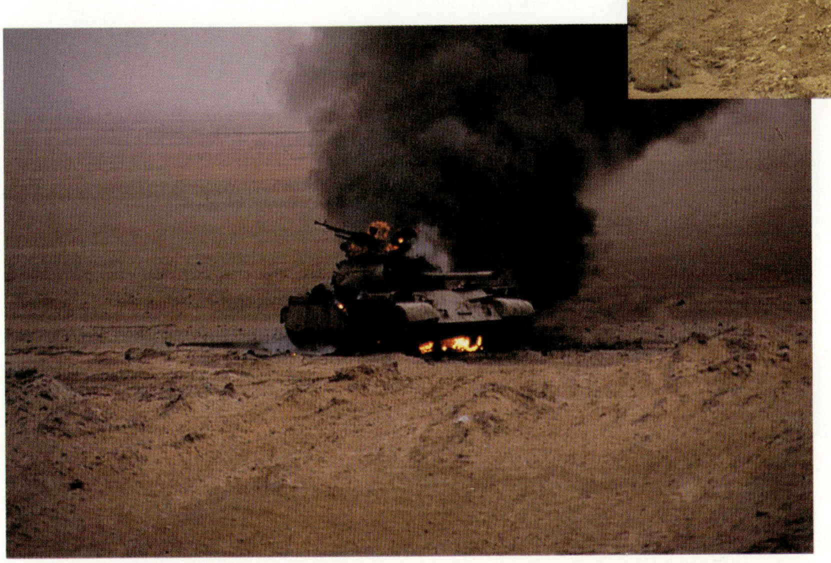

A burning Iraqi Type 69 tank. Iraq had a substantial quantity of the Chinese built Type 69-I and Type 69-II tanks. The Type 69-I is armed with a 100mm smoothbore gun while the Type 69-II is fitted with a 100mm rifled gun. The majority of Iraqi Type 69 tanks were the -II version.(DoD)

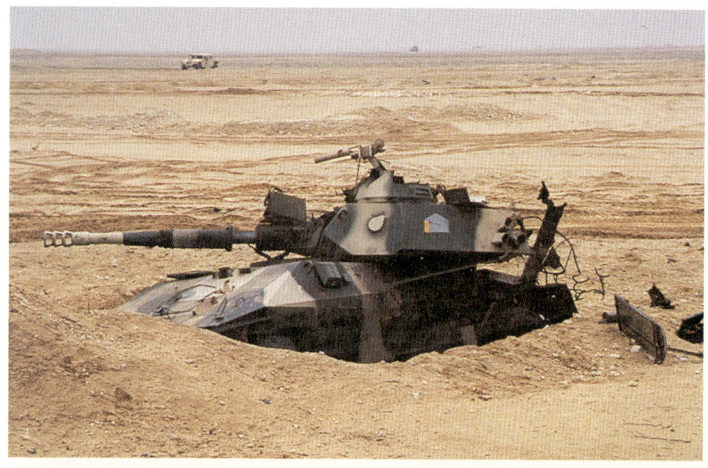

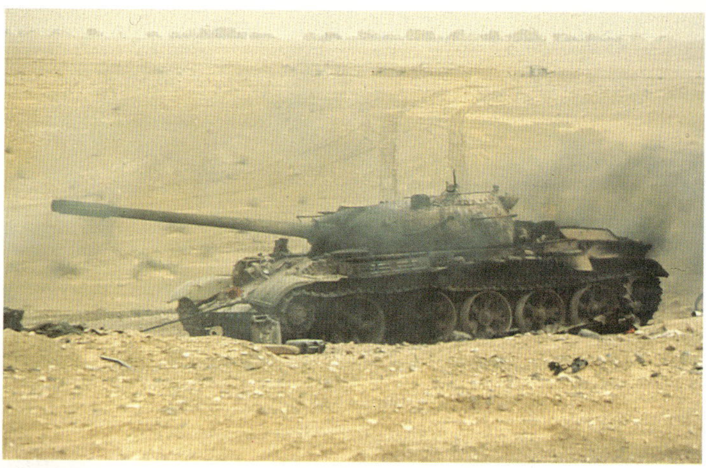

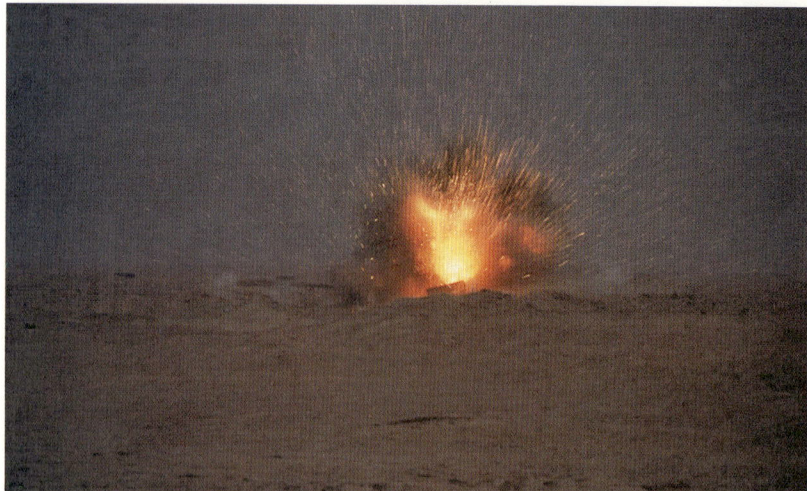

◄▲▲ A knocked out Iraqi EE-11 Urutu armored car built by ENGESA of Brazil and fitted with a 90mm gun. (DoD)

▲ Another destroyed Iraqi T-54/T-55 tank. (DoD)

◄ A destroyed Iraqi armored vehicle being blown up by the American sappers.(DoD)

▼ A British FV432 passes by an Iraqi BRDM-2 armored car with tyres still burning. This BRDM-2 variant was fitted with Sagger ATGW missiles. (DoD)

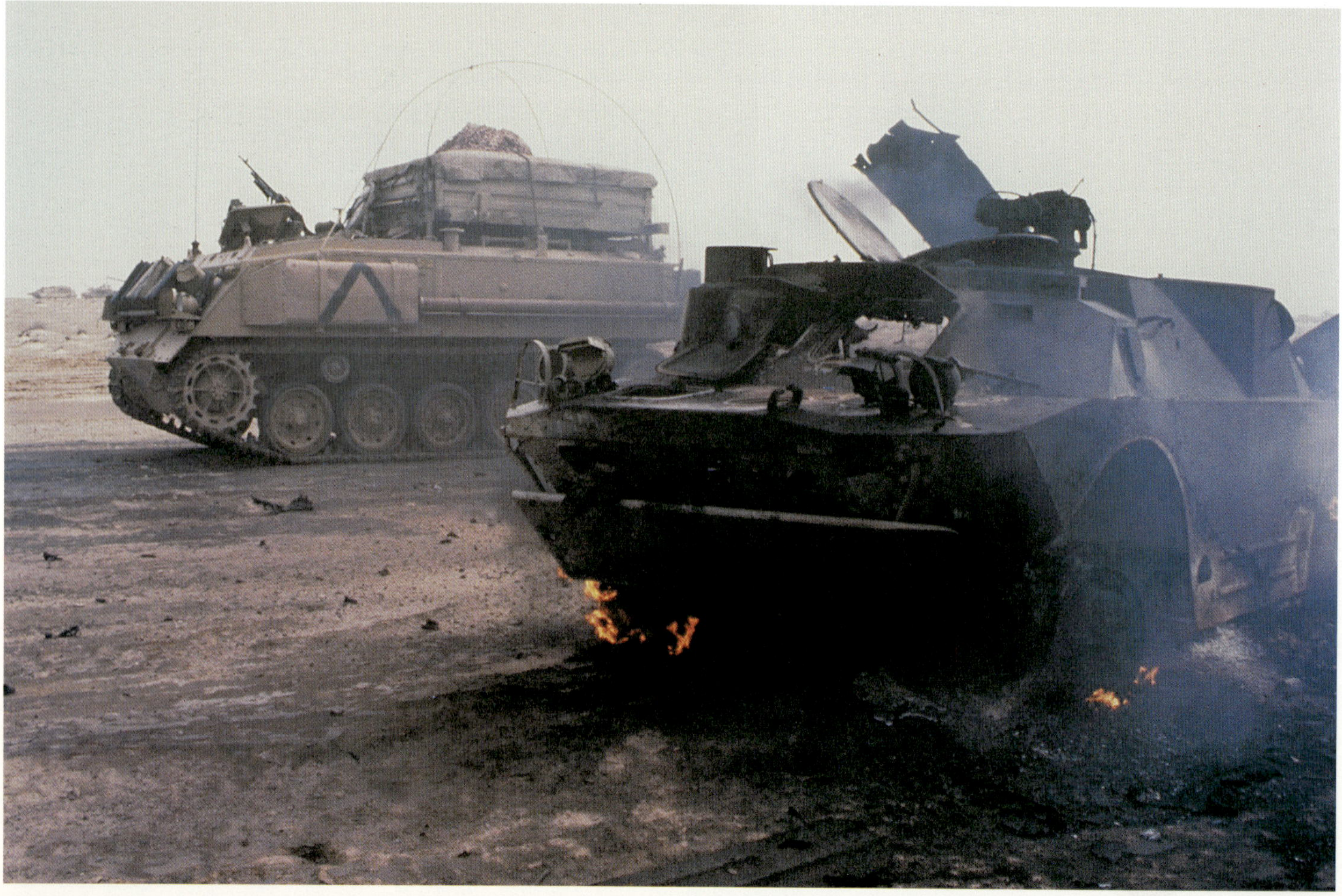

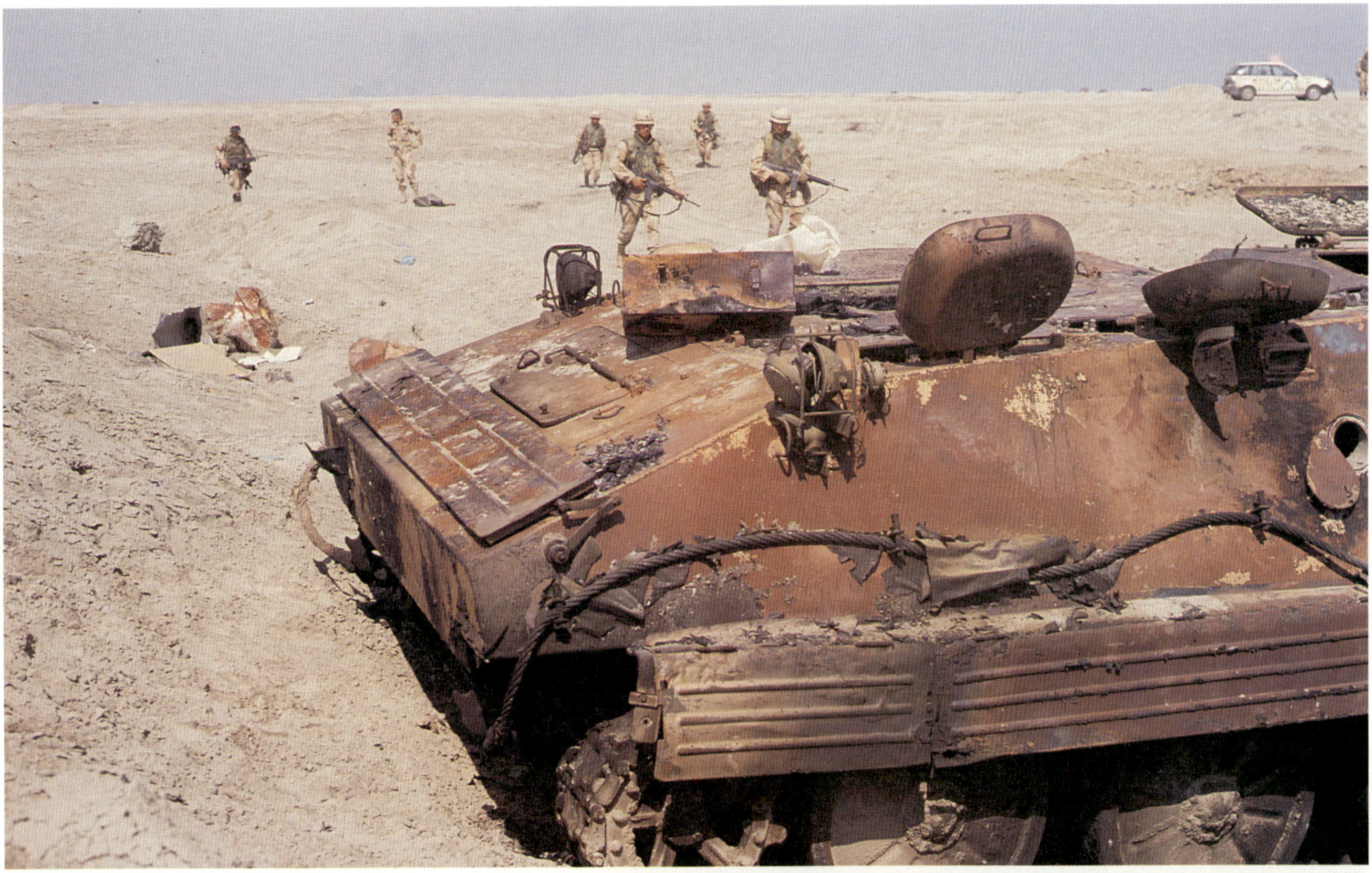

Paratroopers of the U.S. 82nd Airborne advancing cautiously towards the charred remains of a Chinese-built YW531 armored personnel carrier near Souk al Shuhuk.

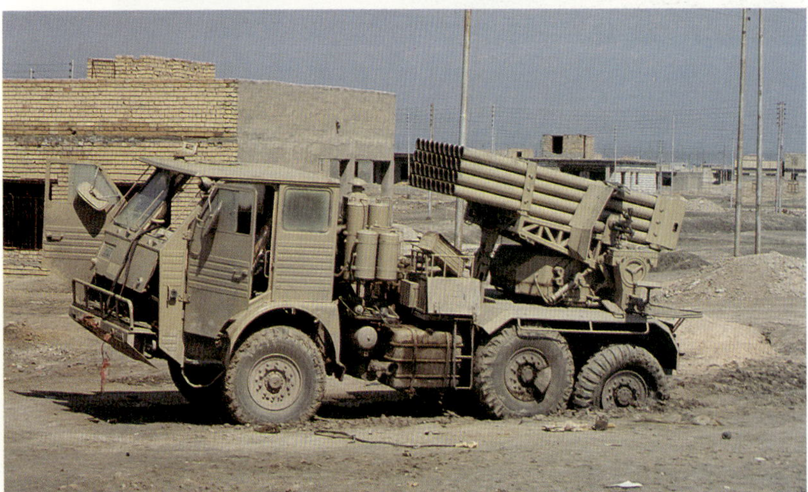

An Iraqi BM-21 multiple rocket system abandoned near the city of Souk al Shuhuk. The Iraqi soldiers often booby-trapped their abandoned vehicles.

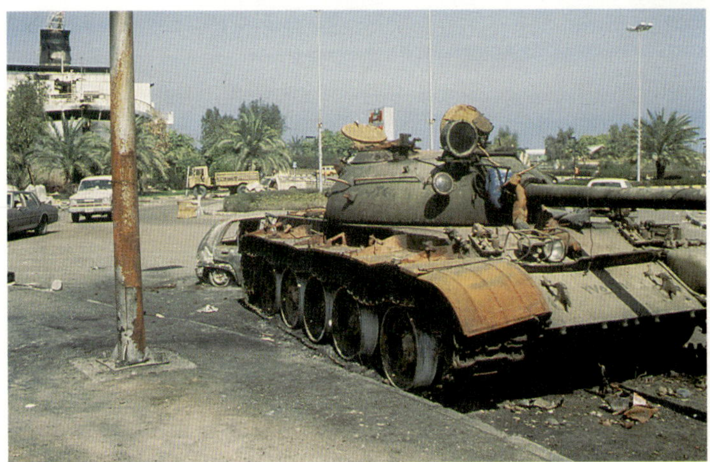

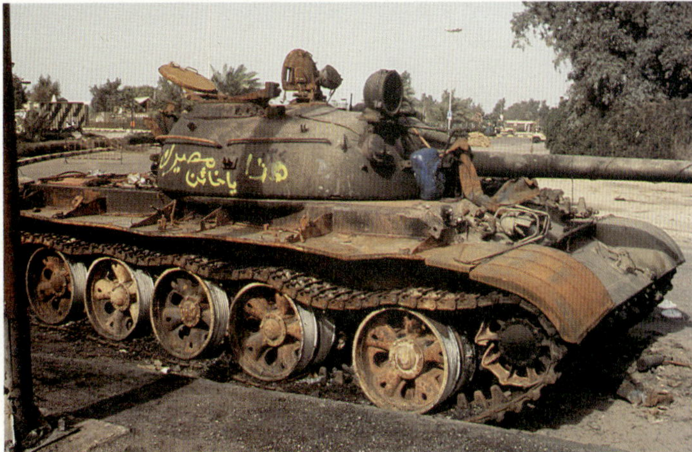

Burnt-out Iraqi T-55s can be seen everywhere. U.S. AH-64 Apache gunships and A-10 Warthog tank-killers inflicted heavy damage to the Iraqi tanks. (DoD)

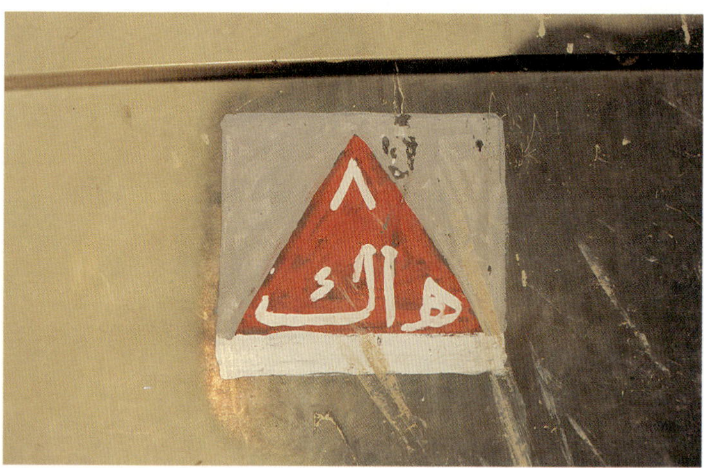

▲   The red triangle on the vehicle is the badge of the elite Republican Guard.

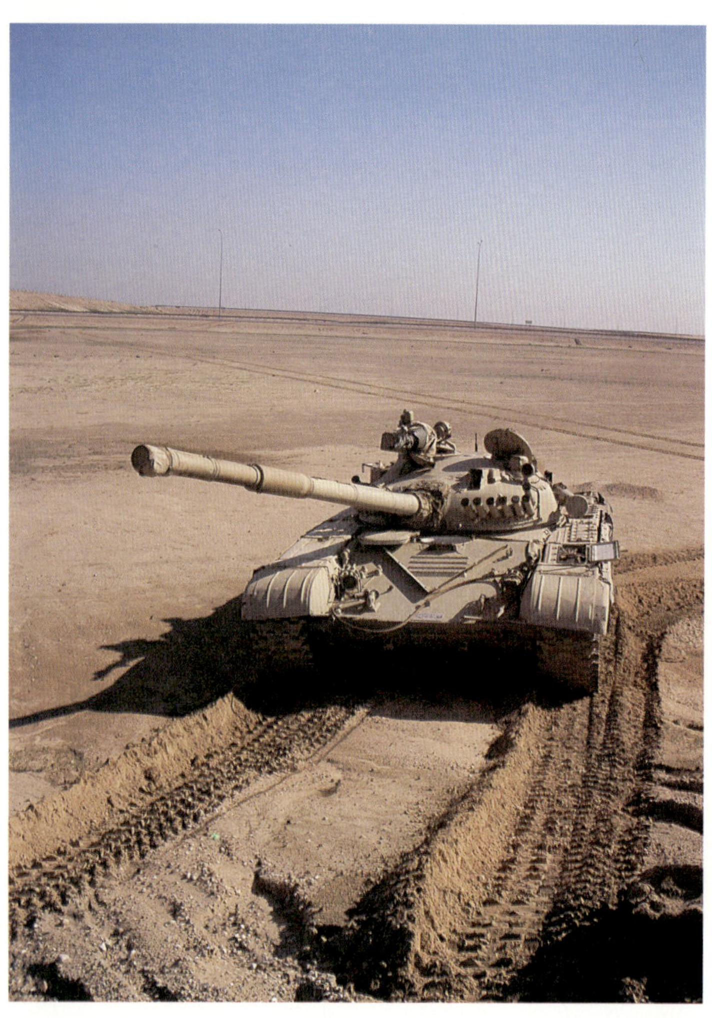

◄   An abandoned T-72 tank of the Republican Guard. The crew of this T-72 never intended to put up a fight, as the gun tube is still covered.

▼   Damaged T-55 tank litters the highway.

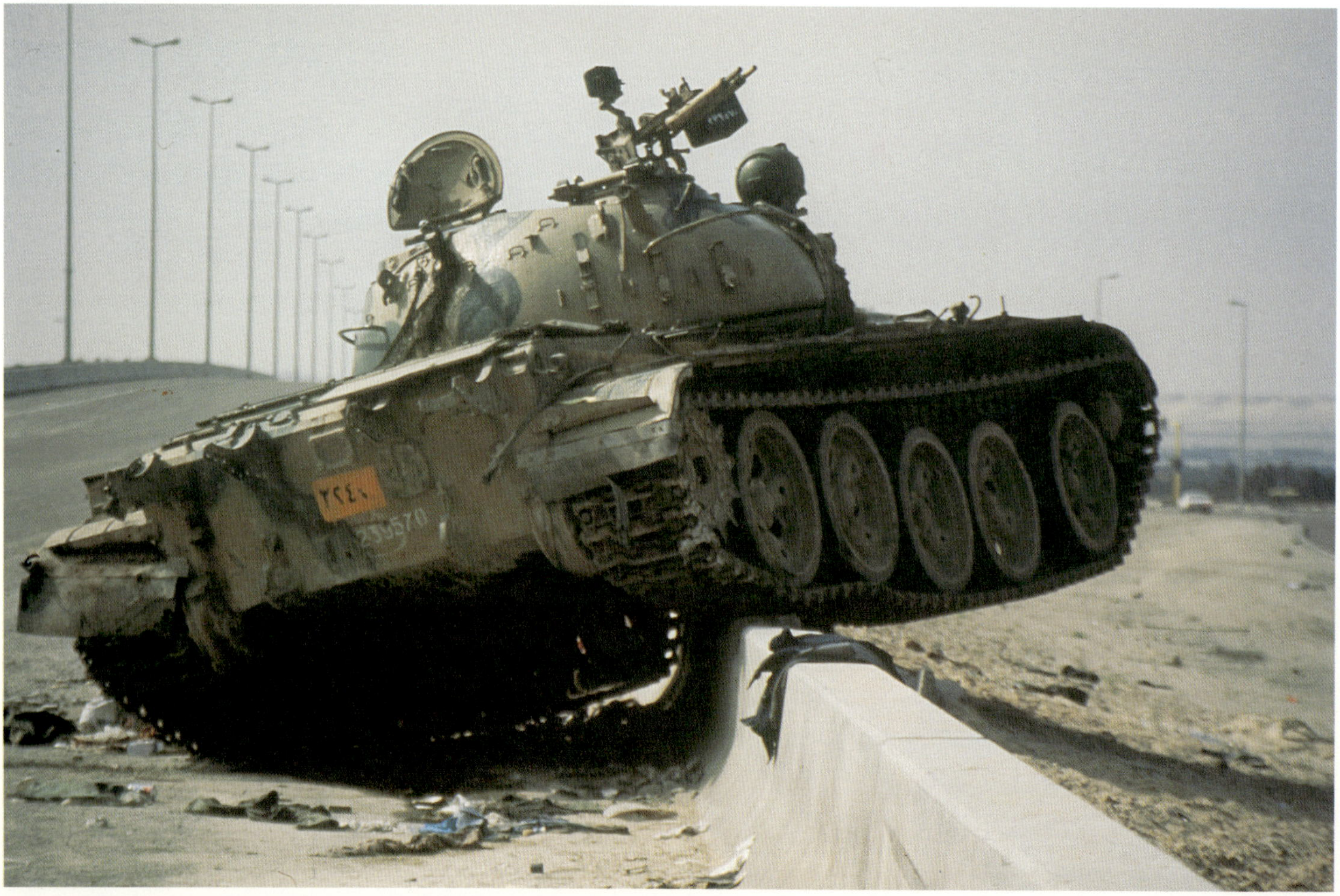

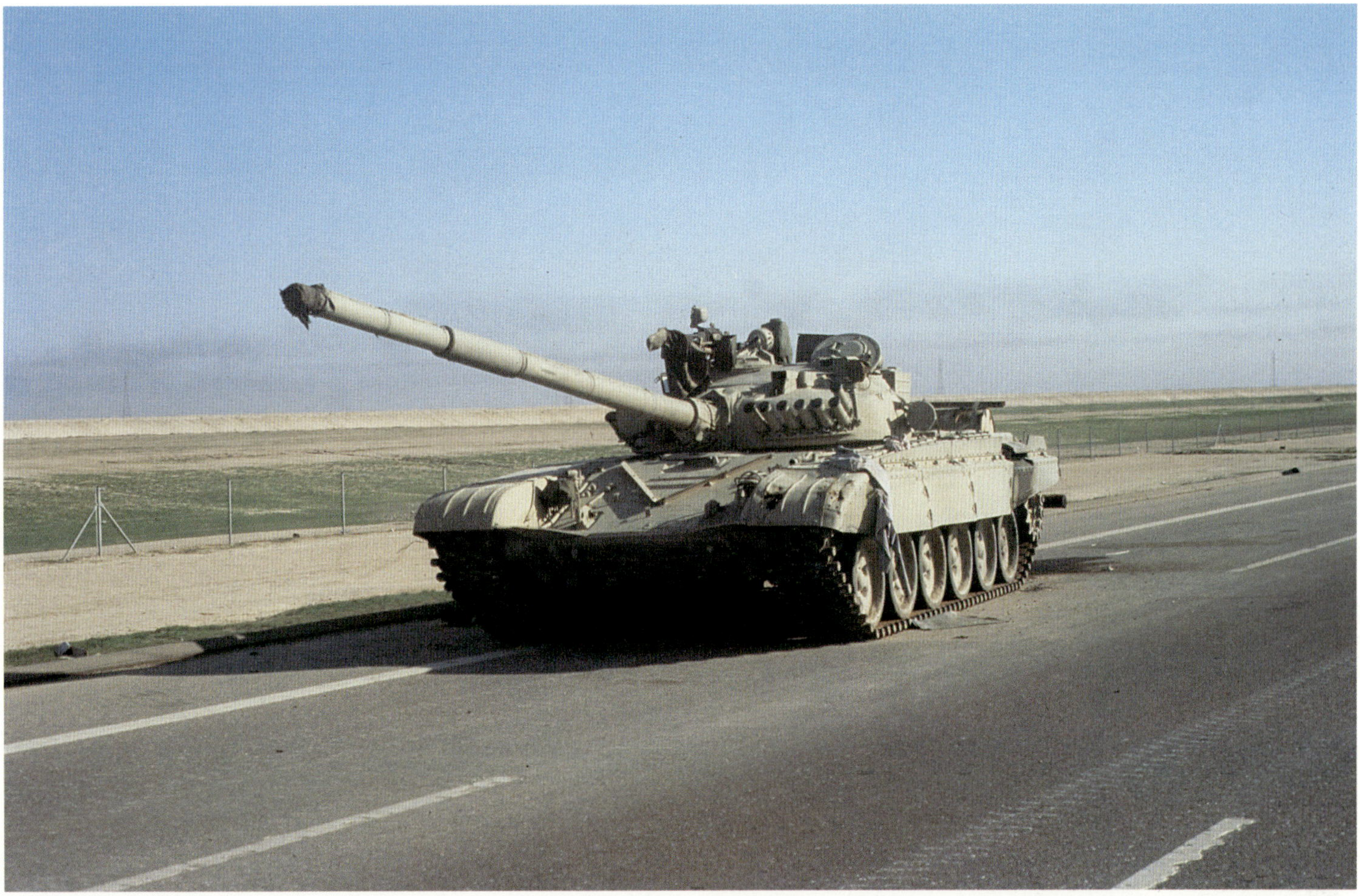

Another T-72 of the Republican Guard abandoned on the Baghdad-Basra highway. It is apparently intact, except for the green circle on the back of the turret, there is no other markings. The tank is called the "Lion of Babylon" by the Iraqi who manufactured some of the components.

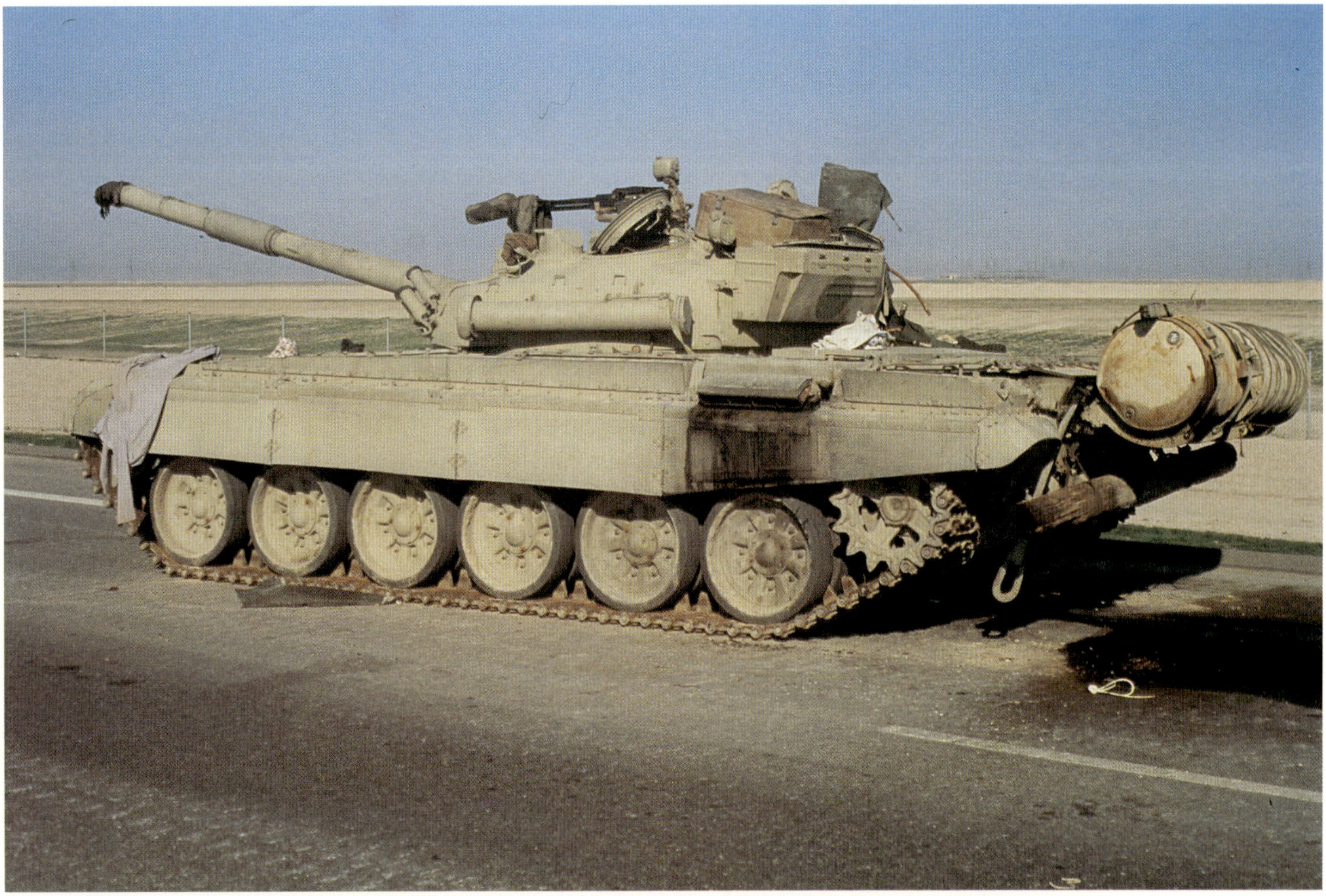

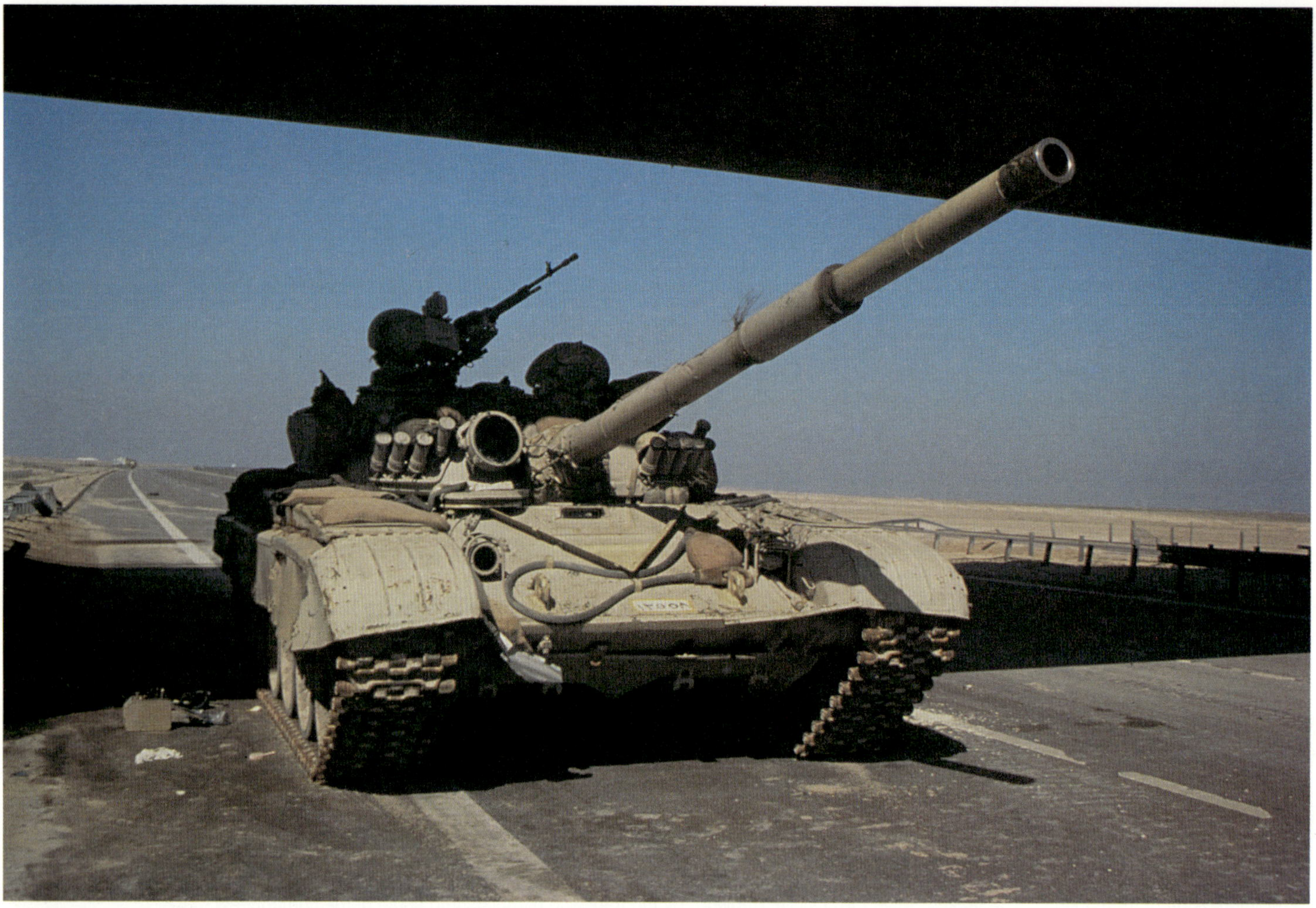

An abandoned Republican Guard T-72 on the Baghdad-Basra highway, sitting still under a bridge. This T-72 was still intact when photographed by the author.

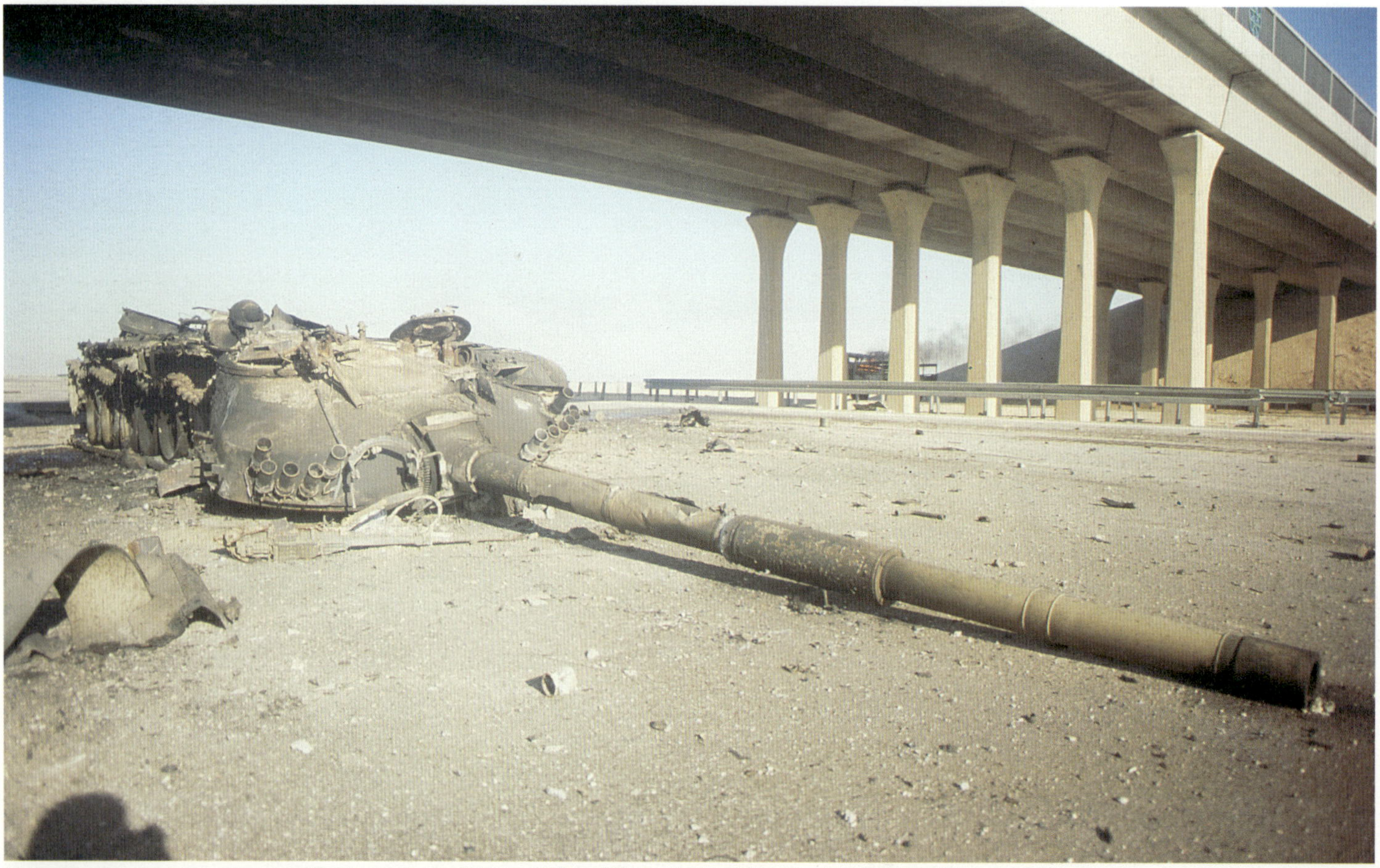

However, the next day, the same T-72 had its turret blown off by a TOW missile of the 24th Mechanized Infantry Division.

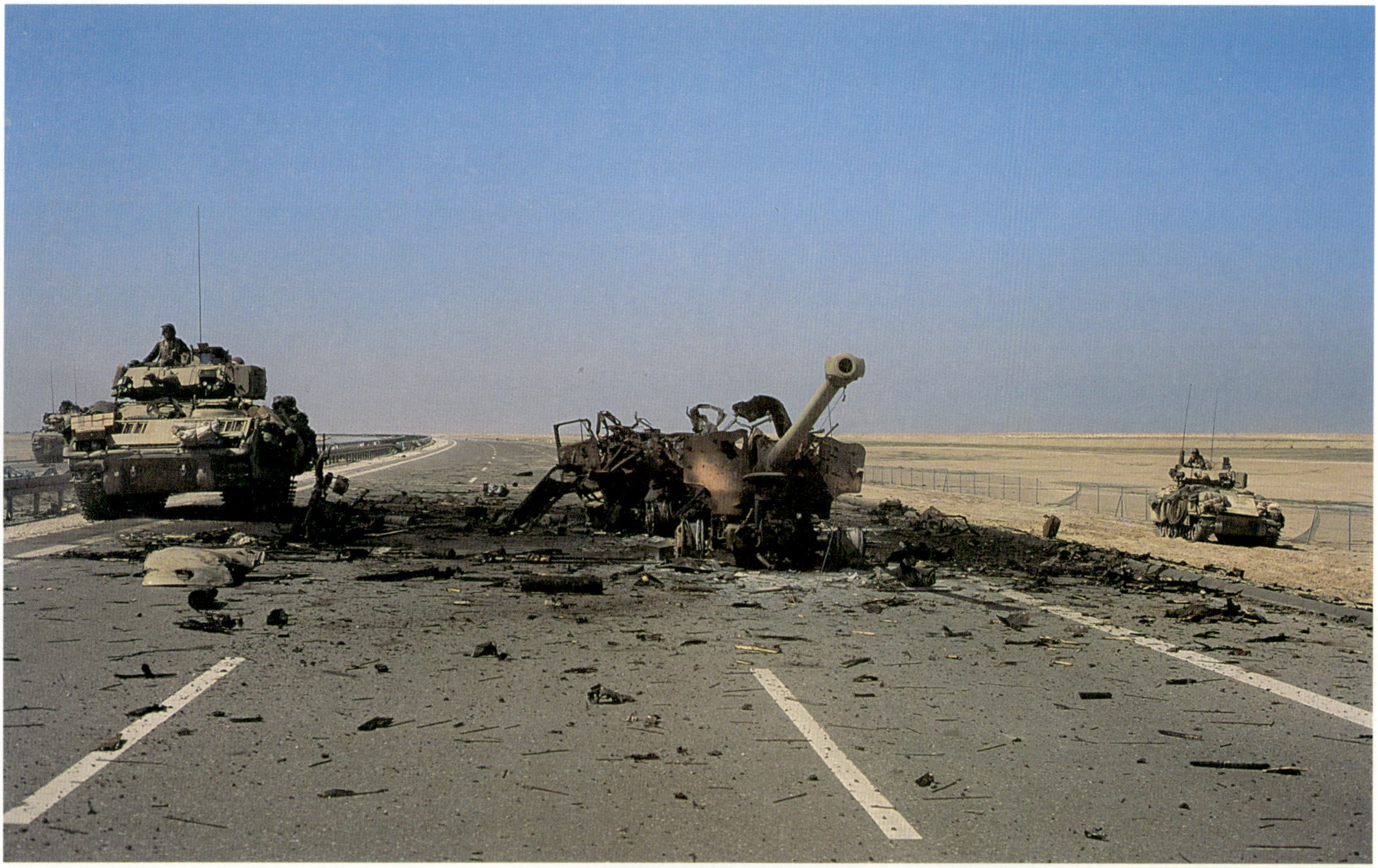

An M-46 130mm field gun and tractor destroyed by American warplanes on the Baghdad-Basra highway. Bradleys of the U.S. 24th Mechanized Infantry Division are passing by the wreck.

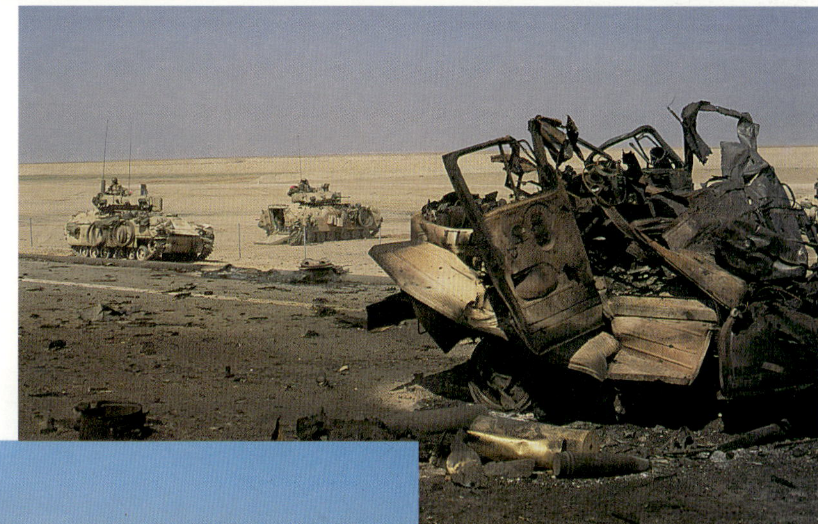

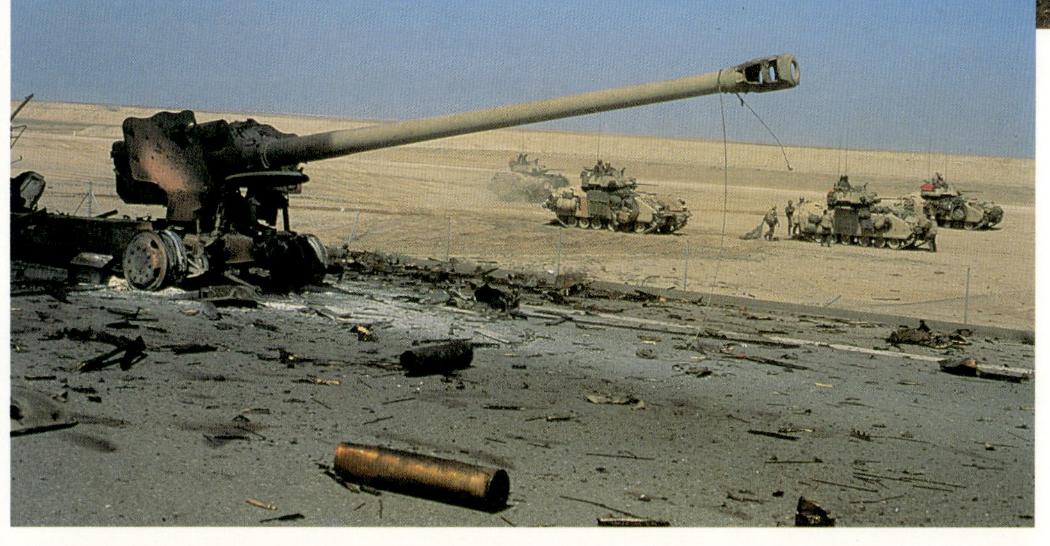

An Iraqi truck carrying SAM-6 AA missiles probably destroyed by air attack litter the Baghdad-Basra highway.

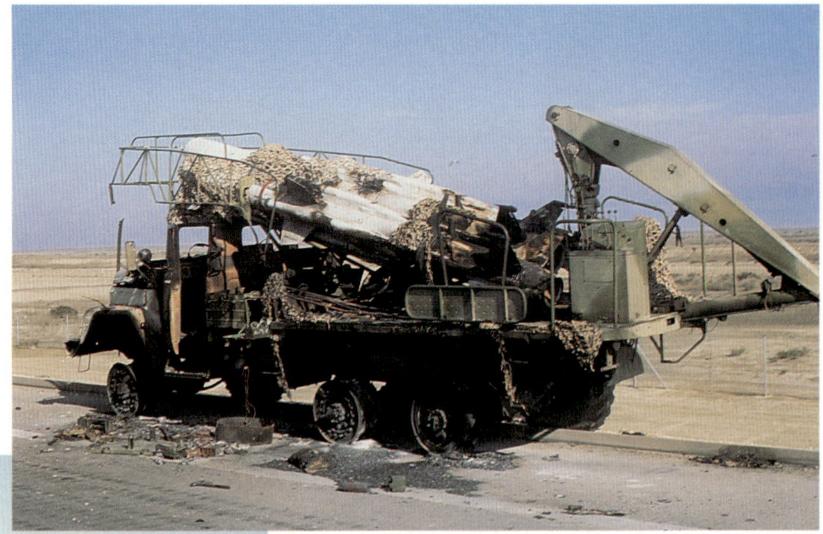

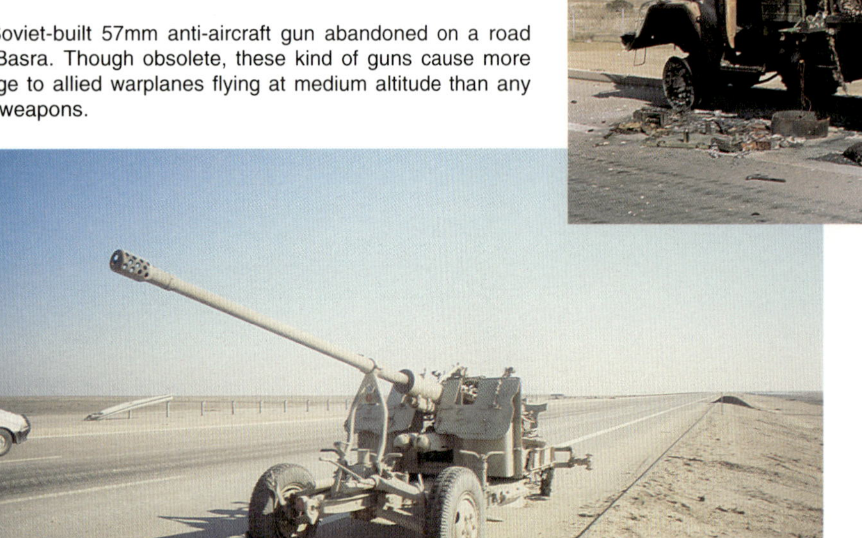

Soviet-built 57mm anti-aircraft gun abandoned on a road near Basra. Though obsolete, these kind of guns cause more damage to allied warplanes flying at medium altitude than any other weapons.

U.S. soldiers holding a flag in front of an Iraqi T-55 tank destroyed at the Rumaila oil fields in Iraq. The T-55 is fitted with a mine plough.(DoD)

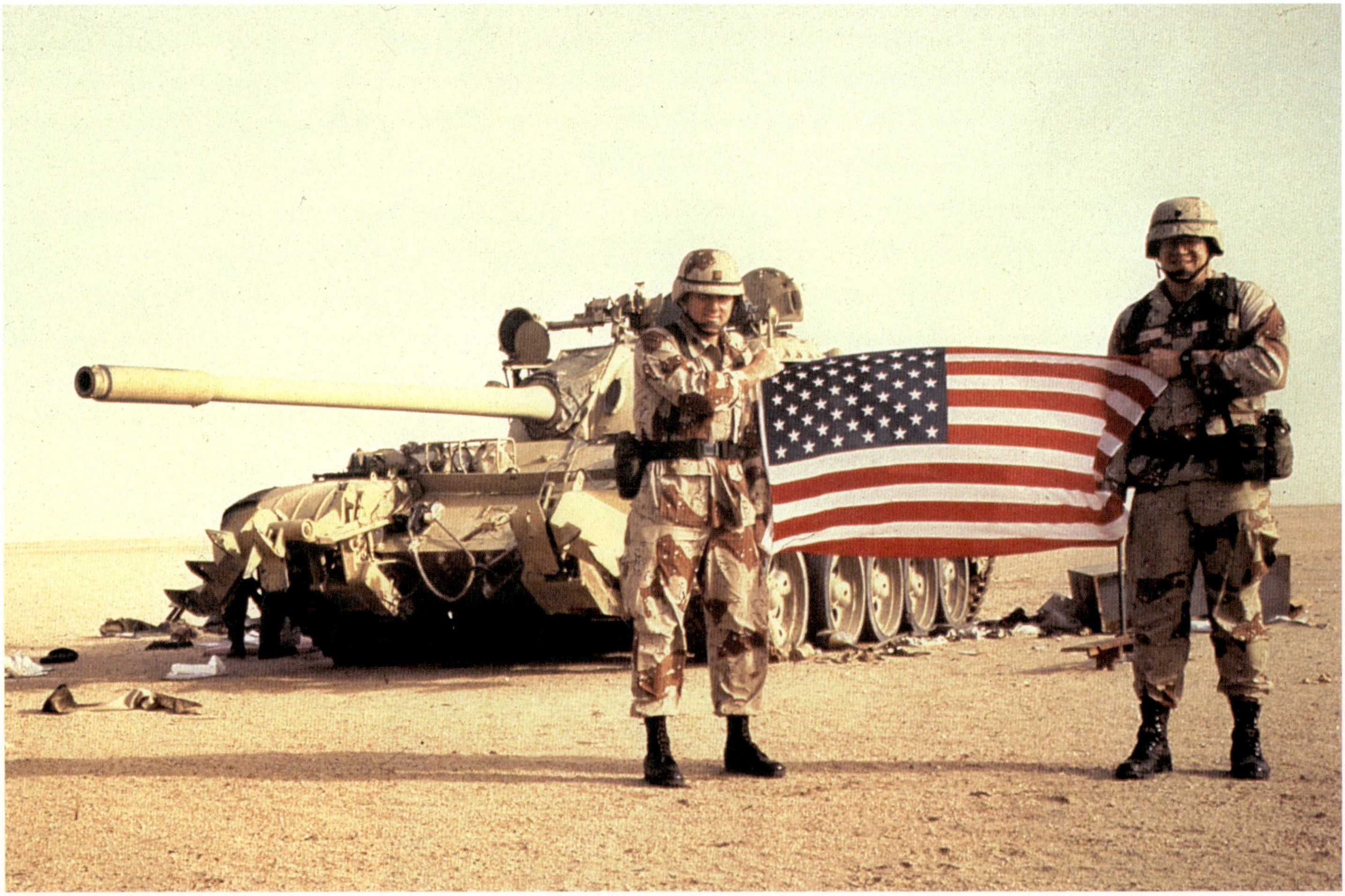

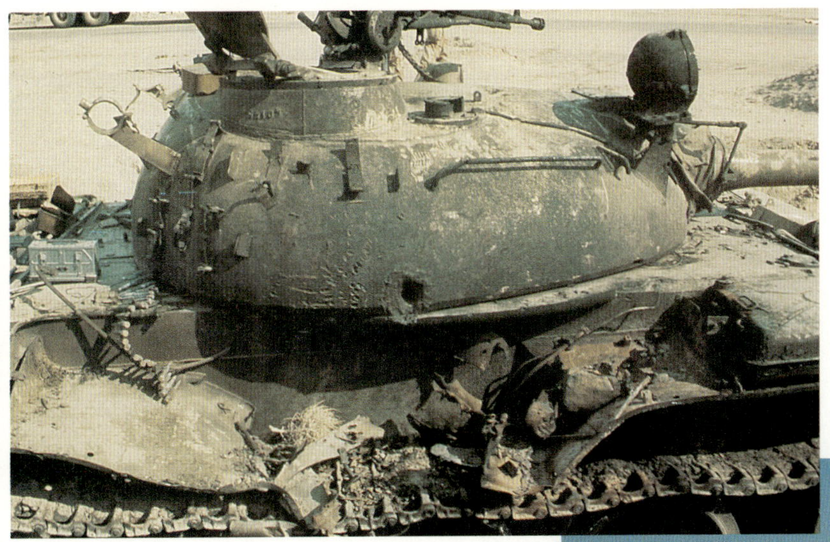

Pictured is an Iraqi T-55 tank hit by an American tank gun right at the bottom of the turret. (DoD)

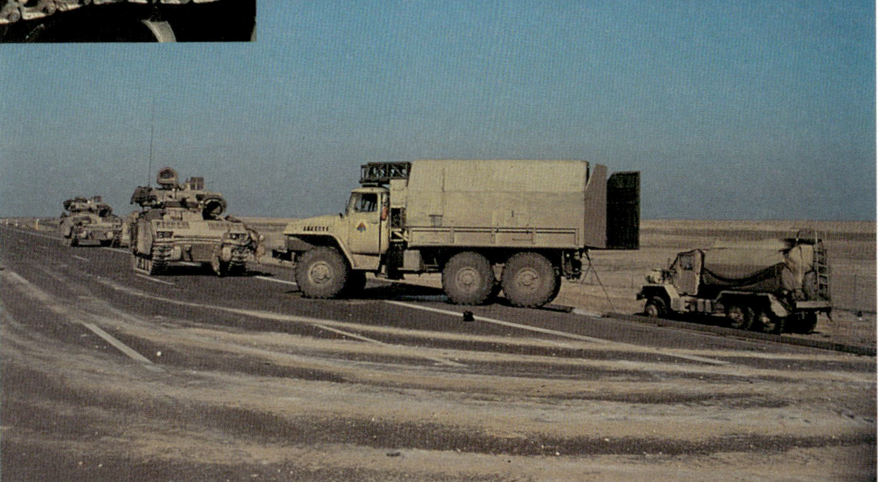

Two Bradleys approaching a couple of abandoned Iraqi trucks.

An abandoned MT-LB.

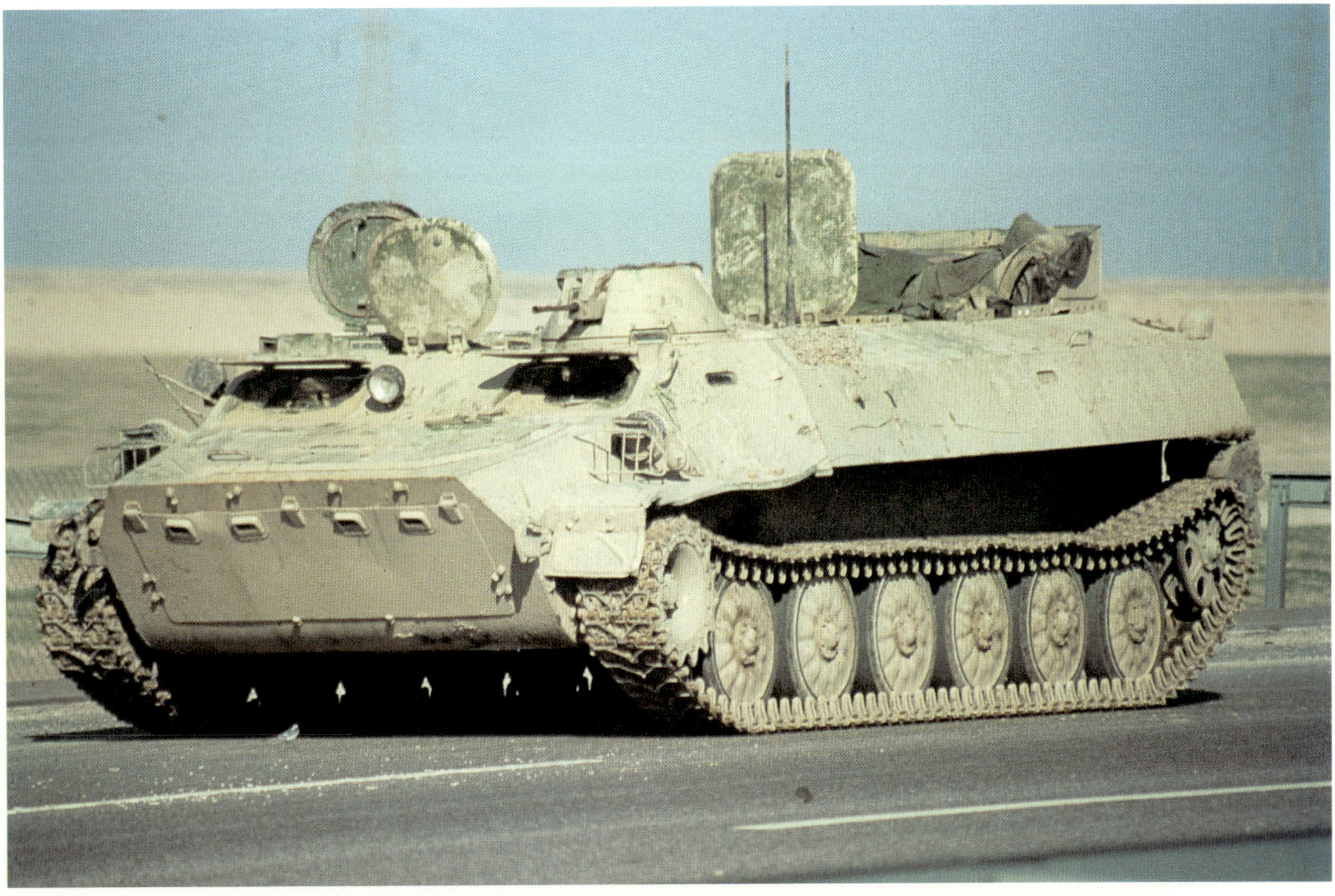

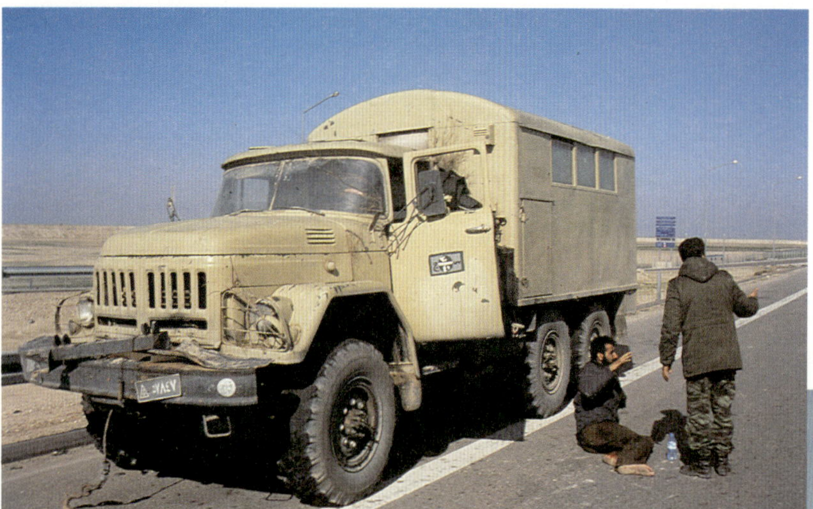

A ZIL-131 (6x6) truck used as a command post. The Iraqis used a lot of these trucks for transporting cargo, personnel and as a prime move for towed artillery. The driver of this truck has been wounded.

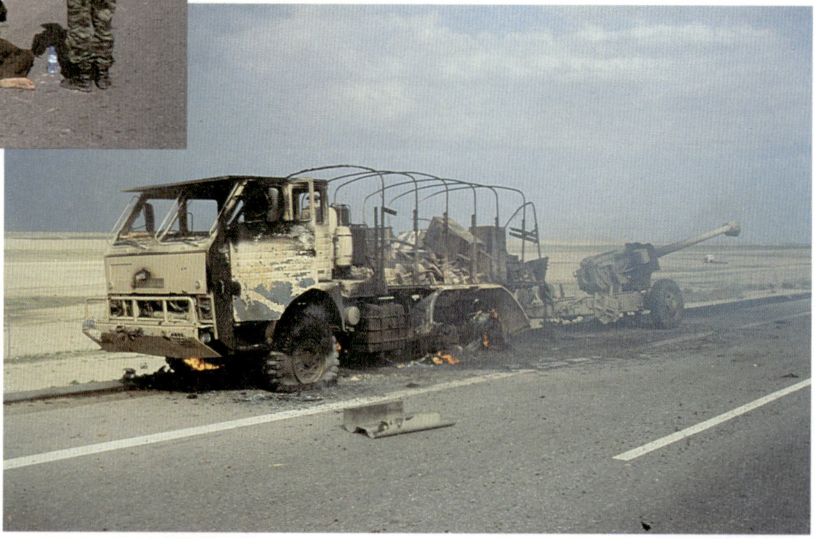

A destroyed 6x6 truck with the 152mm D-20 howitzer on tow.

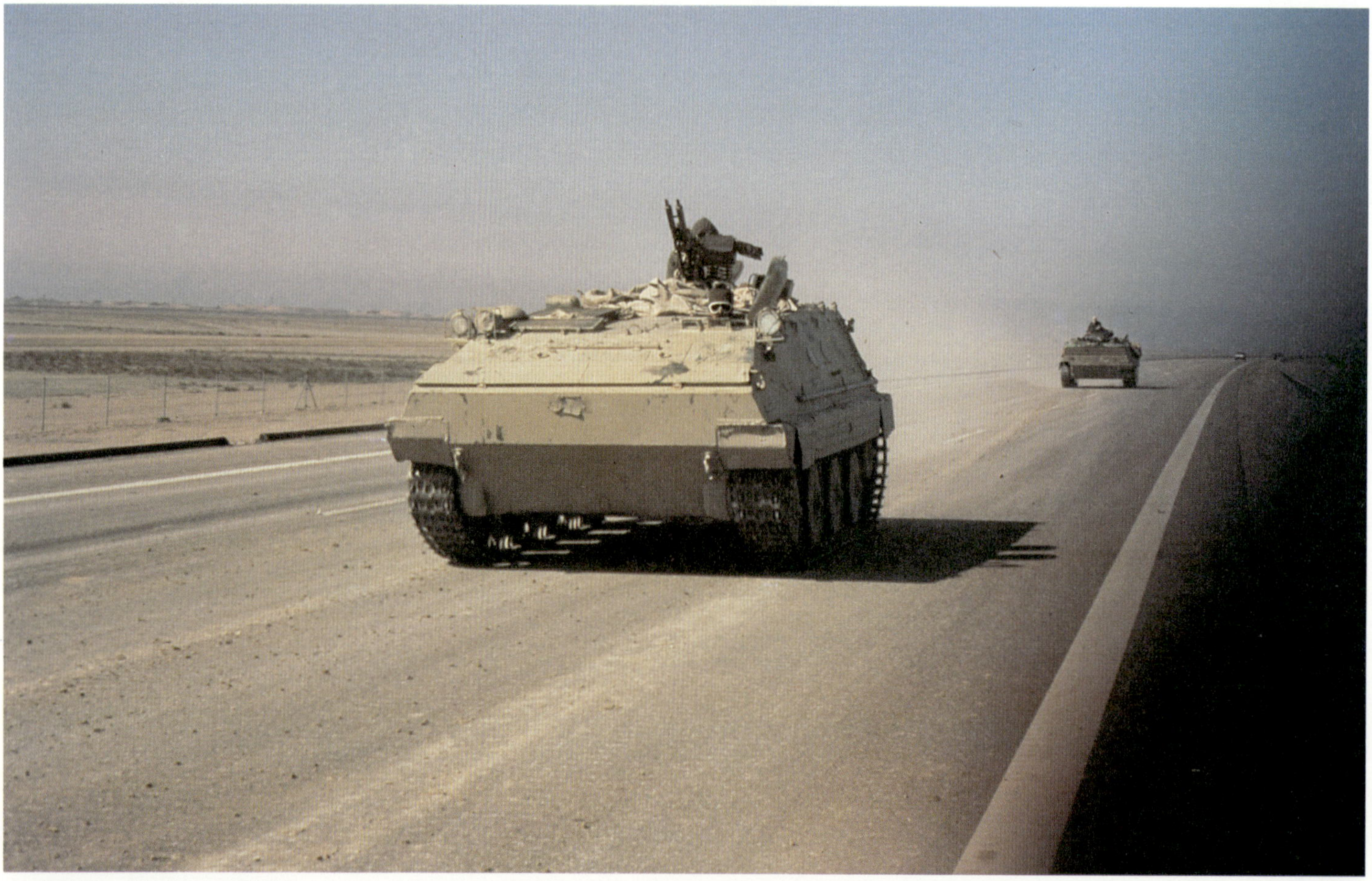

Iraqi Republican Guard YW531 Armored Personnel Carriers approaching the author on March 3, 1991. This was the last shot by the author before his capture by the Republican Guard. The author was put into prison for two weeks, with all his cameras, films and personal belongings confiscated. He did manage to take with him a few roll of films when he was later released. The photos taken by him during the land war were all taken under dangerous conditions, he really risked his life for them. (Ed.)

1:35 Modern AFV Series

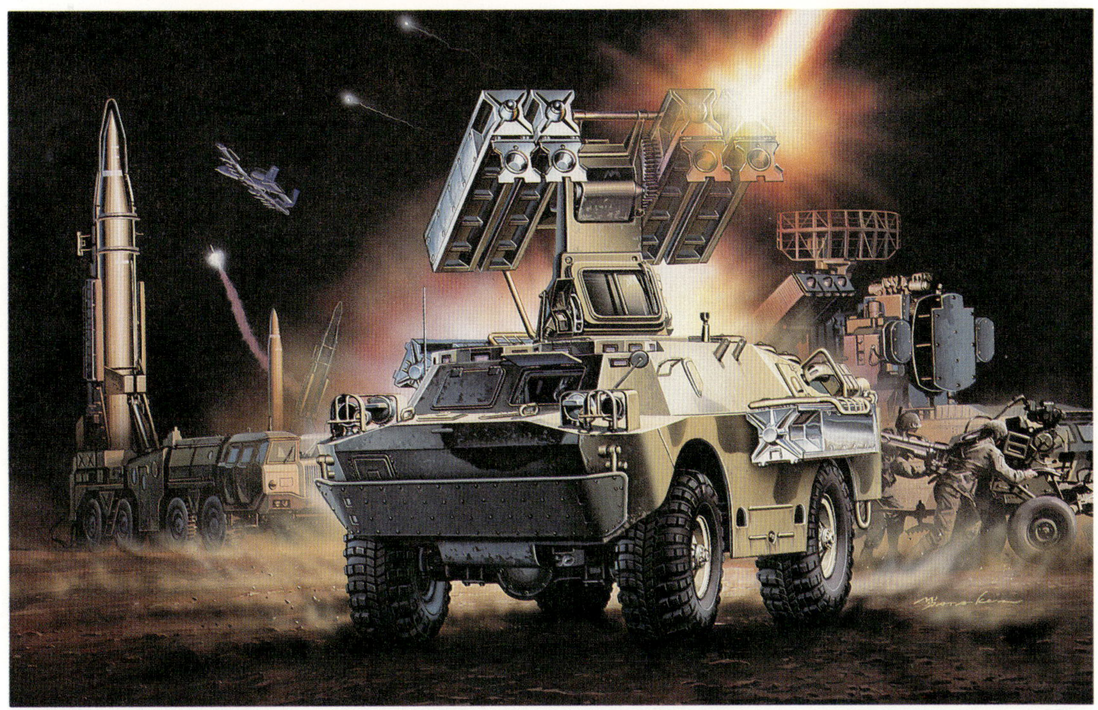

3515 SA-9 GASKIN

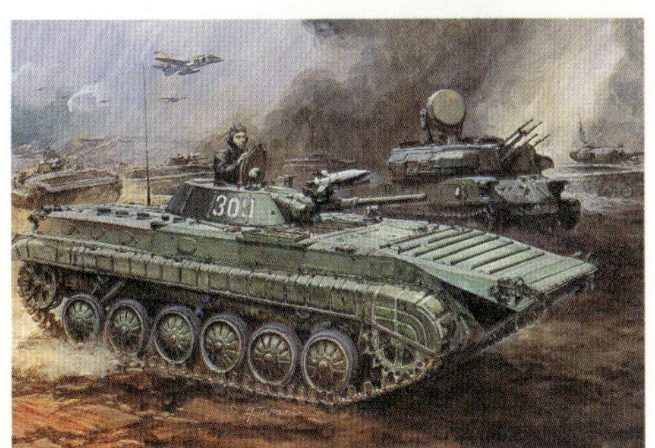

3503 BMP-1

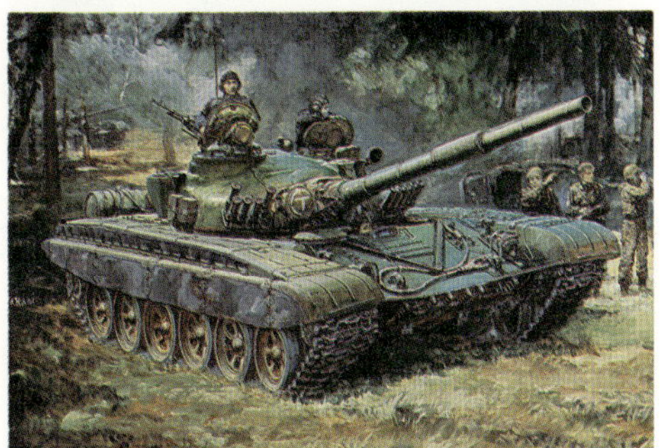

3502 T-72 G/M

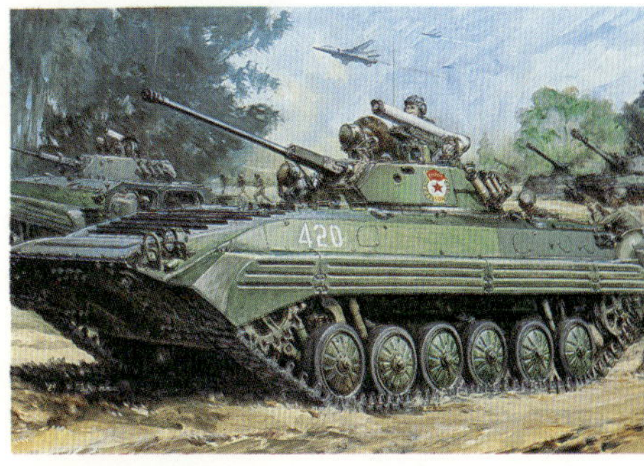

3504 BMP-2

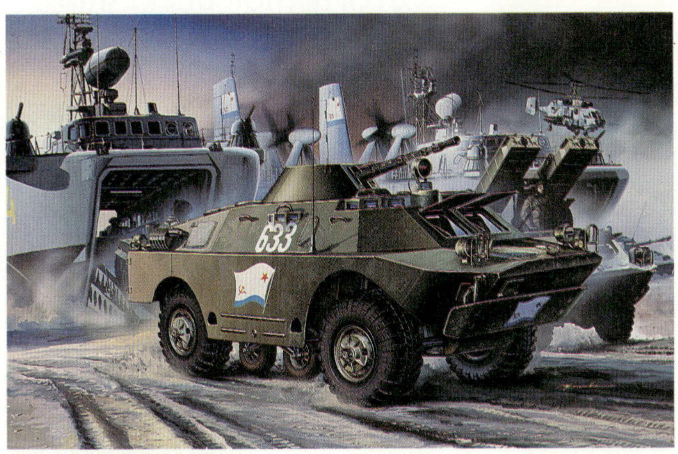

3513 BRDM-2

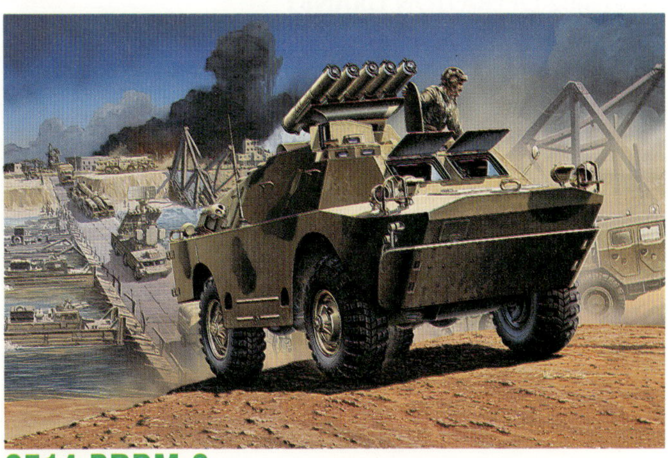

3514 BRDM-3

These models from DML's fine line of 1/35 scale military vehicle kits can now be modeled as equipment of the Iraqi Army that gained such notoriety in the recent Gulf War. All the quality and level of detail you have come to expect is present throughout.

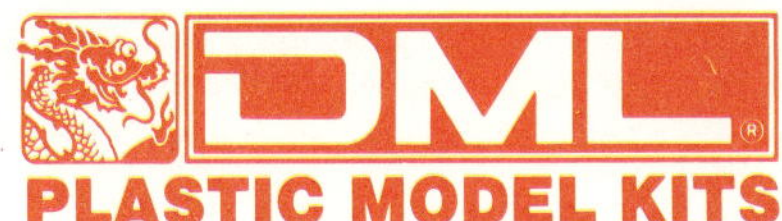